OCT 10 1976

D0450136

WIND
IN THE TOWER

Winnifred
E. Short
Memorial

J. Morehouse

Books by Han Suyin

DESTINATION CHUNGKING

A MANY-SPLENDORED THING

AND THE RAIN MY DRINK

THE MOUNTAIN IS YOUNG

CAST BUT ONE SHADOW

WINTER LOVE

TWO LOVES

THE FOUR FACES

THE CRIPPLED TREE

A MORTAL FLOWER

CHINA IN THE YEAR TWO THOUSAND AND ONE

BIRDLESS SUMMER

ASIA TODAY

THE MORNING DELUGE: MAO TSETUNG AND THE CHINESE REVOLUTION
1893–1954

WIND IN THE TOWER: MAO TSETUNG AND THE CHINESE REVOLUTION
1949–1975

WIND
IN THE TOWER
MAO TSETUNG AND THE CHINESE REVOLUTION 1949–1975

by HAN SUYIN

LITTLE, BROWN AND COMPANY • BOSTON • TORONTO

COPYRIGHT © 1976 by Han Suyin

ALL RIGHTS RESERVED. NO PART OF THIS BOOK MAY BE REPRODUCED IN ANY FORM OR BY ANY ELECTRONIC OR MECHANICAL MEANS IN-CLUDING INFORMATION STORAGE AND RETRIEVAL SYSTEMS WITHOUT PERMISSION IN WRITING FROM THE PUBLISHER, EXCEPT BY A REVIEWER WHO MAY QUOTE BRIEF PASSAGES IN A REVIEW.

FIRST EDITION

T 09/76

LIBRARY OF CONGRESS CATALOGING IN PUBLICATION DATA

Han, Suyin, pseud.
  Wind in the tower.

  Includes bibliographical references and index.
  1. China — Politics and government — 1949–
  2. Mao, Tse-tung, 1893–   I. Title.
  DS777.55.H2975   951.05′092′4 [B]   76–13606
  ISBN 0–316–34288–2

Published simultaneously in Canada
by Little, Brown & Company (Canada) Limited

PRINTED IN THE UNITED STATES OF AMERICA

Wind in the tower,
Herald of the approaching storm . . .

— Chinese poem quoted by
Chou En-lai, 1973

Preface
and Acknowledgments

No complete story of the Chinese Revolution, and of the life of Mao Tsetung, a life inseparable from China's transformation, has as yet been written. I have tried in this book and the previous volume, *The Morning Deluge*, to fill this gap by tracing Mao's background, personal involvement, and the development of his ideas in relation to the events which have changed China so radically between 1893 and January 1976. The present volume, *Wind in the Tower*, starts in 1949, when the Chinese Communist Party and the Red armies under Mao came to power, and depicts the vicissitudes, the struggles, as well as the spectacular rise of China to her present-day importance. The story of the cultural revolution, its meaning, and the vision of Mao which created this phenomenon, are also depicted in full for the first time.

In the last twenty years (since 1956) I have been at least once a year, and sometimes twice a year, in China, and have been personally involved in many aspects of the episodes which are described. Consequently much of the material in this book is firsthand, eyewitness and factual through direct involvement with the people affected by the policies and actions taken by Mao Tsetung and other Chinese leaders in the course of continuing the Chinese Revolution and the building up of a new order. I have not relied merely on documents or studies by experts outside China, however valuable these are, but have tried whenever possible to check them against actual, real events as they took place. It is now widely acknowledged that certain assumptions made by Sinologists regarding the Chinese Revolution, and certain appraisals, are no longer valid. I have tried whenever possible to get at the truth, so as to help in the reappraisal which is going on.

My thanks are due to many researchers, China scholars, of all nations; it is impossible to mention them all. I would like first of all to acknowledge my debt to the late Edgar Snow, whose reports on China, starting forty years ago in 1936, have never been equaled. Mr. Harrison Salisbury of the *New York Times*, one of the first Americans to visit China in the 1970's, has been to me a constant help; his erudition and accurate judgment as exemplified in his books on China stand as a monument to objective and informed scholarship. Mr. Leo Goodstadt, of the *Far Eastern Economic Review*, Hong Kong, has greatly helped me through his articles and his book, *Mao: The Strategy of Plenty*, which is the first economic study to link China's economic policies to the ideas of Mao Tsetung. To Professor John Fairbank and Dr. Richard Solomon I also owe many thanks; Dr. Solomon's book, *Mao's Revolution and the Chinese Political Culture*, was an essential breakthrough in explaining away so much of the distortion surrounding the episode known as the Hundred Flowers (1956–1957) and also in assessing the influence of Confucianism still remaining in present-day revolutionary China.

I have accomplished this work of presenting the Chinese Revolution without any grant or subsidy from any source whatsoever. I thank the government of the People's Republic of China for giving me so many opportunities freely to travel, to interview, and to engage in private (unmonitored, and unaccompanied) conversations with so many individuals in China, even when I disagreed thoroughly with some of the policies being applied. I am, therefore, solely responsible for the description of events, their interpretation, and any errors that may occur.

I hope these two volumes will contribute to the understanding so necessary between the Chinese and the American peoples. For it is upon this closer understanding — whatever the differences in systems — that the peace of the world depends today.

HAN SUYIN

January 1, 1976

Contents

I

THE BUILDING
OF NEW CHINA

1

The Road to the Future

So many deeds cry out to be done,
And always urgently;
The world rolls on,
Time presses.
Ten thousand years are too long,
Seize the day, seize the hour!
— MAO TSETUNG
January 9, 1963

In the spring of 1949, before the last military campaigns of the War of Liberation (1946–1949) between the Red armies under Mao Tsetung and the Kuomintang forces of Chiang Kai-shek had ended, victory was already certain for the former, a military and a political triumph of unparalleled scope. Overnight, China's destiny was changed and also the world balance of power.

In that early, wind-frozen March, the dusty, bleak village of Hsipaipo in North China was host to the Seventh Central Committee of the Chinese Communist Party assembling for its second plenum. The occasion was momentous; the decisions taken would decide the future of China. Countrywide victory was imminent; the People's Liberation Army stood poised, ready to advance into South China. Although Mao Tsetung was to receive an urgent cable from Stalin asking him to desist from prosecuting the war to the end ("Leave South China to Chiang," Stalin advised), he ignored it, and the plenum would back him. In April, Mao would issue orders for the army to advance, and on October 1 the People's Republic of China would come into being.

Mao Tsetung was fifty-six years old. The photographs of that year show him more portly than in his youth, master of the situation, and knowing it. His speeches are free of bombast, but also of self-deprecation. "The Chinese people, one-quarter of humanity, have stood up. . . . From now on no one will insult us again."

3

In this euphoric hour Mao remained cool-headed. This was a mere beginning; twenty-eight years of bitter struggle since the foundation of the Party in 1921 only a prelude. The most difficult work was yet to come: the rebuilding of China. "To win countrywide victory is only the first step in a long march. . . . Even if this step is worthy of pride, it is comparatively tiny; what will be more worthy of pride is yet to come."

Twenty-five years later, in October 1974, Mao Tsetung was almost eighty-one years old. The firecrackers of the October anniversary spread vast bouquets of lights, petals of flame in the Peking sky. A quarter of a century had passed since he had uttered these words, and there had been no turning back. Mao Tsetung was still alert of mind, with flashes of wit and humor as he conversed with the world's statesmen, kings and presidents who now thronged to Peking. He blandly kissed the hand of Imelda Marcos of the Philippines, and satisfied his ever young thirst for knowledge in talks with nuclear physicists.

In those twenty-five years the People's Republic of China had become a giant poised for prosperity and power, an acknowledged miracle. She had confounded all predictions, accomplished what had been deemed impossible. She aroused hope and fervor in the breasts of millions of the dispossessed, and the name of Mao Tsetung was known throughout the world.

But Mao Tsetung was old, and deliberately made it known to his people. He had long ago prepared for death. In the year 1974 all pictures and portraits of Mao in public squares and streets, which until then had shown him almost farcically young and apple-cheeked, were retouched to show his true face, with wrinkles, and white in his hair. Television films of his interviews implacably revealed his aged appearance. Mao himself had asked that he be shown as he was . . . to prepare the people for the time when he would no longer be with them.

Mao's work will remain: his writings, his way of thinking and doing, Mao Tsetung Thought — that body of revolutionary experience and knowledge, practice of day to day revolution, the teaching of a whole people in the science of revolution. Because of Mao, this knowledge is not confined to an elite but has pervaded the minds of the Chinese people, has become a way of living and a way of thinking. China has changed more radically and thoroughly in this quarter-century than any other country in the world, and she has only just begun.

None of this happened without challenge; no moment of these twenty-five years was free from "struggle," contention, controversy, polemics, and even war. Not one day of these twenty-five years but was witness to strife, both overt and covert; continuous high drama.

During this quarter-century the Chinese people transformed the Chinese earth and began to transform themselves. This immense metamorphosis — one-quarter of the world's people live in China — started while the guns were still loud, in that spring of 1949, in the frostbitten village of Hsipaipo. Thirty-four Central Committee members and nineteen alternates assembled to discuss the blueprint of the future. In the shambles and chaos of the devastated country, decisions, a "line," policies were to be devised to cope not only with the enormous immediate problems of famine and chaos, but also to chart the road to the future.

Amid the general exhilaration of a relieved population welcoming the PLA* as liberators, it would have been possible for Mao Tsetung* to institute immediately a far more radical program for change than the one he set out at the plenum. Mao enjoyed immense prestige, reinforced by the astonishing good behavior of the armies he led. "The occupation of eight or nine provinces and scores of big cities will require a huge number of working cadres, and to solve this problem the army must rely chiefly on itself" (Mao, February 1949). Army cadres were to learn to manage industry and commerce, run schools and newspapers, handle foreign affairs . . . and so they did.

But Mao never entertained the thought of a military dictatorship drastically enforcing radical measures. He has no taste for massive "purges" or arbitrary shortcuts. Though he thinks that the true way that governs the world of men is the way of radical change, he would not order change from above, imposing a system on a supine and exhausted people. Mao's way is to teach, to involve the people wholly in every transformation undertaken; to educate them into thinking and wielding power for themselves. Mao's vision was to transform China into a "strong, prosperous, independent, modern industrial socialist state" by combining effective leadership with the broadest participation by the people. A radical transformation of society by compulsion would not work.

The whole emphasis of Mao's speech at the second plenum is on a blueprint for civilian order. The army is to be turned into "a working force" of civilian cadres. The Party must rally as many groups as possible, not only workers and peasants but also the urban petty bourgeoisie

* People's Liberation Army.

and national bourgeoisie,* the intellectuals, all those "who can cooperate with us."

In 1945 the Communist Party had committed itself to a united front
to rally for reconstruction all who could be united, and had proposed a
coalition government in which it would cooperate with the Kuomintang.† On May 1, 1948, in the midst of the war against Chiang Kai-
shek, Mao drafted plans for a political consultative conference which
would gather "all democratic parties, people's organizations and public personages . . . to discuss and carry out the convening of a people's
congress and the formation of a democratic coalition government."
This shrewd tolerance was vindicated by the wholesale and enthusiastic flocking of many members of the Kuomintang, intellectuals, and
even generals of Chiang's armies to Mao's side. Altogether, twenty or
more parties and groups would assemble in the summer of 1949 to form
a coalition as suggested. Twenty-five years later many non-Communists
from such groups would still hold positions in the government of the
People's Republic of China.

Mao is a dialectician; he knows that every situation carries its obverse within it. The very success of the move, rallying so many diverse
individuals and groups, might well drown revolutionary goals in an in-
decisive liberalism; just so, too, were the well-disciplined forces of the
PLA now dangerously swollen with Kuomintang deserters (almost two
million of them).

It was therefore essential to set down a clear line, guiding principles,
for the period to come. Within the Party itself, Mao Tsetung had to
deal with divaricating groups. A strong right wing had as its chief pro-
tagonist the Party vice-chairman, Liu Shao-chi, considered Mao's closest comrade in arms. An extreme left wing, small but raucous, called
for the total liquidation of the bourgeoisie and immediate communism.
And there was the dangerous euphoria of triumph, warping revolutionary will and vigilance. Now the tough peasant guerillas had come to
the cities, would the cities corrupt them? No one better understood the
danger than Mao. He warned: "With victory, certain moods may grow
within the Party. . . . arrogance, the airs of a self-styled hero, inertia
. . . love of pleasure. . . . With victory, the people will be grateful to us
and the bourgeoisie will come forward to flatter us . . . flattery . . . may

* National bourgeoisie: The capitalist sector involved in industry or commerce
using its own assets, and not exporting capital abroad. See also page 40.
† *On Coalition Government*, April 24, 1945. *Selected Works of Mao Tsetung*
(English edition Peking 1961–1965), vol. III.

conquer the weak-willed in our ranks." He warned against the lethal power of "sugar-coated bullets," more dangerous than real bullets, for they eroded the revolutionary will and induced "distaste for continued hard living."

The right wing in the Party was influential. Its arguments appeared rational, and it was backed by many of the intelligentsia newly rallied to the victors. Paradoxically, it could quote Mao to undo Mao; for only a few years back, not thinking victory could be achieved for a decade at least, Mao had spoken of a "new democratic stage" for "decades." And the formula Liu Shao-chi put up was "consolidation of the new democratic stage."

The new democratic stage Mao had talked about in 1940, however, was already outpaced by events in 1949. The phenomenon historians know as the acceleration of history has nowhere been more evident than in the last thirty years, and in China particularly. Mao had felt it when he noted that "the march of events in China is faster than people expected." The outpacing of surmise by events is today an acknowledged fact, but it still catches most men unprepared. Mao had not expected victory in three short years. The situation brought about by the swift and total collapse of the Kuomintang meant that all programs must be updated. "To make revolution when conditions are not ripe . . . is adventurism . . . but not to make revolution when conditions are ripe . . . is unpardonable."

The new democratic stage was already anachronistic. But Liu Shao-chi stuck to the concept of a "consolidation of new democracy" that would last for twenty or thirty years. Bolstered with arguments from Russia's New Economic Policy in the 1920's, he argued that even Lenin had had to brake and reverse himself; China was not ripe for "socialism," he said. And he made it sound "ultra-left" even to talk of socialism.

Mao did not see it that way. He refused to be delayed, as he also refused to be hurried. In his essay *On New Democracy* in 1940 (widely circulated in 1949), Mao had explained that the new democratic stage was a *crossroads* situation; it opened up two possible roads, one towards socialism, one towards capitalism. The decision which road to take depended upon the leadership which prevailed. Hence there could be no "consolidation" of the new democratic stage. The period to come was one of "transition to socialism," said Mao, quoting Lenin, who had made the point that there could *not be* an intermediate stage between the bourgeois democratic revolution and the socialist revolution. Liu

Shao-chi's argument was ideologically incorrect. The time had come to orient China towards socialism, even if gradually. To freeze it into a "new democratic" establishment was to give up the very goal for which the revolution had been fought, to open wide the door to capitalist exploitation.

But, his opponents countered, had not Mao himself, in December 1947, argued that there would be a "prolonged period" of a capitalist small property and middle property class? Liu Shao-chi strongly urged that capitalists, owners of industrial enterprises producing manufactured commodities (such as there were in the pitifully underindustrialized China of 1949), should be "reassured." There must be a rehabilitation period, in which capitalists should be encouraged to return to production. Mao agreed, but these enterprises must be regulated and restricted. They must not be in a position to control the economy, and hence the destinies of the state.

"Chairman Mao struggled against both the left deviationists, who wanted immediate communism, and the right, led by Liu Shao-chi, who wanted the return of capitalism."[*] During the nine days of March 5 to 13, Mao Tsetung fought, for the vision, the orientation, the leadership which would transform China, bring it to power and prosperity, but also and above all to social justice, independence, and the true liberation of the minds of its people. The struggle between two views, two concepts, of what China should become was initiated then.

Once asked by Edgar Snow what he considered to be the most difficult and painful thing in his life, Mao Tsetung replied, "The intra-Party struggle." Yet willfully, deliberately, paradoxically, Mao Tsetung also relied on intra-Party struggle to propel the Party forward, to make its members progress in knowledge and understanding.

The Chinese Communist Party had never been a monolithic entity, not since its birth in 1921. Six times during the years 1921 to 1949 it was subject to internecine strife representing opposite ideological concepts, which on at least five occasions threatened its very existence. In the next twenty-five years, through to 1974, four more major struggles within the Party would occur.

Mao Tsetung, Party founder and Party educator, had devoted years

---

[*] Footnote to speech of Mao Tsetung at the second plenum of the Seventh Central Committee, March 5, 1949. See *Selected Works of Mao Tsetung* (English edition Peking 1961–1965), vol. IV.

to the problem of achieving unity in the Party while at the same time maintaining a dialectic debate within it.

In the long and bitter "major struggle" against Wang Ming, lasting from 1935 to 1945, Mao devised the ways and means of turning intra-Party struggle into a motive force, propelling the Party forward and making it progress. The great rectification (1942–1945)* which climaxed the struggle against Wang Ming had confirmed the efficiency of Mao's methods in dealing with the problem.

These methods — unity, criticism, self-criticism, unity again — eschewed physical violence and arbitrary punishment; Mao is known as generous to his foes (he insisted in 1945 that his defeated opponent Wang Ming should still be given a place on the Central Committee). But this benevolence knows no *ideological* compromise.

Party unity had been achieved in 1945, confirming Mao's position and authority. It was this unity, and the teachings of Mao from 1935 to 1945, which had enabled the CCP to flourish and to undertake the war of liberation, to win a landslide victory in 1949. Mao could not have forged it into the weapon for victory it became without the ideological education he dispensed so strenuously.

But the weapon needs constant overhaul and shaping. Again, in September 1948, Mao Tsetung had taken steps to reinforce unity. For through the years of civil war, dislocation threatened. The diversity of far-flung military operations, the difficulties of communication, had given rise to "independent kingdoms" under military commanders (also CCP members) and "anarchy and indiscipline."

This led to a shake-up (rectification) in both the Party and the PLA in 1948, and also to an unprecedented Politburo meeting, held in September 1948, at which Mao Tsetung reasserted overall ideological authority by drafting a resolution stating the principle of collective leadership.†

The Party committee system was designed to prevent the monopolizing of decision making by a single individual: there would be divergent views, and decisions must be taken by consensus. The practice of "democratic centralism" which Mao repeatedly emphasized during his long career was possible only if debate and contention were admitted as normal, necessary and constant within the Party.

* See Han Suyin *The Morning Deluge: Mao Tsetung and the Chinese Revolution 1893–1954* (Boston 1972), pages 404ff.
† See *On Strengthening the Party Committee System*, September 20, 1948. *Selected Readings of Mao Tsetung* (English edition Peking 1971).

Just as there is class struggle in society, so is this class struggle reflected within the Party, where it becomes an ideological confrontation between two "lines" of political thinking.

There is, therefore, a permanent "two-line struggle," overt or covert, latent or erupting into open crisis, at all times within the Party. And this, far from being untoward, is actually as it should be, for it corresponds to the law of dialectics, the unity of opposites, which is a universal law governing all phenomena, events, and things in the universe. Prevalent ideas and trends are incarnate in *people*, idea bearers, who form groups or cliques. The Party cannot escape this universal law.

"Contradictions exist in the process of development of all things." So long as these contradictions remain on the plane of divergences of opinion, and do not harm the course of the revolution or the Party's existence, they can be admitted. Should they escalate to threaten the Party's existence, to split it, or to deviate the Party from its goal, then major struggles take place.

To see in this permanent confrontation merely a "power struggle" between personalities is simplistic. True, personalities do count; with their foibles, their secret desires, their greed, ambition, capacity for intrigue, jealousy, envy . . . But these personal characteristics are secondary. Class standpoint is the framework upon which is grafted attitude and behavior, which will determine the individual's role in the struggle.

Mao's contribution to revolutionary science is to have devised methods of handling these negative elements so as to fuel progress; to have posited these struggles as necessary and inevitable. The preservation of Party unity is founded on the paradox of incessant struggle within the Party. Without ideological struggle, the Party would become ossified and decay. Struggle guarantees its dynamism; progress can only come through "contradictions" to be solved.

Repeatedly during this last quarter-century Mao would bring to attention the "dark side" of the Party; would enjoin Party members to "use their heads," would speak against blind obedience. But it was only because of the cultural revolution that this knowledge became common among all the people in China, and the notion of two-line struggle within the Party was accepted and evident to each man and woman (and even to schoolchildren). Prior to 1966 no one dared assume that any directive from "on high" could be wrong. The average Party member expected "deviations" and evil to come from below, or from non-

Party people, never from the very top of the Party itself. Today it is no longer so. "Higher authority" is not necessarily correct.

Although little publicized, the two-line struggle at the second plenum* was intense. It was preceded by abundant discussions on economic problems: restoration of production in the cities; the city-countryside relationship; flow of exchanges between city and country-side.

Liu Shao-chi argued that nationalization of the major industries, which under Chiang Kai-shek had been in the hands of the bureau-cratic capitalists as a monopoly, was enough to create a state industrial sector; apart from that the private sector of small capitalist concerns must be encouraged to expand and be given a "free hand." "At the present time it is better to allow the forces of capitalism full play to expand production." This expansion of a private sector would put pro-duction back on its feet, increase employment of workers (many of them now unemployed because of industrial shutdowns), and supply consumer needs. These two sectors, one nationalized, one private, would be kept for two or three decades. This was the meaning of "consolidation of the new democratic stage." The capitalists were "es-sential" for the rehabilitation period. They alone had the knowhow necessary to run enterprises, and the very word "socialism" panicked them — hence it must not be used.

The arguments seemed plausible; the end would have been a system such as prevails in India, which although it dubs itself "socialist" is a nineteenth-century type of capitalism in its exploitative qualities. Though unversed in industrial economics (as he freely acknowledged), Mao Tsetung was aware of the devouring potential of capitalist enter-prise. The coexistence of a state sector (which would perforce be sabotaged by the private sector, as occurs in India, or else be inefficient through lack of knowhow) with a private sector would immensely favor capitalist development. But capitalist expansion would mean ex-ploitation of the workers and peasants: betrayal of the revolution.

"As for the direction of industrial development, some muddleheaded comrades maintain that we should chiefly help the development of private enterprise and not state enterprise, whereas others hold the

* *Report to the Second Plenary Session of the Seventh Central Committee of the Communist Party of China*, March 5, 1949. *Selected Works of Mao Tsetung* (En-glish edition Peking 1961–1965), vol. IV.

opposite view that it suffices to pay attention to state enterprise and that private enterprise is of little importance."*

It all boiled down, in Marxist terminology, to different class stands. Liu, who argued for maintaining "for decades" this ambiguous system, was actually trying to preserve and even to strengthen the capitalist class. He invoked Lenin's New Economic Policy, but this did not impress Mao, who knew his Lenin far better and knew how Lenin's concepts had been distorted in the USSR.

"On whom shall we rely in our struggle in the cities? Some muddle-headed comrades think we should rely not on the working class but on the masses of the poor. . . . Some comrades who are *even more muddleheaded* think we should rely on the bourgeoisie. . . .

"We must wholeheartedly rely on the working class, unite with the rest of the laboring masses, win over the intellectuals, and win over to our side as many of the national bourgeoisie elements as possible . . . or neutralize them. . . .

"Our present policy is to regulate capitalism, not to destroy it, *but the national bourgeoisie cannot be the leader of the revolution, nor should it have the chief role in state power.*"†

Mao Tsetung through reasoned debate and persuasion carried the vote in the Central Committee. The policy of "controlling, regulating, and restricting" though not forbidding capitalism was passed.

Another problem discussed at the plenum, the city-countryside relationship, was also formulated by some right-wing economists as an "industry versus agriculture" contradiction. Liberal economists joined hands with Liu's "Marxist" formulation to argue that the first priority was heavy industrialization; whatever funds there were should be invested chiefly in industrial "rehabilitation." For had not this been the "socialist road" taken by the USSR? They posited the problem in terms of a "contradiction" between urban and rural development; to divert funds to alleviate the immense misery of the countryside would not be "socialism."

Bluntly, this meant a continuation of what had been the hallmark of Chinese society before 1949: domination of city over countryside; exploitation of the countryside majority (over 85 percent of the population) by the urban minority.

* *Report to the Second Plenary Session of the Seventh Central Committee of the Communist Party of China*, March 30, 1949. *Selected Works of Mao Tsetung* (English edition Peking 1961–1965), vol. IV.

† *On the People's Democratic Dictatorship*, June 30, 1949. *Selected Works of Mao Tsetung* (English edition Peking 1961–1965), vol. IV.

Throughout this book, italics employed in the quotations are the author's.

The point is fundamental: throughout the next twenty-five years the problem would recur. Mao Tsetung would never give in on this matter. The countryside must no longer be exploited by the cities. Mao recalled that the bulk of the soldiers who won the revolution had been peasants; and though he had said in 1948 that "the center of gravity of the work of the Party is now in the cities," and enjoined Party members to learn about city work, this did not mean that the city must take priority over the countryside.

Mao's refusal to sacrifice the peasantry for "production and rehabilitation" indicates also his refusal to accept blindly the Soviet Russian pattern. The right wing argued that Stalin himself in 1928 had said that the peasantry must make its "tribute" to the buildup of heavy industry as a priority. But Mao replied that it was not possible to build a socialist industry based on a feudal countryside, or one where cruel exploitation held sway. If the countryside remained neglected and exploited and backward while industry flourished, that would mean capitalism and not socialism, whether a "nationalized" state sector in industry was created or not. "Only through socialism . . . can our motherland free herself from a semicolonial, semifeudal state and take the road to independence, freedom, peace, unity and prosperity," said Mao at the plenum.* And "without socialization of agriculture there can be no complete, consolidated socialism."

In arguing that the peasant must not be sacrificed, Mao was not only standing solidly on the side of the majority of laboring people, but he also had the rank and file of the Party with him. In 1949 2 percent of the Party members were from the working class, 73 percent were poor and middle peasants, and 25 percent were from the urban petty bourgeoisie or were intellectuals or rich peasants. However, this 25 percent were influential; they were literate, with technical and administrative ability, wielding an influence disproportionate to their number, holding administrative posts in the newly liberated cities. Already complaints of the "peasant" ways of some of the army cadres (whose tough guerilla habits were alien to urban ways) had come from these urban-oriented officials. It was at this point that the persistent rumor began that Mao as a "peasant" leader did not understand city problems, nor did his rural warriors.

Liu Shao-chi argued that there should not be land reform, so as not to disturb production, but a return to the rent reduction system operated in Yenan.† Undue socialization in the countryside would bring

* *Monthly Report,* Shanghai, July 1949.
† See *The Morning Deluge,* page 360.

confusion. The peasant was "basically conservative . . . slothful, easy-going . . . only interested in food and profit," said Liu. He favored a "rich peasant" line.*

This contemptuous view of the peasant masses was vigorously resisted by Mao. "Under no circumstances should the villages be ignored and only the cities given attention, such thinking is entirely wrong." Mao conceded that the minds of the peasantry must be changed by "socialist education . . . this is the most important problem." However, socialist education must be accompanied by tangible steps: land reform, and collectivization step by step. This would receive the support of the poor and middle peasantry, 70 percent of China's population.

"Only when each peasant has a farm and three horses can there be socialism in the countryside," retorted Liu Shao-chi.

The arguments would rage for months. Editorials on the two views came out in the local press. "The birth of an economy of rich farmers of the new type is only a natural law in the development of social economy and is not to be feared," clarioned the *Tung Pei Daily*, organ of the Northeast (Manchurian) bureau of the CCP. The Manchurian bureau was run by Kao Kang, a powerful, clever, and energetic man, one of the main protagonists of the Soviet model. His downfall would come in 1954.

"Expansion of industry . . . is of enormous importance. . . . Only when industry has been expanded will it be possible to supply the peasantry with large amounts of manufactured goods and new farming equipment," wrote another daily. "Leadership of the city over the villages means the leadership of industry over agriculture, or the leadership of the working class over the peasantry," ran yet another comment. "To get industry going is to provide employment for the working class, therefore to expand and build up a strong proletariat. . . . This is socialism."

The other view could be found in the *Chang Kiang Daily*, organ of the Central China bureau, which editorialized on July 7: "Rural economy is deplorable. . . . The real power is still in the hands of the landlords . . . it is unthinkable that we can build up industries in the cities when the wide countryside is still handicapped by a feudal economy. . . . It is also unthinkable that we can restore and expand industry before the productive forces in the villages have been liberated."

In the end, it was Mao who would lay down the ideological line in

* See last footnote, page 26.

two masterly documents. His report at the second plenum is today held as an example of how to achieve unity and consensus, and therefore leadership authority, in a complex situation: promoting revolutionary goals with principled flexibility; making timely short-term concessions, but leaving the future wide open and invalidating none of the radical shifts to come.

The plenum finally passed resolutions that the state economy and not private economy should be "in the leadership role," and that agriculture should be led from individual operation to collective development "step by step." Priority for manufactured goods would go to the rural areas; the supply differences between city and countryside were to disappear.

Then happened the curious incident, raised later during the cultural revolution, of Liu Shao-chi's visit to Tientsin.* "When industry and trade were virtually at a standstill in Tientsin, Mr. Liu Shao-chi . . . was sent there to improve the situation. He held a conference with local industrialists and commercial leaders. . . . Mr. Liu said that China had only four big capitalists, namely the Chiang, Soong, Kung, Chen families . . . aside from these China had no big capitalists to speak of. . . . He then encouraged the Chinese capitalists to be big capitalists. . . . He said the Chinese Communist Party will enforce communism in the end . . . twenty or thirty years from now."

Referring to exploitation, Liu had said there were two kinds of exploitation. One was "slavery and feudalistic exploitation" and another "equal value exploitation." He said that while the first must be wiped out, the latter must stay, "for the reason that through this form of exploitation there will develop production, and therefore greater employment.

"He hoped the Chinese capitalists will *go on with the* latter exploitation, and he assured the audience that '*the Chinese Communist Party will not stop you.*'"

At a self-criticism session in 1967,† eighteen years later, Liu would say he had forgotten this episode. Even if one does allow that Liu was trying to rally support from the capitalists, he was certainly doing this in a strange way, dilating on the benefits of exploitation. He brushed off the workers who had congregated and wanted to see him. The

* *Monthly Report,* Shanghai, July 31, 1949, page 20; article entitled *Communist Theoretician Speaks.*
† See *Collected Works of Liu Shao-chi, 1958–1967* (Hong Kong 1968), pages 365–366.

workers were discouraged. "It dampened our revolutionary enthusiasm. . . . Was this revolution?"*

In 1968 Mao would say that he had not been told of Liu's Tientsin
visit at the time. We do not know when he learned of it.†

By June 1949 South China lay open, ready for liberation. Summer
would see the landslide victory of the PLA as it pressed southward; by
the next year all China was liberated.

That June, Mao began to realize that "the imperialist countries"
(meaning chiefly the United States, which had helped Chiang Kai-
shek's regime and committed itself to Chiang's victory) would not
accept the new state of affairs in China. He had expressed throughout
that spring his willingness to establish relations with all countries (including the United States), provided that the "reactionaries" — that is,
Chiang Kai-shek — were no longer recognized. He reiterated in June
willingness to do business and establish diplomatic relations with all on
the basis of independence, respect for integrity and sovereignty, mutual benefit and non-interference in internal affairs. But he knew that it
would be a long time (he hinted then at ten to twenty years) before
the United States would face the facts of the Chinese revolution.

On the eve of the twenty-eighth anniversary of the CCP (June 30,
1949) Mao Tsetung delivered the remarkable speech entitled *On the
People's Democratic Dictatorship*, an ideological document of great
importance, and a definite statement of intent to carry the revolution
forward to its proclaimed goal.

This document provides the foundation for the strategy of development which China would follow; defines the basis of Communist
power, "the worker-peasant alliance"; admits among "the people" (that
is, those with full and total civil rights) the petty bourgeoisie and the
national bourgeoisie; makes clear the essence of power wielding, the
conditions under which the bourgeoisie must not only be tolerated but
also take part in the building of New China. "The national bourgeoisie
at the present stage is of great importance." It posits the main contradiction of the period as that between "the proletariat and the bourgeoisie," but makes it clear that bloodshed is unnecessary; "the method we

---

* Author's interviews with workers in Tientsin in 1969.

† Hsinhua News Agency, Peking, April 15, 1967: report on investigation of
People's Daily regarding the April 1949 visit of Liu Shao-chi to the East Asia
(Tungya) private wool enterprise (now Wool Factory No. 3 of Tientsin). It re-
counts Liu's conversation with Sung Fei-king, the owner, who in May 1950 fled to
Hong Kong with 4 million yuan ($2 million) and died in Latin America.

employ is democratic, the method of persuasion, not of compulsion." The bourgeoisie can be re-educated. Even reactionaries, so long as they do not create trouble, will be given work and allowed to "remold themselves through labor into new people."

Mao Tsetung in this document sums up the history of the Party for the benefit of "young comrades who have not studied Marxism-Leninism and have only recently joined the Party"; refutes the ambiguity of "middle of the road" liberalism, which is clearly equated with the notion of "consolidation of a new democratic stage." The goal is unswerving; it can be achieved only by "leaning to one side," there can be no compromise. "All Chinese without exception must lean either to the side of imperialism or to the side of socialism. *There is no third road.*"

In March, at the plenum, Mao had said that "this period of transition before us is full of contradiction and struggle, the revolutionary struggle today is possibly even deeper than the armed revolutionary struggle of the past." In June he repeats this idea throughout his lengthy speech. Some, he says, believe that "Victory is possible even without international help. This is a mistaken idea." China could not consolidate her victory without help from "the international revolutionary forces." In practical terms, this meant aid from the Soviet Union. In that June, Mao Tsetung began the first tentative negotiations for his trip to the USSR at the end of the year.

The two-line struggle on the ideology and strategy of development continued. It would be 1953 before Mao Tsetung won a clear victory on the definition of the period — "consolidation of new democracy" or "transition to socialism."

In September 1949 Liu Shao-chi was to refer with some asperity to Mao.° "In the course of consultation . . . some delegates . . . suggested including in the common program the topic of the future of socialism, but we did not think it proper to do so, because the adoption of socialism in China will be a serious step to be taken in the fairly distant future."

During the years 1950–1952, Liu would refer time and again to the "distant future" of socialism. But the acceleration of history was on Mao's side. By October 1953 Mao would win; after a series of meetings

° At the Political Consultative Conference, September 9, 1949, when it adopted a common program for the inauguration of the new government. The Political Consultative Conference was called for by Mao Tsetung in 1948. It was to assemble individuals from all political parties, including those members of the Kuomintang who rallied to the Communists (see *The Morning Deluge*, page 498).

the Central Committee would pass a resolution for *The General Line on the Transition Period to Socialism*. And this was the end of "consolidation of new democracy."

In September 1954, in his speech presenting the constitution of the People's Republic of China at the first National People's Congress (NPC), Liu Shao-chi castigated those who "wanted to halt at the crossroads."

Mao had said, and would repeat in 1955 in the continuing battle with Liu: "There are people who after the victory of the new democratic stage have remained at that stage . . . they are still attempting to speak of new democracy and linger at the crossroads, refusing to make the step towards socialist transformation."

Liu now seemed to agree: "The only correct road . . . is to pass from the present society . . . to a society with a unified socialist economic structure, that means transition from the present new democratic society to a socialist society. . . . Some people may perhaps think of maintaining the status quo, taking neither a capitalist road nor a socialist road . . . We all know that China is now in a transition period, building a socialist society . . . this period is also called in our country the new democratic period."

Thus Liu Shao-chi appeared to surrender to Mao's policies. But as the ensuing years would show, he continued to hold on to his own views.

Mao Tsetung . . . Liu Shao-chi. Two names, two men apparently linked by dedication to a common cause. Why did Mao Tsetung, despite his clear knowledge of Liu, despite his bursts of irritation against Liu, keep the relationship going, allow Liu so much latitude and power for so long? Why did Liu become Mao's heir in 1959, only to be expelled from the Party in 1968? Why was the tremendous upheaval of the cultural revolution "entirely necessary and appropriate," and the only means whereby Liu Shao-chi could be removed?

The answer to these questions is the story of China's dynamic building during the past quarter of a century. In this gigantic drama personalities and events intertwine. And perhaps, since the law of unity of opposites holds for all things, there had to be a Liu because there was a Mao. "What is valid and correct can only come to light in struggle against what is incorrect." "All contraries . . . are beneficial."*

What kind of person was Liu Shao-chi? Mao is glowingly, glaringly

* Attributed to Mao. 1959?

accessible, his foibles known, his charisma evident. But even Edgar Snow, who met Liu several times, found him unyielding to description. So did the imaginative André Malraux, whose apt description (to the author, in a personal interview) was: "A gramophone record." Other impressions are similarly unrewarding. "We took him round to visit monuments, hospitals, schools; he never said much, just grunted . . . it was his wife Wang Kuang-mei who exerted herself." No one can remember a memorable quip, sally of wit, from Liu Shao-chi, not even in the heyday of his power.

This shadow insubstantiality is compounded by non-knowledge of his activities for many years at a stretch. For Liu was in the "underground," operating clandestine groups, much of the time between 1935 and 1945.

Efforts to humanize Liu and to render him popular were made between 1959 and 1963. "Primary school textbooks now contain many heroic tales about Liu," wrote Edgar Snow in 1962. "Since 1958 a planned effort" had been made "to prepare people for eventual acceptance of Liu as Party chieftain" (and Mao's heir).[*]

But Liu could never achieve that immediate warmth which characterizes Mao. Tales of Mao's wit, bursts of laughter or anger, acerbic irony or apt quotation abound. He is a living story, a legend and a reality. But Liu needed an organization around him to come alive.

Liu was probably a far abler committeeman than Mao; he was a good apparatus organizer, a lover of order, rules, and programs. Diplomats found him answering questions in a meticulous style, unlike Mao's apparently rambling talk. But Liu had no earthiness; he was at ease only in an office. He was an executive of merit but not a mass leader; a man who needed an organization to buttress him, discomforted by spontaneous or unexpected phenomena.

In short, Liu was a typical mandarin, a Confucianist bureaucrat, such as China produced by the millions during twenty-five hundred years of Confucianism.

Liu Shao-chi's early career has already been depicted.[†] He is said to have first recanted his Communist Party principles in 1925 when arrested by a Hunan warlord. Out of consideration for Liu's landlord family, the warlord sent him the Confucian Analects to read in jail. This brought in Liu a change of heart, and he recanted.

[*] Edgar Snow *Red China Today* (New York 1971; revision of *The Other Side of the River*), page 327.
[†] See *The Morning Deluge*, pages 87, 94, 97, 98–100, 278–283, 439–445.

In 1926 Liu Shao-chi was "secretary for economic demands" in the Communist trade unions of the Wuhan government. He enjoined the workers' pickets to disarm in 1927, and when massacres began fled to North China, and appeared in Moscow for the Sixth Congress of the Chinese Communist Party held there in 1928. In 1931 we find him in Juichin, at the Kiangsi Red base. He took part in the first lap of the Long March (if we believe the 1959 edition of Chen Chang-fong's book, he was there throughout the Long March, but this appears dubious).* After the 1935 Tsunyi meeting which confirmed Mao as the leader of the CCP, Liu returned to North China to begin underground agitation for a united front against Japan. The student uprising of December 1935 in Peking has been mentioned as due to Liu's efforts, but this is now denied. However, Snow states that he arrived in 1936 in Yenan through a letter of introduction written in invisible ink and signed by Liu Shao-chi.

In 1936 occurred the alleged "abjuration affair," which was brought up in 1967 and given much publicity during the cultural revolution. Apparently at the time many Party members later to become prominent as supporters of the "Liu line" (Peng Chen, Liu Lan-tao, Po I-po, and others) were in Chiang Kai-shek's jails. Liu is said to have advised them to save themselves by abjuring communism. It is curious that precisely these people would form the staunch core of Liu's support in the Party in later years. In his self-criticism in 1967 Liu denied responsibility for the affair, though abjurations do seem to have occurred.

What of the relationship between Liu and Mao? This relationship, with its built-in "contradiction," can be dated to 1937, when a disheartened Liu was in Yenan, "holed up to write his reports" as his "good friend" Chang Kuo-tao says.† He produced a long diatribe condemning all CCP policies for the past sixteen years, dubbing them "left adventurism," reproving peasant uprisings as reckless. Liu wanted a merger of the CCP with the Kuomintang, dissolution of the Red Army, and a CCP campaign to "reform the Kuomintang from within."

This capitulationist stance caused "a severe shock" and was called "outrageous" by some Politburo members. Mao, however, sought Liu out, reasoned with him, and brought him around. In the next year we find Liu joining Mao, approving of Mao's united front, aiding Mao in

* See Chen Chang-fong *On the Long March with Chairman Mao* (English edition Peking 1959).

† See Chang Kuo-tao *Memoirs*, serialized in *Min Pao*, Hong Kong, 1968–1969.

the struggle against Wang Ming. From then on Liu became not only a member of the Politburo, in 1939, but also vice-chairman of the Party; by 1949 he was regarded as Mao's loyal ally.

There were personal, practical, and ideological reasons for Mao's behavior. To begin with, Mao's behavior towards erring colleagues is to seek them out, talk with them, persuade them to correct their errors. Mao not only taught this method for Party unity, he practiced it. His authority, and the high regard and respect surrounding him (even from those who disagree with him), were earned by this trait in his makeup, which he has established within Party norms. Backbiting, malice, slander, harsh and cruel treatment towards comrades repel Mao. His struggle against Wang Ming was also against Wang Ming's draconian methods of dealing with Party contradictions. "Save the patient by curing the disease" was Mao's motto. Ideological deviations are a disease, to be cured by patient teaching, persuasion, criticism and self-criticism. Throughout his life Mao Tsetung would never believe that men could not change, or that they would be unwilling to do so once they knew the truth.

Party unity was Mao's overriding concern. To add more antagonism by treating Liu harshly would have strengthened the opposition to Mao. Liu had been frank, openly stating his views. Up to the end of his long and bitter struggle against Liu, Mao would still insist that Liu "did things openly." Mao attributed Liu's pessimism to disgust with the Wang Ming method of handling the Party.

But there were other sound reasons for Mao's gestures. Liu was leading underground organizations in the areas behind Japanese lines, controlled the liaison links with the cities and the urban intelligentsia, inaccessible to the rural guerillas who had Long Marched their way to the base in Yenan. From 1937 onward, intellectuals began to filter in. Many were "processed" by liaison groups behind the Japanese lines, which apparently owed allegiance to Liu Shao-chi. This was not always true; many groups were spontaneously organized and taken over by Mao's own men. But in the first two years (1937–1938) the inclusion of intelligentsia among the administrative personnel of the rural Red bases, to staff the institutes, academies and schools, provided a working link between the two men. Snow remarks that "Liu . . . built up the machine of underground parties in a vast territory stretching from the Yangtze Valley to Manchuria and from the China Sea to the Yellow River while Party membership increased from 40,000 in 1937 to 5,800,000 by 1950 . . . the great majority of these *new* members won promotion under Liu's chieftainship."* Liu thus built up his own head-quarters within the Party, side by side with Mao's. During the same period Chou En-lai headed the West China and South China bureaus in regions entirely under Chiang Kai-shek's rule, far more dangerous and less suitable for recruitment. "Consequently Chou's following among the new recruits was much smaller than Liu's," concludes Snow.

Even if we do not entirely agree with Snow's analysis (and there are as many exceptions to this theory of affiliation as there are confirmations), Liu Shao-chi was by 1949 a force to be reckoned with inside the Party. He was valued by Mao as a hardworking organization man. And there is no better evidence of Mao's concern for Party unity, and the future of the revolution, than that he not only put up with Liu but also gave him power and honor, hoping all the while to "convert" him from his right-wing views. "We should not condemn people out of hand. If they have made mistakes they can change, can't they? When they have changed it will be all right."†

From 1945 onward, when Liu Shao-chi's position as vice-chairman was secure, the occasions on which he opposed Mao multiplied; he seems to have gone on believing until the end that he was right (he died in 1974 of cancer, aged seventy-six). But the climate introduced in the Party by Mao Tsetung, the style of handling Party unity by admitting debate and opposite views, the "struggle by persuasion," is the reason that the "alliance and struggle" situation with Liu endured so long. "We must at all times firmly adhere to and never forget these principles: unity, struggle, unity through struggle, to wage struggles with good reason, with advantage and restraint."

Until 1965, despite many occasions when Mao Tsetung berated Liu Shao-chi (more or less openly), he would not take action against Liu, because he still hoped that Liu was "curable." But when the "contradictions" with Liu grew to a point which Mao Tsetung felt jeopardized the future of the Chinese revolution, he called upon the Chinese masses to topple Liu Shao-chi.

The two men differed above all in their concept of revolution, of what a Communist Party should be. For Liu Shao-chi, the Party was an elite of good and honorable men, assiduously striving for correctness, operating an efficiently honest bureaucracy, acting with objective paternalism towards the docile and subservient people, who had to be

* Edgar Snow *Red China Today* (New York 1971; revision of *The Other Side of the River*), pages 333–336.
† Mao in 1966, speaking of Liu Shao-chi.

"led" at all times. This view, whether Liu knew it or not, was elitist Confucianism, related to the "tutelage" concept under which Chiang Kai-shek had operated during twenty years.

For Mao, the Party leaders *could* err; the Party must, therefore, at all times "struggle" with itself and relate itself to the masses; once it became an elite, it betrayed the revolution. The Party's job was not to do things *for* the people, but to teach the people to become the decision makers, master the policies, and carry them out themselves. "It is to the advantage of tyrants that the people remain stupid; it is to our advantage that they be intelligent."

Liu was attracted and repelled by Mao's talent for fruitful chaos, by his great vision and fire and poetry, by the elemental strength which is Mao Tsetung, yet all the more insistent upon his own aloofness, his self-centered gentleman's pride. "Liu does not enjoy class struggle . . . he enjoys self-cultivation," wrote Chang Kuo-tao.* Liu must have been irked by Mao's combination of uncouthness and elegance, jocose ribaldry and classic wit, all those diametrical opposites which make up Mao Tsetung's personality. The most galling thing of all must have been Mao's immense popularity with the people; even when going against Mao's line, Liu would have to quote Mao to get a hearing.

Liu would never have imagined the cultural revolution; that Mao would risk destroying his own organization to protect the revolution could not be understood by a man for whom the organization was all, the revolution a by-product of the Party. Liu would always be afraid of the tempests that Mao called to birth; the release of the masses' initiative, those immense tidal waves which have shaken China and made her leap forward into her own future.

And yet Liu Shao-chi was also necessary to the inexorable pace which propelled China forward to make up in years for long centuries of stagnation, to the strategy for development within a continuing revolution which Mao needed. A Confucian longing to re-establish a mandarinate through the Party bureaucracy, Liu was yet the person whose "negative" example could be held up to teach the masses of China how things should *not* be done.

Till the end, Mao tried to save Liu from himself. In the furnace of accelerated change, Liu could not but fail; but dialectics also compel us to see in him a man who had his uses, for without opposites there is no progression.

* See Chang Kuo-tao's preface to *Collected Works of Liu Shao-chi* (Hong Kong 1968).

2

The Economic Base:
Agriculture and Industry
1949–1955

We shall . . . open roads yet untraveled.
— MAO TSETUNG, 1958

To anyone who has known pre-1949 China, the most mind-stunning change is the transformation of the countryside. Wide fields, with tree-lined canals crisscrossing their expanse; roads with motorized vehicles jostling horsecarts and handcarts; new houses in the clustered villages, electric light, and a star-scatter of small factories throughout the vast plains; well-dressed, healthy men and women working in groups. Abundance has come to the Chinese village, replacing famine, drought, epidemics, floods and war. "China is the one country which has solved its food problems," declared the agricultural scientist Norman Borlaug. The "green revolution" of the Chinese countryside is the most significant ecological advance yet undertaken by man to make our planet more bountiful and prosperous.

Yet it was a shattered, ruined land, a "blanket torn and full of holes," which the CCP inherited in 1949. Commerce bankrupt or paralyzed; administration nonexistent; cities haunted by starvation, misery and crime; beggared villages; famished millions.

The immediate measures taken to restore normality were effective. The discipline, honesty and efficiency of the victors enthused the population. Food returned to the cities. Hoarding was controlled; bandits — rife on every road — disappeared. "A miracle . . . The new feeling of relief and relaxation can definitely be sensed," wrote Derek Bodde, an American scholar then in China.

But restoration of order was not enough. The deep-seated problem of China's rural areas was the feudal, landlord-ridden agrarian system, "unjust in the extreme." The productive forces of the countryside could not be set free unless the system was destroyed.

In 1946 the Kuomintang Statistical Bureau had stated that China had only 8.06 percent of its total land area of 11,562,598 square kilometers under cultivation, and this area was shrinking because of erosion, mismanagement, droughts, floods, deforestation, wars. Productivity was limited by primitive farm implements, lack of soil care and improvement, lack of draft animals, the poor health and horrifying poverty of a population ravaged by famine and endemic disease (malaria, plague, schistosomiasis, smallpox). In Sinkiang, where only 1 percent of the total area was cultivated (desert oasis), a 46 percent decrease in tilled land had occurred since 1911. Deserts were growing, extending into the loess areas of North China (Shensi, Shansi, Honan provinces). The American experts employed by the Kuomintang government held that the root cause of rural poverty was technical; food production would go up with technological improvement. But the view of the CCP was that the oppressive exploitation of the rural landlord system, and urban capitalism (draining the resources of rural areas towards the cities), were the causes of rural China's backwardness and poverty.

A 1948 study by Professor Wu Wen-hui[*] revealed that landlords composed only 3 percent of the total farm households but owned 26 percent of tillable land; rich peasants, with 7 percent of households, owned 27 percent; middle farmers, 22 percent of households, owned 25 percent; poor peasants, hired hands and the landless, forming 68 percent of the farming population, held 22 percent of the land, and that of the poorest.

This inequality was compounded by the social hierarchy in villages; the absolute power of the landlord and village gentry (petty magistrate, clan heads, police chief). It took 30.9 years for a hired hand to become a tenant farmer, 49 years to become part owner or owner of some land.[†] The proportion of landless peasantry had doubled between 1928 and 1948.

Landlord tyranny was compounded with usury, total authority over contracts for labor, inhuman treatment of tenants as serfs. Fifty percent of the crop, or more, routinely went to the landlord for rent, regardless of climatic disaster; the landlord recovered the value of hired land within nine years. There was no system of legal redress.

[*] *Ta Kung Pao*, Hong Kong, December 18, 1948.
[†] Average longevity was then 32 to 35 years.

Exorbitant levies and taxes fell on tenant farmers, not landlords. No major works to curb floods or drought had been undertaken for decades. Inflation in the last years of the Kuomintang, indebtedness (the seed loan was particularly onerous; twice the amount of seed loaned for planting was to be returned by the autumn harvest), the right of the landlord to serf labor for 120 days a year, his right to take and sell the wives, sons, and daughters of indebted tenants — all contributed to the "backwardness" of the countryside. "Improved techniques" could not solve the situation.*

In the last years of Chiang Kai-shek's rule, galloping inflation had added to the burden carried by China's rural population, and war and the harsh levies of grain to feed the soldiery compelled millions to flee or to become bandits or beggars.†

Throughout 1949 and early 1950, policies towards the rural countryside were discussed with great vigor, and opposition to Mao's insistence on land reform continued. Mao Tsetung did win the consensus against those who wanted only "reduction of rent in kind" (the system operated in Yenan in 1940–1944) and land reform was officially announced in June 1950. Landlordism would be abolished, but the adoption of the "rich peasant" line‡ or "kulak" line which Liu Shao-chi proposed was upheld in the land reform resolution passed that month.

In fact, the "conservative" trend was so strong that in certain areas where peasants had begun to share the land on their own, they were enjoined to return it to the former owners.

Mao Tsetung bowed to consensus. "There should be a change in our policy towards the reach peasants. . . . from a policy of requisitioning the surplus land and property. . . . to one of preserving the rich peasant economy in order to further the early restoration of production in rural

---

* The same thinking, that technical improvement alone can solve the problem, has been practiced in Indian rural areas. It has benefited only landlords and rich farmers in a "green revolution" which has now failed because the unjust social system has produced increased income disparity, and deprivation among poorer farmers, with increase in landlessness.

† Between June 1937 and May 1949, China's monetary issue increased 144.50 millionfold, and prices 8,500,000 millionfold. Land tax in kind in Szechuan, together with government requisitions, totaled 18 million piculs of rice, enough to feed the residents of Chungking (population one million) for twelve years; however, hoarding and corruption still produced shortages. (One picul is equal to 120 chin, or 133 pounds.)

‡ "Rich peasant" line or "kulak" line was a term coined to denote a laissez-faire policy of individual farming. In practice it would have retained landlordism, for new landlords would have arisen from the rich peasants, who would have exploited the majority of landless and poor.

areas. . . . This will also serve to isolate the landlords while protecting the middle peasants."*

Mao urged that land reform be achieved by arousing the peasantry itself to denounce its own exploitation and to rise against the landlords. It was to be an education in politics as well as the accomplishment of needed change. The peasants must do it themselves; the Party could not do it for them. "The peasant must be educated into socialism." Agricultural cooperatives were "the only road to liberation for the people, the only road from poverty to prosperity. . . . Agriculture can and must be led prudently, step by step, and yet actively, to develop towards modernization and collectivization; the view that they may be left to take their own course is wrong. . . . The greatest efforts must be made to organize various mutual assistance cooperatives and for the improvement of agricultural techniques."

Liu Shao-chi's view that the natural forces of the countryside must have a free hand was reflected in his "four freedoms" suggestion: freedom to buy and sell land, to hire tenants, to select crops to plant, free markets and pricing. This suggestion, though not official, circulated at cadre level, and its effect was to diminish the effectiveness of newly formed peasant associations in carrying out land reform.

Liu insisted that "no requisitioning of surplus land and property of rich peasants will be done . . . *This is a long-term policy*. . . . Only when conditions are mature for the extensive application of mechanized farming, for the organization of collective farms and for the socialist reform of the rural areas, will the need for a rich peasant economy cease, and this will take a somewhat long time to achieve" (June 14, 1950).

The land reform campaign swung into action that summer. Represented abroad as a grim purge — although many landlords were spared; only tyrants were tried by people's courts and condemned to death — it started the process of change.†

The land reform teams were made up mostly of army cadres, and intellectuals and students from urban areas who were to be educated

---

* Mao Tsetung *Struggle for a Fundamental Turn for the Better in the Financial and Economic Situation in China* (Third Plenum, Seventh Central Committee, June 6, 1950). Author's translation.

† The author is constantly surprised by the existence of landlords in all of today's communes. Though they were deprived of voting rights, their influence would remain strong for a considerable number of years. In clan villages where all have the same name, and kinship is claimed to enforce feudal authority, a patriarchal connection exists between landlord and tenant. See Han Suyin, *China in the Year 2001* (London 1967).

by participation. "We must forbid the beating of any individual or destruction of property at will; we must start the struggle . . . according to circumstances and to the degree of awakening and organization of the masses. . . . To depart from the realities of the situation and amplify the struggle is dangerous" (Mao, June 6, 1950). In some areas it took weeks, sometimes months, before land reform teams could energize the poor peasants into moving against the landlords; but in other areas the peasants moved spontaneously to smash the landlord system.

Peasant associations based on the 70 percent poor and landless were given the responsibility for proceeding in each locality, and land reform was officially completed by the summer of 1952. Though the landlords lost out, the rich peasant and the wealthier middle peasant remained. They still had better land, better equipment, draft animals, capital, prestige, and influence. Usury was still possible. Trade shops and workshops belonging to landlords went untouched. Big landlords fled to the cities, leaving their landholdings in the keeping of poorer relatives; it would take more years and repeated "struggles" to really change the system.*

Mao Tsetung would not let things stagnate. In 1951 he began one of his many tours through the countryside and by December had initiated a further step. His *Draft Decisions on Mutual Aid and Cooperation in Agricultural Production* (submitted in December 1951) encouraged the formation of mutual aid teams. Mao analyzed the smallholders' mentality: "Their enthusiasm for production manifested itself in individual economy on the one hand, and in mutual aid and cooperation on the other . . . These two trends reflect the dual character of the peasant . . . in particular that of the middle peasant . . . which arises from the peasant being at one and the same time a toiler and a property owner." The key to success lay in actively encouraging the trend towards mutual aid and cooperation. "In no way can the spontaneous forces of the countryside be allowed full play." With the deeply entrenched habits, customs, attitudes of the past, such freedom would mean only a return of exploitation.

Within a year after land reform had begun, exploitation by rich peasants was producing a new rural polarization. Nationwide rural surveys in 1951 and 1952 showed that poor and landless peasants, even

---

* An "ultra-left" tendency also occurred at the time, with landlords and rich peasants totally deprived of land and constrained to flee to the cities or become bandits. Mao also spoke against this extremism.

when given land, could not effectively work it because of scarcity of implements and capital, and were once more falling prey to the wealthier farmers. To resist this retroversion, in Shansi province, in the spring of 1951, the poor peasants banded together to form cooperatives, without any directive from the Communist Party. But within the space of two harvests many poor peasants began to lose their newly acquired land under the "freedom to sell land" circular.* With the Korean War (1950–1953), price manipulation in the cities, under the "free market" theme promoted by Liu Shao-chi, led to a black market and resurgent hoarding. Landlords and rich peasants with connections in the cities (and many were also traders in grain) helped to drain countryside produce towards city speculation.

In Manchuria, Kao Kang, the Party secretary for the Northeast, stuck to the rich peasant line and ignored all Central Committee directives for collectivization, which he qualified as "absurd." Liu Shao-chi wrote a letter to An Tze-wen, vice-director of the CCP Organization Department, dated January 23, 1950: "Only with 70 percent of peasant families owning three horses shall we be able to go on to collective farms . . . at the present time peasant exploitation saves lives . . . not to allow it is dogmatism." (This three horses dream would never have been realized in China's conditions, where in 1949 there were only 107 million hectares for 500 million people in rural areas.) On May 7, 1951, Liu derisively called the few cooperatives which had sprung up spontaneously "isolated islands in the ocean of the countryside." In June an article by Po I-po† called *Strengthen the Party's Political Work in the Countryside* derided the cooperatives. In July Liu called a Shansi province Party committee report on cooperatives "utopian . . . mistaken . . . dangerous." In July at a lecture at the Marx-Lenin Institute for Higher Cadres, Liu expounded: "Such spontaneous forces cannot be checked . . . hiring labor and individual farming should be unrestricted . . . no collectivization before mechanization . . . production and financial reconstruction are top priorities."

Mao was undeterred. "If socialism does not occupy the rural front, capitalism assuredly will" (1951). "Our aim is to *eliminate* the rich

---

* The intra-Party document expounding Liu Shao-chi's "four freedoms" policy; see page 27.

† Po I-po, born 1907, in 1952 a member of the State Planning Commission; alternate member of the Politburo and vice-premier in September 1956; director of the Industry and Communications Ministry in 1961; and vice-chairman of the State Planning Commission, October 1962. He is said to have been one of those who abjured in 1936.

peasant economy and the smallholder economy in the countryside so that all the rural people will become increasingly well off together."

By 1952 almost half of China's arable land had been redistributed (46 million hectares out of 107 million hectares) and 300 million poor and landless had obtained land. The local landlord and gentry apparatus of exploitation was abolished, and committees for village administration were set up, founded on poor peasant associations. But the system also had its problems: commandism,* infiltration by rich peasants or the sons of landlords because of the need for literate cadres. Stories of landlords' sons or nephews in schools in the cities being recruited as cadres for the land reform program and protecting their families were current. And fully half of the students in colleges would be of landlord or rich peasant origin.

The initial land sharing did not solve the basic problem of "four months a year" labor. The countryside suffered not only from demonetization and exploitation, but also from disguised unemployment; the average period of actual labor on the land was four months a year, not through sloth but through backwardness, lack of implements, of crop diversification, of secondary occupations, of infrastructural work with labor-intensive techniques; lack of capital and loans, lack of banking processes to fund rural development, lack of workshops and of enterprises to transform the primary material produced into manufactured goods on the spot, lack of transport to open up untilled land.

"The inevitable result was that a struggle between . . . these two trends . . . capitalism or socialism . . . arose in the rural areas."†

The poor and landless, 70 percent of the rural population, wanted cooperatives. "A rich peasant is like a snake in one's pocket," the poor said. By January 1952, 43 percent of the peasantry had formed mutual aid teams "as a way of avoiding poverty and bankruptcy." Investigation showed that between 1953 and 1954, eight hundred peasant families out of five thousand in one area had been compelled to sell their newly acquired land within a year.

Although mutual aid teams helped with routine planting and harvesting, they were most in demand when everyone was busy on their own fields, including the members of the teams. They could not cope

---

* "Commandism" means giving orders arbitrarily, to be carried out without previous consultation and without allowing any dissent or differing opinion to surface. Mao always fought against this arbitrariness in the Party.

† Mao Tsetung *Cooperative Farming in China . . . Decisions of the Central Committee of the Communist Party of China on the Development of Agricultural Producers Cooperatives,* adopted by the Central Committee of the CCP, December 16, 1953 (English edition Peking 1965).

with farm management or climatic disasters, initiate technical improvement of tools, organize water conservancy projects. The tendency for
their aid to be monopolized by wealthier farmers was also strong.

Again Mao Tsetung toured, investigated. In October 1953 *The General Line for the Period of Transition to Socialism,* passed by the
Central Committee, affirmed collectivization and cooperatives. The
rich peasant economy formally disappeared. The draft on agricultural
production penned by Mao two years previously was passed in December 1953.

It is interesting to note the delay which Mao incurred in having his
suggestions passed. This alone shows how little the image of a dicta-
torial Mao, having his own way all the time, corresponds to fact.

"The struggle in the countryside between the two roads became
clearer in 1953–1954," wrote Mao in 1955. He began to collect an
immense series of on-the-spot reports, vivid and frank, from the poor
peasants and their associations.

"The masses are enthusiastic . . . seething with enthusiasm . . . a
potentially inexhaustible enthusiasm for socialism . . . boundless creative power . . . they can create more and more well-being and happiness for themselves." At sixty, vigorous and vital, still the same young
Mao who at thirty-three had seen the tornado of peasant power and
peasant revolution, Mao walked the Chinese earth, felt the great stir of
new life, and encouraged it with all his might.

Cooperatives were now official, but the pace of their formation was
slow at first. Landlords and rich peasants infiltrated them or resisted
their formation, asserting their own "leadership." Lower-level cadres
sometimes lacked drive and vision, but more often were impeded by
the Liu-controlled party apparatus at a higher level and by conflicting
directives. One such obstacle was the sending of "work teams" from
higher echelons, which discouraged cooperative formation, "dampened
enthusiasm" as Mao put it, in the name of "orderly process."

But Mao Tsetung kept on pushing. He worked in trains, in impro-
vised quarters, pored over figures and reports and plans. "For the first
time the vast majority of the people see their future clearly," said Mao
Tsetung.

The first five-year plan in industry* allotted only 6.7 percent of
investment resources to agriculture. It was drawn on the Soviet model,
that agriculture was "an auxiliary of industry," and no more. How
much of this contempt for the peasant was due to Soviet experts, how

* See pages 51–52.

much to the urban-oriented technocrats of the CCP itself, is not clear. Yet in 1949, 90 percent of China's national output came from agriculture, 10 percent from industry; 97 percent of the budget for the first five-year plan would be funded by the Chinese themselves, overwhelmingly from agricultural production, with only 3 percent from external aid (USSR).

"To complete the technological revolution in agriculture [mechanization and electrification] four or five five-year plans will be necessary . . . [this] *must* be the goal of industrial development," Mao had said in 1952. But the goal of an industry created primarily to develop mechanization and electrification in the rural areas was by and large neglected, though it was inscribed, in the first five-year plan.

Mao's view that only rural collectivization could unshackle and increase the productive forces of China's agriculture (upon whose surplus industrial expansion depended), and that collectivization must precede mechanization, was not a new concept but one based upon his intensive study of Lenin.

Mao is, above all, a Leninist, Lenin's continuator and developer. So much of what Mao thinks and puts in action is an extension of Lenin's lonely battles in the early 1920's against the rising tide of arbitrariness and bureaucratism in the USSR that it is almost possible to see the two men bridging the gap of time and nation, Mao picking up where Lenin was stopped by death.

Already in 1936 Mao Tsetung had expressed an idea basic to Leninism which would guide all the policies he initiated twenty years later: "When it is impossible for the productive forces to develop without a change in the relations of production, then the change in the *relations of production* plays the principal and decisive role. . . . While we recognize that in the general development of history the material determines the mental, and social being determines social consciousness . . . we also, and indeed must . . . recognize the reaction of mental on material things, of social consciousness on social being."* And now he argued that: "In agriculture, with conditions as they are in our country, cooperation must precede the use of big machinery . . . socialist industrialization cannot be carried out in isolation from agricultural cooperation."†

By 1953 Mao was studying the Soviet model as operated by Stalin.

---

* *On Contradiction. Selected Works of Mao Tsetung* (English edition Peking 1961–1965), vol. I.

† *On the Question of Agricultural Cooperation,* July 31, 1955. *Selected Readings of Mao Tsetung* (English edition Peking 1971).

His critical research and comments on Soviet agriculture and industrial methods and policies were not known until the cultural revolution, but hints of his remarks were available in private interviews.

Although Mao averred that he knew "nothing" of industrialization, he was not dogmatic about his inexperience. It was Liu Shao-chi, and the anticollectivist right wing, who proved "Stalinist," quoting the experience of the USSR, emphasizing the priority of heavy industry, without a sober quest of China's practical needs. Liu would uphold the "theory of productive forces" as the motor of change, something which Stalin and his successors also believed.

Yet this theory had been denounced by Lenin as "revisionist." It denied the concept of class struggle as the motor force of historical change; denied the necessity for continuing the revolution under the dictatorship of the proletariat, a major and basic Communist principle. It would permit a new state bureaucracy-bourgeoisie to emerge as the dominant power holder, a new exploiting class.

Mao would opine (in 1958) from his reading of world history that revolutions in the past had begun with changes of opinion, the overthrow of backward ideas, effecting changed relations of production *before* a great or rapid expansion of productive forces had occurred (though there was always "some" development). But to the "orthodox" — i.e., Russian-patterned — this was aberration. Only when heavy industry had expanded enough to turn to rural mechanization could there be cooperatives.

In the typical bureaucratic way of seeming to comply while actually sabotaging directives, a Ministry of Agricultural Machinery was duly set up, with tractor stations planned on the Soviet model, and tractors purchased from the USSR. But they went to the large state farms (three hundred in existence by 1954) manned by demobilized PLA personnel, who enjoyed technical prerogatives. Nothing of the kind could be done in the backward rural areas, where no individual peasant could afford to own or to run or to rent a tractor; and it was also impossible for the early cooperatives to do so with no oil, no technicians, no spare parts.

Yet in 1952, through the abolition of the landlord regime, grain production, only 108 million tons in 1949, was 152 million tons — a yield never reached before in China's history.

Mao Tsetung moved, and five hundred million peasants moved with him to change the earth.

"Everyone has a pair of hands . . ." If everyone moved hands, they could move mountains, tame rivers, make the deserts bloom. Man-power alone had wrought in the past great wonders; why could not conscious mankind, in collective units, its mind made bold to try the untried, work for its own prosperity? All that was needed was "to trust the masses," which meant to explain the policies, arouse the boundless creative power of the people, unshackle initiative, creative energy. Mao's trust in the masses was as intact in 1955 as it had been in 1927. (It is as intact in 1975.) He quoted Lenin: "The Soviet power is strong because the masses know everything, judge everything, and act in full knowledge." This "mass line" was fundamental to victory in any under-taking.

Thus Mao Tsetung in 1953 and 1954, pitting the vast majority of the peasantry — wanting cooperatives, demanding restriction of rich peas-ant and new exploitation — against the Liu Shao-chi line of "pru-dence," which was really stagnation and the maintenance of rural exploitation.

Mao started to grapple with the problem of water conservation. He toured the Yellow River in 1952. "The Yellow River must be tamed . . . the Huai River must be tamed." Too long these rivers had been China's sorrows.

The Huai River project is now completed, ending the menace of flood to 55 million people in an area of 210,000 square kilometers, increasing irrigated farmland by 2,670,000 hectares, providing 1,000 kilometers of navigable waterways and hundreds of electric power stations. All this took fifteen years and was done with very little ma-chinery. The Yellow River conservation projects were tackled and a two-thousand-year menace brought under control; had the masses waited for machines to do it, there would still be famines in North China today.

"Class struggle" surged in the villages. Rich peasants resisted state purchases of grain, cotton, oil at fixed prices; they made contracts directly with city organizations under the "free market" scheme. The revenue of a few rich peasants increased faster than the total revenue of the villages they belonged to. In the early cooperatives (inexperi-enced and shaky), rich peasants encouraged waste and extravagance, withdrew their draft animals or implements at times of harvest or plant-ing, said: "Why worry? If you eat your pigs, the state will give you more. . . . Joining the coop is like acquiring sons. One can lie down and rest. . . . Now you have a guarantee (against hunger), no need to worry."

By the end of 1952, 59,000 households had begun to organize cooperatives. In 1953, 275,000 households. By mid-1954, 2 million households, or roughly 2 percent of the 100 million peasant households of China, were in cooperatives. Eighteen cooperatives existed in 1950; 129 in 1951; 3,634 in 1952; 15,032 by mid-1953; 114,165 by 1954.

But now bureaucracy stepped in: "Drastic reduction by order of 'the Center.'"[*] Cooperatives were disbanded; peasant households returned to individual farming. It was alleged that the cooperatives "worked badly," "had not been well planned." However, some coops refused the order to disband; poor peasant associations resisted the cadres enforcing the order.

In the autumn of 1954 another setback occurred; 70 million piculs of grain, far more than the North China region could supply without hardship, were arbitrarily procured by the State Purchasing Corporation for increased industrial needs. This caused great discontent and had a bad effect on relations between the peasantry and the Party cadres enforcing the levies. As Mao would remark in 1955, relations between Party cadres and the masses became "abnormal" due to arbitrariness, commandism and arrogance.

An angry Mao Tsetung took action. The agricultural tax, fixed at 15 percent of produce, was now lowered to 10 percent, with flexible provision for further downgrading in case of hardship and climatic disasters. The State Purchasing Corporation was overhauled. Extra levies were forbidden. Margins were set in case of adverse conditions, with total remission for distressed areas. Through these measures, and a vigorous propaganda campaign, with "struggle" of the peasant associations against "class enemies," the revolutionary impetus — which was fading in bewilderment and discontent — revived in the countryside. Suddenly the cooperative movement took on an enormous amplitude.

The upsurge also coincided with the return of PLA men from Korea in late 1954. These peasant veterans returned to their villages to become cadres and to lead the collectivization movement. Poor and lower middle peasant associations became stronger, with vigorous, politically experienced ex-PLA men in every community.

Suddenly 650,000 coops came into being in early 1955 (16,900,000 households, 14 percent of the total). But this was only the beginning of what Mao would describe as "a tremendous event" in his preface to

[*] A term used to denote orders from "on high," usually meaning the Central Committee. Yet we shall often see such orders come from only a bureaucratic department or ministry in Peking. See pages 37–38.

*Socialist Upsurge in China's Countryside,** a collection of reports from
the rural cadres and the poor peasants of the conflicts which took place
to launch cooperatives. The book is the most vivid and entrancing story
of a nation changing, of minds groping their way to reason and to
scientific logic.

To each report Mao appends his own comments, pinpointing the
battle against old ideas, against superstition and fear, against rich
peasants and landlords, against arbitrariness and corruption, the failing
and errors of some cadres, the exertions or indifference of Communist
Youth League members: a picture of rural China in the throes of
revolution.

"In three years 85 percent of the 4,343 families in the eleven town-
ships of District Ten (in Tsunhua county) joined semisocialist cooperatives. If this place could do it, why can't others? If you say it is not
possible, what reasons can you offer? *I see only one reason* . . . unwill-
ingness to take the trouble or, to put it more bluntly, right opportunism. . . .

"The people are filled with an immense enthusiasm for socialism.
In a revolutionary period those who only know how to follow routine
paths cannot see the enthusiasm. They are blind. Let something new
appear and . . . they rush to oppose it . . . Let him† walk among the
people, learn what they are thinking, see what they are doing. . . .
That is how to cure his ailment. . . .

"The agricultural cooperative movement from the very beginning
has been a severe ideological struggle. . . . Our most serious failing is
that Party leaders in many places have not bestirred themselves to keep
up with the encouraging situation."

There are stories of wrecking, sabotage, murder, "quite common in
many places," by hostile elements. There is corruption. In Shansi province cadres "were found guilty of corruption and other unlawful practices" — graft and stealing, profiteering, refusing to show the
cooperative accounts to the peasants. The cadres "grow haughty . . .
unwilling to tolerate any supervision" by the peasant associations who
had been empowered, by right, to supervise the cadres. "They go so
low as to help themselves to public funds."

In 1954 and 1955, the rich peasants but not the middle peasants had

---

* *Selected Readings of Mao Tsetung* (English edition Peking 1971), page 421.
Socialist Upsurge in China's Countryside (Chinese edition December 1955; English
edition Peking 1956).
† In the singular in the original. Was Mao thinking of one particular individual?

been refused admission to the cooperatives. But now the wealthier middle peasants gave trouble. They supported, sometimes secretly, sometimes openly, the excluded landlords and rich peasants. Distinction between upper and lower middle peasants was made in 1954. Landlords, rich peasants, and upper middle peasants were now sifted out of peasant associations. Mao called the whole epic struggle "peaceful" because it did not involve wholesale killing, but it was severe. Notwithstanding the scarcity of bloodshed, there were trials and executions for sabotage, arson, poisonings, murder.*

The peasant associations were now maturing — tough, resilient people. Communist Youth League members, active and literate, were sent to each coop to strengthen the administrative framework. There were many problems of management, of remuneration. The work point system came in, but allocation of work point value would cause endless discussions for years.

To live through all this was in itself to acquire thorough knowledge of rural China. Poor illiterate peasants would develop qualities of leadership in a process requiring enormous patience, unswerving dedication, and almost superhuman energy. Through practice, performance, the revolution in the countryside would create leaders who in 1975 would accede to the highest rank in the Party.

By June 1956, 91.7 percent of peasant households were in cooperatives. Despite the dearth of fertilizers and technical aids, grain production would reach 165 million tons that year.

Obstruction continued. In late 1954 a "hacking down" of cooperatives in Chekiang province was suddenly ordered by "high level" authority. Out of 53,000 cooperatives, 15,000 were disbanded in 1955.

This "resolute contraction" (Mao's words) was not by decision of the Chekiang provincial Party committee but by orders from the Center. "At one fell swoop, 400,000 peasant households were returned to individual farming. . . . This was altogether the wrong thing to do, decided in a panic-stricken state of confusion. It was not right either to take such a major step without the consent of the Central Committee." This revealed that Liu Shao-chi's power at the Center was such that his apparatus could bypass or ignore the Central Committee and its chairman, Mao.

* No statistics are available, but the figure of five million condemnations is sometimes quoted unofficially (1 percent of the total rural population). This does not mean executions, which remain very few, as witness the number of former landlords, rich peasants, etc., still in the villages today.

In July 1955 Mao lashed out against "those who obstruct the advance of the economic base." He spoke just after the official announcement of the "major struggle" which purged Kao Kang and other adherents of the "rich peasant line,"* and when there was a shake-up throughout the Party and a counterrevolutionary purge. Mao was putting the finishing touches to his own grand strategy for economic development, which he would expound in 1956.

On the hot afternoon of July 31, 1955, Mao assembled the provincial, municipality, and autonomous region† Party representatives and made a long forceful speech. The fact that Mao spoke to *provincial* personnel, away from the Peking Center, to denounce the incorrectness of orders from "a higher level" and from the Center, was a momentous example of revolt against hierarchic authority. It was unprecedented, and broke with all tradition. All past Chinese administrations had been heavily centralized. Directives "from Peking" were imperial commands. By appealing to the regions to resist orders from the Center, Mao was actually beginning his great battle against power centralization in the hands of the capital's bureaucracy. This action was not a capricious burst of temper, but a well-calculated move in a long-term strategy to decentralize authority and allocate more decision making to the regions. It also set an example. Mao's concept of democratic centralism stressed the right to object to orders which were palpably incorrect. He had already stated this in 1930.‡ Party members must not be "docile instruments"; they must investigate, know real conditions. "You must investigate. You must not talk nonsense. . . . No investigation, no right to speak." "A Communist must always go into the whys and wherefores . . . must use his head and think carefully."

Mao's fact-finding tours had made him aware of a growing unease among provincial authorities, bypassed or ignored by the Center in the plans drawn up. The "tribute" paid by the provinces was heavy, and control of funds was in the hands of the Center.

"Some of our comrades are like a woman with bound feet, tottering along and constantly grumbling to others: You are going too fast. . . . To criticize excessively, blame inappropriately, worry endlessly, put up

* See pages 62–64.
† China has twenty-two provinces, two municipalities (Peking and Shanghai), and five autonomous regions. The fifty-four national minorities inhabiting the autonomous regions form 7 percent of the population.
‡ *Oppose Book Worship*, May 1930. Mao Tsetung *Selected Readings of Mao Tsetung* (English edition Peking 1971), page 40. Mao's whole career is an example of refusal to be servile to authority.

countless taboos and commands . . . this they imagine is the correct policy for guiding the socialist mass movement in the rural areas. . . . This is the wrong policy."

Mao called collectivization *"a revolutionary movement involving a rural population of more than five hundred million and . . . of immense significance for the world. . . .* We must guide the movement boldly and not always fear the dragon ahead and the tigers behind. . . . Treasure every bit of socialist enthusiasm shown, not thwart it." He caustically advised "officials from above" to go down to the countryside to see for themselves what was happening. People did not learn "by attending a training class and listening to a lecturer explain a few dozen rules."

"The leadership is lagging behind the mass movement." The co-operative movement had always overrun the targets set. Coops were in existence *before* they became official. While 35,800 cooperatives were being planned, over 100,000 had been formed, and this response continued.

Mao referred to the arbitrary procurement of grain to cater to industrial demand, which had provoked regional suffering, hunger and discontent in 1954. "Let us remember this. . . . Any neglect or slighting of the peasant's daily life will result in a failure of the collective economy. . . . *Some socialist countries have committed errors in this."*

Mao then swings into severe criticism of "right opportunism," and this is the first time he refers to the right wing *at the Center itself.* "Do not repeat the 1953 mistake of mass dissolution of cooperatives, otherwise you will again have to make a self-critical examination. . . . But some comrades are not willing to listen . . . Some comrades, *proceeding from the standpoint of the bourgeoisie, the rich peasant or the well-to-do middle peasants,* examine the question of the worker-peasant alliance . . . a question of the utmost importance . . . in the wrong way. They think the present situation . . . a very dangerous one and advise us to 'get off the horse quickly.' If you do not, they warn us, you are in danger of breaking up the worker-peasant alliance.

"Everyone has noticed that in recent years spontaneous capitalism in the countryside has grown . . . On the other hand many poor peasants lacking sufficient means for production are still living in poverty . . . in debt . . . If this tendency goes unchecked, the bipolar differentiation in the countryside will get worse . . . under such circumstances, could the worker-peasant alliance continue to stand fast? Obviously not. . . .

"This problem can only be solved on a new basis. The basis is:

simultaneously with the gradual realization of socialist industrializa-
tion, to bring about step by step the socialist transformation of agricul-
ture as a whole."

Thus, in July 1955, Mao bluntly warned Liu Shao-chi. But few in the Party knew whom Mao meant. Few indeed knew, until 1967, that it was Liu who had ordered the disbanding of the cooperatives in Chekiang.

Industry in China before 1949 was pitifully undeveloped. There were only 3.8 million workers, mercilessly exploited, the bulk of them in four coastal cities. A prolonged feudal state for two millennia had impeded the growth of commerce and enterprise. This precapitalist state was followed by colonial domination, with an imported capitalist structure, from the 1840's to 1949.

Colonialism produced in China a class called "bureaucratic compra-dore capitalist." The compradore capitalists were descended from the mandarins of the empire, great landlords wealthy and shrewd enough to invest in western industrial urban enterprises. This external capital-ism, grafted onto the previous feudal structure, made China a "semi-feudal, semi-colonial" country, as Mao had described it. The compra-dore capitalists supported Chiang Kai-shek, and in 1949 controlled 80 percent of China's industry, commerce, foreign trade, banking, rail-ways, airlines, road transport.

After the First World War, which weakened the grip of western colonial domination in China, there had also come into being a small "national capitalist" class. The national capitalists were recognized by the CCP as one of the four classes forming the people, with full rights of voting and representation. They did not ship out their wealth, they were often patriotic, many had been the victims of the bureaucratic compradore class.

In 1949 compradore capitalist enterprises were taken over without compensation to lay the foundation for the state sector of industry. But national capitalist enterprises remained in the hands of their owners. What would happen to them, how long they would be allowed to continue running their businesses, under what conditions, had been, as we have seen, a topic of contention between Mao and Liu Shao-chi at the second plenum of the Seventh Central Committee in 1949.

The take-over for the nationalized state sector comprised 59 percent of all capital in the banks (2,448 banks out of 3,489 belonged to the bureaucratic compradore class). It included the entire railway, highway and air systems, 45 percent of shipping tonnage (another 50 percent belonged to foreign companies), 67 percent of existing electric power, 33 percent of coal mines, 90 percent of steel (total production 140,000 tons in 1949), 45 percent of cement, the entire nonferrous metal industry, and 60 percent of the textile industry.

In 1929 Mao had discussed the great importance of the national capitalist class to China's future development, and its dual character: on the one hand an exploiting class; on the other, patriotic. Its importance to China's reconstruction was its overall fund of knowledge in trade, commerce, business, banking; its links with the intelligentsia, its command of scarce expertise. "We must unite with the national bourgeoisie in a common struggle." But it must not hold decision-making power.

The number of enterprises run by national capitalists in 1949 was 123,165; they employed 1,640,000 workers, including staff. Of these enterprises, 105,275 (70 percent) had fewer than ten workers each; only 164 had more than five hundred.* Seventy-nine percent were artisan and handicraft workshops with no mechanized tools.

Owners of one shop only (also reckoned as "capitalists") numbered four million, of whom only 3.3 percent were companies owning stock, and 96.7 percent were individual small traders investing their own capital. Ninety-five percent of the national capitalists had investments of less than 10,000 yuan (5,000 U.S. dollars at the pegged rate of two to one pre-1949). Only eighty-nine national capitalists in all China had investments of over 1 million yuan; of these eighty-nine, only seven had investments of more than 10 million yuan (5 million dollars).

In Shanghai only eighteen machine shops of more than a hundred workers belonged to national capitalists, of which only seven were completely equipped, the other eleven being assembly and repair workshops. Of 443 knitwear mills in China, only nine were complete, and they belonged to compradore capitalists, who also controlled all imports of foreign machinery from abroad (until Liberation China did not make any machinery of her own) as well as the raw materials from rural areas.

Life had been hard on national capitalists before Liberation. In the widespread inflation they had found speculation, hoarding, corruption, and bribery indispensable to survival. They were "squeezed" by the compradore capitalists. They rallied on the whole to Mao Tsetung but with mixed feelings. Would they now be instantly socialized?

* These figures were published in 1953.

"The bourgeoisie dare not revolt against us," said Mao, aware of this duality. It was entirely possible to effect a "peaceful transformation" of this class, first by putting them back to work, assuring their livelihood (many were in debt), then controlling and regulating their activities without arbitrary expropriation or nationalization and without bloodshed.

Though small and feeble, the class was potentially dangerous, because if given opportunity for expansion and power it would exhibit vigorous resurgence. It was the ideas the class carried, that whole structure of thought, motivation, habit, which constituted the danger, because such ideas, "bourgeois ideas," were to be found throughout Chinese society, urban and rural alike. "The Party is surrounded by an ocean of petty bourgeois," Mao had once remarked.

"After the countrywide victory . . . two basic contradictions will still exist in China," said Mao in March 1949. "The first is internal, that is, the contradiction between the working class and the bourgeoisie; the second is external, i.e., with imperialism."

This internal contradiction could be solved peacefully. There would be both "struggle" against the capitalists — against the idea of profit, exploitation, individual selfishness — and "unity" through persuasion, education, what is called "remolding," to transform their social outlook.

At first "rehabilitation" was a happy period for business circles. *Monthly Report,* a Shanghai English-language business paper, is enlightening on the subject: speculation was checked, money surged to the local banks, state control of food and raw materials effaced hoarding. "A miracle . . . beyond belief . . . kindling of popular enthusiasm never seen in Chinese history." Rehabilitation financing of capitalist enterprises proceeded smoothly, with payment by bookkeeping transfers between the private sector and local administration to avoid venality. Railways, coal mines, electric power began to function again. Payment for workers and staff in enterprises was partly in basic grain.* Three million ex-Kuomintang administration employees were also being rehabilitated, employed or semiemployed, a large burden on the new government.

In June 1950 Mao addressed himself to a serious review of the economic situation. The international situation was "favorable" (that was eighteen days before the Korean War started), but there was an in-

* Workers' wages were paid on an index based on the price of rice, oil, coal, flour and cotton cloth plus basic grain allowances.

crease in the number of unemployed. Land reform, large-scale reduction in government expenditure, administrative and army expenditure (the latter was 35 percent of budget costs), readjustment of industry and commerce, and frugality, economy, would alleviate the situation. Mao emphasized "unified control and leadership" of financial and economic work. Abuses were occurring. Frugality and economy must be practiced and be inculcated, for this was the only way to build socialism. He hinted at venality within the Party, degeneration among Party members, and proposed a "rectification campaign." This was to be done "with open door," soliciting the criticism *of the masses*. It was obvious from what Mao said that this degeneration in the Party was occurring in *urban* areas, and was due to the "sugar-coated bullets" of the astute bourgeoisie, "who will come forward to flatter us."

But Liu Shao-chi spoke of production and growth as compelling goals. "All things center on economic construction . . . many cadres now in the cities still have a peasant mentality, not applicable to city running. Some people . . . think socialism means overthrowing landlords in the countryside."*

Had things remained in this state, it was entirely possible for the small capitalist class to grow very rapidly in influence and then accede to power; for they could suborn and subvert cadres who themselves had become bureaucratic and cut off from the working people. As in the countryside, where the sons of landlords and rich peasants became the bookkeepers and sometimes even the sub-managers of cooperatives, so in the cities, in the reopened schools and universities, young people of the bourgeois intelligentsia were being promoted into administrative employment in the new government.

The private capitalist sector would forever complain of "economic restrictions which hamper production," and this was reflected in the Party press, which in certain cities such as Peking, Tientsin, and Shenyang appears to have been under control of the right wing (Liu in Tientsin and Peking, Kao Kang in Manchuria). Measures to "restrict workers' demands" were being pressed by employers in the name of "production."

Thus Fan Hung, dean of economics of Peking Academy, argued in "Observer Viewpoint"† that the national bourgeoisie "still has a historical task . . . the development of capitalism through exploitation" (reproducing Liu's argument that "exploitation has its merits").

* July 5, 1951. Liu Shao-chi to the Marx-Lenin Institute for Higher Cadres.
† *Kuan Ch'a* magazine, vol. VI, no. 1, October 10, 1949.

"Workers' welfare and their majority employment is inseparable from the right of exploitation," writes Fan Hung. Enough restrictions are present: the private sector is utterly dependent on the state sector for raw materials; hence the changeover from capitalism to socialism will be "easy" through state control . . .

Because of production priority, in August 1949 the Industrial and Commercial Bureau of Tientsin (a state control agency) rescinded control over acids, antimony, aluminum, nickel and other commodities supplied to private industry. This practice of rescinding state regulations in favor of the private sector in the name of "production" was abetted by officials in the state corporations. Since the private sector was run on the 25 percent basis (25 percent of profits for the businessman, 25 percent as government tax, 25 percent for workers' welfare — trade unions — and 25 percent for capital accumulation, expansion and running expenses), decontrol ensured ample profits to the private sector.

Decontrol became prevalent with the onset of the Korean War in June 1950. "Production first" sounded patriotic, but profiteering rapidly took hold. National capitalists reverted to the pre-Liberation pattern of corruption, bribery, nepotism. Businessmen contracted directly with rich peasants for agricultural produce; landlord "refugees" in the cities helped to sabotage government regulations. By the end of 1950 inflation had started again.

The "great patriotic drive to aid Korea and to defend the motherland" built the mental climate to halt this festering corruption. The government publicized war savings and victory bonds; private citizens contributed their gold, silver, jewelry in patriotic gifts. Stringent controls were imposed; special import-export permits, rationing of coal, a revaluation upward of private property and capital assets of private enterprises with increased taxation on private assets; a check on silver hoardings was imposed through a "joint consortium" of state-operated banks and silver houses. Severe penalties were enacted against those who kept false accounts. But a class so versed in corruption and gifted with scheming could not be quelled by such measures.

Stealing of state property, smuggling, tax evasion, shoddy work for the state, slacking on state contracts, using inferior materials, black-marketeering, hoarding, bribery, sending gold to Hong Kong . . . this was cooperation between an inexperienced, ill-staffed state sector (or staffed with erstwhile private sector employees) and a competent, unscrupulous private sector. There was even the exposure of a secret cartel of eight hundred private concerns in Shanghai which controlled the handling of state orders. The solidarity of the bourgeoisie was more effective in destroying the new order than that of the Party cadres was in controlling their activities.

The embargo placed upon China in May 1951* gave the private sector a great opportunity for pressuring the government in the name of assuring production. There were two alternatives for the state: to yield to "economic expansion and production first," thus allowing the private sector to gain the upper hand, or to strike back. Mao Tsetung decided to strike back.

"The old exploiting classes will be attempting a comeback. . . . We must remain vigilant," Mao had said in June 1949. Through greed, the national capitalists brought about the downfall of their class perhaps earlier than expected; they had "raised a stone to let it drop upon their own feet."

In 1951 a widespread purge began against counterrevolutionaries. A rising tide of Kuomintang sabotage (an estimated 400,000 agents were still in China) and attacks upon the mainland from Chiang's forces in Taiwan province were factors in starting the purge. It was undeniably a "brief reign of terror." At least 800,000 people were shot, jailed, sent to labor camps; in Shanghai 20,000 were arrested in a single day. They included gangsters, hooligans, smugglers, dope pushers. "Nightly we heard the trucks roll, carrying off people to be shot."† In the month of June 1951, 11,400 executions were recorded.

Two other drives for cleaning up society took place: the San Fan (three-anti) and the Wu Fan (five-anti). These two movements had specific targets; the three-anti was directed towards Party members who had connived with private capitalists or otherwise become corrupt; the five-anti towards national capitalists who had sabotaged or cheated. The active help of the population was enlisted in these movements, and they were very popular; workers, housewives, shop clerks, all joined in. There were political education movements in class struggle; special citizens' committees to receive complaints and denunciations were set up. The five-anti campaign (so named because it was to wipe out the five capitalist evils: bribery, tax evasion, theft of state property, cheating on government contracts, and stealing of economic information, which included spying) was what Mao called a "decisive

---

* By the United States, after having pushed a motion through the United Nations that China was the "aggressor" in the Korean War.
† Eyewitness.

struggle," and this was the end for the national capitalists as a class.*
But their ideas would remain, among the intelligentsia and within
some Party members.

By 1953, 450,000 private enterprises in nine big and small cities had
been investigated, of which 340,000 had been found guilty of one or
more of the five "evils." Dragged out before popular courts, reviled by
their own kin and their employees, the national capitalists in a short
time "remolded themselves." They wrote a great number of confes-
sions, attended classes in Marxism-Leninism.† Leniency was extended
to those who repented. How happy they were to be helped to transform themselves, saved from their own pernicious vices!! How many
were sincere? Mao was aware that the majority remained "wavering,"
waiting for an opportunity "to return on the stage of history."

The five-anti movement ended in the enthusiastic self-liquidation of
the private sector by the capitalists themselves, who formed a federation and opted for being taken over by the state sector, many of them
on a fifty-fifty basis. Take-over was completed by June 1956, Peking
accomplishing its take-over in twelve weeks. The capitalists were paid
dividends on their assets and interest on their money till 1966; though
dividend payments have stopped, payment of interest on bank accounts continues.‡ Until 1966 capitalists continued as salaried employees — managers or experts — in enterprises, though they earned
no profit. They retained their houses, and life for many continues to be
above the average in 1975.

The three-anti movement against Party cadres was much harsher.
Mao himself called on the people to rise "in wind and thunder" against
Party corruption, waste and bureaucracy, which were changing it into
a new tyranny. A million cadres were expelled or otherwise punished,
and there were summary executions.

Twenty-three years later, in April 1975, this major campaign, "the

---

* By 1953 mass movements — such as destruction of flies and rats, against plague,
for vaccination and city cleanups — had involved some 150 million people. The
campaign against illiteracy (50 million peasants attended literacy classes in the
winter of 1950) lifted the population into a pattern of collective endeavor for
weeks, for months on end. This began the habit of "mass movements" and participation effective in bringing new ideas and habits to such a vast population.

† Pierre Guillain, columnist on Le Monde, interviewing some capitalists in 1955,
said they were still "shaking" with fear. Author's interview with private capitalists in
Shanghai in 1959 found that they still had many privileges and benefits, and would
continue to enjoy them till the cultural revolution. One of the capitalists in 1966
still drove a new imported car; others were millionaires, and their sons and daughters
threw parties, sometimes attended by the offspring of high Party officials.

‡ In addition, there is no individual income tax in China.

first all-out assault against the bourgeoisie both within and without the Party," was recalled for the benefit of a new generation in China which had not seen the beginnings of liberation, to warn them that the seeds of exploitation, of a return to the past, were still present even twenty-five years later, still attempting to corrupt the body politic from within.

Although it was now claimed that the right-wing tendency in industry had been quelled, problems remained, one being industrial organization and management, even on a "socialist" pattern.

Exploitation of the working class was notorious in pre-1949 China. With the revolution, the workers expected a vast change. The contradiction between their aspirations (which led to spontaneous seizure of plants and roughing up of unpopular foremen and managers) on the one hand and the "priority to production" slogan was very apparent.

Trade unions followed the Soviet model, and their very existence nurtured a dilemma. To play their role as representatives of the working class they had to educate the workers into their decision-making role, since socialism means power to the worker. But at the same time the need for "production" required discipline, obedience to orders in a vertical chain of command.

Entrusting responsibility and decision-making processes to the proletariat was brought up by Mao as early as 1950, when he suggested that the Party "rely upon the working class" for its work in the cities. But working class power was not achieved by establishing workers' supervisory councils in factories, nor by organizing trade unions, because the right wing was strong in industry, even in the state sector. Until 1958, the year of the Great Leap Forward, educating the working class for decision and power holding was ignored. Mao's influence in the industrial sector was far weaker than in the agricultural sector.

In Tientsin, factory regulations for the establishment of "normal relations" between capital and labor were promulgated; they maintained the "normal" twelve-hour day with two days off per month only for trade union members! Seizure of power by workers in factories was absolutely forbidden. Under the "production first" slogan, the manager or employer nearly always had the upper hand. The employer was to remain sole judge of a worker's capacity; the apprentice system was maintained (five years' work without pay); "traditional usage" was to be followed in arbitrating worker-management disputes!

Some idea of the restrictions upon workers may be gained through the report of a plenary conference on September 7, 1949, published in the *Tientsin Daily*. The capitalist side retained the right to discharge workers "redundant" to production; discipline was to be strictly observed by workers; working hours were "as per custom"; there would be no wage increases, and workers were to refrain from "high and excessive demands"; welfare would be improved according to existing precedent; female and child labor would be paid equally *for equal work*; there would be the customary vacations — seven days per year at public holidays! Such rules and regulations, issued with the approval of the local Communist Party branch, were bitterly discouraging to the working class.

On April 6, 1950, an article obviously inspired by Mao, entitled *We Must Rely on the Masses in Running the Factories*, emphasized the place of the working class and its role in the running of industrial units and of the country; it recalled that the mass line *must* govern the buildup of industry. It pointed to *"deplorable incidents occurring in Tientsin and in other cities,"* where in the name of production Party members had given in totally to the demands of the employer and "did not care for the welfare of the workers"; where flourished a "bureaucracy" which "has changed nothing of the old system."

The trade union law of June 29, 1950, laid down the structure of trade unions in all enterprises — factories, mines, shops, mills. Labor insurance was set up. Workers were to "participate in the management of nationalized enterprises," and to determine conditions of work in the private sector. A labor constitution promulgated in May 1953 called upon the trade unions to "improve the material and cultural life of the workers": education, recreational facilities, dormitories, nurseries, and canteens. The material life of the workers improved greatly, but the goal, decision-making power within the state, remained unsatisfied until Mao decided to "push" in 1958.

On May 1, 1950, Labor Day, speaking as working class leader, Liu Shao-chi called for "cooperation between capital and labor" and for the workers to "unite with the national bourgeoisie" in production.

Industrial management would provide the clearest battlefield for the two-line struggle, and the story starts with Manchuria. In 1949 industrial development in Manchuria was one-third of China's total. The USSR had retained (through the 1950 treaty of friendship and alliance with China*) bases and control of the Manchurian railway. Kao Kang, chairman of the Manchurian (Northeast) government, went in July

---

* See page 111; also *The Morning Deluge*, pages 522–523.

1949 to the USSR and signed agreements for industrial equipment and technical aid in return for grain, vegetable oils, soybeans. Of the fifty projects of the aid agreement signed in February 1950 between the USSR and China, thirty would be set up in Manchuria.*

By 1953, 80 percent of Russian aid and 40 percent of the Soviet experts were in Manchuria. The Soviet pattern of industrial management was introduced and practiced there earlier than elsewhere, and since Manchuria was China's most powerful industrial base, as well as the arsenal and assembly plant for the war effort in Korea, what was done in Manchuria was broadcast as "the socialist model" to be imitated throughout the country.

Whole industrial plants complete with advisers were imported from the USSR into the Northeast during the first five-year plan, and the proposals made by Soviet specialists were accepted without discussion. Manchuria operated the "one-man responsibility system" or "one-man management," where decision making and factory running were concentrated in the manager, with an advisory panel of technical personnel. The workers thus had *no share* in decision making. A system of individual worker responsibility, piecework, bonuses, material incentives and a vertical hierarchy or organization was practiced. On July 10, 1953, the "one-man management" system was endorsed in a directive from the Ministry of Heavy Industry in Peking as a model for the state sector.

Every aspect of work in the industrial units was catalogued under a different department; all had echelons which could not be bypassed. Nothing could be done through initiative on the shop floor. The Soviet experts would only communicate with the "top," the "responsible" manager. They issued orders and no one dared argue; were they not *the* socialist model?

But one-man management was bitterly resented by the Chinese working class. They reacted badly to the system of "rewards and punishments," the pace of work, the quotas set without regard for differences in capacity of workshops, and without consultation with labor. They disliked above all Stakhanovism, which set them one against the other; the system of electing "model" workers to foreman positions cut across the traditional collective solidarity of the Chinese working class, which likes to work in teams, assuming responsibility for work done.

---

* When in November 1952 the State Planning Commission was created to draft the first five-year plan, Kao Kang became its first vice-chairman. The State Planning Commission was placed on a par with Premier Chou En-lai's State Council.

This new system destroyed group spirit, created conflict. It made for red tape, infinite delays in getting machinery repaired, an inflated administrative personnel, no cohesion or liaison between departments. Top centralization was making the same kind of muddle in China as in the USSR.

Many articles for and against one-man management appeared. Those against pointed to the diminished sense of responsibility among the workers. Machinery waited for a year or more for repairs because no one claimed responsibility for damage in the first place, and no one filled the requisite forms asking for repair.

The fall of Kao Kang in early 1954* and the denunciation of one-man management occurred at the same time. The system was to be superseded by "reinforcement of collective leadership." But on May 6, 1954, the *Outline of Labor Regulations for State-operated Enterprises* adopted by the State Administrative Council laid emphasis on the need for labor discipline and "an increase in labor productivity to match the expanding targets of the first five-year plan." Piecework, which had been instituted "to stimulate production," was maintained. So were bonuses. Punishments for negligence, absenteeism, and other infractions of regulations were enforced. Trade unions were now expected to popularize and to implement government policy.

One-man management was again denounced in the summer of 1955. A new system called factory-manager responsibility *under the collective leadership of the factory Party committee* was made official at the Eighth Congress of the CCP (September 1956). But at the Congress Liu Shao-chi, the person most concerned with industrial development as a former trade unionist, averred that managers, former capitalists, and higher technical personnel had truly undergone a basic change, had acquired a "proletarian outlook through working for socialism"! "In China, the question of which wins out, socialism or capitalism, is already solved," he said; at the time Mao was saying exactly the opposite. The main task of the Party and state was "developing production as quickly as possible," because the major contradiction was "between the socialist system and the backward productive forces of society." This was enshrined in the resolutions of the Eighth Party Congress in September 1956.

What it meant, baldly, was that one-man management, now disguised as "factory-manager responsibility under the collective leader-

* See pages 62–64.

ship of the factory Party committee," would continue. And with it would rise a manager-technocratic elite, a new bourgeoisie.

The first five-year plan was not published until 1955, though it began in 1953. On September 23, 1954, in his report to the first National People's Congress, Chou En-lai had said that the blueprint was "not yet complete and final." It was completed in February 1955, and passed in June.

The main target was to double industrial output, increasing national income 43 percent. Sixty percent of the basic construction work would be designed by Soviet experts, the remainder by Chinese planners working under Soviet specialists.

The plan did succeed in major sectors. By 1957 iron and steel production had quadrupled, coal and cement doubled. The annual growth rate was impressive. If we exclude 1953, the increase was 12 percent a year (1954–1957). By the end of the plan (1957), levies on industry in the form of taxation and profits together accounted for more than 70 percent of total government revenue.

Why then, if results were so brilliant, were many Chinese planners (not only Mao Tsetung) obviously disquieted by the plan? In that very July 1955, when the plan was published, Li Fu-chun, vice-premier and chairman of the State Planning Commission, was questioning certain aspects of its *cost*.[*]

It was not so much the first five-year plan in its concrete, material achievements which Mao questioned. The problem was deeper. It concerned the road China should take in the development of its economy. Chinese planners and economists who agreed with Mao's line of thinking were questioning the value of the Soviet model for China, both ideologically and in economic terms.

"In the ideological field, the question of who will win out in the struggle between the proletariat and the bourgeoisie has not been really settled yet," flatly said Mao in 1956, and again in 1957, asserting a view directly opposite to those Liu Shao-chi expounded at the Eighth Congress. He is still saying it today.

Mao was not sure the Soviet industrial model was really "socialist," judged by its results in Russia, nor was he anything but uneasy at some aspects of the Soviet economy. This apprehension well antedated the

---

[*] Li Fu-chun *Report on the First Five-Year Plan* (Cambridge, Massachusetts, 1962). Li Fu-chun, vice-premier of the State Council and chairman of the State Planning Commission, made the report on July 5–6, 1955.

Sino-Soviet dispute, and was the wellspring and source of Mao's search for another strategy of development for China.

What was the use of "production" and "growth" and "increased output" in industry, asked Mao, if it was not "to serve the people," to build socialism in China?

The capitalist system was just as capable of promoting growth increase, but it was done by the exploitation of the many for the few; it concentrated wealth in cities, draining the countryside. And Mao saw that in China the imported "socialist" model was tending to do the same — that Soviet industrial management did not differ all that much from capitalist management.

"When in doubt, investigate." From practice to theory, searching for the overall strategy of development which would not sacrifice the class which was to take power, the workers, nor their ally in the revolution, the peasantry. Mao toured and read, debated and studied. "When Chairman Mao thinks of something, he does not sleep; he sits up all night, thinking, reading, writing . . . he calls people and discusses the problems with them, sometimes for ten or fifteen hours."[*]

Already in 1955 Mao and his economists and planners were considering a different political and economic development. Criticism of the first five-year plan was current, but it was stifled; "it was not allowed to criticize . . . the unselfish aid of fraternal countries."[†]

For a country as poor as China, for whom frugality and economy were essential, a serious problem was the inflation of the bureaucratic staff in industry. There were two parallel administrations in each unit, the Party leadership and the executive staff. This plethora of cadres became as inefficient (and as formidably wasteful) as in the USSR. For example, in an 800-man factory in 1956, there were 126 administrative cadres, who felt fully busy though they never touched a machine. "They read the newspapers," said the workers. Another problem was that industries under the plan were unable to absorb the millions of youths coming on the labor market every year.

Waste and extravagance in use of materials and machinery, shortages due to ill-planned capital construction, delays in receiving spare parts, decrease in quality of products, unnecessarily large overhead costs are mentioned. But they are secondary to three main issues: first, depolitization of the working class; second, the strains of a capital-

[*] Said by a high official to author.
[†] Author's private interview.

intensive technology on a poor agricultural and backward country; and third, grafting onto an industry an elite (managerial-technical) whose approach had no relevance to the real problems of China. Worse, the monopoly of technology by an elite rapidly entering into the Party, protected and on the best terms with influential top officials, was a threat to the goals of the revolution itself. It was a state bureaucratic bourgeoisie . . . and how swiftly it could seize power!

Because of heavy reliance on Soviet experts, resentful servility pervaded the Chinese personnel. As in India today, where the scientific and technological native is often rejected in favor of foreign expertise, so in China the Soviet expert was "always right." Feelings of hostility on the part of the Chinese remained unspoken. Some of the objectors were trained in capitalist countries and would be accused of antisocialist demeanor if they disputed Soviet experts. There was a colonial flavor in the demeanor of some of the Russian specialists, who lived on a very high scale in China, and this also rankled.

"Old ideas reflecting the old system remain in people's heads . . . we must change ideas . . . through socialist education and changed *relations of production*," said Mao.

From the ranks of the working class itself must come the future managers, engineers, technical experts, the researchers and inventors, proletarian intellectuals both politically aware and solidly scientific — "Red and expert."

Another problem was payment for Soviet loans, machinery and equipment (cost above world prices). Much refunding was in agricultural products (meat, grain, oils, and fruit, etc.) and in rare metals. But indebtedness meant a growing dependence. By 1955 the Chinese were aware that the machinery supplied was not up to world standards except in price.

An anecdote, perhaps apocryphal, throws some light on the heart-searching and questionings in Mao's mind concerning the appropriateness of the Soviet model. It is said that he sent Kang Sheng, old and stalwart Party member,* to the USSR to investigate the tractor stations set up for the kolkhozes. Kang Sheng came back with a negative report. "They are draining the pond to catch the fish," Mao remarked as

---

* Kang Sheng (1899-1975). A prestigious member of the CCP since 1924, he took an active role in the Sino-Soviet dispute. His integrity and ideological correctness were never questioned, not even during the cultural revolution, when so many high officials were criticized.

he heard details of how these tractor stations operated as tax-collecting agencies.

"The problem today," Mao wrote on December 27, 1955,* "affects agricultural production, industrial production . . . the scale and speed of capital construction . . . the coordination of commerce with other branches of the economy . . . coordination of the work in science, culture, education, public health . . . *in all these fields there is an underestimation of the situation.*" If this lag continued, the Party leadership, far from being the "vanguard of the proletariat," would become a bureaucratic, conservative tyranny entrenched in its own privileges, a brake upon the rapid development of the productive forces, an obstacle on the road to progress.

As Mao saw it, the solution lay in transforming men's minds. There must be another way of thinking and doing which would suit the goals of the Chinese Revolution and the concrete conditions of China.

---

* See *Socialist Upsurge in China's Countryside* (Chinese edition December 1955; English edition Peking 1956).

3

The Superstructure,
the Party Struggle,
and Confucius

Regulations alone will not work . . . men's minds must change.
— MAO TSETUNG, 1957

Down with Confucius!
— Slogan of the
first cultural
revolution, May 1919

The "underestimation of the situation,"* the lag in understanding the compelling surge of the economic base, came from the "superstructure," which also encompasses the Communist Party leadership.

"Superstructure" denotes the ensemble of ideas, habits, customs and behavior — philosophical, legal, religious, political, artistic, literary — in any given society, and the institutions through which they function. What are called national characteristics, or the politico-cultural modes of a given group, are covered by that word. In Marxist terms, the superstructure is the "sum total of the relations of production." Like everything else, it is subject to the universal law of contradiction, embodying its unity of opposites. The superstructure will therefore have a dual role: conservative insofar as it represents the classes which are challenged by the new material and idea acquisitions at the economic base; progressive when it represents the latter. Within the Party retrograde individuals, representing the exploiting forces of the past, will cloak themselves in glib Marxist phrases to promote a reversal of the revolution. For to be a Party member does not guarantee that a man's mind has changed.

* See page 54.

The story of the next eighteen years would be marked by Mao's efforts to cleanse the Party, to avoid its degeneration into an exploiting new class, so that the country "will not change color . . . become revisionist . . . or a fascist state."* In his strenuous efforts to revolutionize the superstructure, Mao came up against not only Liu Shao-chi, but also against an embedded political culture — twenty-five centuries of literocratic administration — which is now, in 1975–1976, being vigorously challenged in the great movement against Confucian ideas.

Liu Shao-chi represented a way of thought far more prevalent than it seemed, not only in the Party but in society at large. For him the Party organization was *the* revolutionary line; the Party was *per se* the vanguard of the proletariat and revolution a by-product of the Party's existence. This automatic view of the Party as superior, infallible almost, because it held the "correct" theory, was itself a new Confucianism.

For Mao, it was quite possible to spoil a good system through the wrong methods. To spout Marxist phrases irrelevant to reality was "dogma . . . not as useful as horse dung." Practice linked to theory must validate at all times, through daily action and through the *correct methods,* the theory proclaimed. Hence the emphasis in all Mao's work on practice, growing and learning, adapting to changing situations, and the need for constant education of the Party cadres themselves. Only through this continuous honing of the Party, through practice as the determinant, could its claim to correct leadership be validated. And only practice could ensure the correct political line.

"A basic principle . . . is to enable the masses to know their own interests and unite to fight for them." Constantly Mao expounded the mass line; *to serve the people* was the Party's vocation and dedication, and the quality of its cadres (an important factor in success) could be guaranteed only by the closest integration with the people it served. And there was more. Mao insisted on the right of the masses to "supervise" the Party cadres. By saying this he recognized also the right of the masses to revolt against a Party leadership which betrayed the revolution.

In this conceptualization of the Party and its role, structure, and relationship with the people, Mao Tsetung was breaking with the entire system of Chinese political culture — two and a half millennia of Confucian authoritarianism so deeply ingrained in every Chinese mind (including Party members) that there was no longer a distinction be-

* Mao at the Ninth Congress of the CCP, April 1969.

tween what was "Chinese" and what was Confucian. The problem of the lingering prerevolutionary superstructure affects each revolution, and this old and infinitely resistant past affects the concrete conditions in which the revolution unfolds itself.

Not until 1973–1974 would Confucianism be denounced by name, and the Party really come to grips with the structure of the minds of the Chinese people, among them its own membership. Earlier, there was much denunciation of "bourgeois" and "capitalist" thinking; perhaps more appropriately it should have been "Confucian bourgeois" and "Confucian capitalist," for the capitalism China knew was grafted onto the enduring authoritarian framework of its past feudal ages. Sometimes certain habits (such as a love of bright colors, or a freer attitude towards the other sex) were denounced as "bourgeois" or "capitalist" when they were nothing of the kind, but only different from the Confucian cultural tradition.*

Confucianism classified men as superior and inferior, the learned and the manual laborers, the literocracy and the "small men," as determined by Heaven's mandate. The links of superior to inferior — father and son, teacher and pupil, husband and wife — were immutable. No revolt in this order could be allowed: "Above is knowledge; below is ignorance." It followed that a leadership group such as the Party would automatically assume (until pulled up by Mao) its own absolute superiority. "It is the masses who are intelligent . . . while the intellectuals are often stupid . . . childish," Mao repeated countless times. "A Communist must never set himself above the masses . . . he must learn from them humbly . . . Learn before you can lead." It was not the "heroes," but the masses, "the slaves . . . who make history."

It is Mao who has truly democratized the Chinese revolution; "without democracy . . . socialism cannot be established." He introduced voting in Party meetings, "open door" supervision of Party cadres by the masses, public criticism through "big-character" posters,† and the right of revolt "against reactionaries," even if these were Party leaders. In his eightieth year he would continue to uproot from the depths of the Chinese soul Confucian authoritarianism, docility and submission. "It is wrong . . . blindly to carry out directives without discussing them . . . simply because they come from a higher organ." One can imagine

* In general the peasantry loves bright colors; it is the intelligentsia which equates morality with dullness of attire, a typical Confucian attitude. Only someone well versed in Chinese customs realizes this.

† Wall posters (tatzepao) pasted up by anyone on any street, in factories, universities and schools, villages, etc.

what China would be like, what the CCP would be like, had it been Liu Shao-chi, whose contempt for the "ignorant" masses was flagrant, who prevailed. And how much the tidy-souled bureaucrats of the Party, heirs to the mandarins of old, must have resented Mao for upsetting their prerogatives of authority!

Mao's efforts to unshackle the minds of the people, teaching the many-millioned to enter into their own liberation through their own efforts and not by doled-out knowledge from above, is a landmark. "His claim to be remembered as a leader must rest not on the structural changes he introduced . . . nor on his success in laying the foundations for communism through methods which were moderate and bloodless compared with East European socialist countries. . . . Mao's brand of social engineering to tap the energy and ability of the ordinary people should win him . . . respect.*

The Party after Liberation presented many problems. In 1945 it had 1.2 million members, toughened by austerity, revolutionary practice and armed struggle, by years in the rural bases, and by the great rectification movement led by Mao from 1941 to 1944.† By September 1949 there were 4.5 million members, and 5.8 million by June 1950. The considerable accretion included raw, untried new members who had not been through the Yenan days, ignorant of Party history and even of Marxism-Leninism, as well as "riffraff, landlords, rich peasants, Kuomintang agents," infiltrators of every kind.

The needs of the administrative apparatus, government ministries and departments made the recruiting of cadres (both Party and non-Party) and their training very complex. Millions were required. Where could one get them, except from among the middle school and university students? — and these were nearly all from the urban bourgeoisie or sons of landlords and rich peasants. How to remold this potentially dangerous element? Ten thousand university and high school graduates had already been recruited in the cities in 1949 to cope with the necessary take-over of administrative units in newly liberated provinces. The new government had also inherited three million ex-Kuomintang employees.

The following example illustrates the difficulty of achieving political soundness with technical competence. Out of nearly 4,000 students in training to become government cadres in 1950, 2,100 came from the bourgeoisie, 650 were former Kuomintang employees, 400 unemployed

* Leo Goodstadt *Mao Tsetung: The Search for Plenty* (Hong Kong 1972).
† See *The Morning Deluge*, pages 404–420.

schoolteachers and lawyers, 500 from the Kuomintang police or armed forces, 60 capitalists, 50 landlords, 40 in trade, and only 140 called themselves "workers." Family origin analysis of nearly 3,000 of them showed 800 from landlord families, 800 from the urban petty bourgeoisie, 500 with rich peasant background, 500 national capitalists, 350 from the liberal intelligentsia and from compradore capitalist families, and none of worker or poor peasant origin. Even the "workers" were from impoverished urban petty bourgeois families.

Very soon the new bureaucracy would have its eight grades of cadres, reminiscent of the eight grades of the mandarins of old (and still existing today). Confucianism thrives on bureaucracy, and among the educated the idea of study in order to become an official was deeply embedded. In China every poet, writer, educated man was also an official, whether successful or not, and this persisted into the twentieth century. The word "intellectual" implied possession of knowledge and superiority. It had been through the first cultural revolution (May 1919*) that this straitjacket of officialdom had been loosened; publishing houses began to pay authors for their works, and thus allow them to live without becoming officials.

Bureaucracies inflate spontaneously. A waxing in number irrespective of need or efficiency is especially marked in "socialist" countries, where every educated man is also, in some respect or other, an official. In government as in industry, administrative units had parallel organizations — of the Party for political leadership, and of the governmental executive staff.

The rectification carried out in 1951–1952,† though purging from the Party about a million undesirables, did not solve the problem. A survey of the press indicates the divergent approaches. In some articles the study of Mao Tsetung Thought is earnestly promoted, and in 1951 the first three volumes of Mao's selected works appeared. But Liu Shao-chi's *How to Be a Good Communist,* first published in 1937, was republished and placed on the list of compulsory documents, whereas Mao's selected works were graded as reference material in the Marx-Lenin Institute for Higher Cadres, which was run by Yang Hsien-chen, once closely allied with Wang Ming. Yang had been hostile to Mao's ideas ever since 1938.

It appears that even in the early 1950's Mao was being nudged out of executive activity in the Party, and in October 1966 he explained

* See *The Morning Deluge,* pages 66–81.
† The three-anti (San Fan) movement (see page 45).

how this had happened: "For seventeen years now, I think one thing has been done badly." For considerations of the country's security, and in view of the lessons of Stalin's individual arbitrariness, two channels or lines of work had been established. "I was on the second line, I did not take charge of the daily routine; other comrades were on the first line."

Mao himself acquiesced in sharing authority; "I put too much trust in others." The "others" meant Liu, who had built prestige and authority, along with his selected clique, upon the power Mao had relinquished. The implementation of Party policies rested with Liu Shaochi.

Mao not only suggested mass participation in the Party cleanup (his "open door" policy meant public criticism of Party members by the masses), but also the admission of many more workers as Party members to counterbalance the preponderant peasant and intellectual elements.*

There was popular participation in the San Fan (three-anti) and Wu Fan (five-anti) movements already described. Activists from the working class who took part in the movements were co-opted into the Party. Schools and universities enrolled 180,000 such activists, and crash courses in reading and writing were given to 1.7 million others. The Party had only a 2 percent worker membership at the onset of the movements, but the total number of workers in China was 3.8 million, less than 1 percent of the population. Twenty-five percent of the Party in 1950 were rich peasants and urban petty bourgeoisie; 73 percent were classified as poor and middle peasants.

In 1952 An Tze-wen, then vice-director of the CCP Organization Department, proposed a policy of "raising knowledge and intellectual standards" among new recruits. This sounded excellent, but it could (and in practice did) discriminate against the hardworking, dedicated peasant cadres and favored the urban element. Eight criteria for Party membership were now laid down, and though worker participation was encouraged, admission of intelligentsia and petty bourgeois elements into the Party was also increased. It was decided to stop peasant recruiting for a while.

Mao Tsetung was not against admitting intellectuals; he had time and again emphasized the necessity for their participation. "We must learn from all who know,. no matter who they are. We must esteem

* Mao Tsetung's speech of June 6, 1950.

them . . . we must not put on bureaucratic airs." Unless the intelligent-sia were rallied to work for the socialist cause, the latter would not prosper. But this was a far cry from admitting a preponderance of unreformed candidates from the intelligentsia.

The problem was the dire need for competence in the administration, and out of about 600 million people there were only five million (Mao's own figure of 1957) who had achieved middle school or higher levels of education.

After crash courses in Marxism-Leninism, by 1956 many of the Party recruits from the intelligentsia had moved rapidly into administrative positions at the Center as well as in provincial capitals. "If the Chinese Communists had changed their recruitment policy and allowed all the new intellectual cadres to come into the Party, the Party would probably have soon turned into an elite club," comments Schurmann.[*]

Party recruitment thus was also a "two-line struggle." The concepts that Liu Shao-chi promoted — that collectivization must wait for mechanization; that there must be capitalist exploitation to develop a proletariat before socialism could work — rest upon the fundamental assumption that the working people, the base, are "not ready," and that it is the "superstructure" which is in advance and is socialist, whereas the productive forces are still backward. Thus class struggle is denied as the motive force of revolutionary change; it is "production" and "the economic forces" which achieve the goal of "socialism."

Mao fundamentally disagreed with this view, and criticized it when it was practiced in the Soviet Union. For him it was the superstructure, still permeated with past modes of thought and behavior, traditions, customs, and attitudes, which obstructed the surge of the economic base. "When the superstructure obstructs the development of the economic base, political and cultural changes become principal and decisive."

Party membership, the quality and class standpoint and consciousness of the cadres, their dedication to serving the people, were therefore of paramount importance. If the dominant influence within the party was an elitist, feudal-minded intelligentsia selfishly bent on achieving its own supremacy, the revolution would fail. Lenin had seen this happen and denounced it in the USSR, and Mao saw it as a possibility, ever recurrent, in China's young revolution.[†] Lenin had

[*] Franz Schurmann *Ideology and Organization in Communist China* (Berkeley, California, 1966), page 169.

[†] See Charles Bettelheim *Class Struggle in the USSR 1917–1923* (Paris 1975).

seen the bureaucrats who manned the new departments of the Soviet government turn it within two years into a replica of the old czarist regime. Mao Tsetung would do his best to stop the Chinese Communist Party from being turned into another Confucian, mandarin-like bureaucracy.

When the two-line struggle in the Party grows into an irreversible confrontation, a "major struggle" occurs. This took place in 1953–1954; it was not, strange to relate, between Liu and Mao, but with Kao Kang, vice-chairman of the Communist Party and of the state's central government, and Party secretary of the Northeast (Manchuria)* bureau.

Kao Kang was dubbed Chairman Mao's close comrade in arms, for he had been a local leader in the North Shensi base prior to Mao's arrival there after the Long March in October 1935. His propensity for considering himself not only indispensable but also best fitted to lead the Party, and his ineradicable stubbornness in sticking to his own ideas, had started in 1945. He claimed that Chairman Mao had said: "Only Comrade Kao Kang makes no mistakes." This was pure ironic Mao; since Mao as a dialectician considers that Party members who have *not* committed some mistake "are in great danger . . . they have not been immunized." Errors of ideology, like measles, have to be undergone and cured, to teach humility.

In 1951 Kao Kang, besides keeping his local appointments, became vice-chairman of the Military Affairs Committee, of which Mao was chairman. His excellent relations with the Russians were well known; it was rumored that Stalin had sent him a motorcar for his personal use.† As chairman of the Sino-Soviet Friendship Association he had extolled Russian friendship, even hinting at merging Manchuria with the USSR; "new patriotism means internationalism, there should be no frontiers between us."

Kao's propensity for running Manchuria as his own "independent kingdom" was actively abetted by the Soviet government. Manchuria, as China's greatest industrial center, served as the model for industry. One-man management was copied notably in Shanghai (also an industrial center) by Kao's friend Jao Shou-shih. Jao was Party secretary of the Shanghai Municipal Party Committee, and also head of the East China bureau.

---

* Also known in Chinese as the Three Northeastern Provinces.
† See Stuart Schram *Mao Unrehearsed* (London 1974).

In 1952 Kao and Jao were asked, together with many top-echelon cadres in the provinces, to come to Peking; the Center needed talent for national planning. The draft constitution was being discussed and preparations made for the first National People's Congress. Jao became director of the CCP Organization Department, and Kao chairman of the State Planning Commission — both men rising stars at the Center.

The absence of Jao from Shanghai diminished his local base of influence; but Kao did not give up Manchuria, and flitted between the Northeast and Peking. He continued to assert his independent policies, despite the fact that the Central Committee was now passing resolutions for agricultural collectivization. Kao and Jao stuck to the rich peasant line and ignored criticism of one-man management in industry. It was not, however, these "right-wing" deviations which brought about their downfall; in fact, their views were close to Liu Shao-chi's. But Kao Kang felt sufficiently strong to challenge the Party leadership, sufficiently backed by the USSR to attempt to take power.

Kao Kang and Jao Shou-shih, through a network of fellow conspirators in the Party, attempted a coup. In his subsequent denunciations, in 1955, Kao was accused of having plotted a seizure of power ever since 1945. He had engaged in "splitting activities" which were bound to lead to disruption in the Party.

Actually, Kao Kang was a competitor for Liu Shao-chi's rising control of Party cadres. He accused Liu of having his own "majority" of educated cadres at the Center, and hinted that a good many of them were untrustworthy and should be replaced. Kao Kang probably knew well enough that some of Liu's close colleagues — such as Peng Chen, the Peking mayor, and Po I-po, the minister for Heavy Industry — had been linked with the abjuration affair in 1936–1937, which if true made them renegades. Kao said that Liu Shao-chi, Chou En-lai, and Teng Hsiao-ping should give up their posts while he, Kao, should be the Party's general secretary, first vice-chairman, and premier of the State Council . . . no mean ambition for one man.

Kao Kang averred that there were not one but two Parties, or "two headquarters" in the Party: that of the Red bases, under Mao, and that of the White areas, under Liu. The two had come together. He, Kao, belonged to the Party of the Red bases, which was the "senior Party," he said, and should therefore have more authority. He seems not to have confronted Mao directly, but while in Peking he approached the minister of Defense, Peng Teh-huai. There are rumors (uncorroborated) of a joint letter to Mao, advising the latter to "take a rest."

Some of what Kao Kang was alleging turned out to be correct, but his actions destroyed Party unity, and Mao as Party founder could not tolerate this ambitious intrigue or indulge a feudal satrap conspiracy.

Kao Kang was unlucky in his timing. In March 1953 Stalin died; the Korean War ended in a cease-fire in July; and China's dependence on the USSR diminished. The Kremlin was in the throes of a succession crisis; both Georgi Malenkov and Nikita Khrushchev wanted Mao's support; Kao Kang was cast aside by his backstage instigators. In October, Mao Tsetung's *General Line for the Transition Period to Socialism* won major approval from the Central Committee, marking Liu's policy defeat, but also Kao Kang's personal defeat. In December, Mao Tsetung made a long speech to the Central Committee stressing Party unity; comrades engaged in detrimental "splitting" activities should now repent and "come clean."

But things had gone too far. In February 1954 Liu Shao-chi in a report on Party unity spoke of "certain high-ranking cadres . . . who regard the region under their leadership as their personal property." Kao and Jao suddenly dropped out of sight. They were arrested, and the whole affair seems to have been taken in hand by a revengeful Liu. Kao committed suicide in prison. Jao was not executed but detained. It took over a year to track down the whole conspiracy, including the contacts Kao and Jao had had within the PLA. Peng Teh-huai seems to have done his self-criticism and was not touched in the subsequent shake-up, but seven high-ranking leaders were demoted. The whole affair was reported in March 1955 at a Party conference by the acting secretary-general, Teng Hsiao-ping.

As a result, Liu Shao-chi's hold on the Party became even stronger, for he took over the supervision committees established by Jao Shoushih when the latter was director of the Organization Department. Liu's own nominee, An Tze-wen, saw his power increased; and Liu streamlined special agencies to fight "all corrupt elements . . . and particularly recurrence of such cases of serious harm to the Party as that of Kao Kang and Jao Shou-shih."

The abolition of regional bureaus* followed; this further weakened regional Party leadership and strengthened central power, which is probably why Liu was able to dominate the Eighth Party Congress in 1956. A purge of "hidden counterrevolutionaries," which was exceedingly harsh, took place in mid-1955.

* These were set up at Liberation.

In his *Red China Today*,* Edgar Snow seems to imply that Mao was not happy with the handling of the Kao Kang affair, and that he would have preferred a balance between himself, Liu and Kao. This view is dubious; Mao was inexorable regarding ideological principles, and Kao was close to treachery. But he may have been saddened that an old comrade like Kao Kang should have thus degenerated. He was not there in March 1954 when Kao and Jao were tried, and at the March 1955 exposure of the conspiracy reminded his audience: "In dealing with all comrades who have made mistakes . . . but are willing to change themselves . . . we must help them . . . This is the only constructive attitude towards comrades."

But this major struggle did expose the contradictions within the Party, pinpointed the need for a decisive "line" which would promote vigorously the continuing revolution. It also indicated that "contradictions" between socialist countries (China and the USSR) could also happen.

Mao warned: "There will occur other struggles in the Party, like this one" — a phrase which the Party Central Committee's secretary-general, Teng Hsiao-ping, repeated.

---

* Edgar Snow *Red China Today* (New York 1971; revision of *The Other Side of the River*), pages 328–329.

4

Thought Remolding and the Intelligentsia

To change a system, one must first of all create public opinion; this is true of revolution, it is also true for counterrevolution.

— MAO TSETUNG, 1962

In the superstructure, no sector is considered so important, dangerous, vulnerable, and unyielding to change as that of the intelligentsia: the arts and education. Marxism considers the intellectual a "social engineer," molder of public opinion, idea transmitter, subtly or vigorously influencing society. In a socialist society, the artist and the educator must consciously fulfill an appointed goal: to serve the people, which means to propagate through their activities the ideals and benefits of socialism for the masses. Here the word "propaganda" is not derogatory; it is an accepted activity. "Any person engaged in talking with another person is engaged in propaganda."*

"To cut off heads changes nothing . . . it is what is inside the head which has to be changed." A taboo on killing — such as Mao Tsetung had instituted in Yenan† against the brutal, arbitrary liquidations which Wang Ming had performed (imitating the Soviet Union) — makes the transformation of individual mental makeup all the more important. Mao's firm belief that man can be changed explains both the restraint in bloodshed and the persistent tenacity of the great remolding campaigns throughout the last twenty-five years.

There were approximately five million intellectuals in China, according to Mao's estimate, in 1957 (less than 1 percent of the population). The term is unclear; anyone with a middle school education qualifies: schoolteachers, engineers, doctors, geologists, chemists, university pro-

* Attributed to Mao, 1956.
† "No executions and few arrests" (Mao 1942–1945).

66

fessors, lecturers, research scientists, musicians, writers, painters and journalists. Edgar Snow reports that in 1960 only 20 percent of the Communist Party had had education above lower middle school level — two million out of the (at the time) ten million Party members.*
Newly trained workers, "activists" from spare-time schools and the "people's universities" set up in 1950, are probably included.

Members of the old intelligentsia, pre-1949, were overwhelmingly from a landlord, rich peasant or urban bourgeois origin. They were indispensable for education and cultural activities; they had to be "remolded" while at work, for these sectors could not stop. A majority (90 percent) rallied to the socialist system without being convinced Marxists. A small minority, less than 5 percent, were reckoned by Mao to be absolutely hostile to the regime.

The remolding of intellectuals, Mao warned, would be a long, painful process, taking "many years . . . decades . . . Impatience will not do . . . we must not attempt to change people's ideology by a few lectures or meetings." Meanwhile the Party would demand of the intelligentsia that it serve the socialist system, irrespective of private beliefs. "Some people disagree with Marxism, although they do not openly say so. There will be people of this sort for a long time to come and we should allow them to disagree." Mao thought that if over a period of several five-year plans a fairly large number of Chinese intellectuals accepted Marxism, that would be fine. But only a long process of practice, living and working integrated with the laboring people, would change them. That was why intellectuals should be encouraged to go among the masses. "They should seize every opportunity . . . even if they just go for a walk, to look around the countryside, like looking at flowers while on horseback."

Thousands of intellectuals did go to rural areas, for weeks, sometimes for months. Land reform† saw many step into the villages for the first time in their lives, and it was a salutary and chastening shock for them. But this did not make for integration, even if they were moved by a poverty they had seldom guessed. There were too many barriers, too much contempt for demeaning manual labor; they did not speak the same language, though they used the same words, as the workers and peasants. There is something in "class stand" which is extremely resistant to change, all the more because it is unconscious. Repelled by dirt, discomfort, and rough words, punctilious about their honor and

---

* Personal interview with Edgar Snow in 1968.
† See pages 27–28.

saving their faces, intellectuals were rudely tested, felt easily insulted. The Party cadres did not always exercise towards them the necessary patience, for even in the new system the intelligentsia enjoyed privileges, a higher living standard, emoluments far above those of the cadres in charge of their remolding.

In these conditions, hostility, resentment and suspicion surfaced. The counterrevolutionary drives (1952 and 1955) hit the intelligentsia; even research scientists working at experiments were accused of sending secret reports through "radio" and sometimes their laboratory equipment was smashed or confiscated. Suicides did occur among those who could not stand the harassment, or the "loss of face" in front of people they considered their inferiors. And though their treatment was mild compared to what happened in other revolutions in other countries, the intellectuals did, on the whole, react badly to the surveillance, the lack of deference, the long and tedious meetings at which they had to reveal their souls and misdeeds. Yet within six years this valuable yet suspect minority, indispensable for the construction of New China but dangerous because it could destroy a socialist China, was moving into many administrative positions of influence in departments and ministries.

Today, after twenty-five years, the majority of the erstwhile bourgeois intelligentsia have not only survived but have adjusted to the new society and become more active and productive than ever. What sustained many of them throughout was that in spite of prolonged criticism their lives were not in danger, and above all that most of them loved their country, and this helped them to endure and to survive.

The policy towards the intelligentsia, as defined by Mao, was "unity and struggle." Criticize their wrong ideas, persuade, educate, "remold" them; but do not touch a hair of their heads, and keep them useful, at work. "Ideological reform . . . of the intelligentsia is one of the important conditions for our country's . . . industrialization." He would opine that on the whole engineers and scientists found it much easier to integrate, adapt, and change than graduates of the arts, philosophers, historians, and economists. That was because they were in touch with reality. "Liberal arts subjects are completely detached from reality . . . such students . . . are the most ignorant."

The struggle between the Mao and Liu lines also affected the intellectuals, and for many years they must have despaired of ever knowing or understanding what "the line" was. Too great a severity alternated with periods of complete laissez-faire. "Certain unreasonable features in our present employment and treatment of intellectuals" were mentioned by Chou En-lai in January 1956. "Straightforward administrative measures to deal with writers . . . in a subjective and rigid manner" were offensive (*People's Daily*, 1953). "Many of our comrades are not good at uniting with intellectuals. They are too crude . . . lack respect for their work . . . interfere . . . in scientific and cultural work where this is unwarranted" (Mao, 1957). On the other hand, in some departments "no effort to educate or reform the intelligentsia" was made (Chou, 1956). There was the obverse too: "Alliance . . . between the bourgeoisie which seeks protectors . . . and some high-level Party cadres," a threat to revolutionary purity (1966).*

In education, the wholesale adoption of the Soviet model led to a total change in orientation. Whereas before 1949 almost 70 percent of college students opted for art faculties, the proportions were now reversed. By 1958 only 1 percent of the new university students went into the arts, 35 percent chose to train as teachers, and 60 percent went into engineering, science and medicine. The courses were streamlined, shortened, and reformed; specialization, heavy emphasis on scientific courses, led to some excellent results in numbers of scientific workers trained, particularly needed because particularly lacking. Between 1950 and 1960, 230,000 engineers were trained; fewer than 10,000 had existed in all China in 1949. By 1960 there were 105 research institutes with 7,000 research scientists, whereas there had been only 1,500 in 1949. A twelve-year plan for scientific development reckoned on two million engineers and 10,500 graduate students in specialized sciences by 1967. Eight thousand students went abroad to study, the majority in the USSR. "China's advance in the education of specialists in applied technology has been extraordinary."†

In general education, massive drives to wipe out illiteracy (involving 50 million peasants in 1952–1953) and the creation of many schools (spare-time schools, technical schools, engineering colleges, and people's universities) opened wide the field of education to a large proportion of the young population. Accessibility was, however, still confined to the cities, although with the setting up of agricultural cooperatives many village schools were launched. By 1953 the Ministry of Educa-

---

* See pages 272–273, the May 16, 1966, circular. Documents and editorials during the early part of the cultural revolution were particularly full of this topic.

† Edgar Snow *Red China Today* (New York 1971; revision of *The Other Side of the River*), pages 226–228.

tion claimed that 80 percent of primary school students, 60 percent of middle school students, and 20 percent of college students were of worker or peasant origin. By 1960, 91 million children would be in 737,000 primary schools with 2.5 million teachers and staff, 13 million in middle school. From 1950 to 1960, 431,000 college graduates (including the 230,000 engineers mentioned) were produced.

Superficially, it seemed that a new generation was being trained "under the Red flag," as socialists in socialist schools. But the importation of the Soviet model of education did not change the elitist climate which had pervaded Chinese education. Courses were highly theoretical; material for study was injected into passive students; the continuing emphasis was on committing to memory vast amounts of facts. Examinations (entrance, midyear, yearly, final) relied entirely on memory — no place for imagination, inquiry, initiative, originality. A good student was respectful, submissive, obedient, and the compulsory political courses were entirely devoid of any concrete, tangible object lessons. The boredom of this thrice-weekly catechism was resented.

The rules for middle school students issued in June 1955 by the Ministry of Education but "applicable at all levels" are illuminating. Students must assume a correct posture in class, listen attentively, stand up when answering teachers' questions, sit down when allowed, respect principals and teachers and salute them when class begins and ends, obey instructions, obey teachers, obey rules.

Confucianism was declared "eradicated" from schools, but this program of rules was neo-Confucianism, for above all it promoted docility. Mao exploded. "Our education is fraught with problems, the most prominent of which is dogmatism. The children learn only textbooks and concepts which remain theoretical, they do not know anything else. The method of teaching is squeezing things into them, not arousing their interest or imagination . . . Many children do not even know what cows, horses, chickens, pigs are . . . nor can they tell the difference between rice, canary seeds, maize, wheat, millet. . . . The school years are too long . . . The method of examination is to treat the students like enemies and to ambush them.[*]

Mao became especially angry when he found out that agricultural colleges taught students to do experiments in laboratories, under glass, in cities — where they were sited — "when there is the whole vast paradise of the countryside . . . to utilize their talents." (Experimental

[*] Mao in 1964, to a delegation of educators from Nepal.

fields became, very early, a requisite for each cooperative, not only to teach scientific farming to the peasants, but also for the young.)

Under this type of "socialist" education, not only did contempt for manual labor remain entire, but also all the values and prejudices of the old literocracy were passed on to the young and — what was worse — now infected a sizable proportion of the young peasant and working class children who entered school.

For two millennia the ideal of every peasant child had been to learn to read and write in order to become an official, and this did not change. The whole system of education was impregnated with the idea of becoming an official and escaping manual labor. "In three years a worker's child has forgotten his father and mother" (Mao, 1964 and 1965). Promotion, passing examinations, and a white-collar job at a desk in a city . . . this was the dream which "socialist education" instilled in the young.

In the well-established higher institutions a smooth technique was devised to get rid of workers' and peasants' children. These young people already suffered from the taunts of their professors* and their bourgeois schoolmates — still 80 percent of the enrollment. Now examinations were devised that were impossible for anyone without some classical background to pass; everything was done to make the young worker or peasant voluntarily leave.

One institution which had taken about a thousand children of workers and peasants in 1953 took only 173 in 1957 — and two in 1962. Even in 1974 a case was exposed of a design institute where twelve students of bourgeois or "higher Party cadre" origin were kept, while thirteen of working class origin were, under various pretexts, asked to leave.

On the other hand, the teaching staff, the professors, complained that the new curricula and the admission of workers' and peasants' children forced them to lower their standard of teaching.

By 1955 signs of youth restlessness, due to this cloistered, alienated world and to a lack of understanding of the goals pursued, were evident. The dreadful times of the Chiang regime, when students were hunted and persecuted, were forgotten, the discomforts of the present magnified. The students now became the new intelligentsia, and automatically felt that they should be privileged; they resented being directed to work in places not always of their choosing. Their discontent was subtly fueled by resentful teachers.

* Such as "You smell of manure," or "How can your brain understand anything?"

A report by Yang Hsiu-feng, minister of Higher Education, in June 1956 summarized the problems: too heavy a burden of theoretical study; students "in a flurry" and subject to nervous breakdowns; frequent failures in examinations; too little outdoor exercise; occurrence of tuberculosis, stomach ulcers and "neurasthenia." Professors had too many political meetings on top of preparing assignments. Teachers were exhausted by too many students in class. Yang Hsiu-feng was discreetly arguing for a return to a more "selective" standard for higher institutions; this would mean keeping out more of the workers' and peasants' children. By 1955 there were reports of "gangsters . . . infiltrating into institutions of higher education" for the purpose of arson, sabotage, putting up anti-Communist posters, and other activities.

In those early years, unlike today (1975),* a tight-lipped secrecy was maintained, though there were sporadic references to university unrest. If we remember the high proportion of children from the disgruntled bourgeoisie who formed the bulk of university student bodies, and that almost all the staff were from the bourgeoisie, such unease is not surprising.

It soon became clear that manifestations in the universities were coalescing, no longer isolated. A definite counterrevolutionary movement was feeding on resentment, and gathering strength. Finally, the matter came to a head with an episode called the Hu Feng affair. Since Hu Feng was an intellectual, a writer, it hit the intelligentsia both in universities and in literary and art circles particularly hard.

According to Communist tenets, "Workers in art and literature are cultural fighters, dedicated to serving the workers, peasants and soldiers."

Writers had been greatly persecuted under the military regime of Chiang Kai-shek. The Union of Chinese Writers, established in 1949, counted a membership of four hundred odd. At Liberation there were great hopes that literature would surge forth and that many plays and novels, praising "positive characters" and portraying the achievements of the revolution, would be written.

But it is more difficult to depict positive figures than negative ones, as Chiang Ching† remarked in 1964. The old-style writers did their

---

* University debates on education are made widely known by *tatzepao*; see page 373.
   † The present Madame Mao, better known as Chiang Ching. A former actress, she went to the Red base of Yenan in 1937 to join the revolution. Although she occupied no official post until the cultural revolution of 1966, she seems to have

best. Novels, plays, essays did appear, but most of the writing confined itself to reportage. No writer dared give his own view or opinion of events — far better to just become "a reflecting mirror." And the officials of Culture and Propaganda seemed well pleased.

Excellent physical treatment (large royalties for any work produced, good houses, a style of living far above the average) was meted out to writers. Within the first few years their numbers grew rapidly, with essayists, political critics, journalists and propagandists thrown in, until by 1959 the union counted three thousand writers. Each new work was hailed and sometimes overpraised. Books never sold less than half a million copies. But in speeches to the National Conference on Propaganda Work, which comprised writers, Ministry of Culture officials, and the press, Mao emphasized the long time it would take to change the writers, and how much depended on their personal willingness to integrate, to "come to grips with reality."

But in this sector too there was a touch of schizophrenia. For the man who wielded power as arbiter of literature (and propaganda) was Chou Yang, deputy director of Propaganda, vice-chairman of the Federation of Literature and Art circles.

Chou Yang with three other writers, Hsia Yen, Tien Han, and Yang Han-sheng, had in the early 1930's been in the League of Left-Wing Writers of Shanghai. Chou Yang as its secretary had disbanded the league in 1936 on orders from Wang Ming, and launched the slogan "Literature of national defense." Wang Ming at the time followed a right-wing "opportunist line" of capitulation to Chiang Kai-shek, on orders from Stalin. But the great and famous writer Lu Hsun, although not a Communist, fought against what he called the "four rascals" and proposed instead the slogan "Literature for the masses in the national revolutionary war." This slogan was Mao Tsetung's.* The "battle of the slogans" was part of the struggle between Mao and Wang Ming at the time.

Lu Hsun was very ill, but vowed to fight "to my dying breath"

---

devoted all her time to the theater, films, plays, etc., and to have fulfilled in this respect the role of a stimulant, propagating revolutionary themes and urging artists to abandon feudal concepts in art. After the cultural revolution, in which she played an important role, she remained a member of the Politburo and the Central Committee, but has no official post in the government to date.

* See *The Morning Deluge*, pages 353–354. The literary conflicts of the early 1930's are fully documented in the work of the French scholar and Sinologist Michelle Loi, also in the documents which came out at the cultural revolution. The author herself had a personal interview with Hsu Kuang-ping, Lu Hsun's wife, in 1966, on the matter.

against Chou Yang. The latter after various ineffective pressures against Lu Hsun then called a meeting to criticize him, and published a letter written against Lu Hsun by a high official in the CCP. This "high official," who used a pseudonym, was none other than Liu Shao-chi himself.

In Yenan, however, Mao Tsetung praised Lu Hsun, and a Lu Hsun Academy of Arts was set up there at his death, in 1937. However, Chou Yang now managed to go to Yenan, where he became vice-president of the Lu Hsun Academy! After 1949, with Liu's support, Chou Yang became the most prominent figure in the sensitive sector of propaganda and culture. Why did Mao not object? To this question the answer given (to the author) was: "Chou Yang had made his self-criticism."*

For years writers were subjected to the vagaries of the "dictator of literature," Chou Yang. Kuo Mo-jo, an author of great renown, erudition, and integrity (whose work as president of the Academy of Sciences and as an archaeologist has not hindered him from writing books and plays), gave a warning against Chou Yang in a talk to writers and artists, in May 1950, on the united front in literature and art. He began by praising Lu Hsun, enjoining him as a model. Writers should emulate Lu Hsun's courage, battle against wrong orders, even those given by authorities, as Lu Hsun had fought against the Party officials of the League of Left-Wing Writers, who practiced an erroneous policy. He enjoined the writers to read Mao's *Talks at the Yenan Forum on Literature and Art.*†

But writers and artists were immersed in "remolding," searching for their own souls, going through political meetings, criticism and self-criticism sessions. It would be years before their minds would clear on what was "the correct line," especially when there were two diametrically opposite lines, resulting in bizarrely contradictory policies, and both using the same Marxist language. Their treatment alternated between harshness, when it was necessary for officials of the Ministry of Culture to appear active in the midst of a movement, and total permissiveness when the movement abated. "Chou Yang always took the prevailing wind and rode it."

In such an atmosphere, where backbiting, malice and envy are disguised in political jargon, it is not the forthright, the sincere, the painstaking who triumph, but the opportunist and the timeserver. "We

---

* Author's private interview.
† *Talks at the Yenan Forum on Literature and Art,* May 1942. *Selected Readings of Mao Tsetung* (English edition Peking 1971), pages 250–286.

felt alternately boiled or frozen; pampered and insulted; driven to castigate our ideas and paid enormous royalties for writing shoddy pieces," said one writer. Another wrote that the Party representatives treated them like "monkeys that had to go through hoops."

The most prolific among the writers, Lao She, felt that he could "only write about the past, because I do not understand the present." It was easier indeed to depict the villainous old days under Chiang Kai-shek than to write of "positive" characters in a confusing today. And anyway, the bourgeois writers did not really know the workers and peasants. They tried. But they were inhibited by their class stand from real contact. It would take a new generation of intellectuals, themselves sprung from workers and peasants, to begin to write vividly about the Chinese working people.

Mao Tsetung personally intervened to point out the wrong directions taken by the Department of Propaganda (or of Culture, or both) at various times.

The first occasion was in 1950, when the film *Inside Story of the Ching Court* was shown. This film was praised by Liu Shao-chi and the Propaganda Department, but Mao's wife Chiang Ching saw the film, objected to it, and brought it to Mao's attention. It is a film about the Boxer uprising of 1900; the peasantry is depicted as ignorant, cruel and barbaric because it revolted; the Manchu emperor is shown as saving the country, through the efforts of the Chinese concubine of the German commander invading Peking at the time. This, besides being historically fanciful, was an insult to the revolution.

In 1951 another film, *Life of Wu Hsun,* was also praised. The story is that of a "benevolent" beggar, Wu Hsun, who goes around building schools for peasants, and so on. So anchored is it in the Confucian idea "Benevolence is all" that even Kuo Mo-jo praised the film. (He recanted afterward.)

Mao wrote: "There is a great degree of ideological confusion . . . in cultural circles . . . our writers have not studied history . . . not tried to find out what new ideas appeared." His anger was not directed against the bourgeois writers, but against those who were supposed to guide them politically. "Certain Communists who have *reputedly* grasped Marxism warrant particular attention . . . Is it not a fact that reactionary bourgeois ideas have found their way into the Party? There should be discussion on the film . . . so as to thoroughly straighten out the confused thinking on this question."*

* *Mao Tsetung on Art and Literature* (English edition Peking 1960).

In 1954,* again Mao would intervene, this time on the publication of a critical essay, Study of "Dream of the Red Chamber," the famous seventeenth-century novel, by a renowned historian, Yu Ping-po. Yu Ping-po belonged to the Hu Shih school of philosophy.† Two young writers criticized Yu Ping-po's essay, but found it impossible to get their own paper published in any national daily. Mao Tsetung finally read it in a local university magazine. When he asked why this criticism, which was cogent, had not been given wider publicity, he was told that it was by "nobodies," and hence had been ignored.

This Confucianist stand angered Mao. He wrote a slashing comment to "comrades of the Political Bureau and other comrades concerned" (officials of Propaganda and Culture). The young writers who countered Yu, he said, had provided "the first serious attack in over thirty years on the erroneous views of a so-called authoritative writer." Previously, no one in the position of a student ever dared challenge an authority. Mao Tsetung considered this breakthrough indicative of a new daring, and therefore important.

Mao advised that the root cause of errors such as those of Professor Yu — the Hu Shih school of thought — should be studied and refuted. Yu Ping-po himself went untouched (though much criticized). But, said Mao, Party officials should seriously examine their own ideas. Upon which Chou Yang duly started a "struggle" in the writers' union, the dramatists' union, and all cultural departments against Hu Shih and his idealist conceptions. This meant reviewing and criticizing a great deal of the current writing.

Then the Hu Feng affair burst.

Hu Feng was a Party member, a critic, essayist and polemicist. He objected, however, to Party discipline, and argued for freedom of the "subjective struggling spirit" of the writer. He had had in the 1930's many conflicts with Chou Yang. Hu Feng had always been against any control of a writer's work, and in July 1954 he presented a long report to the Central Committee in which he blamed the lack of good writing on the authoritarianism of the officials (he was not very wrong there). Had this been all, Hu Feng would still be among today's writers. But he now rejected all Marxist belief, ridiculed integration of the writer with working people, and attacked the principles of communism, and also Mao Tsetung.

His words found an echo in the breasts of many a demoralized and

---

* Mao Tsetung on Art and Literature (English edition Peking 1960).
† Hu Shih, a philosopher of the Dewey school. He fled to America in 1949.

discontented writer. Hu Feng then began to organize dissident groups; in the universities his influence grew and his invective-charged essays were passed secretly among the students. It was then that reports of "gangster infiltration" began.

At first Hu Feng was only criticized. He made his own self-criticism in January 1955, but then went back on it and continued to travel and to incite discontent. Arrested in the summer of 1955, he was imprisoned, but his voluminous correspondence with intellectuals throughout China was published in the press.

Because Hu Feng's actions coincided with the major struggle in the Party against Kao Kang, and added to the simmering malaise in the seats of higher learning, the Party suddenly felt threatened by a counterrevolutionary rising in the cities on the part of the disgruntled intelligentsia. And it is true that Hu Feng had become counterrevolutionary. Mao denounced Hu Feng as representing a return of the exploiting classes. The campaign against Hu Feng mounted into a movement called the Su Fan (liquidation of hidden counterrevolutionaries). This was a multipurpose purge in the superstructure, to weed out Kao Kang's supporters, both ostensible and presumed counterrevolutionaries, and also the Hu Feng cliques. It was by all accounts severe; and in 1956 and 1959 both Kuo Mo-jo and Foreign Minister Chen Yi spoke about it,[*] noting its harshness. Mao Tsetung also described it as excessive, although necessary. Kuo Mo-jo told the story of two photographers who were arrested as counterrevolutionaries when a flash bulb unexpectedly exploded during picture taking at a Party function. (They were later released.) Fortunately, as Mao was to remark (in April 1956), the taboo on indiscriminate killing held for a good many cases, and the next two years would see many errors rectified. But the Party apparatus in the hands of Liu was still infected with the paradoxical double-pronged methods of the Soviets: too much harshness coupled with sudden compromises.

A story circulating then has its grim humor. Mao had remarked that possibly 10 percent of cadres in administrative units were counterrevolutionaries or had reactionary thoughts. This resulted in an unofficial pursuit of "10 percent" in each unit who must be found guilty if the zeal of the cadres was to be commended. One small unit found itself in great perplexity, for it had only seven members, and ferreting out seven-tenths of a counterrevolutionary was not easy.

[*] To the author personally.

In November 1955 Mao stopped the purge; forty-five thousand counterrevolutionaries had been found. But four hundred thousand intellectuals had been "grilled" during the movement. In that December Mao Tsetung stated that "the problem facing the entire Party and all the people . . . is no longer one of combating rightist conservative ideas about the speed of socialist transformation. The problem concerns other fields, including culture, education, science, medical work."

Mao was now to launch a new model for socialist construction, a radical departure in its originality and inventiveness from what had so far been done. This strategy of development would involve thorough overhaul both at the economic base and in the superstructure; and for its accomplishment the intellectuals, such as they were, were as indispensable as the worker and peasant masses.

5

The Ten Great
Contradictions and
Relations

On no account should we allow . . . comrades . . . to use the Soviet experience as a cover for their ideas of moving at a snail's pace.
— MAO TSETUNG, 1957

Our aim is to create a political situation which is centralized yet democratic, disciplined and yet free, which has unity of purpose and ease of mind for the individual, dynamic and lively.
— MAO TSETUNG, 1957

The concept of a new strategy of development was not an invention of Mao alone, though its grand vision is his; a good many economists and administrators shared in the detailed programming. Already, in a speech by Li Fu-chun, chairman of the State Planning Commission, in July 1955 the problems and contradictions met in the first five-year plan had been hinted at; by 1956 the second five-year plan was being discussed, and with a growing realization that it should not be "more of the same," but radically different in its whole approach to China's development.

Mao's vision rested on a bone-true knowledge of China, of its strength and weaknesses, seen by a mind both fertile and imaginative. What comes out clearly is the desire to avoid repeating the mistakes of the Russian Revolution, and to accelerate development rather than limping behind a model. Progress meant "learning from past mistakes to avoid future errors." There could not be blind faith, "trailing behind others at a snail's pace." The solution to China's development did not lie in imitating the USSR. When Mao said, "We must learn from the Soviet Union," he meant that both the positive and the negative as-

pects must become object lessons. "Some people never analyze anything. They simply follow the prevailing wind." "The study of the
universal truth of Marxism-Leninism must be combined with the Chinese reality."

Mao is said to be indifferent to economic issues, his focus on revolutionary purity. This is absolute misunderstanding of Mao's thinking.
Politics is economics; and economic growth, progress, production are
inseparable from political aims. Mao firmly believed that socialism,
provided the correct methods were used and policies shaped to actual
conditions, could release in China potential forces for immensely accelerated development, at a speed and to a degree which capitalism
never could attain.

His slogans "Revolution to promote production," "Grasp revolution
and promote production" define his thought. "Politics in command"
does not mean sacrifice of economic growth to political shibboleths; it
means the expansion of growth through political orientation. In the
same way, Mao sees no contradiction between expertise and political
motivation. The term "Red and expert" means that a human being
energized and stimulated by a high dedication is far more efficient,
productive, and "expert" than one who has no such motivation.

Mao's strategy would, inevitably, rest on an ideological foundation:
none other, again, than the theory of contradiction, which is a way of
grasping the essence of a problem, and "seeing a problem . . . is to
begin to solve it." Marxism is dialectical materialism, but its flexibility
and deepening to sharpen perception and understanding of situations
and its application to China's continuing revolution is the unique feature of what is known as Mao Tsetung Thought.

In that winter and spring of 1955–1956 meetings, discussions, conferences were designed towards "The positive mobilization of all
forces, all potential in the country . . . for socialist construction in
accordance with the principles: *More, faster, better, and with more
economy.*"

This mobilization began, in January, with the intellectuals. The send-
off was a keynote speech made by Chou En-lai on January 14, to about
thirteen hundred intellectuals, at a special conference convened by the
Central Committee. Chou bluntly set forth the intra-Party struggle and
its relation to the intelligentsia; the Soviet model and its relation to
China's own specific development.

Far from indicating a laissez-faire policy, Chou said, the meetings

and discussions held with the other eight non-Communist parties*
were to strengthen Party leadership. They were part of the opposition
to rightist conservative ideas within the Party which had resulted in
two apparently opposite but equally nefarious attitudes — one sectarian, the other permissive — representing a "most serious threat" to
the future. Only advance fulfillment of plans and accelerated progress
would prevent "the outbreak of a new war." Unless China speeded up
industrial development she would remain weak, and weakness was a
temptation to imperialist attack.

Chou spoke of self-reliance. China's intellectuals must take over designing, planning, studying advanced scientific techniques, both from
the Soviet Union and from other countries. "We must discard all servile
thinking . . . must not run to the Russian experts for every question, big
or small."

Chou reviewed the specific problems of the intellectuals: lack of
needed books and reference materials, irrational grading, work, and
conditions of treatment. He estimated at 40 percent the number of
progressives among them. He conceded the validity of fundamental
research — a sore point with higher scientists, for it had been denounced as idealism. "Without a definite amount of theoretical scientific research as the foundation, we shall not be able . . . to register
transformation of a basic nature in our techniques." However, even
until 1972, the validity of fundamental research was still a point on
which there was no uniform policy; it was reaffirmed as necessary and
valid in 1972.†

This speech by Chou En-lai heartened and rallied the demoralized
intellectuals, for demoralized they were. It would be followed by a
great improvement in their condition and in the attitude of the Party.
Now the rush for the intelligentsia to enter the Party was on, and
within two years six hundred thousand intellectuals would be admitted. This capriciousness again was the result of the two-line struggle,
with the right wing attempting to win over as many as possible in
order to reinforce its own positions in the Party.

In January 1956 Mao addressed a state conference attended by many
intellectuals, and explained the need to quicken and to intensify development in order to catch up with the advanced scientific level in the
world. "China will emerge a highly cultured nation." In May he would

* Eight other non-Communist parties were represented in the Chinese government
and the National People's Congress.
† Interviews of author with Chinese scientists in 1969, 1971, and 1972.

talk for four hours — a speech which has never been published and which contained the policy "Let a hundred flowers bloom, a hundred schools of thought contend."

Because the speech was never printed, yet several versions of what Mao said exist, it is difficult to do more than extricate Mao's main ideas enunciated at the time. Again in 1957, in the masterly exposé *On the Correct Handling of Contradictions Among the People,*° a section is devoted to the Hundred Flowers. Yet another 1957 speech, delivered at the National Conference on Propaganda Work,† further elaborates Mao's ideas on the role of intellectuals. Both these documents are regarded in China as major canons for economic growth, although they seem mostly ideological and political in content. But this is precisely, a Marxist economist will say, why they are valuable, marking a new way of handling "contradictions" so as to utilize them as the driving force to stimulate progress.

One basic idea which Mao expounded in all three speeches is that the foundations for China's subsequent development lie in solving the contradictions between the superstructure and the economic base by *changing* the superstructure, the ideological and political relations in society. But this transformation of relations cannot be realized mechanically; it can proceed only through "blooming and contending," the full exposure of all existing ideas, through full debate and critical assessment.

But one must first *admit* that there are contradictions, problems of class relations, even in a socialist society. This is where Mao makes a radical departure from the USSR theories. Stalin and his successors denied the role of contradictions in socialist society: "between the leadership and the led . . . even between the government and the people." For them, every problem had been solved and the system was ideal. But Mao had Lenin to back him, for Lenin had been critical of tendencies within the Soviet Communist Party and bureaucracy even in 1922 and 1923. Stalin presumed that any "contradictions" arising must perforce be enemy ones, "antagonistic." "Our bourgeoisie has been liquidated and socialism has already been built in the main," he said in 1935. Hence when problems did arise, harsh suppression was the only way to deal with them. The bloody purges of Stalin were the result. Mao Tsetung, on the contrary, said that classes and class strug-

---

° *On the Correct Handling of Contradictions Among the People*, February 27, 1957. *Selected Readings of Mao Tsetung* (English edition Peking 1971).

† Speech at the National Conference on Propaganda Work, March 12, 1957. *Selected Readings of Mao Tsetung* (English edition Peking 1971).

gle still existed, but the problems arising (contradictions) need not all be "antagonistic." In 1937 he had warned against labeling any dissent an "antagonistic contradiction." Now he would expound more fully on the theme, notably on what he called "contradictions among the people," non-antagonistic, soluble by criticism, "reasoning and persuasion."

For, said Mao, the take-over of the private sector in industry had not eliminated the bourgeoisie; its ideas were everywhere, among the people and in the Party too, though a material base for it did not seem to exist. It was still capable of a return, even through "socialist" structures. The battle against this fluid, intangible ideological enemy could not be a physical pressure or liquidation, but must be on the ideological level, and a very long process.

This concept presupposed that the contradiction between the bourgeoisie and the proletariat, which Mao in 1949 had posited as the main internal contradiction of the present period, was not antagonistic. How could this be? Was not socialism the doom of capitalism, and hence of the bourgeoisie? Quite right, Mao replies, but at the present time all the classes, strata and social groups which oppose imperialism, which support and work for socialist construction, come within the category of the people. The national bourgeoisie and the petty bourgeoisie count among the people;* contradictions with them in the present period are non-antagonistic because they also serve socialism. Only those who resisted the revolution, sabotaged socialist construction, were enemies. It was wrong to enlarge the field of "antagonistic" contradictions, as had been done during the Su Fan counterrevolutionary drive. Good people had suffered thereby. Though there was *theoretically* an antagonistic contradiction, in the *concrete conditions of China* the bourgeoisie had a dual character, and this specific contradiction could be solved as a non-antagonistic one. "We cannot abolish religion by administrative decree . . . we cannot compel people to believe in Marxism." Mao referred to his formula of 1942 — unity, criticism, unity — which had been applied inside the Party and must be extended to deal with relations between the leadership and the masses; it should be used in all factories, schools, government offices in resolving contradictions "among ourselves."

If these non-antagonistic contradictions were not handled properly, or if necessary vigilance was relaxed, then non-antagonistic contradictions could turn into antagonistic ones.

Quite a few people could not distinguish clearly between the two types of contradictions, said Mao, who forbore to state publicly that

---

* As Mao had proclaimed in 1949.

Stalin had not done so, though he said it in private at Party meetings. In China, some "dare not openly admit that contradictions still exist among the people in our country or that contradictions continue to exist in a socialist society." This was another hit at Liu Shao-chi, who in that year repeatedly emphasized that class struggle had ceased to exist in China. This left him unable to solve problems except by either compromise or harsh suppression.

Mao enumerated contradictions: within the working class; within the peasantry; within the intelligentsia; between worker and peasant; between worker, peasant, and intelligentsia; between worker and national bourgeois; within the national bourgeoisie. There were contradictions between government and people though the government genuinely served the people; between the interests of the state, of collectives, and the individual; between leader and led; between the bureaucratic style of work of some cadres and the masses, between centralism and democracy, and between socialist countries.

The class struggle was by no means over; in the ideological field it would continue for a very long time and be "tortuous" and "at times . . . very acute." In this respect "the question of who will win out, socialism or capitalism, is still not really settled." "It will take a long period of time to decide the issue." The influence of bourgeois ideas and of the old society would remain for a long time to come. "If this is not understood . . . the gravest mistakes will be made."

This is where the policy of the Hundred Flowers came in, and it would be a long-term one. Along with it was the policy of "long-term coexistence and mutual supervision" between the Communist Party and non-Communist parties. China's specific conditions, the recognition that contradictions still existed in socialist society, and "response to the country's urgent need to speed up its economic and cultural development" dictated these policies.

In April 1956, at the close of intensive meetings and discussions, Mao would deliver a speech, of which only notes were circulated, to be known as the Ten Great Relations. This speech also was never published, but the notes were circulated again in 1967 and it is abundantly referred to in the press, which indicates its wide diffusion throughout the country.*

---

* Much of what Mao said in that April speech is also found in *On the Correct Handling of Contradictions Among the People*, February 27, 1957. *Selected Readings of Mao Tsetung* (English edition Peking 1971).

The Ten Great Relations focuses essentially on the reshaping of the economy. It is a useful clue to Mao's thinking, from the ideological plane to the practical, from the political line to the economic program in the making. The speech confirms that thirty-seven departments concerned with finance and economics had turned in reports. The ten problems were raised by Mao for one purpose: "to mobilize . . . all active factors and all available strength for socialist construction in accordance with the principle: *more, faster, better, and with more economy.*" The speech is a program for self-reliance, and self-reliance was to become the hallmark of China's subsequent economic strategy.

Mao remarked that the strategy of mobilizing all available strength had won the War of Liberation in 1949; the battle for construction was also a war of liberation, and was destined to unshackle and to emancipate the minds and the potential resources of China.

"What was done to win the revolutionary war cannot be applied to China's construction," was Liu Shao-chi's hostile comment. Throughout that year the hostility of Liu, and of his economists and top-echelon Party cadres, to Mao's concept of how China's progress could be engineered was very evident.

In this speech Mao again demonstrates his use of contradictions. The latter are also *relations* of contraries. What appears negative may be used in a positive manner, not as an impediment but as a further propelling force.

The first contradiction-relation is that between agriculture and industry, between heavy and light industries. As early as 1949 Mao had shown the error of dwelling on the agriculture-industry link as an absolute confrontation. "We have not repeated the mistakes of some socialist countries which attached excessive importance to heavy industry at the expense of light industry and agriculture," he said. Shortages of consumer goods and lowering living standards to provide investment in capital-intensive industrial projects were not appropriate for China. Economic growth there must be concurrent with raised living standards and ample supply of consumer goods, especially to rural areas. Therefore, in order to have a healthy heavy industry, one must paradoxically invest more in light industry and in agriculture. Shortages in living necessities produce discontent, lower morale, and inefficient work; and though heavy industry is a priority, attention must be paid not to sacrificing living standards but to raising them. For economic growth could not be divorced from concern for the well-being of the masses; otherwise progress would be exploitation.

Light industry and agriculture, once stimulated, could produce fund accumulation more quickly than heavy industry; investment in them was not sacrificing heavy industry but providing a stable, healthy source of accumulation for it. "If you want heavy industry badly, then you ought to pay close attention to light industry and agriculture . . . the more the output of light industry, the more fund accumulation for heavy industry."

This was a radical departure from the "all or nothing" inflexibility and conventionalism of socialist planning which after forty years had bred massive contradictions among the people in Russia, shortages of daily consumer goods, and agricultural stagnation. To all this Mao had paid a great deal of clear-eyed attention. And he knew that the Chinese peasantry, who after all had been the mainstay of the revolution and who were so near the bone of subsistence, would not accept any reduction in living standards; nor would Mao foist it upon them. There must be tangible, perceptible rise in living standards to encourage enthusiasm for socialism among the rural majority.

"The experience of some socialist countries has proved that bad management could fail to raise agricultural production even after collectivization." The system was correct, the *methods* were wrong. "In some socialist countries they put too heavy a tax burden on the peasants and lowered agricultural prices in terms of industrial prices." In China this is called the scissors policy, and Mao would fight against it all his life. After many decades the scissors policy would still maintain the difference between peasant and worker, town and countryside in the Soviet Union. Yet socialism was dedicated to eradicating these differences.

The key to capital creation without exploitation was energizing the human factor: human enthusiasm, dedication, grounded not on material incentives but on revolutionary fire. Mao conceded that in all systems the main contradiction was between relations of production (the superstructure) and the productive forces (the economic base). But where he differed radically both with the Soviet Union and with Liu Shao-chi was in their assumption that all the trouble was with the backward productive forces and not with the superstructure of ideas, routine habits, behavior.

The solution was the catalyzing of the revolutionary enthusiasm of the masses to change all ideas, habits, behavior: "The decisive factor is man." Total participation, total arousal, mind emancipation, liberation of initiative and creation . . . "China's people, poor and blank, want to do things, want change, want revolution." This immense fund of human energy could be made to explode into positive action "like an atom bomb" released into fission. But it did mean total participation of the masses . . . "the affairs of a country are the affairs of the people of the country, not of a sect" (Mao, 1950).

China's potential was vast, because she had "the largest internal market in the world." Its development could by itself fuel industrial progress. The key to this expansion would be a steady rise in living standard, increased accumulation and consumption by the rural masses.

Thus Mao in 1956 was reaching for what is recognized by many economists today: that in backward agricultural countries the development of capital-intensive heavy industry leads to a dual economy in which 80 to 90 percent of the population remain unbenefited while an affluent urban minority swiftly modernize. In China this would increase the gap between city and countryside, break the worker-peasant alliance upon which the People's Republic was based, and introduce new and dangerously antagonistic contradictions into society.

The second main idea in the Ten Great Relations is on training for the technical skills required. It was too lengthy and inefficient to use orthodox schooling procedure, which is expensive, highly theoretical, and tending to elitism. "It is not always necessary to have a diploma . . . many inventions in the world are by young people . . . who did not have a formal education." China had, in the coastal cities, reservoirs of skilled workers, even if a small minority. In the new industrial planning 90 percent of the industrial expansion would be sited inland. Why create a contradiction between the new inland industries and the pre-1949 coastal industries by neglecting the latter? The coastal factories had pools of skilled veteran workers, whereas the inland ones started from scratch. Why not utilize these experienced workers to train competent technicians? China needed four hundred thousand technicians.*
Why concentrate only on students for future engineers and qualified technical personnel? "College-trained technicians are lacking in practical experience . . . divorced from practice."

This leads to the relation between education and manual labor, a Marxist tenet. Mao had already instituted manual labor for all cadres

---

* See *Take the Road of the Shanghai Machine Tools Plant in Training Technicians from Among the Workers* (English edition Peking 1968). Engineers who, as ordinary workers, were trained in engineering in this particular plant are found all over China, including Tibet, and their record of work has been excellent.

in Yenan in the 1940's during the great production drive.* Since 1953 he had urged students to participate in rural construction; in 1955 he had called upon the young to deploy their talents in the rural areas. There was plenty to do, but education created barriers, instead of breaking them, between the educated and the rest of the population.

Another contradiction-relation was that between the Center and the regions. "Judging by the present situation, it is necessary to expand the power of the regions . . . it is detrimental to socialist construction if regional power is too small."

Bureaucratic centralization, with forms and reports "like floods," with red tape prominent, stifled local initiative. "To centralize everything, to concentrate on some areas at the expense of others," was utterly wrong, said Mao, directly hitting the Liu economists. For the latter had come up with another program, in which certain regions (132 out of 2,000 counties) were picked for investment because they could give the best returns. This was actually the first, disguised form of "profits in command" which would surge after 1960 with Liu's active support. The suggestion was that the index of profitability was a correct criterion for judging development, and loans to deficit areas should be slashed back. This apex type of economy was really a return to capitalism.

It was better, Mao said, to establish a wide net of industry to serve each locality, run according to local materials and resources and funded by local provincial and county authorities, than to invest only in centralized large complexes, which suffered from transport bottlenecks. "Now there are dozens of hands interfering with local administration, making things difficult for the regions . . . the Center must not put them in a straitjacket. . . . We must promote a consultative style of work with the regions."

This implied a basic change in the administration. Decentralization would be announced that June by Chou En-lai at the National People's Congress, under the slogan "Central planning and local initiative and management." The regions would have more power, leeway, and express their views. This was also a shrewd way to economize the outlay for administration; it allowed production to move more swiftly, and it provided for multi-tiered planning: "Every cooperative and locality should also make its own plan." There would be overall planning, provincial planning, and local planning; and thus a constant dialogue,

---

* See *The Morning Deluge*, pages 358, 359–360.

linking together in a common endeavor, by consultation, the whole fabric of the country, would be promoted.

This was the beginning of the excellent, and now praised, pattern of "small and medium" industrial enterprises scattered into the whole of China's rural areas, serving local needs, relieving the transport problem, providing local employment, stimulating each region to discover and to utilize its own resources, and diffusing science, machinery, and a raised living standard to each village. At the same time it democratized the whole process of command, abolished the vertical imperative chain of orders and made it multi-tiered over the whole of China, involving even the lowest cooperative. Thus the conditions for Mao's cherished idea of democracy in socialism, called democratic centralism, could be established.

And this alternative technology would tap energy and initiative; it would promote the "walking on two legs" concept, using both craftsmanship, traditional methods, indigenous labor-intensive knowhow when machines were lacking, and machinery where available. From 1957 onward, the provinces would keep an average of 70 percent of their revenue for their own development; whereas previously they had only 30 percent, and 70 percent went to the Center.

There was a contradiction-relation between the state, productive units, and individual producers, said Mao. It was necessary to heed it, for the factor of morale. Workers' initiative and morale were important, and a problem existed there. "Every productive unit or individual must have its initiative and individual character." "Is it not better for industrialization if we give necessary benefits to individual producers and a certain amount of initiative to productive units? . . . It would be bad if we centralized everything, took away the factories' depreciation fund, left productive units with no initiative. On this question many of our comrades here may also lack experience." Enthusiastic participation by the workers was necessary, in fact the key to production.

In that year (1956) Mao, although against the principle of material incentives, asked for a 10 percent increase to all workers and also more liberal loans to the newly established cooperatives. Cooperatives are productive units, like factories, he said. "The relationship between the collective and its members must be properly handled. Any inadequacy, neglect of peasant welfare, will result in failure of the collective economy. On this question some socialist countries have made mistakes. . . . We must not . . . make things too hard for the peasant."

"In our country the exchanges between industrial and agricultural goods must . . . *diminish* the differences between the sectors." The peasant was also a worker, and every year his income must rise with the cost of agricultural production. Rational division of earnings between the state, collective units, and the individual could be reached only through consensus and consultation. "The state agricultural tax is not heavy . . . we are prepared to stabilize the total annual amount of the grain tax and grain purchases." This would leave a surplus for the peasantry, to eat and to store in case of climatic vagaries.

There were other contradiction-relations. That between national defense and economic construction was one. In March 1956 Mao Tsetung had spoken to a meeting of military commanders regarding certain harmful "deviations" in the army. As in every other sector, there was a two-line struggle in the PLA. The contradiction — national defense investment versus economic construction investment — is handled by Mao in an interesting way. To get better defense, the funds expended on conventional defense must *diminish,* and more money go into national construction.

Here Mao Tsetung envisages strength as a comprehensive sum total of independence and self-reliant economic progress, reaching an international level in which the development of nuclear energy (and its corollary, atomic weapons) is included. The strongest protection for a nation is its buoyant economic health and advanced technological level. "Do you genuinely want atomic bombs? Then you must reduce military and administrative expenses and increase expenditure for economic construction. If you only pretend to want them, you will not decrease the proportion of (conventional) military expenditure, but decrease economic construction . . . Will everybody please study this question, it is a problem of strategic policy."

Mao castigates "great Han chauvinism," and stresses that "lip service will not do." Abnormalities in the treatment of national minorities must be corrected. Traditionally, for centuries, they had been exploited by the dynastic imperial houses, but Mao always remembered how the Miaos, the Yis, and other nationalities had helped during the Long March. He would continue to push for their welfare, for respect of their customs and cultures, and refuse to apply blanket directives; he would promote, in that year, the announcement of autonomous territory and rights for the national minorities.

Some Party leaders wanted to abolish the eight non-Communist parties, but Mao's policy was "long-term coexistence and mutual supervision." It was again a policy fraught with duality, for "they are the opposition and yet not the opposition." Their existence extended the dialogue; their identity conferred the benefit of a different viewpoint.

In analyzing the relationship between revolutionary and counterrevolutionary, Mao again speaks strongly against physical liquidation. Counterrevolutionaries can be changed; and though vigilance must be maintained, and certainly those who commit very serious crimes should be executed, yet the scope should never be enlarged, and "in future . . . there must be fewer arrests and fewer executions." This did not mean abolition of the death penalty, but its very careful use. Mao seems, in this oblique way, to signify his distress at the recent Su Fan movement and its harshness.

The relationship of "right" and "wrong" in and out of the Party concerned the treatment meted out to the people: harshness and arrogance, or a correct attitude. Mao says there should be integrity and fairness. He repeats his fundamental view that people who have made mistakes must be helped, and not, as in Wang Ming's time, ruthlessly attacked and punished. Mao reasserts his faith that the human being can be changed by patient criticism, persuasion.

In the contradiction-relation between China and other countries, Mao says China must learn "the strong points of all countries . . . previously we had some people, rather muddleheaded, who learned even other people's weaknesses . . . who adopted fashions . . . with no independent views of their own."

In 1957 Mao would stress strengthening solidarity with socialist countries as well as with the countries of the Third World. "As for imperialist countries, we should unite with their peoples and strive to coexist peacefully . . . but not harbor any unrealistic notions about them."*

Throughout his numerous unpublished and published talks in those years, Mao's emphasis is on building China both ideologically and materially, emphasizing self-reliance, frugality, economy.

These months were most intensely active ones for Mao, but also a period strangely muted as to dissemination of what he said. For events had happened which had strengthened the opposition to Mao in the Party, so that by September 1956, when the Eighth Congress of the Party assembled, Mao Tsetung was definitely in a minority. Support for his views and the economic strategy he had outlined in the spring

---

* *Selected Readings of Mao Tsetung* (English edition Peking 1971), page 478.

was lacking. And his speeches were not given full circulation within the Party.

The reason for this eclipse lay in Moscow; for in February 1956 the Russian Party's Twentieth Congress had taken place, with the ascent of Khrushchev and the denunciation of Stalin.

Later, in 1958,* Mao Tsetung was to state that "a gust of foul revisionist wind" had blown from "the north" (Moscow) and had blown many good plans away. For some months after the Twentieth Congress of the CPSU† in Moscow. Liu Shao-chi would shelve Mao's programs, but time was on Mao Tsetung's side.

* In March, at Chengtu.
† Communist Party of the Soviet Union.

6

The Hundred Flowers

Events have their twists and turns and do not follow a straight line.
— Mao Tsetung, *On Protracted War*, May 1938

Certain people in our country were delighted by the events in Hungary.
They hoped that something similar would happen to China.
— Mao Tsetung, *On the Correct Handling of*
Contradictions Among the People, February 1957

For the next eleven years, the two-line struggle within the CCP would be inextricably intertwined with the great campaign which Mao began for ideological purity and which led to confrontation with the Kremlin leadership. Within this war on the ideological plane, the Hundred Flowers and other aspects of Mao's program for development take on their full significance.

The word "revisionism" was first used by Mao as a hint to the Kremlin leadership in December 1956.* Again, in his March 1957 speech at the National Conference on Propaganda Work, Mao warned against revisionism at home. "One of our current important tasks on the ideological front is to unfold criticism of revisionism." However, it appears that until 1963 the Chinese Party in the main did not feel that China could have "revisionists" in its upper echelons.

Denounced by Lenin as the crassest form of opportunism, revisionism is a distortion of the basic principles of communism. It denies class struggle, the dictatorship of the proletariat; it breeds a new elite class from within the Party itself, which in turn becomes an exploiting class and leads back to capitalism — or worse, to what Lenin had called "social-imperialism." And its most pernicious feature is that while practicing capitalism, it cloaks itself in Marxist phrases and slogans.

* *People's Daily* Editorial Department *On the Historical Experience of the Dictatorship of the Proletariat and More on the Historical Experience of the Dictatorship of the Proletariat*, April 5, 1956, and December 29, 1956 (English edition Peking 1957).

The roots of revisionism in the USSR were complex; privately, Mao has conceded that because of Stalin's errors in dealing with contradictions, and his ruthless methods, it had been possible for unscrupulous opportunists to thrive, and plant in the Russian Party a revisionist line even before Stalin's death. This also explains Mao's great concern for correct *methods;* he watched with anxiety the developments in the USSR well before Khrushchev's famous outburst at the Twentieth Congress. "When Stalin was criticized in 1956, we were on the one hand happy . . . but also apprehensive," Mao is reported to have said in Chengtu in 1958, when he analyzed Stalin's errors and also his virtues. "The Chinese Revolution was won . . . by acting contrary to Stalin's instructions."

Mao had always been critical of what he called "blind faith," unthinking acceptance of everything that Russia did because it was "the fount of socialism." He now hoped that "blind faith" would stop in the Chinese Party. The lessons of historical experience must be learned, he said, and Party members must develop their critical faculties. Mao told humorously how he had not been allowed to eat eggs or chicken soup for three years because Russian medical men said they were bad. Then they had changed their minds, and so had Mao's Chinese doctors. When he was painted with Stalin, the Chinese painters "made me a bit shorter [as if] knuckling under to the moral pressure exerted by the Soviet Union at that time." But he also disapproved of Khrushchev's arbitrary and total demolition of Stalin. It too was a kind of pressure, unprincipled, non-analytic, and he only hoped that "blind faith" would not recur.

But if Mao was both relieved and worried, the worry prevailed. Not so, however, with Liu Shao-chi. This does not imply that Liu at any time was in collusion with Khrushchev, but simply that he thought along similar lines. This coincidence of opinion was ironically referred to by Mao in his speech in Chengtu (March 1958) when he alluded to Khrushchev's main thesis at the Twentieth Congress of the CPSU: "peaceful transition to socialism." "Some people [certain Communist parties] were delighted . . . a millstone had dropped from their neck . . . now the world was at peace." Such people were no longer revolutionaries, but wanted socialism to come peacefully, without their own exertions.*

Mao noted that the majority of the Chinese Party did not agree with the manner in which Khrushchev launched his attack on Stalin. How-

* In this general remark, Mao hints at the CCP, but also includes "other" parties, notably that of the USSR — meaning Khrushchev.

ever, the reaction to the "peaceful transition" thesis was far more diffi-cult to gauge. And the net result for a few months was a strengthening of the right wing, led by Liu Shao-chi, opposing the Mao line and saying that "it always smells of gunpowder."

Three things, Mao said, had been "blown away by a gust of foul revisionist wind." They were: the general line or basic policies, pro-moters of progress; the program based on the Ten Great Relations speech; and Mao's twelve-year plan for agriculture, drafted in 1954, twice shelved by the opposition of Liu Shao-chi.

As a result of his increased influence, Liu pushed through a number of his own policies. A directive that there would be no further changes in policies for the countryside for ten years, and the circulation of another "four freedoms"* draft to the grass-roots cadres (without the approval of the Central Committee, as Mao said in March 1958 in Chengtu), were calculated to reverse collectivization when the co-operatives were still frail. The policy of admitting intellectuals to the Party was speeded up, and there was a revision of the Party constitu-tion at the Eighth Congress in September 1956.

Liu's main speech at the Eighth Congress shows his thinking, and the approval of his report by the Congress bears out the evidence that the right wing was then in preponderant position. Liu's speech is full of quiet sniping at Mao. He notes that "some comrades want to lower the rate of development of heavy industry . . . this is wrong." He averred that "the tendency of deviating to the 'left' has manifested itself in demanding that socialism be achieved overnight." On class struggle, Liu's major theme was directly contrary to Mao. Liu spoke of "the decisive victory of socialism." "The national bourgeois elements are in the process of changeover from exploiters to working people . . . the working class has won ruling power throughout the country." The resolution of September 27, 1956, passed by the first plenum of the Eighth Central Committee, spoke of the "decisive victory . . . won in socialist transformation . . . the contradiction in our country between the proletariat and the bourgeoisie has been basically resolved."

In international relations, Liu praised the theses of Khrushchev at the Twentieth Congress and declared that there was definite hope of "an era of peace" and of "relaxation of tension."

---

* Freedom to buy and sell land, freedom to plant crops as wished, freedom for usury, and free markets. First promoted by Liu unofficially in 1952, and reissued in documents emanating from central administrative departments from time to time. This bypassing of Mao, as chairman of the Central Committee, was all the easier since Liu at the Eighth Congress had won the approval of the Central Committee for his main "line," from which specific policies then followed.

Liu derided Mao's fundamental view that changes in relations of production and the superstructure were essential and primary in China. The basic contradiction in China, Liu declared, was "between the productive forces which are backward and the advanced socialist system." This meant that no criticism from the masses who were "backward" could be acceptable; the Party was "advanced," and its leadership must be reinforced.

Neither Liu nor Khrushchev was prepared to rectify and educate the Party by plunging it into the masses and practicing open-door debate and criticism, so fundamental to Mao's thinking. Both saw the Party organization as a power base. And both would initiate an ostensible "thaw" to allow certain privileged intellectuals into the Party, thus producing a fusion of high Party cadres and a technocratic elite.

The notion of the "dying out of class struggle," therefore, far from being more democratic or "liberal," was paradoxically the opposite — a means of reinforcing absolutism through a new class. "Criticism of inferiors by superiors is all right . . . but the other way round, things become chaotic," said Liu Shao-chi.

The new Party constitution produced by the Eighth Congress of the CCP would be called "revisionist" during the cultural revolution. It was very different from the constitution passed by the Seventh Congress in 1945. It deleted any reference to class origin in the recruitment of Party members. "Any citizen" could now apply for membership, and the criteria were vague. All reference to Mao Tsetung Thought as a guide to Party study was deleted.

There appears to have been an attempt made at the Eighth Congress to condemn the personality cult, with oblique references to Mao Tsetung. This was not successful; for it was pointed out by the secretary-general, Teng Hsiao-ping, that the Chinese Communist Party, by following the mass line, had not fallen into the most glaring pitfalls of personality cult; that Marxism recognized the contribution of outstanding individuals; that the personality cult, a legacy of the past, was fought by the Chinese leadership.*

By May 1956, when the Hundred Flowers movement began, there reigned in China an atmosphere of puzzlement and confusion created

* Mao himself, in September 1948, had insisted on the Party committee system, and therefore on collective leadership. Teng Hsiao-ping was to distinguish himself in the polemics against the Soviet Union. Though much criticized during the cultural revolution, he like many others made a comeback, but he was later found "unrepentant" and guilty of again trying to apply the Liu Shao-chi line.

by Khrushchev's two speeches at the Twentieth Congress. Besides his secret anti-Stalin outburst, there was his public speech, which laid down as its main topic the line of "peaceful transition to socialism." The two speeches circulated throughout the Chinese Party and among the intelligentsia in the universities; they also percolated down to the students.

Mao's Hundred Flowers speech, which to date has not been published, was "interpreted" by Lu Ting-yi, director of the Propaganda Department of the Central Committee, in a draft circulated throughout the universities and technical colleges and institutes.* Lu Ting-yi's draft is now said to be a distortion of Mao's meaning. Abroad, Mao's speech was regarded as a desperate gesture to prove that he was not a Stalin, and the whole movement as an attempt at a "thaw," or "liberalization." Yet it was neither. As Kuo Mo-jo, president of the Academy of Sciences, was to point out, Mao Tsetung had already mentioned the necessity of debate, of "blooming and contending," and had launched the slogan "Let a hundred flowers bloom" in 1951.

Lu Ting-yi's interpretation eschews the point of Mao's speech, one that Mao had made in his address to the intellectuals: that is, that the Hundred Flowers movement was motivated by the need to strengthen Party leadership and accelerate development, to consolidate the system.

With events in Moscow shaking the socialist world; with the recent counterrevolutionary purge still vivid in their minds; with the confusion about what Lu Ting-yi (an authoritative spokesman) exactly meant, and the fact that Mao's speech was not published, the intellectuals were loath to speak up, except among themselves.

Kuo Mo-jo, as president of the Academy of Sciences, gave in June his own interpretation of what Mao had said. He made the point that "blooming and contending" must serve socialist construction. There were limits to the blooming, said Kuo, in answer to some queries on how far should one bloom? "A hundred schools contend" was a phrase used two millennia earlier to mark a cultural renaissance, a "cultural revolution" but in a different historical context. "It is not knowledge for the sake of knowledge . . . our aim in blooming and contending is to promote even better socialism."† An article in the *People's Daily* took

* Draft of a speech delivered May 26, 1956: *Let a Hundred Flowers Blossom, a Hundred Schools of Thought Contend* (English edition Peking 1957; second edition 1958).

† June 19, 1956, speech at National People's Congress on the twelve-year plan for science and technology.

exception to Kuo's statement. "All the various schools ought to create each their own sound . . . they should not play just according to one conductor."

By summer there were strikes in factories, disturbances on university campuses. "The immediate cause . . . was the failure to satisfy certain . . . demands . . . which should and could have been met . . . But a more important cause was bureaucracy on the part of the leadership. . . . In the same year, some members of agricultural cooperatives also created disturbances."* All this, said Mao, was mainly due to bureaucratic leadership and lack of educational work among the masses. He suggested, therefore, a "rectification" in the Party and a socialist education movement in the countryside.

Such a movement is a confrontation with the masses. "We should take . . . determined action to get rid of any unhealthy manifestations in our work . . . detrimental to unity between the Party and the people."† Mao's idea was to have a multi-level "blooming and contending," confronting the intelligentsia, the Party, the workers in factories, the peasants in cooperatives; bringing people together to argue and debate; "opening the door to see the mountain before us."

This is really Mao — to bring the most diverse sectors together in wholesale slanging matches; to show up all the ideas, prejudices, good and bad, circulating in society; to prove that "class struggle" was indeed still very acute; to educate Party and people in this mutual confrontation and exposure, to catalyze awareness . . . but this was not at all the idea of the bureaucrats. By June, some mid-level cadres were indignant. "We have fought for everything under heaven . . . now these people want to sit on everything under heaven." The authoritarian streak made them resent the very idea of humbly submitting to mass criticism.

The socialist education movement launched by the Party did not go deeper than the county branch level; it did not reach the grass roots. The cooperatives, meanwhile, were the scene of acute class struggle; by November 1956, 96 percent of rural households were in them, but many problems had not been worked out. And that year the harvest was less than expected (though higher than before). Persistent propaganda by the rich peasants urging the people to consume at will,

---

* On the Correct Handling of Contradictions Among the People, February 27, 1957. Selected Readings of Mao Tsetung (English edition Peking 1971), page 432.
† Speech by Mao Tsetung at the opening of the first plenum of the Eighth Central Committee, September 1956.

because the state would provide, led to a drastic reduction in the pig population (40 percent in some areas). Such defects were now pinpointed by the right wing in an endeavor to prove that the cooperatives did not work. Party cadres at times acted harshly; for instance, in forbidding rural subsidiary occupations as "capitalistic enterprise," and thus reducing the peasant's income.

"Blooming and contending," thwarted at every turn, limped along for a few months. But at the same time a strange permissiveness crept in, and a great many novellas of the most romantic, even pornographic kind appeared. There were condemnations of unsatisfactory health work and failure to protect workers in factories, and a great many minor complaints from students. It would be 1957 before the Hundred Flowers would start blossoming, producing both "fragrant flowers and poisonous weeds."

The events which reversed this downgrading of Mao's ideas and projects, and shot him into authority again, were the revolts in Poland and Hungary in October 1956.

The Chinese have always distinguished between the two revolts. The Polish revolt was worker-led, was not against socialism but Party arbitrariness. Mao sympathized with it, advised the Kremlin leaders not to interfere, and hoped the Polish Party would practice self-criticism, correct its errors, practice the mass line.

Not so with the Hungarian one. At first Mao also sympathized with the first insurrection; but the Chinese ambassador in Hungary watched events closely, and it soon was obvious that the first wave had been subverted and taken over by a counterrevolutionary nucleus inside Hungary, the right-wing intellectuals who had formed the Petofi Club prominent among them, aided by outside forces (American). From Mao's frequent references subsequently to the Petofi Club, one is aware how seriously he weighed the possibility of similar occurrences in China. "Let us see what effect the Hungarian events have had in China. After their occurrence there was some unrest among a section of our intellectuals, but there were no squalls. Why?" It was because counterrevolutionaries had been effectively quelled, said Mao.

The Polish and Hungarian events proved Mao's views correct. There was class struggle, there were contradictions rife in socialist society; and the possibility of capitalist restoration was present. "The Hungarian events were not a good thing . . . But they too had a dual character . . . All socialist countries have learned a lesson" (Mao,

1957). In this strong position, Mao could now push ahead with the Hundred Flowers, and also his other plans.

In January 1957, calls for criticisms of the Party's defects continued. By this time the ferment in the universities had been working, and many articles had been published by intellectuals criticizing this or that aspect unsatisfactory in their view, but there had been no overall attack against the Communist Party. In February, Mao made his famous speech *On the Correct Handling of Contradictions Among the People,* which was not published until June, and then in a revised version, which has led to the accusation that Mao did not inform the intelligentsia there were limits to criticism.* In March, Mao again delivered a long and weighty speech (at the National Conference on Propaganda Work),† which indicates clearly the resentment in the Party at having to submit to mass criticism. Mao reiterated that Marxism grows "in wind and storm," not in hothouses; through debate, not by suppression of debate or dealing in summary fashion with problems. "Listen to opinion, especially unpleasant ones . . . Let people speak up. The sky will not fall . . . If you don't let people speak, you will lose . . . don't think you are always right, as if you alone had the truth . . . as if the earth would stop spinning without you . . . some comrades are allergic to criticism . . . they intimidate others."

Liu Shao-chi and Peng Chen, the Peking mayor, were for restricting Party rectification, which was to begin in April and which would be the target of the "blooming and contending" process, to Party members only. There was no need to admit non-Party people to this exercise. Mao countered: "To open wide or to restrict? To let all people express their opinion freely, so that they dare to speak, criticize . . . debate . . . or to forbid . . . We must choose one or the other . . . We choose (to open wide) because it is the policy which will help to consolidate our country and develop our culture."‡ Inevitably in any such movement "freaks and monsters" would "jump out of themselves . . . thinking their opportunity has come, they will reveal themselves . . . this is a law of history." He fully expected rightist elements, hidden among the people

---

* *On the Correct Handling of Contradictions Among the People,* February 27, 1957. *Selected Readings of Mao Tsetung* (English edition Peking 1971), page 432.

† Speech at the Chinese Communist Party's National Conference on Propaganda Work, March 12, 1957. *Selected Readings of Mao Tsetung* (English edition Peking 1971), page 480.

‡ Speech at the Chinese Communist Party's National Conference on Propaganda Work, March 12, 1957. *Selected Readings of Mao Tsetung* (English edition Peking 1971), page 480.

and in the Party, to expose themselves. Then the Party would realize that class struggle on the ideological plane was very real, and that it was *in the Party* too.

It is at this point that there seems to have been, on the part of the right wing, a deliberate attempt to discredit Mao by pushing the whole movement into one direction only: that is, deliberately obscuring the issues, allowing and giving wide coverage only to the most extreme, the most anti-Party articles, and thus arousing opposition to the whole affair.

Party committees in charge of academic institutes were enjoined to "let everything be allowed." There was no reference to Mao Tsetung Thought in blooming and contending. Mao's address in March had been explicit: constant and arduous revolutionary struggles and social- ist education on the political and ideological fronts (*not* physical purges) were necessary for a long time to come. Criticism was good for the Party. China's transformation depended on CCP leadership, "but we cannot accomplish this on our own . . . we need a good number of non-Party people with great ideals who will fight dauntlessly together with us." One had to find them, to sort out "fragrant flowers" from "poisonous weeds."

In April the tone and volume of criticism meetings rose; by May the intellectual sector began to effervesce, especially the university stu- dents. Looking at Chinese newspapers of the time, one gets a biased picture of what actually went on. Suddenly a great amount of freedom was allowed, and students formed clubs, held meetings, and especially posted *tatzepao* (big-character posters). These *tatzepao* not only cov- ered campuses; they were also found in offices, in administrative de- partments, in factories. Most of the concern of foreign newsmen and China scholars centered on university discontent, as seen through quotations from the most extreme *tatzepao*. Universities were still the stronghold of the bourgeoisie, with 80 percent of the student body of bourgeois origin. The *tatzepao* were of every kind, ranging from com- plaints about studies and "no good jobs available" to demands for "freedom, equality," and more books on the outside world. Each uni- versity or college had a board for these posters, on each a reminder that "criticism must help socialist construction."

Some curious things happened. Posters put up by worker and peas- ant students praising or defending the Party were torn down. Worker and peasant students were beaten or wounded in scuffles, and pre- vented from speaking for the system by groups of students.

Because "rectification" was, he knew, directed toward his own groups in the Party, Liu Shao-chi announced that the movement must be carried out gently as a "breeze or mild rain," and that there would be no punishment of Party cadres or officials.

Criticism and confrontation sharpened as the newspapers aired the intellectuals' complaints in cascades of speeches and articles which had nothing to do with the construction of socialism. Under glaring head-lines Mao Tsetung and Chou En-lai were condemned, enjoined to "get down," and intellectuals demanded to share power with the Com-munist Party. This small typhoon of irrational virulence lasted about three weeks. It distorted the meaning of the Hundred Flowers, because during that time there was no reply, no criticism, no debate.

And yet this was not the total picture. A good many non-Party intellectuals occupied posts in the government and the State Council. Some were ministers, held privilege and office. The eight non-Commu-nist parties enjoyed 25 percent of the seats in the National People's Congress though they represented less than 1 percent of the popula-tion, yet some of their members gave birth to voluble pronunciamentos against the Party. Strangely enough, however, some of the most viru-lent articles and speeches came from Party members themselves.

A very large number of the texts which appeared opposed control of education by the Party; others argued for a parliamentary system com-posed of several parties, who would alternately hold power. On the other hand, there were also some critical speeches which sought to promote better socialism. For example Chang Hsi-jo, a non-Party edu-cation minister, criticized the "Confucianism" of Party cadres who "told the people what to do, but not why." Mao Tun, then minister of Culture (non-Party), criticized the bureaucratism prevalent among Party writers. "Whenever creative writing is mentioned they feel that unless they are sent to a luxurious writers' home in a scenic spot they cannot function." Neither Chang Hsi-jo nor Mao Tun were dubbed "rightists" nor castigated for their criticism.

Historians and philosophers now joined the fray. Some of the history professors stopped their courses at 1911, refusing even to mention the Chinese Revolution. Now they demanded freedom in universities and "government of education by the professors." Philosophers demanded the right to teach any kind of philosophy they wished.

Some serious incidents took place. There were a few murders of Party cadres. Then groups of students openly discussed forming Petofi clubs. Behind them were ex-landlords and gangsters and former members of the now proscribed secret societies. There were two days of public demonstrations by university students in Wuhan. In the provinces the sons of landlords and capitalist families tried to incite factory workers to revolt, but were thrown out of factories. Within the Writers' Federation there was an attempt to resurrect the Hu Feng case; demands that he be rehabilitated were also raised in a few universities.

"These are brave men," stated John Foster Dulles upon hearing of demands made for parliamentarian government by certain members of the Democratic League. In the USSR the Chinese experiment aroused some disquiet. "They were afraid that we were liberalizing," Mao would explain.

Through the Party rank and file, resentment grew as no one publicly rebutted the statements given such wide publicity. "After all, in what way has the Party not taken care of you . . . mistreated you to deserve . . . this intense hatred from you?" wrote one Party cadre. Workers also became restive. They wrote collectively to the newspapers, but their letters were not printed. Non-Party people who defended the Communist Party received threatening anonymous letters. Slogans to "kill all the Communists" were issued by small and hysterical extremist groups. In the Communist Youth League a small number of landlord sons formed juntas to seize power.

There is good evidence that it was Liu Shao-chi and Peng Chen who called the movement to an abrupt halt,* having created the impression they desired — that unless there was control from above, any mass movement would become "chaotic." By allowing this tide of antagonistic articles, and then demanding immediate action to stem it before a "Hungarian-type revolt" occurred, they hoped the Party would reassert its control, and especially that there would be no further targeting upon the Party's right wing.

The *People's Daily* published an editorial (*What Is This For?*) on June 6. The movement ground to a halt. It was not till about eight weeks later that an "anti-rightist" drive began.

Mao Tsetung knew perfectly well that there would be a surge of rightist articles and speeches. Had there not been, he would have been surprised. The apparent volume of dissent did not frighten him. He

* See Richard Solomon *Mao's Revolution and the Chinese Political Culture* (Michigan Studies on China; Los Angeles, California, 1971), pages 268–329, for a most important study of the Hundred Flowers. Author in private interviews and during the cultural revolution also derived repeated impressions that Peng Chen and Liu Shao-chi had shielded their own groups, as the report of Secretary-General Teng Hsiao-ping also would make clear. See page 106.

considered it an excellent lesson for the Party. But he had wanted "rectification" to target upon the right wing in the Party, and now this was being deviated. Although some counterrevolutionaries within the Party were being unmasked (through their actions, for in some cases they led groups to commit murder and sabotage), the main target, the top leadership holding a rightist line, remained untouched and aloof, letting the non-Party intelligentsia do the shouting.

On July 1, in an editorial in the *People's Daily*, Mao's view was again expressed. Such "freaks and monsters" as had come up should be criticized, but non-Party intellectuals who had committed errors should be dealt with more leniently, provided they recanted their errors and mended their ways. Which they did, en masse. For instance, two non-Party officials of the Democratic League, Lo Lung-chi and Chang Peng-chun, who had distinguished themselves by their loudness, made their self-criticism and went unharmed, though they lost their posts and were assigned other work. (They were to be met, attending a theater performance, in 1966.*) To point up his meaning, Mao went to Shanghai and was photographed during a two-hour meeting with non-Party writers and artists, thus putting into action his "unity and struggle" thesis.

The anti-rightist campaign began in the autumn; and though there were a few executions (chiefly for murder) and some dissidents did spells of "educative-corrective" manual labor, the main punishment was being labeled a "rightist." On September 11 a directive entitled *Handle Sternly Party Rightists* said: "There are many rightists who are Party members for ten or twenty years . . . if their existence within our Party is tolerated they will collude with rightists outside . . . to attack and oppose us from within."

Did the Hundred Flowers accomplish its aim? Partly. The movement showed that class struggle was acute, that the bourgeoisie had not made a total conversion, and that the Party was not immune to bourgeois ideas or infiltration. In short, it refuted all of Liu Shao-chi's assertions. The Hundred Flowers also revealed a new method for solving contradictions in a socialist society. Mao had been daring enough, percipient enough, to show how it was possible for a Party claiming to be the vanguard of the proletariat to be infiltrated by an exploiting class and its ideology.

The Hundred Flowers was followed with close attention in many

* By author.

socialist countries. Although none of them* have ever been bold enough to call for mass criticism of their own Party methods as China has done, it was a breakthrough on the need for Party submission to mass criticism, and how this helps it to become truly itself, and not degenerate into another tyranny.

The Hundred Flowers did not stop; it was a long-term policy, and it continued until 1958. But after September 1957 it was the turn of the workers and peasants to put up their *tatzepao* and to criticize rightist ideas. This prepared the mental and ideological background for the Great Leap which was to begin.

Mao Tsetung had now proved to the Party where its deficiencies lay; and from September 1957 onward a number of higher-level cadres carried out their self-criticism "before the masses." This broke down their apprehension and also the Confucian idea that no "superior" could be criticized by an "inferior." It promoted a new attitude in Party members. Mao utilized this swiftly to launch a re-education of the Party through manual labor, breaking down the biggest barrier of all — the barrier between mental and manual work. By September, eight hundred thousand cadres were doing manual labor in the co-operatives. The socialist education movement, which had stopped, was now vigorously promoted. All cadres at the lower level, in factories and in cooperatives, would henceforth participate in manual work in their units.

Through the Hundred Flowers, and the "pulverization," as one observer put it, of the right-wing groups in the universities, it was possible to start the revolution in education which Mao had contemplated since 1953.

Liu Shao-chi in his report at the Eighth Party Congress had emphasized "productive skill and professional ability . . . the basic object of all Party work is to satisfy to the maximum . . . the material and cultural needs of the people." This deft phrasing did not solve the problem of training successors for the continuing revolution. After the anti-rightist campaign, a million young students from colleges and universities would be doing manual labor, starting the essential integration with their own people to guarantee revolutionary motivation for the next generation.

We do not know whether Liu Shao-chi went through another self-criticism that autumn; he now appeared completely won over to Mao's

* Except Albania.

ideas. We do not know whether his conversion — even if temporary — was genuine. It was certainly not motivated by fear, though it might have been by self-preservation, both in status and in influence. Mao's leadership style was consensus; and the respect and affection with which he was surrounded was based on the recognition of his integrity of purpose. Whatever the private talks which Mao and Liu may have held at the time, unity once more pervaded the Party. In February 1957, at the third plenum of the Eighth Central Committee, an overwhelming consensus in favor of Mao's strategy of development reversed the 1956 stand.

The report of the secretary-general, Teng Hsiao-ping,* praised the "great national debate" which Mao had launched. A revolution in the superstructure was essential; in other words, a cultural revolution. It was more necessary to rectify within the Party than outside it, yet there had been "reluctance to take action against some veteran Party members who should have been demarcated as rightists." However, Mao still considered his differences with Liu Shao-chi a non-antagonistic "contradiction among the people," to be dealt with by criticism and persuasion and self-criticism, until the realization that it had become an "enemy" contradiction could no longer be avoided.

Teng Hsiao-ping's report emphasized the need for a revolution in education, pivotal for transformation of the superstructure. The proletariat must bring forth its own intellectuals, both "Red and expert." Manual labor for all students and graduates from educational institutions, to integrate them with the peasants and workers, would be an essential part of education. Mao's three criteria, already mentioned in 1939, of practice for the young in class struggle, struggle for production (labor), and scientific experiment (innovation, self-reliance, and participation in the technical revolution) would be applied to each and every student. "During a certain period . . . we assigned to leadership organs at various levels too large a number of young intellectuals who had not been steeled in productive labor."

In the factories, working class enthusiasm rose with the anti-rightist campaign, which for the first time allowed workers to criticize the

* Report on the rectification campaign by Teng Hsiao-ping, general secretary of the Party's Central Committee, September 23, 1957, to the third plenary session (enlarged) of the Eighth Central Committee. Released by Hsinhua News Agency in English on October 19, 1957. This report was most important in charting the new "general line" for tthe Great Leap Forward of 1958; i.e., the notion of "Red and expert," castigation of "free markets" opened in September 1956 in rural areas (the Liu "four freedoms" directive), the triple alliance, and denunciation of "rightists" in the Party.

administrative elite. Workers' posters covered factory walls, and this was the beginning of their emancipation. Mao Tsetung, visiting factories and seeing the innumerable letters of opinion which plastered the walls of every workshop, would write in 1958:

> *Only in wind and thunder can the country show its vigor.*
> *Alas, the ten thousand horses are all muted.*
> *O Heaven, bestir yourself, I beseech you,*
> *And send down men of many talents.*

The third plenum passed resolutions based on Mao's suggestions for industrial management. All decisions in factories must have the workers' participation. A triple alliance of administrative cadres, technicians and workers must be organized in each, and the first two grades must do actual workers' labor at least twice a week to maintain close ties with the people. Rules and regulations that stifled initiative should be abolished or revised. Workers' committees under Party leadership must overcome bureaucratism. Workers must participate in management.

The twelve-year plan in agriculture, shelved the preceding year for the second time, was also passed. The socialist education movement in rural areas was to promote understanding of this plan and its scientific and economic principles. In the preceding winter, because of the confusing two-line struggle and rightist bureaucratism, there had been an influx of population from the countryside into the cities. Now the rural people were persuaded to return; loans were given to needy cooperatives, and a nationwide program of irrigation, which provided millions with work in the slack season, was begun. Handicrafts and subsidiary occupations were collectivized and stimulated.

The provincial governments were happy with the changes. Decentralization assured them of retaining a majority of their funds; they vied in producing documents which would mesh in with the overall plans, and these make interesting reading. Most praise the socialist education movement as making clear the difference between the socialist and capitalist roads; many describe the left and right tendencies in the Party. "A number of comrades have not yet grasped the directives . . . they do not understand that to overcome difficulties, they must rely on the masses," writes one particularly forthright report from Chekiang. This report also drew attention to the need for "keeping the doors of educational institutions open for workers' and peasants' children," who otherwise were eliminated or humiliated, and for giving priority enrollment in administration to cadres from worker-peasant origin or who had done manual labor.

Some of these reports also voice what must have been a growing feeling among the hardworking, dedicated, and on the whole honest Party members. They complain of the mass of contradictory directives and the morass of paper through which the low-level cadre had to wade, trying to figure out what he really should do. There is "dispersionism," writes the Chekiang paper. "Certain important directives of the Party Center and certain important measures formulated by the Provincial Committee are not firmly carried out . . . due to . . . failure to exercise concrete guidance."

The Hundred Flowers and the socialist education movement, together with the Party rectification and the anti-rightist campaign, did promote a new and better relationship between Party and people. "The revolutionaries must transform themselves if they want to transform society . . . making the self the target as well as the promoter of revolution," writes another report.*

In May 1958, to conclude the "blooming and contending" in the intelligentsia sector, Liu Shao-chi mentioned "exchanging hearts . . . between Party and intellectuals, workers . . . and peasants." This led to a rather curious scene in Peking, when university intellectuals paraded with hearts of cardboard, silk, or velvet to Party headquarters to signify that "we give our hearts to the Party, the Party gives its heart to us." We do not know who originated this procedure, or whether it was really useful, but it was quite clear to anyone visiting China then that a far better atmosphere prevailed. Two years later, many people dubbed "rightists" would have this label removed and re-enter normal life.

Whatever the imperfections and limits of the Hundred Flowers, Mao Tsetung had originated something new. "The tree wants to be quiet but the wind is restless." The Party, under its right-wing influence, did not wish to be disturbed, but now it had to accept being constantly overhauled and shaken.

"The east wind prevails over the west wind," said Mao Tsetung in 1957. The phrase is not political in origin; it emanates from the famous seventeenth-century romantic novel *Dream of the Red Chamber*. Neither is it racist; for the east wind brings warmth and rain; the west wind freezes the Chinese plains. Mao Tsetung adapted this figure of

---

* This is a quotation of Mao's words (1957?).

speech to mean that the wind of revolution must blow down the wind of revisionism, which was coming from Moscow.

Armed with this great east wind, in November 1957 Mao Tsetung led a high-powered Chinese delegation to the USSR, to attend celebrations of the fortieth anniversary of the Russian Revolution.

7

East Wind, West Wind: China, the USSR, and the United States 1949–1957

It takes more than one cold day for the river to freeze three feet deep.
— Proverb quoted by MAO TSETUNG, September 1963

Mao Tsetung's attitude towards the Soviet Union is that of a reasonable Communist, whose duty is to criticize errors, to support with friendship and materially anything that promotes the socialist cause. Mao Tsetung went to Moscow in 1957 prepared not only to rejoice and to congratulate, but also to reason and to debate.

Relations between the Soviet Union and China and between China and the United States cannot be dealt with separately; since the 1945 Yalta conference a triangular relationship has existed. In early 1945 Mao had hoped that the United States, which he then considered a democratic country, would help in China's reconstruction, but the United States chose to back Chiang Kai-shek and refused to face the inevitability of China's revolution. In 1949 Mao had reiterated that the People's Republic of China was prepared to have diplomatic and trade relations with all countries provided the latter did not aid the "Chinese reactionaries" (Chiang Kai-shek).

However, no such relationship with the United States occurred. Mao Tsetung then gauged that it might take ten years, or perhaps twenty, for the United States to emerge from its obsession against "Red" China. This dictated a course prudent and unprovocative, yet firm and unyielding. Meanwhile, China's industrialization would have to rely upon the USSR. And Mao went to Moscow to see Stalin in the winter of 1949–1950 not only to seek aid, but also for other reasons.

"In Moscow, I struggled for two months against Stalin." The latter had been unwilling to sign a treaty; unwilling to recognize the Chinese Revolution — he called it a "fake." "Only when we shouldered the burden of the Korean War was Stalin convinced." Meanwhile, Mao was forced to agree with the hard terms Stalin made, in return obtaining the abrogation of Stalin's treaty of friendship and alliance with Chiang. The Korean War increased China's dependence on the USSR, and so did the American embargo in 1951. "We could not manage the planning, construction and assembling of heavy industrial plants . . . we had no experience . . . all was imported uncritically" (Mao, 1958).

The hostility of the United States expressed itself in a steady torrent of worldwide propaganda against China, in military threats, in a ring of bases around China, and in the continued protection of Chiang's refugee regime in Taiwan province — Chinese territory — together with the patrolling of Taiwan Strait by the Seventh Fleet.

A history of the irrational anti-China obsession of that time will appear, one day, amazing to the American people themselves. "The heart of our present policy is that there is to be kept alive a constant threat of military action vis-à-vis Red China . . . by Taiwan and other Far Eastern groups, and militarily supported by the U.S. . . . the U.S. is undertaking to maintain for an indefinite period . . . American dominance in the Far East."*

But the world was rapidly changing, and after the stalemate in Korea came the Geneva conference of spring 1954, which coincided with the defeat of the French colonial forces in Indochina and the liberation of three more Asian countries — Vietnam, Laos, Cambodia. Nothing could now stop the emergence of the Third World. At Bandung in April 1955 twenty-nine nations gathered, and though they appeared timid enough, yet the will to national independence and sovereignty was there.

At both Geneva and Bandung the People's Republic of China was represented by Chou En-lai, and it became obvious that no problems in Asia could be solved without the participation of China.

Towards the United States, Chou En-lai reiterated China's stand at Bandung: "The American people are our friends. We do not want war with the United States . . . the Chinese government is ready to enter into negotiations with the American government to discuss relaxation of tension in the Far East . . . especially in the Straits of Taiwan." But

* Walter Spencer Robertson, U.S. Assistant Secretary of State for Far Eastern Affairs, 1954.

Taiwan was Chinese territory, and the PRC would not abrogate her sovereign right to liberate her own territory by any means she saw fit; nor would she ever accept the "two-China policy."

Despite the hostility, and China's vigorous denunciations of American imperialism, there was also the necessity for communication between the two countries. At Chou En-lai's suggestion, meetings at ambassadorial level were initiated in August 1955. To show goodwill, China liberated some American airmen (not all) captured on spy flights in the Northeast. In May 1956, in another goodwill gesture, Chou En-lai expressed readiness to grant fifteen American journalists visas to visit China. But this was refused by the State Department in Washington.

Meanwhile, in the USSR, Stalin's death had led to a crisis of succession in which both Malenkov and Khrushchev sought Mao's support. Malenkov, desirous of ending the Cold War, had initiated policies of "detente" with the United States, but without success. Khrushchev appeared, at the time, a hard-liner compared to Malenkov, but this stance was skin-deep; in reality the deep internal problems of the USSR, problems which had not and could not be solved without a thorough overhaul of the Party and its methods, were already being used in a way which indicated a reversal (revisionism) in both internal and external policies.

It is not necessary here to study the underlying causes that dictated the choices which Khrushchev and after him Leonid Brezhnev were to make. But it is certain that Mao had studied them deeply, and was worried and disturbed about the trend of policies in the USSR years before the Twentieth Congress took place in February 1956.

In September 1954 Khrushchev and Bulganin had paid a visit to Peking. At the time there had been, on the part of Mao, a "test of intention," which consisted in the shelling of some small islands off China's coast, garrisoned by Chiang Kai-shek's forces. Although a great clamor of invasion was raised, and Eisenhower asked and obtained from Congress authority to "engage in whatever operations may be required," the United Nations allies of the United States now refused to budge; and Chiang Kai-shek, though "unleashed," in Eisenhower's picturesque phrase, also refused. Chiang had always preferred the Americans to do his fighting for him. Shrewdly, he knew his allies and protectors; should he fail, he would be discarded and replaced. The hullabaloo died down, but Khrushchev showed some trepidation.

Khrushchev's perturbation seemed to Mao all too reminiscent of Stalin's attempt to induce Mao to desist from pursuing the War of Liberation ("Leave South China to Chiang Kai-shek") for fear of atomic retaliation by the United States (1946). Mao had given then his famous interview to the American writer Anna Louise Strong: "Imperialism and all reactionaries are paper tigers."* Khrushchev feared that Chinese action might jeopardize the negotiations by which the USSR was attempting to end the Cold War.

To Mao, the USSR desire for *exclusive* dialogue with the United States (Khrushchev emphasized that there were "only two large powers in the world") was reminiscent of Yalta. Khrushchev might try to make agreements in the name of the whole socialist camp. The test of intention in the shelling of the small islands had been as much a test of USSR intention as of U.S. intention, a gentle reminder that China did not want any deals made at her expense. For now the line of military demarcation in Korea had become a political boundary, with the agreement of the USSR; and Mao Tsetung, who is vigilant and knows history well, did not want a repetition of this horse-trading: another demarcation in the Taiwan Strait.

In other ways, however, Stalin's death had removed many causes of friction, as the Russians themselves hinted. Within days of his demise, a Chinese delegation which had been cooling its heels in Moscow since the previous October had concluded an agreement for 141 large-scale industrial projects; and Mao, until then ignored, was called "a great Marxist theoretician" by *Pravda*.

The Peking talks in the autumn of 1954 achieved substantial gains for China. Russian garrisons in Manchuria were removed, joint-stock companies transferred to China, Port Arthur and Talien returned, and a credit of 170 million rubles negotiated. Initial steps for an exchange of nuclear knowledge were started; shortly afterward Chinese personnel went to the USSR for nuclear training, and a small-scale atomic reactor was built in China.

While Mao thus obtained release from the "undue interference" of Stalin, Khrushchev obtained Chinese support for the policies of the USSR. In fact for many years, despite the growing dispute, China would support the USSR in the policies she considered would lead to peace and relaxation of tension, but without compromising or jeopardizing principles and the rights of other nations, notably those of the Third World. In October 1954 the USSR proposed to twenty-three

* Talk with the American correspondent Anna Louise Strong, August 1946. *Selected Readings of Mao Tsetung* (English edition Peking 1971), page 345.

European governments and the United States the convening of a conference on European security, and China supported this move.

The important outcome of Khrushchev's visit to Mao was a solemn agreement to hold mutual consultations "on all matters of common interest pertaining to the socialist camp . . . in order to engage in concerted action . . . to maintain peace." This meant that in any moves which involved China directly or indirectly, or negotiations with the United States on world affairs, China must be consulted, as she would be affected. Both Molotov and Bulganin referred to China as "an equal partner." Equality between all socialist countries, respect for their sovereignty and territorial integrity, and non-interference in their internal affairs were written into the joint communiqué issued.

But it was soon obvious that Khrushchev would not honor the clause on "equality." He remarked to Chancellor Konrad Adenauer of West Germany in July 1955, at a five-power meeting in Geneva, that China might become "a worrying problem for the West." Khrushchev was a political animal, and until his uncontrolled bizarre moods would compel his demotion, he was also thoroughly unscrupulous. He was certainly aware that an America haunted by the vision of China as the main enemy was advantageous to the USSR in its burgeoning imperialism; it would be some years before Mao realized the dishonesty of the man. He seemed for a while to place great hopes in Khrushchev. "With cooperation between our two countries . . . I am convinced that all the aggressive plans of imperialism will come to nothing," Mao wrote.

In return for support of Khrushchev's foreign policy initiatives, Mao asked in early 1955 for a declaration of support regarding Taiwan, but despite the treaties and military alliance pact, this was not forthcoming. It would become increasingly obvious that the focus of attention for the USSR would be Europe, where she sought "detente," and that the price she was only too willing to pay would be a tacit acceptance of U.S. military presence and activities in Asia. This would make it possible for Dulles to fashion the Southeast Asia Treaty Organization (SEATO), which needed for its rationale the bogey of a Red China bursting at the seams and intent on invading Southeast Asia (the domino theory). Thus would the ground be prepared for the subsequent war in Vietnam.

China's first five-year plan, whatever its defects, did lay the foundations for her heavy industry, but she seemed in 1955 more than ever under Russian influence, from architecture to the army, from the ballet to bathrooms, from food to furniture. And yet it was precisely in 1955 that Mao was fashioning his economic strategy based on self-reliance, which would depart from the Soviet model.

Two months after the April 1955 Bandung conference, in which the USSR had not participated, Khrushchev started an Asian tour which asserted Russia's place as also an Asian power. The focus of the tour was India, where the USSR contracted in February 1955 to build a steel plant. The Indian subcontinent, with its great wealth and the strategic importance of the Indian Ocean, was a major consideration in this wooing of India. By 1960 Soviet aid to India would be three times as much as to China.

In February 1956 the Twentieth Congress of the CPSU took place, and Khrushchev delivered his two speeches, one public and one secret — the secret one being the startling outburst against Stalin which rocked the socialist camp. The condemnation of Stalin diverted attention from the new line of peaceful transition to socialism, which was the burden of Khrushchev's main speech. Khrushchev had now enunciated a new general policy for the socialist camp without consulting the Chinese, in defiance of the 1954 agreement.

Khrushchev's speech is a hurly-burly of imprecise statements. "We want to be friends . . . [with the United States] and to cooperate with them in the struggle for the peace and security of the people . . . as well as in cultural and economic sectors . . . peaceful transition to socialism . . . is now possible . . . the forces of peace are so strong." He warned that any war, because of nuclear weapons, would mean the hideous destruction of the whole human race; therefore war must be avoided at all costs. Peaceful economic competition would "bury imperialism," and this was the only course.

Denunciation of Stalin was a psychological ploy, allowing the Moscow leader to smuggle in the attractive thesis of "peaceful transition" by using Stalin's grim purges as a foil. Some old Party members in France and other European countries, where parties had almost become bourgeois establishments themselves, were delighted. As Mao said mockingly: "A millstone had dropped off their necks . . . the world could be at peace." How bourgeois they had become they themselves were not aware. "The world can only go towards relaxation of tensions . . . one can see the prospect of a durable peace . . . cooperation between all states," echoed Liu Shao-chi.

Mao was disquieted. The sum of Khrushchev's seven-hour rambling was that in order to avert a world holocaust, nothing must obstruct an arrangement between the two big powers. And this meant, bluntly, that no national liberation movement which might threaten imperialism would be supported by the USSR, as it might destroy the "understanding" between the two big powers upon which rested world peace.

This was the setting up of a dual hegemony to rule the world, and even worse than Yalta. It was also a grotesque distortion of Marxism, for Khrushchev abundantly misquoted Lenin to bolster with ideological principles his thesis, which Mao called revisionist. "The Twentieth Congress was the first step along the road to revisionism," Mao wrote in September 1963.* The Kremlin leader sought to subordinate all revolutionary movements to the national great power interests of the USSR and its "capitulation" to the United States.

There was also the question of Stalin and the personality cult. While agreeing about Stalin's many errors, "the complete negation of Stalin, on the pretext of combating the personality cult, and the thesis of peaceful transition to socialism by the parliamentary road . . . are gross errors of principle," Mao said.†

Yet we find Liu Shao-chi asserting at the first plenum of the Eighth Central Committee (September 1956) that "the Twentieth Congress . . . is a political event of world significance . . . It has condemned the personality cult," while Teng Hsiao-ping defended Mao, recalling that Mao in September 1948 had drafted the resolution ensuring collective leadership, "a long-established tradition in our Party."‡

Two months after the Twentieth Congress of the CPSU, Mao had already indicated to the Russian ambassador in Peking his disapproval. "We do not agree . . . with the total denunciation of Stalin . . . There are other matters . . . on which we do not agree."

The first Chinese document in the Sino-Soviet ideological dispute appeared on April 5, 1956.§ Called unwieldily *On the Historical Experience of the Dictatorship of the Proletariat*, it is a consensus work in which Mao's views are considerably attenuated. But its major theme is that socialist society still contains class struggle and many contradictions. It reminds the Russian Party that Stalin, although arbitrary, counterposing his individual authority to collective decisions, was not

* *On the Question of Stalin*, September 13, 1963. This is the second of Nine Comments, starting with *The Origin and Development of the Differences Between the CPSU and Ourselves*, attributed mainly to Mao and published between September 6, 1963, and February 10, 1964.

† Ibid.

‡ *On Strengthening the Party Committee System*, September 20, 1948. *Selected Readings of Mao Tsetung* (English edition Peking 1971), page 360.

§ Besides the Nine Comments, there were other documents, letters, etc., to a total volume of around two million words.

always incorrect. Eight months later, in December, after the events in Poland and Hungary, another document appeared: *More on the Historical Experience of the Dictatorship of the Proletariat.* This one, in its forthright explicitness, bears Mao's stamp.

"A further train of events has caused us concern. . . . Who is our enemy, who is our friend?" This rhetorical question repeats what the young Mao of March 1927 had written in his first protest against erroneous Party policy, *Report on an Investigation of the Peasant Movement in Hunan.* *

In this document Mao provides a long explanation of "contradiction." The main contradiction of the present period is between imperialism and socialism on a world scale; all others — between socialist countries, between comrades within a Party, between Communist parties — are secondary. "Life is complicated . . . it is possible for classes with fundamentally conflicting interests to unite to cope with a main common enemy." This was the basis for a world united front of all exploited nations, irrespective of their political systems, against imperialism.

But non-antagonistic contradictions could turn antagonistic when one side gradually goes over to the enemy; there were such instances in the history of both the CPSU and the CCP. "Certain comrades" were focusing on errors and mistakes, not on the main successes of the Russian Revolution and its essential correctness. To negate all that Stalin did was to negate the revolution; this was what imperialism hoped for; had not Dulles recently stated that "a change of character of the Communist world now seems within the realm of possibility"?

Stalin committed many "errors": alienation from the masses, illegality, killing of great numbers of good Communists and citizens; great nation chauvinism. "Stalin lacked the spirit of equality, let alone the desire to educate the mass of cadres to be modest . . . sometimes he even mistakenly intervened in the internal affairs of certain fraternal countries and parties." Nevertheless, he was a valiant Marxist-Leninist. This showed that even with a correct theory and system, much harm can be done when the wrong strategy, wrong methods, wrong style of work are used. The cure for this "subjectivism" was the mass line. Some Communists, however, were now fostering "a revisionist trend. . . . According to them it is possible to build socialism without going through a proletarian revolution . . . (peaceful transition)." This was "more dangerous than dogmatism."

* See *the Morning Deluge*, pages 143ff.

As in the first document, in *More on the Historical Experience* there is an insistence on unity in independence of Communist parties and countries, and the necessity for eradicating national chauvinism.

Khrushchev's prestige had been damaged by the uprisings within the socialist camp; it was China who helped the USSR at this hour to maintain unity. Chou En-lai went from country to country, calling for unity and solidarity, in order to initiate the process of open dialogue which Mao thought was the best way to solve contradictions.

Within the CPSU itself there was objection to Khrushchev's denunciation of Stalin. "Stalin's name is inseparable from Marxist-Leninism," Khrushchev was constrained to remark at a reception at the Chinese embassy in Moscow in January 1957. Again Mao Tsetung gave him the benefit of the doubt. Perhaps Khrushchev had been too hasty, abrupt . . . but he might still undertake his self-criticism.

In Peking, Mao received many visits from Party leaders in European and Asian countries. He explained his concepts, emphasized self-criticism by the Party leadership, mass line methods, open-door criticism by the masses. The Italian Party chief, Palmiro Togliatti, had the impression that Mao defended the Twentieth Congress because Mao's practice towards a "comrade" was not to talk behind his back. Mao remarked that the situation in the USSR was that of a pan boiling, compressed too long; "When one takes the lid off, hands get burned."

When the Hundred Flowers was launched in China, in May 1957, Soviet Marshal Kliment Voroshilov was sent to watch the event. "This has never been done in the USSR," he said disapprovingly.

The November 1957 celebrations of the fortieth anniversary of the Russian Revolution saw Khrushchev in a much stronger position. In June a move to depose him had been defeated. In August the USSR successfully tested her first intercontinental ballistic missile; in October and November she sent up the first two successful earth satellites, Sputniks I and II. This revelation of Soviet might induced further reflection in Washington. George Kennan, who had favored a working partnership with the USSR, suggested a policy of military disengagement in Europe: "The entire area can in some way be removed as an object in the military rivalry of the great powers." And ambassadorial talks, initiated at Chou En-lai's suggestion in 1956, with China were temporarily suspended.

Sixty-four delegations of Communist and workers' parties assembled to attend Moscow's lavish and impressive celebration; a vast display of Soviet military might impressed those present. The meeting of so many parties was a good occasion for frank exchanges, because the disarray within the parties, the confusion of many Party members, was obvious.

From the very start, Mao's stand was that no resolution of one fraternal Party could arbitrarily represent the general line of the international Communist movement. The Russian leadership had prepared a draft declaration, as had the Chinese. Mao's speech was a detailed analysis of the changes in international relations since World War II.*
His intention was to start an ideological debate among all parties. "Unity, struggle, criticism and self-criticism . . . and unity on a new basis."

It was necessary to have this debate, as the Russian leadership indicated it considered its own line binding upon the whole socialist camp. Mikhail Suslov, a Party ideologue, had made a speech some months earlier on the universal principles guiding the building of socialism, in which any reference to equality between parties had been omitted.

Mao began by first listing world events which proved the irresistible current of history in favor of socialism and world revolution. The defeat of Hitler and Japan, the victorious revolution in China, the truce in Korea, the Vietnam victory over French colonialism, the Suez victory with withdrawal of the Anglo-French forces, the withdrawal of colonial powers from Southeast Asia and Africa, the national liberation movements in Algeria and elsewhere . . . all these were armed struggles, and the excellent situation prevailing was due to these armed struggles. "I consider . . . that the east wind prevails over the west wind." The socialist camp was objectively stronger than imperialism. The emergence of socialist states and the Soviet development of nuclear missiles all indicated this growing strength.

The present period, Mao continued, was characterized by national liberation movements in Asia, Africa, Latin America. These struggles would now occupy the forefront of the battle against colonialism and imperialism. Imperialism was beset with contradictions, some very acute. But in order to ensure victory, correct strategy and tactics must be utilized. Here we find again Mao's emphasis on the methodology of revolutionary science: nothing can be left to chance.

Some people held that nuclear power determined everything. Mao disagreed. In 1946 he had said the atom bomb was a paper tiger. He still thought so. Now it was even less probable that nuclear bombs would determine the issue of any war. For the USSR also had atom bombs and was achieving nuclear parity with the United States.

* Editor's note, *People's Daily*, July 20, 1963.

Proletarian internationalism must provide help and support to the national liberation movements, the wave of the future. The superiority of the socialist camp must be used on their behalf, not on behalf of one country or a few countries. Such a policy of resolute support would stop aggression and war everywhere and make the socialist camp a true bulwark of peace.

Imperialism was already on the defensive, not on a wave of expansion; it fought to maintain the status quo. Mao posited aid to national liberation movements in the Third World as the main factor for the general line. It was precisely on this point that Khrushchev was not only vague but hostile. A dialogue with the U.S. entailed toning down the national liberation movements, regarded by imperialism as the main challenge to its domination.

In the years to come Khrushchev would distort Mao's meaning by calling him "intent on promoting war . . . bellicose . . . needing a psychiatrist." Mao never suggested military provocation, but pointed out that the U.S. was preparing for small local conflicts in Latin America, Asia, Africa, in which the manpower would not be American but local.*

The population factor was on the side of the emergent Third World. There were fully one billion people in the "socialist camp"; the industrial nations of the West contained only 400 million. Mao had discussed this matter with "a foreign statesman who appeared in dread of nuclear war" (Nehru). He had told Nehru that if imperialism started a general war, of course one must defend oneself, but he did not think the United States would begin a *nuclear* war. Nehru appeared persuaded that the United States would stop at nothing and would go for "total extermination of humanity." Mao had replied that he did not think so, but that should this happen, at the worst one-half of the population of the globe would be exterminated. However, this would not stop resistance; the other half would remain and "imperialism would dig its own grave." "We do not want war, not for a single day," Mao repeated. But the best way to prevent war was through the correct strategy and tactics of defense, and this meant supporting national liberation movements in the "intermediate zone" — the Third World. Imperialism drew its strength from the raw materials it controlled in the Third World. To deny it these resources would be to deprive it of strength.

"Strategically we should despise the enemy, but tactically take him

* Discussion on the "limited new strategy" and counter-guerilla tactics were being debated in the U.S., and Mao followed the discussion with great attention.

seriously." The world had reached a turning point; the awareness of the world's peoples, their desire for independence, were very strong and would increase.

The Russian argument was that the strength of the socialist camp was such that there would be no local conflicts; U.S. imperialism would choose a general war, striking at the USSR first. And this could only be avoided by a policy of "peace." Restraint upon national liberation struggles and local conflicts was necessary because they might escalate into global conflict.

Another argument was that unless a nation was industrialized and produced abundant steel for weaponry it could not wage war against a highly industrialized nation. This argument had already been proved wrong by the victory of Mao's guerillas in China, and in Indochina in 1954, when the forces of Ho Chi Minh had won against modern, well-equipped French colonial forces. It would be proved wrong in Algeria, and again in Vietnam. A small undeveloped country, said Mao, could beat a large industrialized one. There was the factor of logistics, but above all the factor of morale. A just war enjoyed the support of the world's peoples. "The decisive factor is man, not weapons."

In April 1959 Chou En-lai would again state Mao's view: "Asia, Africa, and Latin America, which used to be the imperialist rear, have now come to the forefront in the fight against aggression and imperialism. But the imperialist forces will not step down from the stage of history of their own accord." China was therefore ready to give support and assistance to the full extent of her capabilities to all national independence movements.

In 1958 aid programs from China to the Third World, soon to surpass in scope the aid programs of the USSR, would begin.

"Where necessary, Comrade Mao Tsetung . . . waged struggles against . . . the leaders of the CPSU . . . in order to help them correct their errors."*

The draft declaration prepared by the Russians was altered. The original had proclaimed that the defense of peace was the most important world task. The "historic decisions of the Twentieth Congress" were to be rammed through the sixty-four parties attending the USSR fortieth anniversary celebrations in Moscow. The Kremlin leaders evoked Czechoslovakia as the example of a country which had operated a "peaceful transition to socialism." The Chinese pointed out that the Prague uprising of February 1948 was a continuation of the war of

* September 6, 1963. See note on the Nine Comments, page 116.

resistance against Hitler led by the local Communist Party, and that the Soviet army had also intervened "decisively." The Chinese draft refuted the thesis of peaceful transition. The declaration that emerged was a compound. It concluded that imperialism was the chief danger; that war was always possible as long as imperialism existed; and that even if peaceful transition was possible (Lenin had said that it was an extraordinarily rare occurrence) a class in power never gave up power willingly. The Chinese obtained other amendments: the internal source of revisionism was bourgeois influence; the external source was "capitulation" to imperialism; revisionism represented the "principal danger" at this period of history. Solidarity was stressed, the joint struggle of socialist forces with national liberation movements, the working class in all countries, and the peace movements.

The Moscow meeting ended in a flourish of unity, assurances of unbreakable friendship. The Chinese indicated support for Khrushchev's negotiations with the United States as evidence of peaceful intent, but they conveyed their view that their moves were tactical, since "imperialism will never lay down the butcher's knife" of its own accord.

Khrushchev was enraged. He may have thought that Mao Tsetung would not oppose the Russian draft because, in that very October, the Russians had signed with a Chinese military delegation, led by Peng Teh-huai (the Defense minister and a warm supporter of the sovietization of the Chinese army), an agreement to exchange information on nuclear weapons and to deliver a sample atom bomb to the Chinese. But at the same time Khrushchev was engaged in preliminary talks with the United States for a nuclear test ban. Khrushchev had added a codicil to the Soviet proposal: the question of forbidding nuclear tests should be separate from the problem of disarmament and of total interdiction of nuclear weaponry. This would leave the field open for nuclear expansion in the U.S. and the USSR, but would stop other countries, when and if they managed to have nuclear weapons, from testing them.

In that December, a campaign through Soviet-supported peace organizations would begin, stressing the horrors of nuclear warfare. It would have a great emotional impact in Europe and America, but almost none in Third World countries.

Long and numerous were the discussions in the CCP that winter. Mao Tsetung was not optimistic after his Moscow visit. It only confirmed his urgency: China must accelerate her development in the full expectation of having to go it alone; accelerate her own independent nuclear deterrent. Mao now foresaw that the time might come when the USSR would "exert pressure" on China.

"Ever since the Twentieth Congress of the CPSU we have watched with concern, as the CPSU leadership took the road of revisionism. Confronted with this grave situation, our Party had scores of times and for a long period considered: What should we do?

"We foresaw that if we criticized . . . they would certainly strike at us vindictively and cause serious damage to China's socialist construction . . . but should Communists take a stand of national egoism and not dare to uphold truth for fear of vindictive blows?"*

In January 1958 Mao Tsetung indicated that he wished to relinquish the post of chairman of the Republic.† He wanted to give himself more time to pursue the important issues at hand: the ideological struggle with the USSR and other Communist parties, which Mao saw as absolutely essential for the future of humanity; the great experiment in China itself; accelerated development to bring China into the modern age as a strong, prosperous, industrialized socialist country.

Nothing is valid that is not justified in practice; and Mao Tsetung had just seen socialism gone wrong in the USSR because of the wrong methods, the wrong style of work, the wrong people come to power. China was to prepare to go it alone, finding strength and power, heroism and genius, in her own people.

* September 6, 1963. See note on the Nine Comments, page 116.
† Mao was chairman of the PRC, chairman of the Chinese Communist Party, and chairman of the Military Affairs Committee. See also pages 152–153.

8

The Great Leap Forward and the Communes, 1958–1959

Men have to be changed. . . . If we do not win this battle, there is no hope for socialism.

— *Peking Daily*, September 18, 1957

Upon Mao's return from Moscow at the end of November 1957, the Central Committee met and the general line of the Great Leap Forward was passed: *To carry out the technological and cultural revolution simultaneously with the socialist revolution on the political and ideological fronts; to develop industry and agriculture simultaneously with priority development of heavy industry; to develop central and local industries simultaneously under central leadership, overall planning and in coordination; and to develop large, medium and small enterprises simultaneously. To build socialism, faster, better and more economically by exerting efforts to the utmost and pressing ahead consistently.*

Though misjudged for many years, few today will disagree that China's development, her autarkic self-reliance, her prosperity, are due to the broad lines of the Great Leap Forward, the methods invented during those extraordinary years 1958 and 1959.

"My purpose is to get people to dare to speak out with vigor and invincible force, like Marx or Lu Hsun, freeing themselves from inhibitions," Mao said in 1958.

"Corruption, lawbreaking, the arrogance of intellectuals, the wish to elevate one's family by becoming an official and not dirtying one's hands, all these are the thinking, culture, customs and habits which brought China to where we found her. They must disappear. The thinking, customs, culture of a proletarian China which does not yet exist must appear" (Mao, 1965).

In the fourfold accelerated revolution within the Chinese revolution which was the Great Leap Forward, both the material environment and men's minds were to be changed. The cessation of struggle was sheer wishful thinking. Mankind's advance was never-ending struggle. The notion of stability was a desire for stagnation. It was on the principle of changing man and of a constantly progressing revolution that Mao based the concept of the "leap." Individually, the "leap" set the standard of "Red and expert." To posit a contradiction between political acumen and technical ability was a fallacy. Proletarian virtue must replace bourgeois pursuit of personal ambition and greed.

The "leap" was a war against complacency, superstition, prejudice, bureaucratic procrastination, as well as against Nature. To remodel the Chinese earth; to remake Chinese man.

It was the first time an undeveloped country, out of its own potential and people, would speed its own development, wresting itself out of inertia, ignorance, submission. "We shall teach the sun and moon to change places . . . we shall create a new heaven and earth for man."

The experiment's success is due to Mao's entrusting the masses of China with their own destiny, arousing them to create and to transform their society, their earth and themselves, by their own efforts. And this lesson unshackled minds to an extent we are only beginning to gauge. Yet the concept and proposition that a socialist state needed the upheaval of revolution within itself was unheard of.

On January 28, 1958, Mao would elaborate the concept of the continuing revolution. "The Hunanese have a proverb: There is no pattern for straw shoes, they shape up as one weaves them. The ideology of continuing revolution continuously stimulates the enthusiasm of the cadres and the masses. There is no final stage; mankind progresses like the universe, in a never-ending spiral." Mao did not even view communism as a finality. "Even when Communist society is reached . . . the nature and form of the revolutions (within it) will be different from those in class society, that's all."

Mao's contribution to mankind would be that he opened wide the doors to mass self-understanding and self-humanization. Knowing mankind in its infancy, he did his share to catalyze its maturity.

Mao's twelve-year agricultural plan was the backbone of the rural drive. It divided China into three regions with average yield estimations: 500 catties of grain per mu* north of the Yellow River; 800

---

* 1 catty = approximately 1.2 pounds.
 1 mu = 0.1518 acre.

between the Yellow River and the Yangtze; 1,000 south of the Yangtze River. These norms have now been reached and surpassed. The plan was condensed into an eight-point agricultural charter which rural cadres were to propagate and practice: water conservancy, fertilizer application, soil improvement, seed selection, close planting, pest control, improvement of farm tools, improved field management.

Cadres were to form triple alliances with the peasantry and agrotechnicians, discussing everything together. The experimental field was to be the focus for the dissemination of scientific agricultural methods. Problems of livelihood, such as income distribution, work points, planting, quotas, were to be jointly discussed with coop members "with debate by reasoning."

1958 was also the first year of the second five-year plan. Ten percent of investment resources went to agriculture; 60 percent to heavy industry. However, Mao had made it clear that plans had to be revised every year, sometimes more often. There should be overall planning and multi-tiered plans, level after level. Local conditions would affect plans. Provincial committees should investigate, inspect, submit comparative plans, both the best and the worst from counties, districts, villages. This would give every level a voice in the discussion, eschew arbitrary quotas, and keep the perpetual imbalance* of progress a challenge and a spur for more progress.

In 1958, with the advent of the communes, one billion yuan would be assigned to them by special request of Mao (report by Li Hsien-nien on the budget of 1958). 1957 had seen a good harvest of 185 million tons of grain, outstripping the target set and 50 million tons above the 1952 level. A target harvest of 200 million tons for 1958 was set in February. It would be raised in August and again in December.

Within this framework the technological revolution and agricultural mechanization would begin. With decentralization, funding for mechanization was by each locality, each collective on its own — a radical departure from the Soviet scheme. The cooperatives were to work out an equitable balance, which would enable them to accumulate funds towards purchase of their own machinery. To permit this, agricultural taxes were lowered from 15 to 10 percent (they average now 5 percent, as they were never raised and production has doubled), and there was no other tax. Thus "self-reliance" was instilled in each village.

---

* "Disequilibrium or imbalance is absolute and permanent, equilibrium is transient and relative." Mao Tsetung *Sixty Points on Working Methods*. Draft resolution from the Office of the Center of the CCP, February 19, 1958. Jerome Chen, ed. *Mao Papers* (London 1970), page 57.

During this time scientific education in care and maintenance of machinery was expanded by sending technical personnel to teach the peasantry, and through the wide dissemination of small and medium industrial plants in the rural areas. Here again a distortion occurred. Tractors from the tractor stations set up on the Soviet model by the Ministry of Agriculture were now dumped on the cooperatives who on the basis of past performance appeared able to pay for them. But no one to run or maintain them was provided. Two years later these tractors were withdrawn, but the installments paid were not refunded to the cooperatives.

The heart of any economic system is the accumulation-consumption balance. Mao spoke of it forcefully. Every sector should understand and grasp the notion. Self-reliance is based on awareness of this balance. The refusal to exploit agriculture for industry was no sentimental peasant bias; it was bad economics to make any sector confident that it would be funded by the state; this bred bureaucracy, waste, and inefficiency. It did not release maximum energy and initiative. Through imbuing every cooperative, factory, commercial concern, every school, university, even every administrative office with the necessity for combating waste, feeding its own staff insofar as possible, and balancing the ratio of production to consumption, self-reliance became a built-in goal.

The way to destroy compartmentalization — between mental and physical labor, town and city, industry and agriculture, school and societal environment, official and common man — was a shifting interchange of roles. "We must adopt an attitude of genuine equality towards cadres and masses and make people feel that relationships among men are truly equal . . . Red and expert, politics and techniques, are the unification of opposites . . . In future, schools should have factories and factories should have schools."* Mao's vision was the all-round man, who could be either worker or peasant, also an "intellectual," and shoulder a gun when necessary. This was restoration of the whole man, not amputated by specialization, caste, or prejudice.

A widespread diaspora of small industrial enterprises throughout rural areas began. These small enterprises would not only industrialize China in depth, bringing consumer goods cheaply to the villages and preventing shortages; they also produced a change towards scientific thinking, boosted the revenues of cooperatives, and swiftly expanded

---

* Mao Tsetung *Sixty Points on Working Methods*. Draft resolution from the Office of the Center of the CCP, February 19, 1958. Jerome Chen, ed. *Mao Papers* (London 1970), page 57.

the country's potential with a low capital investment. They were regionally funded and controlled, cut administrative costs, solved local employment problems, prevented the rush to the cities so obvious in other poor countries. They would bring to the peasantry, on its own home ground, a chance of other skills, of liberated minds and diversification of work. Finally, they would expand light industrial products, consumer goods, fertilizers, agricultural implements and other needed articles without straining transport facilities.

In the factories the socialist education movement was specifically directed towards breaking down reverence for science and servility towards scientific "experts." Ke Ching-shih, mayor of Shanghai, a staunch supporter of Mao's policies, said in 1959: "Before the Great Leap Forward, certain comrades considered science and technique as something mysterious; they had a blind trust in a few experts and in books; they looked with contempt upon the practical experience of the workers . . . on the other hand, some workers and (low grade) technicians had an inferiority complex and their minds were imprisoned."

Paralyzing respect for knowledge bearers is favorable to the rise of elitist management. Machines were still foreign wonders. To make scientific thinking as common as breathing, to make any child in China unafraid of taking to pieces and putting together any motor, needed an education in *daring*. The slogan was coined by Mao: "Dare to think, to speak, to do!"

The slogan "Walk on two legs" — use both modern and indigenous methods — stimulated workers to accomplish with whatever means were at hand, propelled the technological revolution by bridging the gaps with ingenuity.

There was a precedent for this, the great self-sufficiency drive in Yenan in 1940–1942,* when making do had developed into a science. Now dynamo casings were made of ceramic instead of steel (not as hardy but cheaply replaceable); windmills generated electric power; lathe belts of handwoven jute replaced imported rubber belts. Initiative was born of stress and want, and a vast ensemble of performance, fertile, chaotic, incalculable, made a "leap" in the mind inevitable.

To explode people into energy, said Mao, was the aim. The nation was like an atom, tight around its nucleus, hemmed in by codes of conduct now inappropriate. It needed fission for explosion. PUSH OUT THE WITHERED, TAKE IN THE NEW . . . WALK ON TWO LEGS . . . TURN OVER

* See *The Morning Deluge*, pages 358–360.

YOUR LIFE . . . DON'T CRAWL BEHIND OTHERS AT A SNAIL'S PACE . . . DOWN WITH ALL FOREIGN FRAMEWORKS* . . . SELF-RELIANCE . . . STRIKE THE IRON WHILE HOT . . . BETTER GET IT DONE IN ONE STROKE THAN DRAG ON . . . The slogans were painted on every available wall — railway stations, schools, village houses — even carved into rock hillfaces.

"To catch up with great Britain in steel and iron production within fifteen years or so" was a slogan born in December 1957. Great Britain had represented, especially in Shanghai, the industrial center of Middle China, unattainable height of science. "Now all the heights have to be scaled. . . . The word is dare. . . . Cast out fear." These words found their echo in millions of minds. And everything was attempted, at once. For a new vocabulary of boldness creates a new mode of thinking, and man is affected by his own construct, language. Words are emotion-forming, and passion carries man forward into his discovery of himself.

Vast water conservation works began in the winter of 1957–1958. They gave birth to the communes.

Communes started spontaneously in Honan province, where a scheme to bring water across the Taihang mountain ranges to irrigate 80,000 hectares of dry plains started.† The employment of nearly 100 million peasants in irrigation projects demanded elaborate manpower organization. The peasants' associations took the initiative in merging their labor power for the construction of the Red Canal, 1,500 kilometers long, across the Taihang range.

Mao heard of the Honan mergers and in April went to visit the Tsi Li Ying commune; at the time the name "commune" had not yet been decided on, and the Tsi Li Ying peasant associations were holding discussions on what to name the newborn merger. Mao approved the name "commune." Other mergers then occurred. Mao went to see some in Shantung in June. He was asked by a journalist what he thought of the communes, and replied that they were "a good thing." Like wildfire Mao's approval spread; by the end of the year 26,000 communes were formed, to divide up into 72,000 by 1961.

"This is a new creation of the masses," said Mao. The communes followed the old *hsiang*‡ pattern, replacing *hsiang* administration; thus

---

* This was particularly meant against stifling rules and regulations made by Soviet experts in the factories, which choked all initiative and creativeness.

† The area had suffered from drought for thirteen years out of fifteen. It is now one of the most prosperous regions in China.

‡ *Hsiang:* the traditional basic unit of regional administration, used in pre-Liberation China to organize manpower for water conservation works, etc. It was an area

a traditional administrative division became a new production unit. This was practical; the *hsiang* area was based on foot travel, and China was still unmotorized in 1958.

Lyrical articles appeared on the communes. For weeks processions of peasants would file to county township administrations to register demands for setting up communes. The celebrations would fill the streets with color and music as joy added to the exhilaration of a new epoch in the making.

TEACH WATER TO CLIMB THE MOUNTAINS UP TO HEAVEN, shouted the slogans in the arid lands. Mao was very happy. "I have seen the great enthusiasm of the masses for socialism. . . . With this enthusiasm and Party leadership nothing is impossible. . . . The masses are the real heroes."

Top-echelon leaders went cheerfully to labor. Chou En-lai was seen shoveling coal and pushing barrows. Even Peng Chen, Peking's mayor, was photographed planting a tree, in the afforestation program. "Some comrades . . . eat their fill and sit dozing in their offices all day. . . . Their platitudes make people sick," Mao had written in 1955. Now the dozing and the replete were digging; they had stopped "simply heaving a sigh" and saying things were impossible.

Liu Shao-chi appeared the most vigorous champion of the Leap Forward policies. It was he who announced the official adoption of the Leap at the May 1958 National People's Congress. He toured the countryside in the summer, proclaiming his enthusiasm. He now went too much to the left. "Communism is near at hand," he said. He upbraided comrades who had magnified defects in 1956, although he had been among them. "In a flurry of opposition to this so-called reckless advance some people even had misgivings about the principle of achieving greater, faster, better and more economical results. . . . Many of these comrades . . . have learned a lesson. But some have not yet learned anything. They say we'll settle accounts with you after the autumn harvest. Well, let them wait to settle accounts. They will lose out in the end!"

There was implicit threat in Liu's words for anyone who raised criticism, doubt, or misgivings. This would promote the extravaganza which did much harm to the Leap. "The conservative view which overlooks the development of the economy or fails to exploit financial

---

within which distances to canals or roads being built could be covered on foot, without too much hardship, by the villagers recruited for this work.

resources better, but wants to overcome financial difficulties by cutting down on essential expenditures, cannot solve any questions." He endorsed Mao's view of imbalance; spoke of it as a U-shaped development, high at the beginning and end, low in the middle; derided the desire "to trim the toes to fit the shoe" or "to give up eating for fear of choking." And now he demanded absolute obedience from cadres to Party directives. His injunctions made many cadres fearful of being called "rightists," which resulted in great leaps of imagination in reporting grossly inflated production results. Thus the leadership went on to plan with figures which bore no connection with reality.

In August 1958, at Peitaiho, the assembled Central Committee passed a resolution officializing the commune. The Peitaiho resolution's tone is moderate; it warns against communes becoming too large, demands rational arrangements with the county as the unit for planning, warns against compulsion and commandism, speaks of first taking up trial points in all counties, then gradually extending the movement. "The merger . . . must be closely combined with current production. The movement must not affect production adversely . . . there is no need for the hasty change of the system of collective ownership into the system of ownership by all the people" (from socialism to communism). The system "from each according to his ability, to each according to his work" was to be retained in the new organization.

The communes were to accelerate socialist construction, making active preparations for transition to communism, but they were not a shortcut to communism. "There is no need to deal with the question of private plots of land, scattered fruit trees and so on in great hurry." Peasants were to retain individual ownership of houses, personal belongings, gardens, poultry, pigs and private plots.

Despite this caution, utopian documents began to pour forth. Some communes spoke of everyone becoming a university student within ten to fifteen years; of mechanization within ten years; of meat and rice and motor cars in plenty.

The commune did have advantages; it could expand production swiftly, accumulate funds through labor-intensive projects faster, make the best use of resource potentials, have a large labor force with flexible application for projects. The commune was defined as the basic unit of production, and as such would combine agriculture and industry, commerce, education, health, military affairs and culture (schools, technical colleges, veterinary clinics, hospitals). It would increase employment, consolidate collective ownership, foster large numbers of local cadres both "Red and expert," provide experimental space for scientific farming, support small and medium industries either alone or in cooperation with other communes. It could start small hydroelectric works for power, establish flour milling and grinding (thus relieving women and draft animals of this work), promote small fertilizer plants, diversify agricultural pursuits. It enjoyed its own decision-making process, managed its own affairs within the overall plan. It was empowered to make contracts with industrial and commercial concerns, to have its own bank accounts, branch banks and savings apparatus. In the following years the establishment of state projects, roads and railways on commune ground would have to compensate for commune land utilization. It was the basic funding organ for the mechanization of agriculture, could train its own technicians, set up its own repair and maintenance shops. Since the commune is an agro-industrial unit, coordination and mutual assistance, based on socialist brotherhood, between city and countryside, industry and agriculture, were to generate rural industrial units within the communes.

The enthusiasm of the masses was at its height that summer. Wells were sunk, irrigation canals dug, dams and roads built, hills dotted with trees, gullies filled and uplands leveled. People initiated projects that were never dreamed of before. One small brigade* sited in particularly stony, unproductive land started a mind-shaking project. Its forty-odd families went to a riverbed some miles away and scooped earth in baskets day and night, bringing it back to thicken their own soil. Today, seventeen years later, they have quarried away their limestone mounds and hillocks, sold the stones as ballast for railway building, and out of the funds built small industries. The children, through habit, still go on jaunts to bring back earth in their pockets. And they have planted fifty thousand trees.

Early in May 1958 the Chinese press carried illustrations of small model hydroelectric apparatus that could be made simply; also of smelting plants and blast furnaces of the primitive type. The large industrial complexes and plants were overhauled; workers repaired machinery in disuse or stored; they contacted other factories offering needed machinery or technical help. Workers' committees were formed and insisted on the "triple alliance." Groups of workers went down to

---

* A brigade is part of a commune, which has three levels of production and ownership: production team, brigade, and commune (except in Tibet, where there are only two levels, brigade and commune).

the countryside to begin "laying eggs," a proliferation of small factories of all kinds. The railway trains were overcrowded with traveling worker groups, all carrying out self-given projects. "No one thought of money or reward."

Hundreds of thousands of volunteers, from students to peasant apprentices, flocked at their own expense to factories to learn the rudiments of techniques. Many veterans and retired workers came out to cope with the demand. A feature of the newfound pride and dignity of the worker was the voluntary giving up of bonuses and material rewards. An unprecedented hundred thousand technical personnel and "engineers" from among the working class were trained during the Leap in crash courses, and through "practice."

Now all the brakes, the "rules and regulations" of each plant, were challenged. Glowing reports of workers inventing, repairing, or improving machinery filled the papers. The wisdom, intelligence, creativeness of the proletariat were brought out all the time; there was derision for engineers with book learning and diplomas but little practical experience, criticism for the technocratic elite "who always say it cannot be done." Confronted by worker power, elite administrators went to labor on the workbench side by side with the workers. Every factory became also a festival. Industrial plants beat all records in production and in construction of new equipment.

Geological prospection was galvanized; volunteer groups of students together with peasants and workers went out to discover minerals. This nationwide search for resources was to prove extremely successful. Many of the mineral deposits now being mined, as well as oil in areas said to contain none, were then discovered. Today's industrial pattern in China is due to the 1958 Leap; three out of four of today's thriving industries owe their birth to the Great Leap Forward. An incredible total of eight hundred thousand small industrial production units (though not all viable) were organized in the two years 1958–1959.

In city streets, factories and workshops were set up to liberate the women. When cooperatives were formed, there was a labor shortage at harvest and planting time. The women came out to work as members of the cooperatives, with work points, voting rights, full economic independence, no longer working unpaid for the husband and his parents. Now urban housewives voluntarily came out of their houses to engage in productive occupations on their own, achieving economic and political equality. The Leap Forward was popular with women of every age, as were the commune and factory kindergartens, nurseries,

mess halls which were erected. Woman's liberation fueled revolutionary advance, and this would become very obvious during the cultural
revolution eight years later. "Without emancipation of women," Mao
said, "socialism could not be consolidated." It is estimated that about
forty million urban housewives who had not worked previously outside
the home started to do so that year.

The great steel campaign, perhaps the most criticized of all Leap
manifestations, began in late October 1958. Travelers through China's
hinterland describe the scene:* traveling workers erecting factories in
the countryside, disseminating information on the building of pig iron
and steel furnaces. "Long lines of peasants, schoolchildren and ado-
lescents were marching to the iron-working and coke-burning furnaces
down by the railway station . . . through night and day the bright red
glare of steel-making furnaces was seen." Six hundred thousand such
coke- or coal-burning furnaces were set up, conveniently or incon-
veniently, in railway sidings, disused temples, large courtyards, schools,
sports grounds. By 1961 five thousand would be restructured into
modernized furnaces and steel converters.

Most of the steel and pig iron produced — altogether over seven
million tons of pig iron and three million tons of steel — was low-
grade. But the aim was to drive home the importance of steel making,
to emphasize the "walk on two legs" principle. The drive also built new
roads to newly opened coal mines. At one time or another about 90
million people went through the experience of trying their hand at
making steel. The campaign lasted about four months.

At the same time as these changes in rural areas and industry orientation, a large amount of capital construction was going on. According
to the second five-year plan, 1,200 high-capital investment projects
were to be built or completed in 1958, employing about half a million
people, and with an investment of over seventeen billion yuan. As
these two expansions proceeded together, no less than 18 to 21 million
peasants became "workers," a loose term to signify they went into the
construction industry — buildings, roads, cement and bricks, carpentry
— or were recruited for work in the large factories which were under
construction but whose equipment had not yet arrived. In many cases
the equipment would not come for some years.

The working force by 1957 had risen to 23 or 24 million from four

* See Rewi Alley *China's Hinterland in the Leap Forward* (Peking 1961), pages
6, 9, 13, etc.

million in 1949,* including apprentices and administrative staff, workers in semimechanized factories, and handicraft workers such as carpenters. In 1958, one year later, the figure rose to 45 million, including rural factories and street factories.† According to Anna Louise Strong, 17 to 18 million rural peasants entered "new factories" in that year alone.‡

The Great Leap Forward also began the revolution in education. Mao's irritation with academic education is well known. "This higher education, what a joke! From primary school to university, sixteen, seventeen, twenty years . . . the students don't know how workers work, how peasants plow . . . the more they learn, the more stupid they become!"

In early 1958§ Mao Tsetung, in a document embodying many practical working methods for the political and economic strategy envisaged, suggested that there should be part-time work and part-time study schools and colleges; that if possible all technical middle schools and colleges should set up workshops and farms for production, so as to become self-sufficient, or partly self-sufficient, in supplying daily necessities.

There was sound economics behind this suggestion, for education is a burden on a poor country with a high percentage of its population in school. And China's population was now younger than ever because of the efficient public health drives, lowered infant mortality rate, and high birth rate. By 1974 China would have 170 million children from seven to fifteen in primary and lower middle schools.

Criticism of the "bookworm knowledge" of "academic authorities," to break Confucian reverence towards "the teacher," was a feature of the Leap. About two million cadres and two to three million students from colleges and universities were "sent down" to labor in 1958–1959, and one million higher intellectuals (university staff, teachers, etc.) also

---

* 3.8 million according to some reports.

† Small factories or workshops in every street of every town or city supply the local population with anything required — handmade saucepans, baskets, socks, household necessities. They provide employment chiefly to the residents of the street without obliging people to travel long distances for supplies. Many of them are also repair shops (for bicycles, etc.), tailoring or laundry shops, and a large proportion also turn out spare parts for larger factories. Some of these street factories also make goods for export — wickerwork, handicrafts, toys.

‡ Interview by author in 1962.

§ Mao Tsetung *Sixty Points on Working Methods.* Draft resolution from the Office of the Center of the CCP, February 19, 1958. Jerome Chen, ed. *Mao Papers* (London 1970), page 57.

went, some to work on large projects such as the Sanmen Dam on the Yellow River.

Subservience to foreign models was castigated. Emphasis on the wisdom and knowledge of the masses prepared the way for the integration of the intellectual with his own laboring people. School years were now to be shortened. Technical colleges and their staffs provided the knowledge to erect new factories; groups of workers entered the universities to study and also to lecture to students. Experts were sent down to participate in the projects whose blueprints they had drawn up.* Linkups of departments of engineering, physics, chemistry, with industrial plants were achieved, promoting the technological revolution.

The part work, part study agricultural universities were born that year, notably the one in Kiangsi province, which would become a model for others. Mao Tsetung inspected it and later wrote a letter of congratulation. He also visited the universities in Tientsin, in Wuhan, where the students themselves had asked for a part study, part labor system. He suggested that agricultural schools establish links with cooperatives and sign contracts with them "so that theory and practice can be unified."

This turning of consumers into producers or part producers made sense. It cut down the education bill, brought home to youth the importance of thrift, avoiding useless spending and especially waste of both public material and private funds. In Kiangsi the students built their own dormitories, planted food for their own consumption, became 60 percent self-sufficient.

Thus the continuing fourfold revolution, whatever its mishaps and mistakes, was a success: by an immense effort, one-quarter of humanity was making a two-millennia leap from Confucian China to modern China, from prescientific thought to scientific thought, breaking all barriers and questioning all accepted values, creating a new economic framework and new societal relations, a new way of thinking and being.

Decision-making power was wrested, partly, from the hands of a new managerial technocratic elite and placed in the hands of a worker-peasant alliance. Although there would be a reversal in 1961, the cultural revolution would pick up where the Leap left off.

* Previously they remained in the cities, not even bothering to see what was done on the spot.

The barrier between mental and manual labor was partly dissolved. Workers did learn philosophy; peasants did make scientific experiments. Workers lectured young students in universities; so did old peasants. Thousands of articles written by workers and peasants came out in the press. Never had this been seen in China before.

Poetry too. Ignored by the officials of Culture and Propaganda, peasant and worker poetry came out in wall posters, in local newspapers, by the million in factories and communes. The Chinese peasant has always had a propensity for the rhymed couplet; revolutionary fervor, like love, stimulated memorable phrases which have remained part of the new language of defiance, daring, and hope.

In such a torrent of activity, with so much genuine emotion behind it, it would be surprising if exaggeration, bombast, did not take place. Thus, even the laws of gravity were pronounced null, as "foreign framework," by a provincial worker. Principles of physics and chemistry were disputed. Although this was not followed up, the desire to "reappraise" was encouraged. Liu Shao-chi was also carried away; he believed an agrotechnician who showed him a bare mound of a few square yards and told him that he would be able to reap ten thousand catties of grain from it through "close planting."

Mao himself was more than euphoric. "Throughout the country the Communist spirit is surging . . . the political consciousness of the masses is rising rapidly." In September he was irritated by a few comrades "unwilling to undertake a large-scale mass movement in the industrial sphere. They call it . . . irregular and disparage it as a rural style of work and guerilla habits" (he was referring to the projected steel-making campaign). Yet it was also Mao who, in March, had said: "Right now there is a ten-force typhoon of enthusiasm. . . . We must not impede this publicly, but within our own ranks, we must . . . damp down a little . . . We must get rid of empty reports and foolish boasting . . . but serve reality." Now Mao Tsetung himself appeared swept off his feet.

In 1960 he told Edgar Snow that he had really believed some of the claims made. In the *Observer* of April 28, 1961, Snow quotes Mao as having said that within one or two years there should be available for each person per year 1,650 pounds of food grains and 110 pounds of pork. These figures would mean a production of 514 million tons of grain and 100 million tons of pig fodder, a utopian surmise.

In the midst of this euphoria, the targets which had been set were raised and raised again. Though Mao had said, "Everything which is capable of achievement we must endeavor . . . But that which cannot be achieved we should not try to do," there was "forcing" of figures in reports.

Suddenly, in that September, a spate of discussion on whether the commune system was actually a shortcut to communism set in; whether Liu's "Communism is near at hand" had to do with it, no one is certain; but Liu did nothing to stem this "ultra-left" tide. The "withering away of the state" and of the Party, a hallmark of the reaching of the Communist stage, to be replaced by fully autonomous communes as basic units of communism, was discussed in provincial papers in October. On October 7 *Peking Review* proclaimed that in Honan, which "more than any other province has given shape and substance to the people's communes, all commune members now get their food free and many other free benefits as well." In communes which proclaimed "communism" everything was free, including haircuts. A dispatch of October 16 from Nanking reported a record daily output of 671,490 tons of coal — equivalent to twice the annual production in 1957 — for one county. A yield of soybeans 143 times the national record of 1957 was declared.

The very people who later would attack Mao for the excesses of the Great Leap Forward contributed their share of irrationality. Peng Teh-huai, the Defense minister, spoke of peasant houses with curtains at the windows and television sets. Claims of 4,000 catties of grain per mu, ten times the amount which the experimental fields then yielded, were made in Honan (this would be 480 bushels per acre, a figure never yet attained).* Some commune administrations went berserk and distributed accumulated funds and loans, purchased television sets and radios, built cinema houses, even where electricity was not yet available.

A few voices were raised in caution. Li Hsien-nien, the Finance minister, after touring the communes in Honan, reported problems. He criticized the "everything free" rampage, and also the unwieldy size of some communes. The average commune was not supposed to comprise more than 2,000 households. Those in Honan contained 7,500 to 8,000,† creating problems of management, information, distribution and labor allocation.

---

* 1 acre = 6.5 mus.
 2½ acres = 1 hectare.
† Average rural family: 5.7 individuals, making a commune of more than 40,000.

Articles arguing that "all China should be one commune" kept coming out. The cadres afraid to be called rightists if they seemed cautious applied blanket-wise all the slogans, allocating labor massively for water conservation and steel making, while ignoring the paramount tasks of harvesting, grain storage, and preparing winter sowing. The abolition of private plots, the slaughter of pigs for festivities to mark the advent of communism, the death of ill-cared-for draft animals, the abandonment of craft occupations such as making baskets and hand-carts and daily utensils occurred. Experimental plot figures (doubled and tripled for good measure) were quoted as actual figures. "The leadership did not get accurate accounts of exactly how much," said Chou En-lai in 1959.

The autumn grain harvest reached 250 million tons in planting, the largest China ever had, but this was vastly exaggerated. Hence the year's end target figures were hoisted to 375 million tons of grain for 1958 and 525 million tons for 1959! "The 1958 crop was truly terrific," writes Anna Louise Strong;* "nobody knew how big. . . . At the time the peasants were also organizing the communes, putting all China on ball bearings in the three summer months by hand . . . going sixty million strong to make steel, seventy million strong to build reservoirs . . . they estimated the harvest they had . . . then went off and left part of it lying ungathered in the fields. The Chinese leadership believed the figures and acted on them for almost a year at all levels."

This massive grain harvest was obtained at the expense of cash crops, all fields being diverted to grain. In the south, banana plantations were leveled for rice planting. Even the women students and cadres who came out to help with the harvest could not compensate for the acute labor shortage which developed that autumn and early winter. "Communes sold grain lavishly to the state and later found they had not kept enough to eat. . . ."†

The figures were exaggerated also because there were no weighing machines available, all figures were guesswork; the usual handcarts, horsecarts and wheelbarrows had gone to infrastructural work and it was impossible to gather the grain; there were not enough people or baskets or granaries; there was no labor to thresh the grain, which is still done by hand. The dislocation of labor power was compounded by the steel drive, the expansion of capital construction, the setting up of medium and small factories, and the water conservation works.

* Anna Louise Strong *China's Fight for Grain* (Peking 1963), pages 3–7.
† Ibid.

More problems were produced by the "everyone a soldier" militia movement. "Young men eligible by age and all demobilized servicemen should be organized into militia and put under constant military training," said a September 4 editorial in the *People's Daily*. A call for the liberation of Taiwan and the second Middle East crisis° helped whip up militia fervor. Men and women went into the militia; this now provided its own exaggeration. Some communes were actually militarized, with peasants getting up to bugle call, marching to the fields in squads and companies. To beat targets, volunteers were called for to work around the clock and they did. The results were deplorable; some young cadres even died of exhaustion.

Fortunately, this militarization was ended in about ten weeks. By the end of October, Mao Tsetung, constantly touring and investigating, was both confident and perturbed. He knew there were excesses in reporting, but did not yet know their scale. He called for truthful investigations.

A Central Committee meeting was held from November 2 to 10 in Chengchow. After it, Mao wrote to cadres at the provincial, district, county, commune, brigade, and team levels a circular letter which dispels the idea that Mao was pushing to extremes: "The production quotas must be realistic, regardless of the instructions issued by higher levels. You should ignore them, and pay attention only to realistic possibilities . . . To brag about 800, 1,000 or 1,200 catties per mu is sheer bombast."†

As to close planting, one of the tenets of the eight-point agricultural charter, Mao the peasant realized its possibilities and also its dangers. "Stiff and rigid orders from above are not only useless but also harmful. Such orders should never be issued . . . Planting must not be too sparse nor too dense . . . [there must be] a more scientific . . . realistic . . . standard . . . according to local conditions."

Who was issuing these stiff and rigid orders? There were other meetings in November and December, where repeatedly Mao called for scrutiny. "Some of the lies are squeezed out by a higher level which brags, oppresses its subordinates, makes life difficult for the lower levels." "One must not praise what cannot be done . . . liars do harm to themselves."

Provincial Party secretaries gave few hints of trouble; the difficulties

° Which occurred in 1958 (see page 149).

† These claims were being made in areas where average production in 1957 had been 300 catties.

were transient; Liu's U-shaped development theory was cited to rationalize the shortages. Reports of a bountiful harvest stifled disquiet. Later an official would say ruefully that "there were 230 million tons of grain, but 120 million tons of stones and rubble." Regional heads were chary of criticism, as no one wanted to be called a rightist lacking in enthusiasm, or "throwing cold water" on the people's red-hot enthusiasm. The decision to transfer funds and control to the regions had been passed in April; and to be too critical might mean a lack of self-reliance . . . and self-reliance is the essence of the Leap.

Mao called another meeting in Wuchang between November 21 and 27. This was a preliminary to the sixth plenum. He opposed the setting of the very high targets suggested by Liu, which "were unrealistic . . . like Buddhas set up for worship," but he seems to have been overruled, and the targets for 1959, based on exaggerated reports, were enhanced: coal from 30 million tons to 270; machine tools from 28,000 units to 90,000; grain from 185 to 375 million tons for 1958 and to an unimaginable 525 million tons for 1959. The publication of these targets in itself quelled all criticism and increased the tendency to report impossible attainments.

During the cultural revolution, the responsibility was laid at Liu's door. In May 1958, right after launching the Leap, he appeared at a conference held by the *People's Daily* on the subject: "Can Party members have personal feelings?" Liu had extolled what he called the "Party spirit," total subservience to Party directives, and abrogating or ignoring one's own apprehensions. This, to be denounced as the "docile tool theory," was contrary to Mao's repeated injunctions that a Party member must use his own head, and that the best way to sabotage orders was to carry them out blindly. In Liu's favor, it could be said that he did so in order to streamline the organizations' efficiency, since "dispersionism" was then the complaint. Liu could never grasp that Mao's exhortations to discuss and debate made for *more*, not less, inner-motivated discipline.

The sixth plenum of the Eighth Central Committee met in Wuhan from November 28 to December 10, and scrutinized all the reports which came in. Mao was disturbed by the claim that communism was being achieved; he called this "irresponsible . . . debasing and making a caricature of the noble idea of communism." It was another way of saying that class struggle had ceased to exist. It was anarchism.

Another resolution on the communes was issued by the plenum. "In

1958 a new social organization appeared, fresh as the morning sun above the broad horizon of East Asia." The resolution noted achievements, but warned that consolidation would take time, and that "good-hearted eagerness" was not sufficient. "We should not groundlessly make declarations that the communes will enter communism immediately."

The following weeks were filled with directives, all indicating Mao's urgent attention to methods, details, checkups. Wages, supplies, democracy, style of work were to be attentively managed; draft animals must be given sufficient food and rest, "as otherwise they lose their reproductive powers." Provincial committees were enjoined that peasants should not be made to work more than eight hours a day . . . at the most twelve at the busiest season; there must be food and care; mess halls must give people enough to eat; the private plots which had been abolished in the Communist phase were returned, they were still a necessary supplement to peasants' income. Accounts and accounting were checked by investigation teams. Strict adherence to truth was enjoined.

The lower cadres cannot be blamed for the woes of exaggeration. Faced with gigantic administrative, economic, organizational problems, with manpower recruitment, the steel drive, setting up workshops, agricultural problems, the socialist education movement, routine administrative work and accounting, propaganda and leading the masses, they did wonders. A good many worked themselves into ill-health.

Admiration goes to the Chinese working people, who gave all of themselves, in an unbelievable maelstrom of activity, to break the chains of stagnation, misery and ignorance. Without the Leap, today's China would not be.

And Mao was at one with them. Even in the hard years to come, the people never lost their faith in Mao Tsetung. "We trust him, because he trusts us."

9

The Tenth Year: 1959 and the Second Major Struggle in the Party Since 1949

Achievements are great, problems are considerable, but the future is bright.

— Mao Tsetung, July 1959

Modernization of the People's Liberation Army and the establishment of an air force and navy were the aims of the People's Republic of China in 1949, a "unified system, unified organization and unified discipline." In June 1950 Mao complained that army expenditures were too high, 35 percent of the budget, and asked for cuts. The Korean War began ten days later. It would effect a great change in the PLA, but not one welcomed by Mao.

Within six months of China's entry into the war (October 1950) the Chinese volunteer contingents were being trained with modern Soviet weapons. When Peng Teh-huai, minister of Defense, in charge of the Korean volunteers, came back as the "hero" of the Korean War, this veteran Long Marcher, whose many quarrels with Mao in the past were notorious, began "sovietization" of the PLA.

But the PLA as Mao had conceived and founded it* was not the Soviet Red Army. To Mao this was a model inappropriate to China, but Peng Teh-huai thought in terms of a conventional, professional, highly technical force, which would have required a massive industrial foundation to support it, and long-continued dependence for weaponry on the USSR.

* For the founding of the PLA and the Party-army-masses tripod, see *The Morning Deluge*, pages 191, 199, 203, 479.

The Soviet model began an erosion of the *political* foundation of the PLA, and this was even worse than gold-braided uniforms, boots, and other paraphernalia imported from the Soviet Union and in which the Chinese peasant-soldiers were now clad, to their great discomfort.

The PLA was founded as a people's army to fight a people's war, at the service of the political goals of the Party. The Party commanded the gun. The PLA was also the cradle in which Party members and cadres were raised and trained during the decades of armed struggle. The tripod Party-army-masses was the strength of China's revolution.*

Political education of the soldier was essential; democracy in the army (soldiers' committees, equality between officers and men) had been enforced by Mao during twenty years. Mao's military writings inform and infuse these decades; and for him modernization does not mean depolitization. Peng considered Mao's thinking rustic and outdated, and the "socialist" Red Army the acme of perfection. He objected to having politics in command, political courses, and army political commissars.

With Peng Teh-huai in command, several thousand officers were sent to the USSR for study. Five thousand Russian advisers were at one time or another in the Chinese forces and military industries. The Chinese assimilated doctrines and practices very different from those Mao had inculcated. New regulations on discipline started in July 1953: strict obedience to orders; punishment for infractions. The "mass line" was no longer practiced; officers were now distinctly superior to their men. Mao had always made the point that soldiers' committees should represent the soldiers; that there must be democracy, discipline consented to voluntarily through Party discipline. But now the soldiers' committees vanished; the command hierarchy was based on military obedience; a system of compulsory conscription was introduced; the time of service in the army was extended; military academies were set up; elite officers enjoyed special housing and other privileges; political education was almost dispensed with; political commissars were ignored or not appointed; some found that no transport was supplied them and so could not visit the soldiers' camps; Party representatives at company level vanished. In February 1955 recruiting for officers began to shift to the intelligentsia — the young university students — because of the "cultural level" required to master the latest scientific techniques. Peng called political studies "a waste of time."

* See note, page 143.

These changes eroded the links between officer and soldier of a people's army, destroyed the relationship between the army and the people, which was even more dangerous. Some garrisons rode rough-shod over civilians, took over houses or land and began requisitioning supplies and forcibly recruiting labor. The concept of Mao that the army is also a work and production force was downgraded. "There is a definite conflict between participation in national construction and training" and civilian work, said Peng Teh-huai. In 1955 the budget for the armed forces was still 33 to 35 percent of the total. "Anything that may weaken war preparations and training is impermissible," said the Defense minister.

Another casualty of sovietization was the people's militia. Mao Tsetung had insisted that "the people armed" were the basis of the socialist system. Peng did not. And by 1956 Mao realized clearly that the Chinese armed forces were not only materially dependent for weaponry upon the USSR, but also could be subordinated to the Soviet concept of an overall war. Mao stuck to his view; in 1946 he had said there would be no attack by the United States on the USSR, and that the confrontation between the socialist camp and imperialism would be in the "infermediate zone," the Third World and Europe. China was part of the Third World, but the USSR was not, and Mao did not want to see China become the devastated battlefield (directly or indirectly) for the two great powers, even in a distant future. He did not want China involved in wars not of her choosing, forced to fight in conflicts which had nothing to do with socialism but would be part of a world power game between the United States and the USSR.

Unless China herself was attacked, China was not going to fight, but this did not mean preparation for defense could be ignored. And defensive strategy involved thinking in terms of the next war, not the last one. A nuclear deterrent, because it was obvious that the two large powers would not give up nuclear might; a generalized people's militia for defense in depth; a highly politicized and diversified army with closest links with the militia and the people — this was the foundation of an active modern defense.

The concept of military power in the West and in Russia is that strength lies in the capacity for inflicting wholesale death. But to Mao, power is not the accumulation of lethal capacity. Mao's view is that of Sun Tzu: "The best general is the one who obtains maximum results with a minimum of bloodshed." To wrest victory by locking one's enemy into inability to attack is the acme of the art of war.

In the Ten Great Relations speech,* Mao had spoken of the contradiction between economic construction (which also implied atomic energy) and defense construction. Too expensive a conventional army impeded progress in economic construction. "We have a considerable defense force . . . We do not have atom bombs, not yet . . . Do you genuinely want atom bombs? Then you must reduce military and administrative expenses and increase expenditure for economic construction . . . it is a problem of strategic policy."

Mao's dictum that the decisive factor is man, not weapons, does not mean that he despised weapons. But weaponry must be tailored to Chinese conditions, to the aims and goals of China's socialist construction. China's predominant need is for peace. No invasion of any kind or aggression against anyone will ever be contemplated, and the PLA must never become an army geared to such activities.

A knowledgeable people, aware and totally participating, becomes through its militia a vast sea in which an invading enemy drowns. The army is the most mobile and technical component of such an armed people. Interchangeability between worker and peasant and soldier; the merging, as fish in water, of the army among the people, militia in every village, factory, city; vast and well-stocked shelters in case of nuclear or other bombardment, to protect the whole population; military training as part of education itself; self-sufficiency in basic staples in each region; self-supply in ammunition and basic weapons in each region; centralized command and decentralized initiative for mobile defense . . . this was the new strategy to come into being. The control of nuclear power in such a pattern must be in Chinese hands . . . no other finger on the trigger, no dangerous and provocative "nuclear umbrella."

Mao's insistence on self-reliance in nuclear power and deterrence must have surfaced first in 1954, at the time of Khrushchev's first visit to Peking. Khrushchev was backed by commanders of the Russian Red Army, and Khrushchev's posture towards the United States that year was far more pugnacious than Malenkov's; he spoke of more credits for the armed forces while Malenkov sought openly a detente with the United States and disarmament, and armies never like disarmament.

The United States strategy, with containment of China, reinforcement of bases in Japan and in Taiwan with nuclear missiles, had been

* April 1956. See page 90.

studied very seriously in the Soviet Union. In the debate on military strategy potential, Chinese participation for "unity of action" and "joint defense" had been amply debated. Perhaps it was then conceived that China should play an active role in an enlarged Warsaw Pact. Khrushchev's visit to Peking was also a probe of China's intentions and defense capabilities. The question of sharing of nuclear knowledge came up and Khrushchev had to agree to sharing. Yet two years later he would use the same words, "destruction of world civilization," should nuclear weapons be used, as had Malenkov. And he would seek accommodation with America, detente in Europe, and offer to Eisenhower the withdrawal of the USSR from her Asian commitments.

The problems of military strategy and of nuclear deterrence were also argued at length in China's military circles. Peng Teh-huai appeared in favor of a "partnership" in nuclear matters with the Soviet Union. But Yeh Chien-ying, another Long Marcher and a most respected figure, argued strongly that China should have her own modern (nuclear) weapons. Despite this insistence, Mao also stated again on March 10, 1955, that atomic weapons could not decide the outcome of a war.

In January 1955 Peng invited Soviet commanders to view mass solidarity maneuvers in China, with air, land and naval forces cooperating. Ten marshals of the Chinese army were created that year; they wore uniforms copied from the USSR: medals, gold braid, huge caps.

But by the next year criticism of the orientation of the PLA became outspoken. On March 24, 1956, an article entitled *Strengthen Party Committee Leadership Over Battle Training* indicated that Peng would be curbed. In September, Tan Cheng, head of the General Political Department, made the point that democracy and political work in the army were neglected. "High technological units have not time for political meetings," retorted Peng Teh-huai. Tan Cheng said that blind obedience was being enacted, and the army was estranged from the people, the Party and the government. He attacked bookishness in army education, training systems and methods not corresponding to reality, foreign experience "mechanically applied." Yeh Chienying in May had already stated at a military college lecture that the study of "advanced Soviet experience" should be intelligently combined "with our own excellent traditions . . . we must also study the military doctrine of the capitalist countries, that we may know our enemy."

The army went through its own "blooming and contending" movement in 1957, pointed reference being made throughout to "those who weaken Party leadership." "Whenever our army separates itself from Party leadership the revolutionary cause will suffer" was the burden of an editorial in the *Liberation Army Daily* on July 1, 1958. On August 1, Army Day, the old veteran Chu Teh, who had been commander-in-chief during the Long March, wrote about "some people . . . who have . . . a one-sided high regard for technique and despise ideology." The movement for renewed solidarity between army and masses, with the slogan "Every man a soldier," occupied several months of the Leap.

Concurrently, after the agreements in Moscow concerning exchange of nuclear knowledge were signed in October 1957, plans for production of an independent deterrent were hastened as a "triple alliance" of Academy of Science scientists, military commanders, and members of the Central Committee was formed. Mao lectured on military strategy in early 1958 to several gatherings of PLA commanders. "Let us work on atom bombs . . . I think ten years will do." And the reorganization of the people's militia which took place began to reshape significantly the armed forces along Mao's line.

"The imperialists are pushing us around. . . . In addition to regular armed forces, we require a tremendous number of militia. . . . Thus they would find it difficult to move a single step."*

The PLA again became a work and production force. In 1956 the PLA, 2.6 million strong, had done only 4 million man-days of labor (roads, state farms, canal digging). But in 1958, 59 million man-days were contributed. Army expenditure was cut by 30 percent in 1957 and another 20 percent in 1958. "Irrational" tendencies to occupy houses and appropriate land were drastically curbed; officers lost their privileges; thousands of them went back to the ranks to work at "manual labor." The PLA was also used in the spring planting of 1959 to combat drought. Veterans set up primary schools, ran literacy classes, helped establish maintenance and repair shops in communes. Sapper regiments blasted mountainsides, built roads, reservoirs, hydroelectric plants. Thus the PLA was taken back in hand and Peng Teh-huai was not pleased.

At the same time the intensive research for nuclear deterrence was proceeding, on the diplomatic front China endorsed a resolution of the Afro-Asian People's Solidarity Conference in Cairo that Asia and Africa be nuclear-free zones. On February 4, 1958, Kuo Mo-jo as spokesman

* Mao, September 1958.

for the PRC expressed the hope that such zones would be set up, but warned that unless there was an immediate ban on manufacture, stockpiling and testing of nuclear weapons, the difference between nuclear and non-nuclear powers might lead to "other countries not remaining without nuclear weapons."

In March and April, China continued to call for atom-free zones in Asia and the Pacific, and the banning of manufacture, stockpiling and testing of nuclear weapons, while Khrushchev was seeking America's cooperation in banning atomic testing but not manufacture or stockpiling of nuclear weapons.

In June 1958 another Middle East crisis occurred.[*] In Lebanon, in Iraq, revolutionary movements took place. British troops landed in Jordan and U.S. marines in Lebanon.

On July 19 Khrushchev called for a "summit" meeting between the USSR, the U.S., France, Great Britain, and India over the crisis, but when balked accepted the reconvening of the U.N. Security Council to discuss the situation, although he had refused it previously. The People's Republic of China could not agree that a situation involving Arab states which recognized her should be put before the Security Council, where China's seat was occupied by representatives of Chiang Kai-shek, and this with the approval of the USSR. The Chinese ambassador in Moscow conveyed this to Khrushchev, and the latter flew to Peking, arriving on July 31.

Some reports say this second Khrushchev visit occurred at the same time as the "second Taiwan crisis," because shelling of the offshore islands started again; but it was only after Khrushchev's departure that the Chinese demonstrated once again, by this token action of shelling the Quemoy and Matsu islands, their right to liberate Taiwan as they saw fit. The first shelling, in September 1954, had not provoked "massive American retaliation." The 1954 mutual defense treaty between the United States and Chiang Kai-shek had subsequently eliminated Quemoy and Matsu as well as other islands in the China seas from its scope.

In Peking there was rank disapproval of Khrushchev's attempt to settle the Middle East crisis by artful summitry. "Nothing can be saved by yielding to evil, and coddling wrong only helps the devil," the *People's Daily* wrote on July 20. We may assume that Khrushchev's meeting with the Chinese leaders was tempestuous. Khrushchev seems to have expostulated over the dangers of imminent nuclear war. He

[*] The first was the Suez crisis of 1956.

said he had information on U.S. aggressive intentions, and suggested that China allow naval bases to Russian submarines and ships, that Russian experts and military staff be located in certain Chinese sites, all the better to implement the accords of November 1957.

This meant, under the phrases "unity of action" and "implementing the defensive alliance between the two countries," Russian control of China's nuclear deterrent. "In 1958 the leadership of the CPSU put forward unreasonable demands designed to bring China under Soviet military control . . . These . . . were rejected."* In Mao's view the United States, despite its missile bases ringing China, would not start a nuclear war because China had no intention of aggression anywhere. (Perhaps Mao did not add that Khrushchev's plans were just the prov-ocation which would alarm the United States and probably start some-thing.) The U.S. was not allowing Chiang control of nuclear weapons in Taiwan. It was on this occasion that Khrushchev first hinted that China should accept an accommodation with the United States over Taiwan, promising not to use force to liberate the island. But this was contrary to China's principles of sovereignty.

"In an exceedingly warm and cordial atmosphere . . . the two parties recorded complete identity of views . . . any new war would be a disaster but should the imperialists provoke war . . . this would permit their complete downfall." Thus the final communiqué. Khrushchev en-gaged himself in "firm support of the just struggles of the peoples of the United Arab Republic, the Republic of Iraq and the other Arab countries as well as to the national liberation movements of the peoples of Asia, Africa and Latin America. . . .

"Whether war can be averted or not does not depend solely on the goodwill and *one-sided* efforts of the peace-loving peoples," said the communiqué. After Khrushchev had left, the Chinese took up the ar-gument again. "*Some people* feel that peace can only be won by abstaining from resolute imperialism and colonialism."

An article, *The Forces of the New Are Bound to Defeat the Forces of Decay*,† quoted Mao: "The emergence of the atomic bomb marks the beginning of the end of U.S. imperialism. The reason is because it relies on nothing but bombs. But in the end the bomb will not destroy the people. The people will destroy the bomb."

On August 23 the shelling of Quemoy and Matsu began. The usual

---

* On the Origin and Development of the Differences Between the CPSU and Ourselves, September 6, 1963.

† By Yu Chao-li, possibly a pseudonym? Mao?

clamor and fury about a bellicose China ensued, but by September ambassadorial talks with the U.S., suspended since December 1954, were resumed.

On September 7, fourteen days after the bombing of Quemoy and one day after the U.S.-China talks had resumed, Khrushchev sent a message to Eisenhower that an attack against China would be "an attack against the USSR." On the 19th he again stated that if aggressors should use nuclear bombs on China, the Soviet Union would use hers to defend China.

By then it was clear there would be no conflagration. These efforts by Khrushchev to appear as defending China against U.S. imperialism (and American nuclear weapons) were considered by the latter a propaganda ploy. The Chinese-American talks were now transferred to Warsaw. The debate inside the United States on the "China question" was growing. But the hysteria of the McCarthy period, though gradually dying down, and the Chiang Kai-shek lobby in Washington, were still too strong to permit any shift in policy. Mao Tsetung fiercely denounced U.S. imperialism, which had "done too many bad things," and reiterated support for the Third World and its national liberation struggles.

At the Twenty-first Congress of the CPSU (January-February 1959, in Moscow) Khrushchev affirmed that there were no divergences with China; the two were in total agreement — the implication being that only "some people" were dogmatists. However, he was more fluent than ever on the decisive responsibility of the two great powers, the USSR and U.S., for peace.

The keynote of the Twenty-first Congress was the transition to communism in the USSR, the impossibility of a return to capitalism, the dying out of class struggle. "There is no danger of restoration of capitalism in the Soviet Union. Socialism has triumphed here totally and definitely . . . the question of building socialism in one country has ended in total and definitive victory." Liu Shao-chi was to echo Khrushchev in his article *The Triumph of Marxism-Leninism in China,* published in the *New International Review — Problems of Peace and Socialism,* a Russian-sponsored magazine, on September 14, 1959.*

In a concluding speech, Khrushchev wistfully pleaded for a visa to the U.S., praising Eisenhower (who had just stated there was no inten-

---

* Also in *Ten Glorious Years* (Peking 1959), page 1.

tion of inviting Khrushchev), recalling happy memories of meeting Eisenhower in 1955 at Geneva, and the "Geneva spirit." "I'm not going to ask for a visa . . . but it is a question of human rights . . . I don't understand for what misdeed I can't benefit from the right to visit [the U.S.] which is granted to so many" — from the head of a state adverse to issuing passports to its own citizens, a comical complaint.

Anastas Mikoyan, first deputy premier of the USSR, went to the United States in the spring, and later that year Nixon, Humphrey, Adlai Stevenson all took trips to Moscow. It is reported by André Fontaine* that it was on Nixon's advice that Eisenhower invited Khrushchev to visit the United States in September.

Why did Khrushchev challenge Mao and his principles at the Twenty-first Congress, singling out Mao by dividing the "dogmatists" from the Chinese Party?

In January 1959 Mao's resignation from the chairmanship of the People's Republic (though not from chairmanship of the Military Affairs Committee and of the Party) was announced, stunning many people in China. Abroad it was interpreted as a "demotion" for Mao. It seemed that Mao's "stiff-necked" opposition to the Khrushchev line had caused this replacement of Mao by someone "more pliable" and better liked by the Russians, Liu Shao-chi.

The facts are different. On Mao's return from the Moscow meeting in November 1957, many conferences were held in China which not only debated the Leap but also discussed problems arising from a continuing dispute with the USSR, and the possible results if it worsened. Mao blamed some of the swift degeneration of the Russian Party upon the fact that Stalin had not prepared any successor for the revolutionary cause in Russia. And from then on, Mao began increasingly to ponder the problem of "successors to the revolution." He also realized that the Moscow encounter was only a beginning; there would be prolonged and very serious ideological debate on the international level. This was a struggle "which may last one thousand years."†

For all these reasons, Mao Tsetung in January 1958 had prepared to give up the chairmanship of the Republic. This would relieve him from a considerable amount of formal protocol. Not that he did not enjoy it; his wit and humor, his forthright remarks enlivened the Peking diplomatic circles. But there was work of great importance to do. Even then

---

* André Fontaine *Histoire de la Guerre Froide* (Paris 1967; English edition *History of the Cold War*, 2 vols., New York 1968, 1969).

† Attributed to Mao, and repeated in many interviews, private talks, etc.

he had begun to question whether it was necessary to have a "chairman of the Republic."* "Before September this year the question of my retirement . . . should be raised . . . concentration on [the duties of] chairman of the Party will enable me to save much time . . . Please explain all this clearly to cadres and the masses so as to avoid misconstruction." The announcement was made a year later, in January 1959, and in that April, Liu was formally confirmed as chairman of the Republic.

It seems that Khrushchev believed that Mao was being demoted. In any case, he would shortly thereafter engage in action encouraging to the opposition to Mao within the Chinese Communist Party itself.

In January 1959 the first admissions of temporary shortages of nonstaple foods were made; there was no surplus to sell to the state, as the communes were short. In that year and the next year also, the peasantry would keep all the food it grew and consume it without selling to the state, so that there were shortages but not serious famines in the cities. The situation reversed pre-Liberation experience, when cities were fed while millions died of hunger in the countryside. The cause of the current shortages was understandable; in 1958 the peasants had sold too much to the state, and gone short themselves.† The government used up its reserves to feed the cities, and started to purchase grain from outside sources in 1960.

Given one good harvest in 1959, all would have been well, but several disastrous events occurred in that and the two following years. Climatic disasters were the worst in a century, with an appalling two-year drought in the North and West and nightmare floods in the South. Twenty percent of North China was parched. Added to this would be internal and external conflicts: a major Party struggle; a rebellion in Tibet, armed clashes with India. "For a while our enemies rejoiced, thinking we had failed."‡ Havoc and disaster were the only reports about China, to which were added "bellicosity and aggression."

In February 1959, at another work meeting to examine the shortfalls in agriculture, Mao said that the relations between achievements and defects were "as between nine fingers and one . . . One learns the piano

* This post is now (1975) abolished.
† There had been again too much requisitioning of grain by the State Purchasing Corporation, based on the high (and mendacious) production figures for that year (1958).
‡ Mao Tsetung, 1962. Also quoted to the author by Foreign Minister Chen Yi, in an interview in 1963.

by playing it." Chou En-lai enjoined that the rate of increase should not be in percentages but in absolute figures. There was still great confidence and enthusiasm among the people. Directives went out for spring planting, "shock brigades campaigns" for manure collection, in which the PLA, schools, town dwellers, all participated.

The first harvest of 1959 was very poor; the second would also be meager. Added to the climatic disasters were soil alkalinity problems from hasty irrigation projects, and insect pests. These were to ravage a fair proportion of fields in Middle China, because of the destruction of many birds in the "away with all pests" campaign in the spring of 1958 to eliminate flies, rats, and sparrows.

Chou En-lai's report at the National People's Congress in April gave figures of achievements but also introduced cautionary notes. One thousand more industrial and mining enterprises than plans called for had been started in 1958, whereas only 537 had been put into operation during the whole of the first five-year plan. 1958 had shown a gigantic all-around Leap Forward, and 1959 would continue so. However, there were defects: raw materials, metals, electric power and transport capacity lagged behind the demands of economic development. Readjustment was necessary in capital construction distribution, allocation of equipment and supplies.

The manpower dislocation was to be tackled. It was now under the unified command of the central authorities that the increase, transfer and employment of technicians, engineers, and other qualified technical personnel would take place. The slogan which introduced this return to centralization was "The whole country like a game of chess." There had been too much decentralization, leading to an anarchic state which disorganized planning and designing in plants.

Provincial and county authorities in charge of industrialization now contracted directly with large industrial complexes for equipment and expertise, and this competed with demands for the same expertise and equipment by major plants being built. Although the number of engineers had now quadrupled, demand for them was still greater. There was competition between the two levels of industrialization for experienced workers.

The flux of 17 million new workers drafted from rural areas to fill the future factories and workshops had not only to be stemmed, but also a good deal of it reversed. Surplus occasional workers must return to agriculture, and it was also forbidden to take away, for infrastructural work, more than a certain portion of the peasantry; 80 percent in each commune must, in times of agricultural need, be there in the fields to carry out the essential tasks of harvesting, sowing, planting, reaping.

1959 was the tenth year of the People's Republic, and the elation, the enthusiasm and the hope of the working people was still buoyant. But at the top level, in Peking, uneasy rumors began to circulate, indicating increased tension in the "two-line struggle." Some attributed this to Mao's having given up the chairmanship; others to events in Tibet* or to the escalating dispute with Nehru over the Sino-Indian border. The real isue, however, was the squeeze which Khrushchev was beginning to put on China that spring.

It began with an apparently innocuous demand in March-April for reconsideration of "joint defense measures" and "unity of action." And this dialogue opened precisely when there was trouble in Tibet. The Tibetan tribe of Khambas, instigated by foreign agents (the CIA, with the connivance of Indian intelligence men), operating from Kalimpong in India, started a rebellion with weapons parachuted in, and in March the Dalai Lama departed, unhindered, for India.† The Indian government granted him asylum, which China did not object to, though she strongly protested against the subsequent propaganda for the Dalai Lama in which Indian diplomatic missions abroad took part. Deteriorating relations with Nehru over demarcation of the Sino-Indian border were also a factor of brewing dispute which Khrushchev would utilize.‡

So much for outside enemies. Within China, in June, a "historical" article entitled *Hai Jui Upbraids the Emperor* was published in the national press. It was written by Wu Han, a historian and the non-Communist vice-mayor of Peking, and was about an upright official, Hai Jui, who had chided a Ming emperor for his tyranny. Hai Jui thus apostrophizes the emperor: "The last ten years or so have been chaotic . . . in earlier times you did a few good things, but how about now? Your mind is dogmatic and prejudiced. You think you are always right . . . the whole country has been dissatisfied with you for a long time."

---

* See Neville Maxwell *India's China War* (London 1970); also see *Concerning the Question of Tibet: A Collection of Documents Concerning the Tibetan Question* (English edition Peking 1959) for a full account of the Tibetan putsch.

† See *Far Eastern Economic Review*, Hong Kong, September 5, 1975, pages 30–34.

‡ Western accounts of "Chinese atrocities" in Tibet have never been proven, nor have they gained credence among knowledgeable experts anywhere. They are based solely on one nonwitness — that is, the Dalai Lama himself, who at The Hague, before a court of jurists, recounted events which allegedly occurred a few months after he had left Tibet. (Report of the court in hands of author.)

Wu Han added sentences to what Hai Jui had said, phrases not in any historical archives extant. This was plainly an attack against Mao, in the tenth year of the Republic. Its timing left no one in the top level of the Party, or among the intelligentsia, in doubt as to who was to be upbraided.

This article would not have been published without powerful back-stage support for Wu Han. The immediate supporter, as many knew, was Peng Chen, the mayor of Peking, whose hostility to Mao's views dated back to the Hundred Flowers. And behind Peng Chen was Liu Shao-chi.

Mao must have been aware of the impending confrontation in the Party. "We unite, and then after we have carried out our work for a while, ideas diverge, and this is transformed into struggle. . . . Once more there are splits . . . as soon as we talk about unity, there is disunity . . . to talk all the time of monolithic unity and not to talk about struggle, about contradictions, is not Marxist-Leninist."* Although Mao must have known from which direction the attack would come, he took no preemptive action of any kind. In that tenth year he had to make decisions of great importance. And it seemed as if the whole world was against China.

But Mao was steadfast. Even Khrushchev, referring to Mao's visit to Stalin in 1949–1950, said that Stalin had found Mao "someone unbreakable, who did not fear him." In the summer of 1959 Mao was preparing himself for the eighth plenum of the Eighth Central Committee, where, as everyone knew, matters of great import would have to be thrashed out.

That summer, for the first time in thirty-two years, Mao revisited his native village of Shaoshan, his old home, and the pond where he had begun swimming. A photograph shows him with his relatives, all peasants, barefoot, as are all peasants when working in the fields. He also went back to Juichin, the base in Kiangsi province where the Long March had started. This pilgrimage to the past was a way of fortifying himself for the onslaught to come. His poem "Return to Shaoshan," written on June 25, shows both nostalgia and buoyant hope:

> *Memories a fading dream; age-old the pain,*
> *Remember the gardens of thirty-two years ago.*
> *Here the Red banners rose, the spears of slaves were brandished*

* In March 1958, at Chengtu.

Against the cruel whips of black-handed tyrants.
Sacrifice emboldens resolution,
Dares to make the sun and moon shine in a new heaven.
Gladly I watch the heavy swell of grain,
See heroes of the plowed earth walk home in twilight mist.

Like Antaeus, he touched the earth and was strong again, vital with the spirit of his people.

At the end of June, Mao Tsetung went to Lushan, the cool and beautiful mountain resort where the Central Committee was to assemble for its eighth plenum. Lushan was the old residence of Chiang Kai-shek. Mao Tsetung composed another poem as he sat in a wicker chair in the garden, contemplating the valleys below.

One peak swooping birdlike above the regal stream,
Four hundred twists to its tree-clad top.
Here I survey the world beyond the seas;
Mellow winds splash rain, sky and river melt.
Pillared clouds veil the Yellow Crane nine-pronged waters.
In which Wonderland has the poet Tao gone,
Perchance to fields in Peach Blossom paradise?

The meaning of the last two lines is that the poet Tao, who invented a utopian "peach blossom land," should now return to see China, which is becoming such a land.

Thus Mao renewed his faith; and to struggle against petty men was no worse than a hard swim in the sullen storm-tossed waters of the Great River. "Going against the tide gives one courage and resolution. There are so many rivers in China; can they not be used?"

The initial attack on Mao at the plenum came from Peng Teh-huai, minister of Defense. Peng had left China in April, during the session of the National People's Congress, to attend a meeting of ministers of Warsaw Pact powers. For several weeks he toured the USSR and East European countries in order to "learn advanced modern techniques."

Before his departure, the Chinese Politburo had received another demand from Khrushchev pressing acceptance of unity of action and "joint defense": Soviet use of Chinese military and naval facilities in return for nuclear knowledge; joint nuclear bases in China under Soviet advisers; allied economies intimately linking the two countries in partnership. The latter was a fifteen-year plan which the Russian experts had drawn up in 1955–1956 for Chinese industrial takeoff in 1967.*

While the Politburo studied this ultimatum — for it was one — Peng left Peking on the same day as Chang Wen-tien,† vice-minister of Foreign Affairs and an observer at the Warsaw Pact meeting. Both men were confirmed by the NPC in their offices in absentia.

While in the Soviet Union, Peng Teh-huai was courted; he heard the Leap and the communes deplored as "petty bourgeois adventurism." Although in January he had seemed entirely pro-Leap, he was now "discouraged." At the same time he was more impressed than ever with Soviet weaponry. Perhaps the memory of old quarrels with Mao, and the long conversations he had with Russian friends, made him decide to "speak up." But it is quite certain that Peng would not have attacked Mao as he did had he not been assured of support within the Party; and this support must have come before he left for the USSR, for during his visit he had with him a draft of his critical comments. In Tirana, Peng met Khrushchev and showed him (and some other Russian leaders) the text of his criticism of the Leap, the communes, and other Mao policies. We do not know what Khrushchev said exactly, but he must have promised support. On June 13 Peng Teh-huai was back in Peking. And on June 20, having received a negative answer to his ultimatum of April, Khrushchev abruptly canceled the agreement for sharing nuclear knowledge.

The Politburo, of which Peng was a member, sat in meetings throughout late June. Mao's opposition took heart. The mighty USSR had canceled the agreements. Did not this prove Mao utterly wrong?

In July, Peng Teh-huai toured China, investigating and collecting data against the Leap. So did Chang Wen-tien. So did others. They were preparing a case against Mao. It is in this context that Wu Han's *Hai Jui Upbraids the Emperor* becomes meaningful. It showed Peng Teh-huai that he had moral support two months before he delivered his attack against Mao.

Peng arrived in Lushan and started lobbying the Central Committee

---

* The same pattern of "linking economies" in a fifteen-year plan was proposed by the USSR to India in 1974 and partly accepted.

† Chang Wen-tien was one of the original Chinese "twenty-eight Bolsheviks" said to be trained by Stalin to take over the Chinese Communist Party in early 1930. Although he had sided with Wang Ming against Mao, he later came to Mao's side, and became vice-minister of Foreign Affairs and a member of the Central Committee. See *The Morning Deluge*, page 227 and others.

members as they assembled in preliminary discussions for the enlarged plenum. He lobbied the numerous generals and marshals invited to attend, as well as regional representatives. A Russian observer team was also in attendance. On July 14 Peng Teh-huai circulated his "letter of opinion." On the 17th Mao received a copy of it. On the 18th Khrushchev in Poland attacked the communes and the Great Leap Forward as "petty bourgeois . . . fanatic . . . adventurism." Peng had used the same terms in his letter of opinion. On the first of August, Army Day, articles appeared in the Russian press lauding Peng Teh-huai. Khrushchev's overt attempt to topple Mao was not revealed until 1963, and then obliquely, when the Chinese wrote that Khrushchev had expressed "undisguised support for anti-Party elements in the Chinese Party" at the Twenty-second Congress of the CPSU in October 1961. The struggle at the Lushan plenum was not only an intra-Party confrontation. It now had implications of collusion with a foreign — even if also socialist — power.

While the plenum was in session, the Chinese Communist Party magazine *Red Flag* came out with a strange article entitled *Peaceful Competition Is an Inevitable Trend* (August 16), which indirectly took up the Khrushchev thesis.

Peng Teh-huai's letter of opinion was an attack on all Mao's policies, which had been approved by the Central Committee and therefore were the Party line. The Leap, the communes, the steel drive . . . "Hasty . . . waste of resources and manpower . . . we have not handled the problems of economic construction in so successful a way as we dealt with the problem of shelling Quemoy and Matsu and quelling the revolt in Tibet." He called the effort petty bourgeois fanaticism. "In the view of some comrades, putting politics in command is a substitute for everything, but it is no substitute for economic principles."

Peng described the sufferings of the people; the masses were hungrier than they had been in the period 1933–1953 (*sic!*). If rations were not improved, there would be riots and uprisings. A Hungarian type of uprising might occur in China, and then it might be necessary to call for help from the Soviet troops.

A minister of defense who submits a memorandum criticizing the head of his party to a foreign statesman, who states that there might be cause to call upon a foreign army's help, would in any country and under any circumstances be relieved of his post.* Peng Teh-huai's

---

* "Certainly Peng's letter was not merely an innocent statement of opinion, since Peng had written to the Soviet Communist Party three months earlier, criticizing

attack was not an honest criticism of the Leap; it was an attack on the basic principles of socialist construction, upon all of Mao's concepts; it implied also an attack upon Mao's stance against Moscow's military demands, which Mao was preparing to resist even at the cost of losing Soviet aid.

Others rose to speak against Mao. There were two strands of opposition to him: one was the "military club," military commanders in alliance with Peng; the other, officials in civilian departments who disapproved of Mao's policies toward the USSR. Both groups assailed his economic policies. The harvest that year would be only 160 million tons, 25 million less than in 1957. Peng even opined that there should be "no investigation of personal responsibility," thus appearing not to attack Mao personally. But this very phrase showed he wanted to put the onus of everything on Mao.

The debate occupied almost the whole of the three weeks allotted to the plenum to review problems and fashion policies.

"You have spoken much," commented Mao wearily, after listening to all his opponents. "Permit me to talk a little now, will you?" He added that he had taken sleeping pills, as he could not sleep, in the last three days.

Mao said that some in the audience were very sensitive to criticism, but that was wrong. They should listen to words, all words, whether correct or not. In his impetuous youth he had been impatient, but now he had learned to listen. "I advise you to stiffen your scalp," to endure all that was said. "I must stiffen mine." It was indeed a pity that more critics, such as for instance some famous rightists of the 1957 Hundred Flowers, could not come to Lushan and join in the torrent of criticism. He would certainly listen to them.

But what he had heard was "muddleheaded." It was also long-drawn, like a protracted war. Yet at the end, the universe did not sink, heaven did not collapse. In truth there had been bad times; there would be more. Everyone had become anxious and tense, including himself. The bad times would last for a while, some months, but they would be overcome. The masses, the cadres, were still full of enthusiasm; they supported the Party.

Enthusiasm was necessary and one must not dampen it. At least 30 percent of the cadres were activists, and 40 percent just followed the

the great leap forward policies" (Lois Dougan Tretiak, *Far Eastern Economic Review*, November 30, 1967).

mainstream; the other 30 percent were passive or somewhat hostile. It was not a good idea to publish *all* the mistakes made, as Peng and others suggested. Every commune probably had made some, and this would dampen enthusiasm and give a one-sided picture of the situation.

The whole effort had been called petty bourgeois fanaticism. It was not the petty bourgeoisie but the poor and lower middle peasants and the workers, about 70 percent of the population, who had accomplished great things. Was their enthusiasm petty bourgeois fanaticism?

Certainly the "Communist wind" extremism of 1958 had produced reversals, but in the spring this had been rectified. Communes had been overhauled, accounting checked. Millions of peasants had received an education in political economy; they had realized that total egalitarianism was impracticable. Within a month abuses had come to an end. This proved the effectiveness of the Party, "great, glorious and correct." Peasants did not know economics, but they were now learning fast; they had acquired experience. "Taking away the fat pigs and the fat cabbages of prosperous teams to share with poorer teams" did not work well, and now they knew it.

Mao recalled how, since November 1958, he had called for inspections and checkups. But people sent down from Peking "talked and talked," but did not listen to the problems and had made no adverse comment. Yet now they were upbraiding him and "three generations of my ancestors."

Mao appealed to the waverers in the Party to make up their minds. They must choose which side they were on. He recalled that he had spoken at the Nanning and the Chengtu conferences in the spring of 1958 on the "ill wind of revisionism which in 1956 had blown away many good things." If one criticized the mad fanaticism of the Leap, why not also castigate the dismal pessimism of 1956? Yet Mao had not put any labels on pessimistic comrades. The problem had been treated as one of methodology.

The inflated targets for grain established at Wuhan in December 1958 had not met his approval. At the Shanghai April conference some comrades (Chou En-lai, Li Hsien-nien?) had asked for a readjustment of targets, but others had disagreed.

But, Mao said, he himself had been responsible for doubling the target for steel, and for the steel drive. It created "great trouble" when 90 million people went to smelt steel, abandoning other work. The responsibility was his. "I have committed two crimes . . . calling for

10,700,000 tons of steel and the mass smelting of steel." And there had been transport difficulties — "Coal and iron won't walk by themselves . . . I had not thought of that."

Marx too had committed errors, hoping for the revolution every day in Europe. He had first opposed the Paris Commune of 1871, later supported it. There had also been failures in the course of the Chinese Revolution; the Long March, when most of the Red bases had been lost, had started as a retreat. Was all that bourgeois fanaticism? As to the Leap: "We have paid the price for learning . . . enabled the people of the entire nation to learn a lesson . . . blown some Communist wind . . . Now you should analyze your own responsibility . . . and you will feel better . . . your stomach will feel more comfortable if you break wind."

Mao read a letter of criticism from a Party member pointing out defects in the Leap. "Highly pertinent." This man had the courage to speak, but was not a plotter. There had been criticisms by the Central Committee itself of errors and shortcomings. Yet those who now attacked him had not said a word in November 1958 in Chengchow, nor protested against raising of targets at the Peitaiho conference in August 1958; not a word at the Wuchang conference in November, nor in Peking in January and February 1959, nor at the Shanghai meeting in March-April. Now they presented their objections. Why now? This required thinking about.

Mao agreed that overall planning had gone by the board. The Planning Commission had given up planning; the Statistics Department did not function — it could not. Coherence and cohesion had been lost; the crunch had come with transport. Mao had not involved himself in planning; he did not exercise control (the executive work was done by Liu Shao-chi). But he would not blame others. Let all responsibility be his, and let him be cut off from having any posterity.*

And now Mao lifted the whole issue to the ideological plane. Rightist sentiments, ideology, activities had become rampant in the Party. Although this had not reached the point of a wholesale anti-Party attack as in 1957, there was resurgence of "right conservatism," overestimating errors, condemning everything, lacking confidence in the revolution. "The Khrushchevs oppose . . . these three things: Hundred Flowers blooming, people's communes, and the Great Leap Forward . . . we must use these things to challenge the entire world, including opponents and skeptics within our Party."

* The worst of curses in old China. Mao uses this phrase ironically, but also perhaps in grief — he had lost more than one child during the arduous days before 1949.

Some people, Mao went on, had spoken of a possible uprising. They really meant an uprising from the right — the landlords, rich peasants, counterrevolutionaries. If it succeeded, the nation would become a bourgeois nation and China would change color. But then he, Mao, would go to the countryside and lead the peasantry to overthrow the government. He would build another Red Army if he thought the PLA would not follow him. "But I think they will follow me."

The audience was moved to the core. They knew that Liu Shao-chi, not Mao, was in charge of daily implementation of directives. As one, the plenum rose to pledge loyalty to Mao, and support. Peng Teh-huai and his backers had lost.

Chang Wen-tien had already written to Mao, asking to come to see him. Mao wrote back: "How come you got yourself entrapped in the military club? What purpose do you have in mind this time? You have so assiduously and extensively searched out dark [incriminating] material . . . like treasure. But two days after you spoke you became so panicky and perturbed . . . I think this is a relapse into your old sickness."° Perhaps he suspected that Chang Wen-tien while in Moscow had seen Wang Ming, the leader of the twenty-eight Bolsheviks. Mao's great struggle against the Wang Ming line had taken fifteen years; Wang Ming had remained, at Mao's request, a member of the Central Committee. He had finally left China in 1956 to live in Moscow, where until his death in 1973 he wrote virulent articles against Mao.

Mao rose to speak once again. "After coming up the mountain, I expressed these three sentiments: Achievements are great. Problems are considerable. And the future is bright." Suddenly there had been this frantic attack by rightist opportunists. It was an attack on the Party, the socialist movement, on the 600 million people. "The struggle that has arisen in Lushan is a class struggle . . . the continuation of the life or death struggle between the bourgeoisie and the proletariat in the process of the socialist revolution during the past decade." This would continue for twenty, fifty years, and there would be many more struggles. The problem of Peng Teh-huai and his supporters resembled the Kao Kang and Jao Shou-shih problem of 1954. Peng Teh-huai was but yesterday a man of great merit, but people were ignorant of the complexities and the deviousness of their own past history. This lapse had its deep roots in their own unreformed ideology.

It was, however, necessary to keep Peng Teh-huai and those with

° Mao here means, by sickness, political deviation. As noted earlier (page 158, note), Chang Wen-tien had, for a while in the 1930's, followed the Wang Ming line.

him in the Party, to give them every opportunity to repent and to change. "It is necessary to have some leeway, to have warmth and a springtime, instead of keeping them always out in the cold."

The Lushan confrontation was an intensely emotional episode. Chu Teh's exclamation "And to think that we all ate out of the same dish in the past!" gave the note of grief at the rift between the men who had fought together since 1927. Liu Po-cheng, the famous one-eyed general of the Long March, also expressed his feelings. "I see now that to become a real Marxist it is necessary to change one's very bones."

It is not known when Mao learned of Peng's consultation with Khrushchev in Tirana. But he mentioned the matter indirectly on September 11 at an enlarged session of the Military Affairs Committee: "It is absolutely impermissible to go behind the back of our motherland and to collude with a foreign country." In 1967, when full details of the struggle against Peng Teh-huai were published, its world revolutionary context became widely recognized. Peng's attack had come "when the reactionary forces at home and abroad were exploiting certain transient and partial shortcomings. . . . An attack at such a juncture launched from inside the Central Committee of the Party is clearly more dangerous than an attack from outside the Party." The activities of Peng Teh-huai and others had been purposive, prepared, planned, organized, a continuation of the Kao Kang and Jao Shou-shih affair.*

Lin Piao now replaced Peng Teh-huai as minister of Defense. And in August an anti-rightist campaign opened in the press. From then until year's end, denunciation of right opportunists in the Party occurred daily. But the opposition remained strong; nothing was done, especially in Peking, to curb the covert attacks against Mao. In this campaign the mayor of Peking, Peng Chen, and Chou Yang, vice-director of Propaganda, were the ones who surreptitiously encouraged the sniping which Liu Shao-chi appeared to ignore.

Wu Han continued to publish "historical" studies. In September he wrote *On Hai Jui,* a panegyric on Hai Jui's courage and unbending spirit even after he had been dismissed. "If you have a spear you have to use it. Why not throw it? If it hits the target it may at least hurt a little . . . my articles all have their target."

On August 26 Chou En-lai reported on the "readjusted" 1959 plan. "Facts prove that the simultaneous development of large, small and

* Resolution of the eighth plenum of the Eighth Central Committee at Lushan, August 17, 1959; published August 1967.

medium industrial enterprises and the use of both modern and indigenous methods, walking on two legs, have their advantages . . . the enterprises are widely distributed; it takes less time to build them . . . it forces an extensive survey of resources, and economy in the use of transport . . . The steel drive is a magnificent spectacle . . . part of the people's understanding how to transform China from a poor and blank country into an industrial state . . . unparalleled in Chinese history." The 1958 grain targets were corrected from 375 million tons to 250 million tons. "Due to lack of experience in assessing harvests under condition of bumper crops, inadequate allocating of labor power . . . which led to rather hurried reaping, threshing . . . the calculations were a bit high." But industry continued to leap; it had doubled output in the first six months of 1959.

Peng Teh-huai dropped out of sight but was named to a fairly high regional post, and he remained a member of the Central Committee. He seems to have written to Mao asking to "go down" to labor in the countryside, but Mao said he was too old; he could spend time going around inspecting communes if he wished. He would be arrested by Red Guards in December 1966 and publicly "struggled" against and paraded through the streets in July 1967. He is reported living in retirement in Szechuan province.

On a cold September day Mao swam in the Miyun reservoir, a creation of the Great Leap Forward. He was again bracing himself, this time for Khrushchev's visit to Peking for the celebration of New China's tenth anniversary. Khrushchev was coming to China straight after his Camp David talks with President Eisenhower.

10

The Years of Endurance: September 1959 to September 1962

When people see only what is under their feet, not what lies above the mountains and beyond the seas, they are likely to be as boastful as the frog at the bottom of the well. But when they raise their heads to see the immensity of the universe, the kaleidoscope of man's affairs, the splendor and magnificence of humanity's cause, the wealth of man's talents, and the abundance of knowledge, they become modest.
— MAO TSETUNG, 1962 or 1963

What we are dedicated to is a world-shaking task.
— MAO TSETUNG, 1963

The years 1959 to 1962 are murky and confused, a season of divaricating statements and divergent policies. The whole world appeared to be against China and predicted her failure; she was beset at home with climatic and agricultural disasters, as well as sustaining major confrontations with both the United States and the Soviet Union. She was labeled bellicose, aggressive, expansionist, and Mao a megalomaniac and tyrant; it was difficult to discover any accurate, much less sympathetic, portrait of China.

In a by no means impartial western press, the event deemed the utmost "evidence" of China's danger to the world was the border conflict with India. Only now, fifteen years later, has the prevalent picture of a peaceful democratic India attacked by a bellicose invasive China given place to a more balanced view.° But in 1962 the minor border conflict, for such it was, was played up. The episode's interest lies in the close link it reveals between India and the USSR, leading to what almost amount to joint operations against China.

° See Neville Maxwell *India's China War* (London 1970).

166

The good relations established between India and China between 1951 and 1956 deteriorated in 1957. Nehru then seconded the "nuclear terror" thesis of Khrushchev, but there were more immediate reasons for this change of attitude, which even Indian journalists have exposed. India's need for massive aid from both the U.S. and USSR dictated a policy of hostility to China. "Nehru is using intransigence towards China as a gambit to obtain more aid," stated one Indian writer. Although Tibet is internationally recognized as a region of China, and in 1954 Nehru had so recognized it, by 1958 the Indians and Chinese were exchanging notes, at first polite, but gradually colder, on the parachuting of weapons and money by the CIA to the Khamba rebels in Tibet.* The CIA conducted intrigues from Kalimpong and other sites controlled by the Indian army. The connections of the Dalai Lama's brother with the CIA were notorious. To Chinese protests, the Indian government replied that India was a country with freedom of movement and freedom of speech.

While canceling agreements with China, the USSR increased aid to India, so that by 1960 India had received three times the amount loaned to China. In 1958 Nehru offered to "mediate" the Taiwan affair between the United States and China and took the Khrushchev line that the situation might "explode into nuclear war" unless China gave way. Chou En-lai thanked Nehru for his intended good offices, but China wanted no intermediary.

The first open clash between Indian and Chinese border patrols occurred on August 26, 1959. On September 6 the Chinese Ministry of Foreign Affairs approached its Russian counterpart, pointing out that the USSR should not "fall into the trap prepared by Nehru," who was utilizing the Soviet Union to pressure China.

On September 9 the Russian ministry prepared a statement on the border clash. The Chinese ministry asked the Russians to abstain from publishing the text, because Premier Chou was writing to Nehru requesting negotiation of the border dispute. The Russians ignored this Chinese request and published their statement that very night, providing the first public indication to the world that relations were tense.

Six days later Khrushchev had his Camp David summit with Eisenhower. The U.S. State Department knew of the unilateral cancellation of agreements concerning nuclear knowledge, "a gift," as the Chinese called it, to the American President.

* See *Far Eastern Economic Review*, Hong Kong, September 5, 1975, pages 30–34. See also Neville Maxwell *India's China War* (London 1970).

The reasons for the Russian attitude were many. There was fear that negotiations over the disputed India-China borders* might lead to a demand for negotiations on the Russo-Chinese borders. Russia's long-term power strategy focused on the Indian Ocean. The deliberate choice of India as its major Asian territory for economic expansion, in the USSR's course as the dominant world power to come, dictated this betrayal of a "fraternal" country.

Coincidence again: as the border clashes with India escalated into bloodshed in August, unpublicized border clashes occurred on the USSR-China frontier in Sinkiang. But this was not published in the American press; China was the Enemy, whose image had to project international danger.

The Camp David summit between Eisenhower and Khrushchev was a thundering success. Khrushchev projected volatile exuberance. Eisenhower described him as a "dynamic, extraordinary personality. Now he has made great dents in the original concepts of this [Marxist-Leninist] doctrine."

Khrushchev arrived in Peking on September 30, the eve of the tenth anniversary of the PRC. Mao Tsetung met him at the airport. Khrushchev appeared jolly. Mao was affably courteous.

Khrushchev's speech at the formal anniversary reception insulted his hosts. He extolled the Camp David spirit; exalted the "free exchanges" he had with the U.S. President, who was a man who understood well the necessity for diminishing tensions. "Force must not be used to test the stability of the capitalist system." The next three days were spent in acrimonious slanging matches behind closed doors. Khrushchev took up the Sino-Indian border clash, blaming China's "aggressiveness," and refused to shake the hand of Marshal Chen Yi, the foreign minister, saying he "disliked militarists." "There are more dead on the Indian side than on the Chinese side . . . the side with more dead is the side which had been suffering aggression." He emphasized the terrors of nuclear war; boasted that only the USSR could stop the U.S. from making such a war upon China.

The Chinese reminded Khrushchev that the subjects to be discussed had significance for the future of the world; that nothing must be done lightly. Chou En-lai tried to explain the Chinese stand on the Sino-

* Borders between India and China, like those between Russia and China, were established by arbitrary colonialist decisions, or by the "unequal treaties" which had been denounced in China since 1911.

Indian border, but Khrushchev brushed the maps aside and said, "You can't make history all over again."

"We have not forgotten what . . . Khrushchev said about the question of Taiwan . . . in October 1959. He said . . . it was an incendiary factor . . . because the U.S. supported Chiang and the Soviet Union supported China there resulted the atmosphere of an imminent great war . . . He further said that there was more than one way to solve every complicated question . . . For example, after the October Revolution there was established in the Soviet Far East the Far Eastern Republic, and Lenin recognized it at the time; this was a temporary concession . . . later it was united with Russia. This absurd view was rejected . . . whereupon the Soviet leader made a series of speeches hinting that China was 'craving for war like a cock for a fight.' "*

"When the masters quarrel, the servants are shaking in their shoes" is a phrase which escaped Khrushchev when he referred to "the two greatest states in the world, on whom depend war and peace." There was no joint communiqué when he left Peking on October 4.

The American writer Anna Louise Strong saw Mao that winter.† Thirteen years had passed since the interview Mao had given her in 1946, in which he had coined the phrase: "The atom bomb is a paper tiger . . . imperialists and all reactionaries are paper tigers." Miss Strong for years kept the memory of this second unrecorded talk for a book she was writing, but her death at eighty-six (in 1971) prevented its publication.

In their talk, Mao had surmised that Russia might now change color,‡ become "revisionist, take the road to capitalism . . . Russia will now try to strangle us, to choke us." But China would not knuckle down. It concerned "our children and the children of the world's people for a thousand years, whether to be slaves or free." The revolution must not be betrayed. Now the burden of revolution was upon China, and she must not falter through fear or selfishness. There would be difficult times, but in the end the peoples of the world would triumph. It was in the Third World that history was being made, and China was part of the Third World.

The entente of the U.S. and USSR would also entail rivalry and conflict; "they both collude and contend"; never would either trust the

* First Comment, September 6, 1963 (see note, page 116).
† On Hainan Island, during a brief holiday.
‡ Interviews of author with Miss Strong, 1964, and again in 1969, when she was preparing for publication a book with Mao's remarks in it.

other or sleep in peace. At each moment, everywhere, there would be confrontation; this would lead to an escalating arms race between the two; a maximization of lethal weapons. And this would impoverish imperialism, yet make it ever more rapacious . . . and the world's peoples would increasingly resist them, "including the American and the Russian people."

Meanwhile, neither of the two great powers would engage in war with China, because this would mean giving a big advantage to the other. China was "tough meat." Of course, it was possible that both of them, together with India and Japan, would attack China. But this would mean a great deal of preparation. The Chinese people would defend themselves, and in the end there would be revolution in India and Japan, in America and Russia. "The time is not far off when the Third World will rise, and the peoples of the world will throw off their chains."

The year 1960 began badly: an iron-hard winter without snow, followed by two hundred days of drought. The Yellow River shrank until it was a pencil thread lost in sand. Forty million hectares of cultivated land were affected. In Shantung peasants replanted grain five times. Townspeople came to help, including schoolchildren, forming long chains to carry water to the fields. The South was flooded, immense seas drowning the crops. Summer hail killed off the wheat in Hopei and Honan.*

And then the communes showed their worth. Fifteen million people in Shantung planted turnips and sweet potatoes to make up for the destroyed wheat crop. Eighteen million in Honan formed an anti-drought army, with four hundred thousand cadres from the cities joining in.

Mao insisted there should be no procurement of grain or other staple food from the affected regions. As a result, there were shortages in the cities and stringent rationing. Pig cholera took its toll of the depleted pig population, and the staple diet in Peking that winter was cabbages.†

Purchases of wheat from abroad for the cities began: 2.5 million tons in 1960, 5.8 million tons in 1961–1962, and 5.6 million tons in 1962–1963. The foreign exchange required amounted to 33 to 39 percent of

---

* *The Times*, London, November 9 and December 30, 1960, *China's Long Battle Against Record Drought*. The article quotes the areas affected as 230,000 square miles, half the cultivated land in China. See also *Far Eastern Economic Review*, September 19, 1960.

† Author's personal experience while in China in 1959, 1960, 1961, 1962.

China's total foreign exchange earnings, yet the shortfall amounted to only 3 to 4 percent of the total harvest, and China continued to export rice, one to two million tons, to Albania and to North Vietnam.

Khrushchev was on the warpath. In December 1959 he decried the arrogance and bellicosity of "certain" Chinese leaders, the "Trotskyism" of the communes "due to one man's influence." In a confidential note to Communist parties he accused China of having hindered his "peace" activities. He then made another Asian tour, arriving in India on February 14, 1960, the tenth anniversary of the Sino-Soviet treaty of friendship and alliance. He extolled India, promised abundant new aid, and encouraged Nehru not to negotiate the boundary dispute with Chou En-lai.

At a meeting of the Warsaw Pact nations in February, Khrushchev stated that nuclear knowhow from the USSR would not be put in the "hands of madmen." The meeting gave its imprimatur to "disarmament." It suggested an entente with the United States on peaceful use of the Antarctic, peaceful exploration of outer space, cessation of nuclear testing, as well as a European security conference.

The Chinese observer at Warsaw, Kang Sheng, stated the Chinese position. The United States still pushed ahead with arms expansion, establishing and expanding missile bases in various places, claiming to be ready at any time to resume nuclear testing. China had supported genuine disarmament initiatives all along. "The Chinese government has to declare to the world that any international disarmament agreement and all other international agreements which are arrived at without the formal participation of the Chinese People's Republic and the signature of its delegate cannot, of course, have any binding force on China." Khrushchev could not, in negotiations with the U.S., claim to represent the socialist camp.

Negotiations on the prohibition of nuclear tests in the air were now advanced. Both the U.S. and the USSR were ready for underground tests. But America refused to be entirely bound by any agreement, appending a codicil that "where national interests dictated" it would resume nuclear testing in any way and at any time convenient to itself.

The agreement on prohibition of nuclear testing in the air was finally concluded in September 1963, and was described by Stewart Alsop* as directed at stopping China from producing her own nuclear armament.

---

* Stewart Alsop "The Real Meaning of the Test Ban," *Saturday Evening Post*, September 28, 1963.

It would neither prevent nor limit the continued development and piling of nuclear weapons by both great powers. "The Chinese Communists, who have alleged that the test ban agreement is a plot to manacle China by denying it nuclear weapons, have understood the real meaning of the test ban . . . President Kennedy and his inner circle of advisers have agreed in principle that China must be prevented, by whatever means, from becoming a nuclear power." The treaty was an implicit understanding (between the U.S. and the USSR) on what was known in current Washington cryptology as the "nuclear sterilization of the Chincoms."

"The 'sterilization' will ultimately require force . . . but not very much force . . . thanks to the U-2's the intelligence community knows precisely where the two main Chinese plants are." The operation would be "no more serious than a tonsillectomy."

Mao Tsetung had only one weapon, ideological debate, in the campaign he now undertook to uphold Communist principles. The Russians had many weapons against China: economic pressures; political pressures; their allies in Eastern Europe could also squeeze China; their new relations of relaxation with the U.S. threatened China; inciting Nehru to frontier clashes with China would influence world opinion against China.

But ideology was the only weapon which *could* in fact be efficient, in the long term, provided the logic and validity of Chinese reasoning could be made known, and events confirmed them. Mao had said that "a new idea . . . always arouses opposition at first. It must be talked about, not to a small circle of people, but to everyone, day in and day out." The only way to defeat revisionism was through "reasoning it to death." Mao decided to reason it to its very end, "a thousand years" if necessary.

For the ninetieth anniversary of Lenin's birth in April 1960, *Red Flag* and the *People's Daily* published *Long Live Leninism*, a lengthy article which exposed the fallacies of the Twentieth Congress line, and which Mao had begun during the major struggle at Lushan. It was the first overt challenge to the USSR as the fount of ideological correctness.

Just as Liu Shao-chi's *The Triumph of Marxism-Leninism in China* (September 1959) repeated Khrushchev's line that socialism had won and that the system was irreversible, the publication of Mao's *Long Live Leninism* six months later was its refutation. It cites Mao's 1945 speech, in which he had said that there would not be war between the

USSR and the U.S. "This propaganda is a smokescreen by which the reactionaries in the U.S. mask the real contradictions, which are between the U.S. reactionaries and the American people, between U.S. imperialism and other countries, capitalist countries, colonial and semi-colonial countries." It was in this intermediate zone (the Third World, and now also Europe) that the collusion and contention of the two imperialisms would be manifest. "The decisive conflict of our epoch is that which opposes the imperialists to the peoples of Asia, Africa and Latin America who struggle for their emancipation."

Chou En-Lai stated:[*] "The decision [to challenge the ideological correctness] is not one taken by China for her self-interest; it is forced upon us . . . it is for the whole world of the exploited, all the world's peoples, whether China is to enjoy now a temporary well-being, but mortgage the future of humanity . . . we cannot sell out, we cannot betray, this is far too serious. We therefore have to give our views in a principled manner."

In early 1960 Khrushchev went to Hungary and to Poland to obtain support for another summit with Eisenhower in Paris in May. He asked the Chinese for "silence" while he conducted delicate summit negotiations. "We must shout on the contrary," Mao is reported as saying. "Can it aggravate tension if we explain the true state of affairs to the Chinese people and to the world public? Can hiding the truth help peace and help relax tensions?"

The May summit collapsed because an American U-2 reconnaissance plane was shot down over Russia; the resulting furor within the USSR showed the opposition there to Khrushchev's plans. Khrushchev accused Washington of exercising pressure, threatened retaliation, but maintained his Paris trip "with a pure heart and pure intentions."[†]

In Paris, Khrushchev was dealt another blow: Chancellor Konrad Adenauer and President Charles de Gaulle indicated their right to discuss every issue in international affairs as equal partners with the U.S., Britain and the USSR. Both de Gaulle and Adenauer had misgivings about the proposed European security conference, although Khrushchev dangled the promise of a pact or entente between the Warsaw Pact and NATO countries. On the American side, presidential elections were due that November, a bad time for any foreign initia-

[*] Author's interview (1960).
[†] André Fontaine *Histoire de la Guerre Froide* (Paris 1967), pages 377–393. (English edition *History of the Cold War*, 2 vols., New York 1968, 1969.)

tives. Khrushchev demanded an apology from Eisenhower and issued an ultimatum. He got nothing, and returned to Moscow. Meanwhile, the pressures within the USSR itself would begin to accumulate. The Soviet Red Army was hostile to disarmament. It would be October 1962, at the time of the Cuban crisis, before serious "talking" resumed between the U.S. and the USSR with a new President, John F. Kennedy.

In that May, Mao Tsetung, speaking off the record to several delegations from Latin America, said the conference in Paris might have been a good thing if "the main point, that is, that peace depends mainly on the readiness to carry on armed struggle by the peoples of the world," was maintained.

That summer Peking-Moscow divergences became very obvious at an international trade union meeting in Peking (June 1960); there were sharp exchanges between the delegations. Some Asian parties then suggested a reunion of twelve parties from socialist countries at the Romanian Party Congress in late June to thrash out the differences. But such a conference, with a majority of East European countries, would automatically vote with the USSR. Mao countered with a proposal for an international conference of all parties, with "ample preparation" to debate thoroughly the points at issue. To prepare this conference, the parties present at the Romanian Congress in Bucharest could exchange views, but not take any decision.

On June 10, 1960, in reply to *Long Live Leninism*, the Russians republished Lenin's *Left-wing Communism — An Infantile Disorder*. "Some people" were "thickskulled opponents of peace," wrote Otto Kuusinen; peaceful coexistence had been Lenin's policy and it had been creatively developed at the Twentieth and Twenty-first congresses of the CPSU.

At the Bucharest conference the Russians circulated a letter dated June 21, addressed to the Chinese but handed out to all attending parties, accusing the CCP leaders of "fractionalism," and asking that the other delegations criticize China publicly. There had been intense lobbying by both delegations, but this practically ordered a course of action. Khrushchev appeared at the Congress and made a heated speech on leftists, lunatics and maniacs who opposed peaceful coexistence, on politicians who didn't take account of present-day situations . . . warmongers. . . .

Peng Chen, the Peking mayor who led the Chinese delegation, distributed the Chinese reply. "There are differences of principle between us . . . we must adopt a serious attitude to reach a unanimous conclusion . . . The attitude of Comrade Khrushchev is patriarchal, arbitrary and despotic. He tried to exert pressure so that we should submit to his views . . . which are contrary to Marxism-Leninism. Our Party will never agree to erroneous views. It will never obey the conductor's baton."

The Soviet press, claiming that the Bucharest conference had confirmed the theses of the Soviet Twentieth and Twenty-first congresses (in fact the Albanian, Indonesian and North Vietnam delegates had not agreed) now printed articles hinting at economic pressures against "dogmatists." "Could anyone imagine the successful construction of socialism going on in present-day conditions even in so great a country as, let us say, China, if that country were in a state of isolation and could not rely on the collaboration and aid of all other socialist countries?"*

In July the Soviet Party served notice on China that within one month the 1,390 Soviet experts in China would withdraw and "suspended" 343 contracts, 257 projects. The withdrawal was timed with the knowledge that the harvest would be grimly under par that year (161 million tons). At the same time the USSR refused, for the next eighteen months, to supply any spare parts for equipment; there was also a demand for payment of debts for military equipment supplied during the Korean War.

"At Bucharest, to our amazement, Khrushchev took the lead in organizing a great converging onslaught on the Chinese Communist Party . . . It will not do for certain persons to behave like the magistrate who ordered the burning down of people's houses while forbidding the people so much as to light a lamp.

"The leaders of the CPSU brought more pressure . . . to extend the ideological differences to the sphere of state relations . . . In July recalling all Soviet experts within one month . . . tearing up hundreds of contracts and agreements."†

"Your perfidious action disrupted China's original national economic plan and inflicted enormous losses . . . You were going completely against Communist ethics when you took advantage of China's natural calamities."‡

Faced with this staggering blow to industry, the Chinese kept silent

---

* A. Titarenko in *Sovyetskaya Latvia*, August 16, 1960.
† First Comment, September 6, 1963. See note, page 116.
‡ Letter of February 29, 1964, from the CCP to the CPSU.

for three years. Chou En-lai would tell Edgar Snow that this withdrawal was "according to plan." The *People's Daily* on August 13, 1960, editorialized that "some people . . . at home and abroad" were trying to sabotage the Chinese revolution, but they "will not succeed."

Who were the people "at home" trying to sabotage the Chinese revolution?

Within China, the acute two-line struggle on economic policies was characterized by a plethora of economic articles, by delays and confusion. Two forces at work in every sector made for a dizzying avalanche of contradictory directives and resolutions.

The "black line of Liu Shao-chi" prevailed in industry and agriculture, though never completely. It is easy but erroneous to attribute to the "return to realism and good sense" and to "pragmatism" China's very swift recovery after the three very difficult years 1959–1961. For by 1962 it was obvious that China was pulling through, and by 1965 foreign economists were wondering whether she was ready for another Leap.

All the evidence is that the return to vigor was due to the spirit and achievements of the Leap. China was reaping in 1962 the fruit of the frantic industrial expansion of 1958–1959. By then, 83 percent of China's usable industrial equipment had been produced by the backbreaking efforts of the Leap.

But the Leap had required the industrial underpinnings supplied by the first five-year plan, which, whatever its other defects, did lay the foundations for industrial expansion. In the same manner the period after 1960 benefited from the Leap. Of the 921 major projects undertaken during the first plan, 428 were completed by the end of 1957 and 109 were near completion. In 1958, 500 new projects were completed and another 1,000 initiated. Industrial production by the end of 1959 had attained the 1962 targets of the second five-year plan in steel, coal, electricity, crude oil, metal cutting tools, cotton and paper production. The accelerated effort could not be maintained because equipment broke down and there were no spare parts,* and also because of the agricultural shortfall, but it had been an attempt "to scale heights yet unclimbed."

The Leap had also pinpointed the necessity for chemical fertilizer plants — a gap in the first plan. This now became a priority sector.

* Because of the USSR's refusal to supply spare parts for the equipment supplied during the first five-year plan.

1960 recorded continued industrial momentum in the first half of the year, particularly in electric power. Twenty-four major hydroelectric works and seventy-six thermal were undertaken by the Leap. A 20 percent increase in light industry in metals, plastic, chemicals, rayon synthetics was registered by 1961, and by 1963 an elevenfold increase in electricity supplied to rural areas (70,000 kilometers of high-tension lines, of which 45,000 had been strung in the Leap).

The most significant breakthrough was the discovery of new oil fields, which made China self-sufficient in oil by 1964 and is now turning her into a major oil producer and supplier. The Taching oil field, discovered entirely by the Chinese themselves, with its "self-reliance" spirit, remains a landmark and a model cited throughout China even today. From 1.3 million tons of oil produced in 1959, China would move to self-sufficiency by 1964, and top 50 million tons by 1974.

Soviet sabotage made retrenchment (called readjustment) imperative. Mao Tsetung viewed this readjustment as a necessary short-term measure, while Liu Shao-chi and the more "orthodox" economists tried to negate the long-term strategy of economic development Mao had unfolded and to return to more academic methods for the building of "socialism."

An article by Ke Ching-shih, mayor of Shanghai, denounced "economism" in October 1959. (Lenin had coined the term: theoretically it meant the "lagging of conscious leaders behind the spontaneous awakening of the masses."*) Ke Ching-shih castigates "some comrades" who think they can decide whether construction can be fast or slow, ignore the mighty power of mass action, replace the mass line with administrative decrees and technocratic regulations. The technological revolution is not the property of an elite technocracy; "it rests upon the masses being informed and enlightened."

"A number of groups grabbed the chance to impeach . . . the validity of Mao's economic philosophy and to run the nation on a command basis through the Communist Party instead of through mass participation," writes Goodstadt.† A characteristic of those groups was a return to the Liu Shao-chi pre-Leap policies. The emphatic note of profit as the standard by which production would be measured was contributed by Sun Yeh-fang, director of the Economic Research Institute of the

* V. I. Lenin *Economics and Politics in the Era of the Dictatorship of the Proletariat,* quoted by Ke Ching-shih. Also see Charles Bettelheim *Class Struggle in the USSR 1917–1923* (Paris 1974).

† Leo Goodstadt *Mao Tsetung: The Strategy of Plenty* (Hong Kong 1972).

Chinese Academy of Sciences. Sun Yeh-fang had been trained in the USSR, and in 1961 visited Soviet economists and returned to impart the Soviet economist Liberman's practices, boasting that he would "out-Liberman Liberman." He compared Mao's planning to that of "a chieftain of primitive tribes . . . with no head for the law of value." Politics in command was "a lazy man's idea." He denied class struggle. "The most important internal contradiction in a socialist economy is that between labor and product . . . value and use-value." All targets except profit targets should be abolished. "The writings of Sun Yeh-fang and similar groups were anti-Mao in style as well as content to such a degree that it was almost a deliberate insult to the Chairman."[*]

But it was not possible to return entirely to pre-Leap situations. The Leap had changed China. The working class had tasted power; a host of complaints about management had come out. With Sun Yeh-fang, Liu restored piecework, bonuses, and material incentives, issuing industrial regulations called the Ma Industrial Charter, based on the regulations in the Soviet Magnetogorsk Constitution. In August 1960 Li Fu-chun, chairman of the State Planning Commission, protested against this leap backward. The abolition of regulations and systems detrimental to production development had evoked the enmity of reactionaries both at home and abroad, and of modern revisionists, he writes. The gross output value in industry in 1958–1959 was 3.6 times that of the first five-year plan, demonstrating the vigor of the expanding base, which had compelled changes in the superstructure: decentralization, administrative improvement, time rates and not piecework, cadres participating in labor and workers in management, the triple alliance in schools (administrators, teachers, students), expanded collective welfare, increased personal income.

There was "still a big kingdom of necessity unknown to us in the socialist revolution," said Li Fu-chun, quoting Mao, who quoted Lenin that "freedom is understanding and solving the problems of the kingdom of necessity." There was still "blindness . . . some people still covet things big and modern . . . look down on small enterprises using modern or indigenous methods: walking on two legs."

The main thrust of the new economic policy was to put profit, "the forces of the market," in command of production. This may work satisfactorily in a capitalist, affluent society, but in a society where the prime need is to develop a living standard to create markets, profit

---

[*] Leo Goodstadt *Mao Tsetung: The Strategy of Plenty* (Hong Kong 1972).

becomes the worst possible means, leading to the impoverishment of the masses for the benefit of the few.

The word "profit" itself has a different meaning in a socialist society; it refers to the accumulation surplus in industry or agriculture and is always collective: state, province, county, etc. China's pricing system, as in every autarkic socialist country, is an arbitrary one; thus "profit" is an arbitrary measure of production and of efficiency.

"Comrade Mao Tsetung is the man in our Party who pays the greatest attention to seeking truth from reality," said Li Fu-chun. The new technocrats did not understand multi-purpose use of resources; they did not use the initiative and creativeness of the masses or seriously study techniques, and they cast aside the concept of self-reliance.

Ignoring the importance of supplying daily necessities, and the strategic significance of the small and medium enterprises, was a defect of profit economics. This secondary industrialization network was oriented to stable supply of necessities for local populations. If China were bombed, the large urban complexes would be destroyed, but the network of small and medium plants would assure regional self-sufficiency. China would be like a ship with many watertight compartments, unsinkable.

In March 1960, to indicate his disagreement with the return to material incentives which had already begun, Mao went to the great steel complex of Anshan in Manchuria.* The Leap had produced there a mighty workers' movement, the construction of two China-made blast furnaces, the opening of new mines. Anshan workers participated in the steel drive, organized a triple alliance of cadres, workers, and technical staff, and set up small and medium industries in rural areas. Mao walked through the complex, spent two days there, then assembled the administration, technical staff, and workers and spoke at length. What he said has become the Anshan Constitution for socialist industry, opposed to the Ma Industrial Charter promulgated by Liu. But it was not publicized until ten years later, in 1970.

"Politics in command." Without political orientation "one is like a body without a soul." Steel was made to serve the people, above all the countryside mechanization. There must be democratic Party leadership, mass line movements, initiative and consultation at all levels; participation of administrators in labor, of workers in decision making;

---

* The first steel plant there, erected by the Japanese, had been remodeled and much expanded with Soviet aid, technicians and machines under the first five-year plan.

reform of archaic rules and regulations; the triple alliance; promotion of the technological revolution; innovation by the workers; no blind faith or servile imitation; a truly scientific and critical attitude towards all industrial processes.*

As usual, obeisance was made to Mao's words. Interpretation and implementation, however, would decide the outcome. Party officials ordered Mao's speech "for study." Twelve regulations were issued which in practice bypassed all clauses except the triple alliance.

Decentralization was now eroded; rigid central command took over once again. Six regional bureaus of the Central Committee, for more effective central control, were set up. Reductions in capital expenditures, but first and foremost closures of small and medium enterprises, now took place. The ninth plenum of January 1961 recorded a directive for reduced construction in heavy industry, stress on consolidation. The speed of development was readjusted. And in December 1961 Liu Shao-chi issued to all cadres in factories, upon the advice of his team of technocrats and economists, the Seventy Articles of industrial policy. According to these, all industrial units not showing a profit should stop operation immediately. Piecework and bonuses were made official. Recruiting of new workers in the countryside was to be stopped for three years. The factory superintendent or manager was again the "person responsible."† Study time for political and cultural purposes was cut down to half an hour a week. A system of punishment and rewards was instituted. There could be no tinkering by workers on machines and no repairs or "innovation" unless in the presence of a qualified engineer; there must be strict obedience to orders, "discipline" of labor must be instituted.

Assets would be invested only in those sectors where efficiency and production was highest. There should be freedom in a free market to purchase raw materials and to dispose of output. "Factories which make money should be rewarded. . . . Those who lose money should be refused loans. . . . If you do not give workers a raise . . . they will not produce . . . with money one can make even a ghost turn a millstone," said Liu Shao-chi.

"Those branches of industry that do not give quick returns are cut back or halted . . . while priority is given to branches whose immediate help to agriculture or immediate returns from consumer will increase

* *People's Daily*, March 23, 1970, on the celebration of the tenth anniversary of the Anshan Constitution.

† One-man management.

the rhythm by which gains in agriculture feed industrial gains." These words are from Po I-po, minister of Heavy Industry, to Miss Strong in 1964.* The rural areas were no longer the priority target for manufactured goods. Consumer industry would cater to urban consumption. The sentence "immediate help to agriculture" was sinister; mechanization of agriculture was now retarded. That as late as 1964 these policies continued to be promoted shows how tenaciously the right wing countered Mao's line.

Shortage of investment resources, absence of foreign aid, were now seen as reasons to increase consumer goods for domestic and *foreign* markets — in essence, the production of luxury goods for foreign markets to compensate for grain purchases, which were projected as continuing even after recovery in 1962. But catering to foreign markets for foreign exchange to buy grain meant a dangerous slide into new dependence upon food imports, while Mao's main preoccupation was to make China invulnerable to outside pressure . . . and food is the most compelling pressure.

At this point the dangers of the new economic policy became most obvious. But such was the strength of the right wing that despite this obvious weakness in its rationale, it continued and persisted in its policies until 1965.

What makes the industrial picture in these years so confusing is that industry was divided into two different systems, with some complexes following the Mao line and others the Liu line. As a result, there would be two classes of workers, sometimes in the same industrial plant. Some workers would remain affected by the material incentive motivation; others, for the most part in the small and medium factories, following Mao's revolutionary industrial management. This would lead to conflict within the working class itself during the cultural revolution.

How can one evaluate the Soviet withdrawal of experts of July-August 1960, which inflicted such damage to Chinese industry?

It is certain that great harm was done, especially in the larger complexes. The Wuhan steel plant stopped functioning, Anshan was 80 percent paralyzed. Until 1966, a great many buildings for projected industrial plants would stand empty of workers and machinery. In 1961, visiting China, one was struck by the number of factory chimneys from which no smoke belched. But by 1969 they were all at work.

* Anna Louise Strong *Letters from China*, vol. II (Peking 1964), letters 11–20 (pages 44–60).

The Soviet sabotage, though temporarily crippling, had its beneficial side. It was now impossible *not* to practice self-reliance, ingenuity, resourcefulness, "walking on two legs," initiative, consultation. Equipment was kept going; by cannibalizing spare parts from some of their own machines, factories struggled on, running at 60 or 70 percent. And under these circumstances the triple alliance *had* to be maintained. Engineers were so much in demand that there had to be promotion from the working class itself.

Mao's call for self-reliance went deep into the working people. With their backs to the wall, the workers performed prodigies. This was not due to material incentives; it was due to a real awareness among the working class.

The main confrontation between the Mao and Liu policies occurred in the small and medium rural and provincial industrial network. The provinces and regions had furnished the bulk of investment for this alternate network. Even counties had invested in industry. The shutdown of any enterprise which did not show a profit created great discontent and hardship, as no money was returned to the regional investors; groups of unemployed workers were returned en masse to agricultural pursuits.

But something unexpected took place. The small and medium enterprises, in a number of cases, refused to close down. Supported by local cadres, they went on to "serve the people." This phenomenon resisted a heavy-handed rectification to enforce obedience in 1961.

During the cultural revolution numerous stories of resistance to closing down circulated.* A small factory in Hupeh which had begun to produce dynamo equipment in 1958 was ordered to make coal stoves in 1961. It returned to dynamo making, enlarged and expanded during the cultural revolution. A plant for electronic equipment near Shanghai refused to close; it is now a thriving concern, graced by a mango which is kept in preserving fluid under glass. Mao received some mangoes from a Pakistani delegation in 1969 and distributed them to enterprises and factories which had followed his line.

Although the "walk on two legs" policy was restated by Mao in February 1960 — "it is absolutely possible to operate a large number of small enterprises with greater, faster economic results" — by December 1961 the shutdowns had taken their toll, especially in remote or poorer provinces. What the workers described later as "control, choking,

---

* These stories had not been published at the time the events took place (1960–1965).

suppression" was carried out by investigation teams which judged a factory's viability by its accounting, not by its services to the people.

Agriculture was disrupted by the two-line struggle. Granting loans and technological aid only to those areas which showed "returns" (the 132 regions chosen by Liu Shao-chi) meant polarization. Poorer regions would get less, both in manufactured goods and in loans. With profit as the incentive, manufactured goods would automatically go first to urban areas, where salaries and circulating money were in abundance, or to the more wealthy rural counties. But the Leap had shown the dependence of industry on agriculture, and this relationship could no longer be denied. Agriculture, the foundation of the economy, would remain the major preoccupation. But there could be a return to the rich peasant line, favored by Liu in the early 1950's, if it were assumed that such a system would produce more.

The priority Mao had put on collectivization leading to rural mechanization and industrialization was downgraded, despite the lip service paid to it. Mechanization and electrification of agriculture would take "several five-year plans," and there was no need to collectivize the peasantry; let it just *produce*.

"The peasants have gained nothing from the collective economy . . . we must fall back . . . both in industry and agriculture, even to the extent of . . . allowing individual farming," said Liu Shao-chi in 1961.

In 1962 tractor stations were set up again on the Soviet model, the state claiming ownership and management. Tractors and farm machinery sold to the communes were removed,* but the money spent for them was not refunded.

The "four freedoms,"† first circulated in 1951, then in 1956, were again propagated among the cadres for "study." (They had been announcements issued without consultation with "other colleagues," Mao had stated in 1958.) They were now modified into the "three guarantees and one reward." The extension of private plots encouraged individual farming and destroyed the collective; the land for plots, originally no more than 5 percent of the total cultivated land, now rose to 15 or 20 percent. The free markets turned into lucrative black markets. Small enterprises were to be wholly responsible for their own profits

* November 1962: Decisions Concerning the Adjustment and Improvement of Tractor Station Work. From *Documents of Chinese Communist Party Central Committee: September 1956 to April 1969* (Union Research Institute, Hong Kong, 1971), vol. I.

† See page 27.

and losses; many went bankrupt. The fixing of output quotas on the basis of individual households meant piecework, and farming out jobs to households. The return of woman to the status of household adjunct, not a member with full rights, began to destroy the liberation of women. It made the peasantry withdraw their children from school to put them to work, and the school dropout increase, especially of girls, was marked. In the name of economy no new schools were built in rural areas; a good many were closed as "serving no useful purpose."

A policy appeared increasing acreage for industrial crops and lowering it for grain. This departure from the strategic policy of having each locality self-sufficient in grain, ensuring basic food in case of war, did not work well; transport scarcity occurred and hardship followed. Itinerant peasants began leaving the countryside, hiring themselves out to labor in cities. Procurement methods became harsh; a system of fines and punishments for "under quota" production was instituted, and "rewards" for "over quota."

The production teams, assured as the basic accounting unit in 1960, were unable to hold their accumulation funds. A struggle to raise living standards with less money made communes eat into their savings. The result was that no general improvement of living standards for the collective could planned, even if a minority of individual peasant families became better off.

A widely held view that the private plot was the salvation of the economy after the Leap is incorrect. Documents which reveal the actual hardships in the countryside show, for example, that in one county where private plots accounted for 11.3 percent of the land, the food grains produced on them were only 5.4 percent of total output.

The rectification campaign of early 1961 shifted the blame for shortcomings in the Leap to the lower cadres, although Mao Tsetung and Chou En-lai had stated that the Center "must take full responsibility for all errors." The movement encouraged rich and upper middle peasants to voice their rancor — as legitimate grievances — against the cadres. It returned influence to landlords and rich peasants. The cadres became resentful. They shut their eyes to what was going on, "not daring to render active leadership any more." Nine cadres in Paoan county, from the Hsinwei production brigade, wrote that since rules and regulations were constantly changing they had better "do nothing and thus never be wrong."

Liu Shao-chi issued the Sixty Regulations for agriculture, a pendant to his Seventy Articles for industry. These officialized the "three guarantees and one reward" policy. The power of the commune to organize labor was rescinded; total control of each production team as to land, tools, and labor power was fixed; accounting at team level was to last for thirty years. The mess halls were abolished. The communes were forbidden to open or run any new enterprises; no enterprises must remain save "those directly serving agricultural production."

In November 1963 an Agricultural Bank was created, ostensibly to effect low-interest loans, totaling 670 million yuan, to the rural areas. Through financial control of the rural areas, in the name of "stopping waste and practicing economy," the bank would effectively starve out the persistent small industrial enterprises, recall previous loans in areas where the peasants were recalcitrant and pursued the Mao line. A *People's Daily* editorial of January 1964, entitled *Advance from Victory to Victory*, on the inauguration of a new agricultural policy under which resources were to be centered on certain key agricultural areas, "to push forward irrigation projects and other types of capital construction and extend the area of farmland on which crops are protected and output stable," would confirm this polarization into two categories of countryside, the one being deprived at the expense of the other.

Had these policies been continued for some more years, the gap between city and countryside, Center and province, worker and peasant, Party and masses, would have widened. As in industry, there was a surge of resistance. In some communes the "three guarantees and one reward" policy was rejected by the peasant associations, who clung to the collective. Party cadres and activists led the peasant associations against the directives, which favored rich peasants. Thus the two-line struggle divided the land; some communes followed the Liu line, some the Mao line.

Despite this latent turmoil, agriculture by 1963 had recovered from the three bad years. In rural areas too the Leap had begun to pay off. Local irrigation projects continued and better crops were reaped; the small industrial network could not be made to disappear, and hydroelectric works, medium and small, began to alter the pattern of labor in many villages.

The new economic policy was not the only manifestation of the Liu line. The shift from output targets to profit targets, the changeover from control by Party leadership to control by managerial staff, meant that "expert rather than Red" became the sought-after ideal. It meant depolitization for the young; the accent on technical excellence; a return to personal ambition, anxiety for success, selfishness and not service. It displaced the focus for progress and prosperity from revolutionary endeavor to technological efficiency. It inevitably and very swiftly set education back to before 1958.

The first thing that went by the board was manual labor for the higher intelligentsia, although lip service continued to be paid to it and "a month a year" of labor was officialized. Students sent out to labor were surrounded by careful regulations.* Manual labor became a farce. On the other hand, because of the stringent food conditions in the cities, urban denizens were being evacuated to the countryside, especially those of peasant origin. It is reckoned that three to five million people were enjoined to go to live in rural areas.

The link between factory and technical college was dissolved. So was youth integration with worker and peasant. A Ministry of Higher Education and one of Lower Education operated two types of education; the lower one continued to show interest in the part work, part labor educational system begun in 1958, but the best teachers, equipment, material went to the projects for training specialists — and the youth selected for these higher institutes tended to be sons and daughters of higher cadres and the bourgeoisie.

Personal excellence, ambition, good connections, and a desire to become "a high-level cadre" replaced self-sacrifice and a revolutionary sense of unity. Teachers went back to teaching in the peremptory, no-argument manner. Examinations returned.

Another "hundred flowers" now blossomed in 1961, but it was a very different movement. No more mass supervision; no more "open door" and *tatzepao*. It assembled intellectuals in symposia. These had received, during the three bad years, special rations of oil and meat. Now they were encouraged to hold "meetings of immortals," or round-table talks. (The term "meetings of immortals" was coined by the erudite Wu Han, vice-mayor of Peking, playwright, and author of the *Hai Jui* articles, who found this classical title becoming for these distinguished discussions.) The intelligentsia could, through such gatherings, become "socialist" without losing face — that is, without being subject to criticism — by "mutual assistance and mutual enlightenment." The questions debated ranged from literature to education, from philosophy to the reform of language. "Let a hundred flowers blossom and a hundred

---

* To make sure they did not work too hard. For instance, they were not allowed to lift heavy weights, and girl students were given eight days off per month during their periods.

schools of thought contend *in academic research,"* wrote *Peking Review* on March 24, 1961. This restored the privileged role of the literocracy as an authoritative group.

The Culture and Propaganda departments were active supporters of this "blooming." The ubiquitous Chou Yang, ever alert to shifting power, made official speeches of pompous and unimpeachable correctness, and unofficial speeches which contained reverse instructions. "Among the most vigorous challengers of Mao's policies were the top officials in the Propaganda Department's literary establishment, the very people who directed the imposition of controls on the intellectuals in the earlier periods," writes Merle Goldman.[*]

In August 1962 at a meeting of the literati in Talien, Chou Yang attacked Mao's line in art and literature, the Great Leap Forward ("a great tragedy"), the communes ("rash action"), mass campaigns ("rustic peasant style"). He sponsored writers who claimed that the shortcomings and errors of life must be depicted, that middle characters (not proletarian heroes) must be described. But to foreign visitors he spoke impeccable Mao-ese.

In the summer of 1962 *How to Be a Good Communist* by Liu Shao-chi was reprinted as compulsory reading for all cadres. The new edition was to run into 60 million copies, whereas Mao's four volumes sold only 14 million copies.[†] Nowhere in this revised edition of Liu's work was there mention of the dictatorship of the proletariat. The Party, by "self-cultivation" (a Confucian notion) of its individual members, can maintain its ideological purity and create a proletarian state. There was no mention of the battle against revisionism in which Mao was engaged. The Thought of Mao was not mentioned. There are veiled references to the "impetuosity" and "destructiveness" of some comrades — "the one who considers himself as a Marx or a Lenin . . . who demands veneration . . . who has not really been selected but considers himself a leader."[‡]

In November 1962 Liu Shao-chi went to Chufou, the birthplace of Confucius, and there paid respects to the memory of the sage. A symposium was held, attended by prestigious philosophers, historians and writers, to restore Confucius to veneration. Confucius and his disciple

---

[*] Merle Goldman "The Unique 'Blooming and Contending' of 1961–62," *China Quarterly*, no. 37 (January-March 1969), page 69.

[†] In some organizations, thirty people had to share one Mao volume to read. Author's personal contacts.

[‡] In his self-criticism, Liu said: "In 1962 when *How to Be a Good Communist* was reprinted, this was revised for me by someone else."

Mencius were considered worth emulating, and by 1963 pictures of both would be in the Historical Museum of Peking.

Attacks on Mao continued and amplified. A play entitled *The Dismissal of Hai Jui* appeared, once again by Wu Han. First published in November 1960, staged in Peking in February 1961, Wu Han's play went further than his previous essays, for a chant is repeated by a chorus of actors portraying peasants: "Return to us our land! Return to us our land!" A forceful way of demanding a return to individual farming.

Wu Han and others wrote on Confucius, praising his moral outlook, the qualities of loyalty, devotion, integrity which irrespective of class should be "passed on" to youth.

Teng To, former editor of *Red Flag* and *People's Daily*, Lin Mo-han, director of the cultural department of the Peking Municipal Party Committee, and Liao Mo-sha, a journalist, wrote a series entitled *Evening Talks at Yenshan*, which ran for about eighteen months (1961–1962) in the *Peking Evening News* and was also reproduced in *Frontline*, the theoretical fortnightly of the Peking Municipal Party Committee. Teng To's attacks on Mao were filled with innuendo, satire, using historical figures to deride Mao.

Teng To, Wu Han, and Liao Mo-sha also published a widely reprinted column entitled *Notes from a Three-Family Village*. One article, *A Special Treatment for Amnesia* (No. 14, 1962), is particularly excoriating: "People suffering from amnesia . . . do not keep their word . . . it leads to abnormal pleasure or anger . . . finally insanity. . . . Such a person must be put to rest, must not talk or do anything. . . . In the past the cure was to pour dog's blood on the sufferer's head." The Leap was ridiculed in the anecdote of a farmer who had one egg and dreamed this egg would hatch many chickens and procure him wealth. In another article occurs the phrase "Winter will soon be over . . . all things will show vitality in the thaw." Mao's sentence "The east wind prevails over the west wind" was mocked; in an article entitled *Big Empty Talk* Teng To wrote: "I want to offer my friends who are fond of big empty talk some advice: read more, think more, talk less."

A philosophical controversy on the theory of contradiction also took place. Yang Hsien-chen, vice-president of the Marx-Lenin Institute for Higher Cadres in 1949 and chief instructor for theoretical studies for higher cadres, in the late 1950's had begun philosophical controversy on the non-identity of thought and reality, on the "two categories of identity" and other philosophical themes. His arguments countered Mao's dialectical approach to ideological problems. Mao Tsetung countered these ideological attacks, although he ignored the persistent satire and malice of such works as *Three-Family Village*.

In May 1963 Mao would make a speech: *Where Do Correct Ideas Come From?* It was a philosophical thesis on conceptual knowledge and the process of cognition, which needs the test of practice to accomplish "leaps" in getting closer to truth. "Among our comrades there are many who do not yet understand . . . that matter can be transformed into consciousness and consciousness into matter." This phrase, which subsumes Mao's dialectical mind and is the underlying theory for the cultural revolutions, was opposed strenuously by Yang Hsien-chen, who expounded that contradictions could be resolved by "uniting their opposites" (two unite into one). Yang affirmed that the link between the opposites in a unity could not be split; and that the correct application of dialectics, the correct solution of contradictions, was how to reunite two opposites.

Yang's theory was not only the reverse of Mao's; it was also an attack on Mao's ideological battle with Khrushchev. It opposed Mao's policy of no compromise with revisionism, and it came at a time when Mao was saying that a split could not be avoided: that true Marxist-Leninists must form new Communist parties and withdraw from "revisionist" parties. While Mao carried on the polemics with the USSR leadership, he was being contradicted in the most authoritative institute for training Marxist-Leninist theoreticians in China.

In 1971* the link between Yang Hsien-chen's philosophical theories and the economic thinking of Liu Shao-chi was exposed. It was then revealed that since 1949 Yang had supported Liu's policies by giving them a "Marxist" foundation. First in the transition period (1949–1955), when he upheld the necessity for "composite sectors" in the economy; second, during the Leap period (1957–1960), when he denied the dialectical identity between being and thinking (that a change in thinking could actively transform the material world); and again in 1964, when the "two unite into one" theory was calculated to stop Mao in his battle against revisionism in the USSR. These philosophical and economic battles were part of one and the same struggle, indivisible as Mao's confrontation against "revisionism" on the international plane and against "revisionism" in China.

* *Peking Review*, February 2, April 26, May 24, 1971.

11

Mao Tsetung Against Revisionism, 1960–1962

I am a person with many shortcomings . . . I have only begun recently
to study economics, but . . . I study with determination, and will go on
till I die . . . otherwise when the time comes for me to see Marx, I shall
be in a fix. If he asks me questions I can't answer, what shall I do?
— Attributed to MAO TSETUNG, 1959

In the autumn of 1960, aghast at the implications of a split between
the USSR and China, the Indonesian, Vietnamese, Italian and Japanese Communist parties had pressed for an all-parties conference. A
twenty-six-strong drafting committee, representing twelve Communist
parties in power and fourteen not in power, was to prepare a joint
platform to restore unity, and organize a meeting in November of 1960
in Moscow.

In the preparatory gatherings the Chinese submitted a draft with
five proposals which asked for strict adherence to the declaration and
manifesto of the 1957 Moscow meeting; respect for the equality between all Communist parties and all socialist countries; settlement of
all disputes through comradely and unhurried discussion on all important questions of common concern; a clear demarcation to be made
between imperialism, "the enemy," and socialist countries; and adequate and full preparation for "a program of united struggle against
imperialism."

But Khrushchev was a man in a hurry. He wanted another summit
meeting with the President-elect of the United States. The American
elections took place in that November, and Khrushchev was determined to meet the new American President, John Kennedy, with a
massive demonstration of solidarity in the socialist camp to strengthen
his hand.

Eighty-one Communist parties assembled in Moscow in November

to begin the lengthy discussions. The Chinese delegation was prestigious: Liu Shao-chi; Teng Hsiao-ping, the secretary-general; Peng
Chen, the Peking mayor; Kang Sheng, and many others.

The original draft proposals submitted by the Soviet side to the
drafting committee banned "factionalism," reiterated the peaceful
transition theory, and made majority decisions binding upon all parties.

Teng Hsiao-ping expressed the Chinese line. He accused "modern
revisionists" of violating the 1957 declaration and of capitulation to
imperialism. He insisted the minority could not be bound by majority
decisions because "the minority was sometimes right" (Mao's words)
and what applied inside a party could not apply between fully equal
and independent parties. No one could ram through hurried decisions
on weighty matters. Teng Hsiao-ping cited Lenin, who had been in the
minority in his great battle against revisionism in the Second International, yet had been correct.

Voluminous articles in the Chinese press explained what the debate
was about. The principal target was the concept of peaceful transition
to socialism. "For the proletariat and the masses to take political
power, smash the old reactionary state machine, is one thing. It is quite
another, having taken power, to proceed to the peaceful socialist transformation of the system. . . . Only when the former [state of having
taken power] exists can the latter be done." "It is muddleheaded to
confuse these two." "No Marxist-Leninist Party . . . advocates . . . resort
to war between states to spread revolution, and least of all the Chinese
Party . . . the modern revisionists and certain muddleheaded people pit
the revolutions in the various countries against world peace, alleging
that revolution cannot be carried out if world peace is to be preserved.
This is preposterous."

After three weeks of wrangling and hours of speeches, a document
emerged from the eighty-one-party conference containing clauses
which Mao still considered too much of a compromise. The final statement referred both to armed struggle and to the peaceful "parliamentary road" to socialism, but did not make commitment to the latter
binding upon parties, as Khrushchev had sought. The sovereignty of
each socialist country was reasserted, and the socialist camp was defined as "a social, economic, and political cooperation between sovereign states." Khrushchev's power to speak in the name of an assembly
of countries was thus curtailed.* The USSR Communist Party was

---

* See "The 1960 Moscow Statement," *World Marxist Review* (Moscow), December 1960.

referred to as the vanguard and not as the leader of the world movement.

A paragraph in the torrentially long declaration is worth noting as probably due to Mao. It says that historical experience proves that capitalist ideas remain in the human consciousness even after the installation of socialism, therefore all parties should continue education of the masses and of their own parties. But the Soviet leader also inserted a clause stating that "the restoration of capitalism has been made socially and economically impossible" in socialist countries, contradicting Mao's view that "who will win out, socialism or capitalism . . . is not yet settled."

The declaration was a hodgepodge, and lassitude may have been a factor. But the conference had shown that the Chinese thesis had a dozen parties siding with it. Even the majority support to the USSR, despite the reverence and prestige with which "the fount of socialism" was still regarded, was not entire; there was a fairish middle section of parties who, disagreeing with China, would nevertheless not agree totally with the USSR. Among the latter, the Italian Party would distinguish itself with a diffuse theory of polycentrism and a quarrel with the Chinese and Russian parties.

Mao would later state that by admitting partly the thesis of peaceful transition, the Chinese Communist Party had laid itself open to criticism. This was the last time that China would, for the sake of conciliation, accept even part compromise, he said. Chinese newspapers reiterated that the principle of the minority submitting to the majority was valid within a party, for discipline, but could not apply to relations between equal parties or between sovereign states.

The Chinese watched the American presidential election with as much attention as the Russians, and with no little anxiety. Since 1958 relations with America had not improved, although the shelling of the offshore islands had revealed many critics of American foreign policy within America itself, and they would become more numerous as the McCarthy hysteria abated. But the Chinese felt that Kennedy was far more militarily adventurous than Eisenhower.

In 1959 the *Washington Post* reported that some senators (Warren Magnuson and Clair Engle) were calling for a moderate revision of China policy; "the Red China taboo shows signs of having passed its peak some time ago." But the China issue was not a pressing political issue in the election campaign. "This is not a proper time for the recognition of Red China," stated Kennedy. He also said that he hoped to bring China into the nuclear test ban negotiations.

On September 8, 1960, a *Peking Review* editorial condemned the American attitude; more than a hundred ambassadorial meetings had been held since August 1, 1955, when the talks began; yet on the three items on the agenda — Taiwan, return of American prisoners, trade and cultural exchanges and reciprocal visits by journalists — the U.S. was obdurate. There was renewed vigor in the condemnation of U.S. imperialism, as a warning to Khrushchev that the Chinese too were talking with the Americans, but that they were unyielding on matters of principle.

It is certain that Mao thought Kennedy, in spite of his liberal reputation, more aggressive towards Asia than Eisenhower. Mao freely expressed his opinion of Kennedy in talks with visitors during 1961–1963. "Kennedy would dare to do what Eisenhower would not do." Kennedy gustily announced "new frontiers" for the U.S., and Mao predicted that the U.S. would now re-enter Asia militarily. The Chinese entertained little hope of America's changing her China policy soon. "It will take a few more lessons of history for imperialism to weaken, but its nature will not change." Kennedy's statement that "our task is to rebuild the strength of the free world" heralded toughness to come.

For some months in early 1961 the Sino-Soviet dispute subsided. In January Khrushchev appeared conciliatory in a speech at the Supreme Soviet. "We must not talk about who won or who lost at this eighty-one-party conference."

Those who approached Mao then saw him confident and well, though reported abroad as ailing. He worked prodigious hours, preparing massive documentation on Marxist-Leninist theses in order to "reason revisionism to death." He saw many delegations, from Asia, Africa, Europe, from Japan and Latin America, and gave them hours of his time. To all he expounded the need for struggle against imperialism, and China's support for national liberation movements. Chinese aid projects went out to many Third World countries, and Mao refused to cut down aid. "Even if we go trouserless, we will uphold proletarian internationalism."

During those troubled months Mao seems to have taken comfort in the famous classic tale *The Western Pilgrimage*. As others seek solace in some cherished novel, childhood tale or holy book, Mao turned to the great story that has fascinated generations of Chinese children. Like *The Pilgrim's Progress* or Homer's *Odyssey*, *The Western Pilgrimage* is a saga, a long and arduous journey through many difficulties in quest of truth. In this case it is based on the real travels of Hsuan Tsang, a Buddhist who in the sixth century went to India to seek the

Buddhist scriptures. The novel, fantastic and delightful, first appeared in 1650 and has never stopped circulating since. The latest edition, in 1972, saw ten million copies sold in a week.

Throughout the novel the abbot Hsuan Tsang is overshadowed by the fantastic, unforgettable figure of the Monkey, an ape with supernatural gifts and eyes like carbuncles of fire, who despises heavenly laws and earthly bureaucrats, breaks into Paradise, burning the files of mortals (after which no one could die on earth) and eating the (forbidden) peaches of immortality. Condemned to burial under a rock for many thousands of years, he is released to accompany the abbot on his perilous journey in search of truth. Many adventures befall them; Hsuan Tsang regularly falls into traps and ambushes laid by wily demons, wicked devils, and is every time rescued by "the great sage equal to heaven," a name which the Monkey has awarded to himself.

The Monkey, a well-beloved folk figure, is the epitome of man, in all his fearlessness, intrepidity, revolt. Vital, boisterous, rude, yet devoted, the Monkey sees through the counterfeit and the dissembling.

Mao seems to have identified the battle against revisionism with this search for truth, and himself (a little) with the Monkey. Perhaps someone said of him that he was a great troublemaker, and Mao's retort might well have been that he was "without law or heaven," a self-deprecating pun, meaning an unrepentant rebel,* like the Monkey. By 1961 episodes from the novel were being played in opera houses and shown in movie theaters in China, especially one depicting the Monkey's struggle against a devil which assumes the guise of a beautiful maiden, but is actually a skeleton of white bones.

That Mao was thinking of the Monkey is clear in a statement to Edgar Snow in 1960: "It is correct to say that we, on our part, will shoulder the responsibility of world peace whether or not the United States recognizes China . . . We will not defy all laws, human and divine, *like the Monkey King who stormed the palace of heaven.* We want to maintain world peace. We do not want war."†

In the summer of 1961 Kuo Mo-jo, the erudite president of the Academy of Sciences, wrote a poem to Mao:

---

* This phrase Mao also quoted to Snow in December 1970, saying he was *wu fa wu t'ien,* which Snow translated as "a monk with a leaky umbrella" — not altogether a correct translation. See Edgar Snow "A Conversation with Mao Tsetung," *Life* magazine, April 30, 1971, pages 46–48.

† Edgar Snow "Red China's Leaders Talk Peace — On Their Terms," *Look* magaine, January 31, 1961, pages 86–88.

Disorder reigns,
Man and demon, good and evil are confused.
The Abbot was kind to foe and spiteful to friends.
Endlessly intoning prayers,
Three times he let the demon flee.
He deserves to be hacked to pieces!
The wise monkey plucks but a hair and conquers.
All praise to his timely teaching,
Even the pig overcomes his ignorance.

The Monkey is the discerning Mao, piercing through the disguise of the "white-boned devil" — revisionism. The Monkey could turn each hair of his body into a small fighting monkey, a pun on Mao's use of his Chinese brush to write polemical articles against revisionism, and also on his name, Mao, which means "hair." The pig* represents those who care only for immediate material gain, therefore incipient revisionists. But is the abbot Khrushchev?

In November 1961 Mao would reply to Kuo Mo-jo.

Thunderstorms shake the earth.
A malignant demon is born of white bones.
The deluded abbot is not beyond teaching;
But the wicked spirit works great havoc.

Wrathful, the Golden Monkey swings his massive cudgel,
And the jade firmament is cleared of dust.
Today call upon the Sagacious Ape,
For miasmatic evil again mists the world.

In Mao's reply it is not so clear who the abbot is; one begins to suspect it is no longer Khrushchev alone but also the revisionists in China itself whom Mao had in mind. He still considers them "not beyond teaching." "The Abbot should not be torn limb from limb. It is good to follow a united front policy with *those who stand in the middle*," Mao wrote to Kuo Mo-jo. And certainly Khrushchev was not "standing in the middle" by then.

In October 1961 the CPSU held its Twenty-second Congress. Mao Tsetung sent a cordial message, and Chou En-lai led a delegation to

* Also a character in *The Western Pilgrimage*.

Moscow for the occasion. The new Russian Party program was promulgated. It said that the USSR was already "a State of the whole people" and its Party "a Party of all the People." Communism was now being built. The dictatorship of the proletariat was no longer necessary, since there were no more classes. The program called for material incentives as stimulant to production. In his speech Khrushchev offered a nonaggression pact between Warsaw Pact and NATO countries, a European security conference, and repeated his line of the "parliamentary road to socialism." "The working class can, even before capitalism is overthrown, compel the bourgeoisie to carry out measures that transcend ordinary reform."

And then Khrushchev attacked by name Albania, absent, uninvited, and since the summer of 1961 deprived of aid, experts and machinery as China had been. On December 3, 1971, the Albanians would reveal why. In the summer of 1961 Khrushchev had demanded that Albania allow him to install missile sites there in order to dominate the Mediterranean. Albania had refused. Hence the economic reprisals. The USSR, said Khrushchev, would not give in to "Albanian dogmatists" *nor to anyone else* on questions of principle. The naming of Albania, a deliberate provocation, was a very serious matter.

Chou En-lai sat, expressionless. There was excited speculation. Would Chou defend the Albanians and be responsible for a split? Or would he ignore Khrushchev's attack and sacrifice Albania to "unity"?

On the next day Chou replied: "We hold that a dispute or difference arising between fraternal parties should be resolved patiently . . . in the spirit of proletarian internationalism. Any public, one-sided censure of any fraternal party does not help unity." The CCP hoped for unity on the basis of mutual respect, independence and equality between parties. He then left the platform without shaking hands with Khrushchev. The next morning Chou went to Moscow's Red Square to lay wreaths on the tombs of Stalin and Lenin. He left Moscow the following day, alleging pressing matters in Peking. Within a fortnight the body of Stalin was removed from Red Square. Chou was received at the Peking airport by Mao in person as a gesture of approval for his stand in Moscow.

Khrushchev now chose to reactivate the war of words with China because of the "summit" with Kennedy he hoped to gain thereby. This exercise has now become devalued through repetition, but at the time Khrushchev made it sound as if the world would explode into war unless he had his summit. He must see Kennedy. There was acute tension over Berlin. The Russians had started a series of nuclear underground explosions and upped the military budget; so had the United States. The Wall was erected between East and West Berlin.

Khrushchev blamed Mao and his intransigence for his failure to make headway with Kennedy. The growing power of the Red Army within the CPSU Central Committee exerted pressure for a "hard line." There was the discomfort of finding the Chinese theses discussed in each Communist Party; the CPSU's infallibility was questioned. A chain reaction of new ideological and political ferment had started and threats could not stop it. In the USSR, Molotov had written to the Central Committee to criticize the program of the Twenty-second Congress; others, like Bulganin, also disagreed.

Kennedy was definitely proving more aggressive; there was an ugly war brewing in South Vietnam, where American military advisers were sent. Ngo Dinh Diem was proving another Syngman Rhee; there was an undeclared war in Laos . . . all of Indochina was threatened.

In November 1961 Alexei Adjubei, Khrushchev's son-in-law, director-editor of *Izvestia*, on a visit to the U.S. saw Kennedy, who put forward harsh demands: unification of Germany on American terms; the western powers must occupy West Berlin; there must be "effective inspection" within Soviet territory of its armaments before disarmament could be considered; the U.S. must have the right to oppose the government of Castro in Cuba; the "independence and neutrality" of Laos must be respected; the USSR should cooperate in keeping the peace for "twenty years" in Asia, Africa and Latin America (the latter clauses meant that the U.S. and USSR must cooperate to put down the "brush-fires" of national liberation movements everywhere in the Third World); and there must be a "free choice" for the peoples of Eastern Europe.

At the same time a conference in Geneva was being held on the Laotian situation, covering as well the brewing war in other parts of Indochina. The Chinese found an approachable Averell Harriman, quite a different person from Dulles. "Should the U.S. withdraw its armed forces in the Straits of Taiwan and in Taiwan the dispute could be settled peacefully," repeated Foreign Minister Chen Yi, present at Geneva. The conference on Laotian neutrality did not bring peace to Indochina, and the U.S., who did not sign the Geneva agreement, introduced more weapons and troops into the area; but it did provide an opportunity for meetings, and Khrushchev realized that public opinion in the United States was changing, demanding more "flexibility" in the policies towards China. What if America chose the dialogue with China rather than with the USSR as its priority?

Meanwhile, the need to form a world united front against aggression and imperialism was stressed by Mao on all occasions. Chou En-lai negotiated successful frontier demarcations with Burma, Nepal, and Outer Mongolia. Only India and the USSR remained obdurate on the need to delineate borders. "Try as hard as I might, I could not bring Nehru to see that it was in our common interest for us to sit down and talk quietly and arrive at a satisfactory settlement," said Chou En-lai.*

Mao and Chou were laying the strategy of a united front of the "intermediate zone," irrespective of national political systems, against imperialism, whatever its source. Kennedy was well aware that China was a challenger in a field where America was particularly vulnerable — American domination of sources of raw materials in the Third World. He looked to Khrushchev to subdue China in this. 1962 was to be known as the year of "containment" of China. With Dean Rusk now at the State Department, did America also hope the USSR would help in this containment?† The growing number of votes for China's admission to the United Nations led to a motion suggested by the United States (December 1961), presented by New Zealand, specifying the question of China's representation as one of "importance" requiring assent by a two-thirds majority of the General Assembly. China angrily denounced this decision, but it was a measure of China's influence and prestige in the Third World.

In April 1962 Mao, receiving the secretary-general of the All-African People's Conference in Peking, warned that there would be rapid escalation of U.S. militarism in Southeast Asia. He said Kennedy was merely "putting more ropes around his neck . . . lifting a stone to drop it on his own feet" in Vietnam.

"Khrushchev is hitting his head against nails," he commented, watching Khrushchev's antics to get a summit with Kennedy. A major clash between China and the USSR took place at the Afro-Asian Writers' Conference in Cairo in February 1962. The marked support which China got from Third World delegations did not go unheeded. At Punta del Este, where the foreign ministers of the Organization of American States met in January, the U.S. delegation was able to get interventionist resolutions passed regarding Cuba. And then in the

* Interview with author.
† See David Halberstam *The Best and the Brightest* (New York 1972).

erstwhile Belgian Congo* Russia suffered a defeat. Khrushchev had to do something, force a parley on Kennedy, subdue the rising criticism in the Third World. It was clear now that the triumph or disaster of the policies of China, the USSR, and the United States would, in the final analysis, be played out in the "intermediate zone."

Again a coincidence. In the summer of 1962 border conflicts erupted between Russia and China, and also between India and China. Jawaharlal Nehru, the Indian prime minister, continued to refuse border negotiations except on his own terms, and also continued to lay claim to large tracts of territory which had not previously been included in maps as Indian.†

In November 1961 Nehru, who had continually accused China of being expansionist, made charges of incursion. Hostility escalated to active military preparation (called in India the "forward" policy) for a showdown with China. The Indians relied on intelligence which described China as on the verge of collapse; in May 1962 Nehru talked of China's "continuous bad harvests" and the resulting "explosive situation."‡

Against the advice of some Indian generals, Nehru and his socialist defense minister, Krishna Menon, planned a military initiative in the Himalayas. Although Chou En-lai had shown himself conciliatory,§ Nehru felt in need of a "show of force." In the same month Khrushchev would have his "show of force" over Cuba.

Just as Khrushchev was disturbed by Chinese inroads in ideology, Nehru was moved at China's growing popularity with the non-aligned nations. Nehru considered that India must be head of the non-aligned, and in September 1961, at the summit conference of non-aligned states in Belgrade, there had appeared a man in a frenzy, brandishing the specter of nuclear warfare and calling for peace at any price. He was termed a "man of peace" by the western press.

Border clashes between the USSR and China also took place in the summer of 1962 in Sinkiang. "In April and May 1962 the leaders of the CPSU used their organs and personnel in Sinkiang, China, to carry out

* Now called Zaire.

† See *People's Daily* Editorial Department *The Revolution in Tibet and Nehru's Philosophy*, May 6, 1959.

‡ China had good harvests from 1963 onward.

§ Offering "to maintain the status quo of the border, and not seek to change it by unilateral action or by force, and making partial and provisional agreements through negotiations." See *The Sino-Indian Boundary Question* (Peking 1962), page 75.

large-scale subversive activities in the Illi region and enticed and coerced several tens of thousands of Chinese citizens into going to the Soviet Union." The national minorities in Illi were told by Soviet radio to flee because the Chinese would massacre them. Panic, through Soviet agents, was created. The Chinese kept quiet about these incidents, but they were well known in India.

On October 8, 1962, the Soviet ambassador in Peking was told by the Chinese Foreign Ministry that India was about to launch a massive attack on the frontier. Soviet helicopters and planes were being used for transporting military supplies to the border. "Should India attack we would defend ourselves."

The American ambassador to India, John Kenneth Galbraith, had also warned his government about these preparations but did not attempt to exert a moderating influence on India. It would be left to General Maxwell Taylor to blurt out the truth at a meeting of the Senate Foreign Relations Committee, later that year.

On October 10 there were patrol clashes; on October 12 Nehru instructed the Indian Eastern Command to "drive out" the Chinese; on October 14 the *People's Daily* published a formal appeal: "Mr. Nehru, it is time to withdraw from the brink of the precipice." "We will fight to the last man, to the last gun," replied Krishna Menon. Heavy artillery attacks from the Indian side took place. On October 20 and 24 the Chinese made proposals for the peaceful disengagement of troops and for negotiations, as well as for a cease-fire. India ignored the calls and on October 20 launched a massive advance. The Chinese troops moved on October 22.

By November 16 the Chinese counterattack had pushed the Indian troops back and penetrated into Indian territory. The world clamored "aggression." In India panic set in; there was no preparedness for the swift debacle. On November 21 the Chinese unilaterally ordered a cease-fire and withdrew their troops to twenty kilometers behind the line of actual control as it existed on November 7, 1959. China then announced the freeing of captured personnel (six hundred) and the return of all equipment without compensation. A call for resumption of negotiations was made by Chou En-lai. In China itself the action was compared to a famous episode in the Three Kingdoms, when Chinese troops seven times captured and seven times released Mong Aw, a Burmese princeling who carried raids into China. Mong Aw then repented and became a friend.

Pravda, on November 25, wrote that the attack had been from the

Indian side and that the proposals by the Chinese government for negotiations were "constructive." But on December 12 Khrushchev, at the Supreme Soviet, said, "These areas . . . have very little population . . . it is impossible to believe that India wants war."

There followed some months of diplomatic exchanges; other Third World countries wanted to mediate.* But India's attitude has been that no negotiations can be entertained unless the Indian claim to contested territory is first accepted as valid. "India's refusal to negotiate weakens the legitimacy of her resort to arms," has noted the English historian John Gittings.† The border has remained "inactive" now for over twelve years.

Despite adverse propaganda, China's unilateral withdrawal enhanced her prestige in the Third World. It destroyed Nehru's credibility and caused the resignation of Krishna Menon. China's refusal to exploit her victory, adding magnanimity's halo to victory's laurels, seems to rankle still with some Indian diehards. Nevertheless, in India itself, the army generals whose good sense had not prevailed wrote a small spate of books on the subject. Nehru was to die two years later, embittered by this self-sought defeat.

The shattering event in the autumn of 1962 was the missile crisis in Cuba. This crisis was Khrushchev's means of getting the dialogue with the U.S. going. Checkmated in the Congo, thwarted by China, confronted by Kennedy combativeness, with escalation of American military activity in Southeast Asia, with increasing restiveness among the "satellites," with the Berlin crisis, Khrushchev designed the Cuba maneuver to focus world attention upon the *indispensability* of dialogue between the two superpowers, who alone could make war and peace for the rest. It would place the USSR as equal, the sole valid partner of the U.S. in a dual hegemony over the globe.

The Cuba crisis remains a many-sided historical episode. Castro's own testimony is conflicting. In January 1962 he received from the Russians a report that Kennedy had asserted the right of the U.S. to intervene in Cuba, since a Communist state in the Caribbean destroyed the world balance of power (the declaration at the Punta del Este meeting). The Cuban government then concluded an agreement with

* See Premier Chou En-lai *Letter to the Leaders of Asian and African Countries on the Sino-Indian Boundary Question*, November 15, 1962 (English edition Peking 1973).

† In private interview with author, and also in his lectures and articles on the subject.

the USSR for defensive weapons. The invasion attempt at the Bay of Pigs in 1961 had been a fiasco; would there be another U.S. attempted invasion in 1962?

In September U.S. spy planes over Cuba detected missile silos; on September 13 Kennedy warned Khrushchev that if offensive weapons, a danger to U.S. security, were installed, necessary measures would be taken. Khrushchev assured Kennedy that there were no offensive weapons in Cuba. Castro himself was to tell a French journalist on March 23, 1963, that the USSR had proposed missiles in Cuba to "reinforce the socialist camp." (This report was later denied by Castro.)

On October 14 and 15 spy planes photographed the cigar-shaped missiles and their storage silos. But Kennedy, after the Bay of Pigs, was chary of CIA reports and their accuracy. "The Russians can't be such fools." For a week he hesitated, but on October 22 informed Prime Minister Harold Macmillan and President de Gaulle, and at seven that night, on television, the American people. The decision to blockade Cuba, to inspect all Soviet ships on the high seas, and to prepare for war was announced. Kennedy warned that any missile attack anywhere against the western world would provoke "total retaliation" against the USSR. This was indeed, or so it appeared, nuclear confrontation! It terrorized many in the West and in Japan, where some writers even contemplated suicide before the last day of the world.*

Everything now seemed to depend on Khrushchev and Kennedy. On October 24 the Tass agency issued a serious warning to the U.S., asserting all material on Cuba was defensive and refusing inspection of ships on high seas. A terrified Bertrand Russell implored the powers to desist. Khrushchev wrote to him that the USSR would not give in to "the law of the jungle," but hinted that a summit meeting would restore peace. Russian diplomatic personnel in England appealed to the British to arrange a summit. And suddenly, on October 25, Soviet boats sailing for Cuba were ordered to return home.

Kennedy called for Strategic Air Command deployment. Khrushchev gave in on the 29th, offering to withdraw the missiles from Cuba if the U.S. would withdraw its Jupiters from Turkey, accepting inspection of Soviet ships in return for an American "guarantee" not to invade Cuba.

Castro had not been warned. The tragicomedy had been played on his territory but above his head. "We are not a pawn in a chess game," he shouted. "The Cuban people are very angry." It took Mikoyan three

---

* Author's personal experience in Japan.

weeks to pacify him. Now the fear lifted; people felt relieved. Khrushchev was called "a man of peace."

Kennedy's prestige increased; he had maneuvered well. The episode was represented as an example of "reciprocal concessions," a pattern for all similar crises throughout the world. Thereafter, summits and crises would take place frequently, until they became almost a repetitious pantomime.

"The CPSU Central Committee . . . possessed trustworthy information that armed aggression by U.S. imperialism against Cuba was about to take place. We realized with sufficient clarity that to rebuff aggression, to defend the Cuban revolution effectively, we had to take the most resolute measures." This "stern rebuff" had secured, claimed Khrushchev, Cuba from invasion.*

The Chinese proclaimed support of "the heroic Cuban people" and organized massive demonstrations against U.S. imperialism, but withheld comment on the horse-trading that went on. Now they showed disapproval. "Nuclear weapons in the hands of socialist countries should always be defensive weapons against nuclear threats . . . in contrast to the imperialists, socialist countries have no need to use nuclear weapons for blackmail or gambling and must not do so." "The Soviet leaders never weary of asserting that there was a *thermonuclear war* crisis in the Caribbean Sea . . . Before the Soviet Union sent rockets into Cuba, there did not exist a crisis of the U.S. using *nuclear weapons* nor of a *nuclear war* breaking out."†

Khrushchev then accused Mao of wanting and hoping for a head-on clash between the U.S. and the USSR. "Did we ask you to transport rockets to Cuba? Did you ever consult the Soviet people or other socialist countries about it?" retorted Mao. Only confidence in the people, in the masses, not nuclear weapons, is "the determining force in the development of history."

After the Cuba affair Mao was indignant; he realized that Khrushchev's course was set. The Albanians warned that "true Marxists" could not coexist with revisionists in the same party. It was at this time that the decision was taken by Mao to expose Khrushchev and revisionism. And this decision also coincided with his decision to battle openly revisionism at home.

But in both cases he would give the opponent yet another chance.

* Letter of CPSU, July 14, 1963, published also in China (English edition Peking 1963).

† Chinese statements of March 8 and September 1, 1963, published in all Chinese newspapers and translated by Foreign Language Press (Peking 1963).

Thus in December and January, at the Czech and East German Party congresses, a proposal for yet another all-party conference was agreed to by the Chinese. But Khrushchev opposed it, though he called for a halt to the polemics.

While this went on abroad, the homegrown revisionists were also mounting an offensive against Mao.

The Central Committee held its ninth plenum in January 1961. "Readjustment, consolidation, filling out and raising standards" indicated the end of the Leap.

The Party now had 17 million members, and of these 80 percent had come in after 1949 and 70 percent since 1953. A rectification "to strengthen the ties between the Party and the masses of the people" was started in 1961. There were rumors that Mao had made his own self-criticism and asked that it be published. But this was formally opposed by the Politburo.

Rectification placed the onus for mistakes upon provincial Party secretaries and middle to low level cadres. This did not satisfy Mao. In January 1962 he said: "I have criticized certain phenomena and certain comrades, but I have not named them for shortcomings and mistakes in the last few years. The primary responsibility should be borne by the Center; at the Center the primary responsibility is mine. . . . If we are to promote democracy we must encourage others to criticize us and listen to their criticisms."

Then occurred what is known as the Meeting of the Seven Thousand at an enlarged work conference in January 1962.* During the cultural revolution it was called a "black" meeting, dominated by the "revisionist" or "capitalist-roaders" of the Party.

The object of the meeting was to decide, on the basis of twelve years of socialist construction, the policies for the future. In this thorough reappraisal of all that had gone before, it was Liu Shao-chi who was to make a general report on all aspects of economic policy, and especially on the last four years (the Leap and after). According to cultural revolution reports, the meeting was preceded by the "Chang Kuan Lou plot," so called from the name of a pavilion in a Peking park where apparently some adherents of the Liu line gathered in a working committee to collect material and to compile a file against Mao.

Liu Shao-chi's draft report, instead of being first studied by the

* Comprising the Central Committee, provincial regional Party secretaries, State Council ministers, etc.

Politburo for emendation and correction, was given directly to the Seven Thousand assembly to be discussed as it stood. Liu was critical of the communes, organized "in great haste as the result of the subjective desire of a few people." He implied, from the reports gleaned during the rectification campaign in the Party which had taken place in 1961, that the Party's unpopularity with the masses was due to enforced collectivization. In one brigade half the labor force had slipped away to do odd jobs for extra money. "Collectivization has done nothing for the peasant." In Anhwei and Honan provinces 20 percent of the land had returned to individual ownership. To remedy the situation, Liu presented his Sixty Regulations for agriculture (see page 184). Again he stressed that production was the top priority.

Turning to industry, Liu was also critical of the last four years. (At a subsequent Supreme State Conference in February he would say that it would take ten years to make up for the disasters of these years — yet they were due in great part to the Soviet withdrawal and natural disasters.) He presented his Seventy Articles for industry for formal approval.

The moment of decision had come: to abandon (even if gradually) the general line, the communes, and the ideas, structures, and methods of work of the Leap; or to go forward with them.

Liu "came forward in person and launched a frenzied attack" against the general line is the way cultural revolution reports describe the scene. But from Mao's speech on January 30 at the work conference one does not get altogether this impression.

Mao expressed himself as pleased at the open discussion, the liveliness . . . "this is democratic centralism . . . it is the mass line. . . . First democracy, then centralism. . . . The method of discussion, reasoning, criticism and self-criticism." He mentioned "incorrect handling" of lower cadres by the top leadership; "they should all be cleared and rehabilitated . . . so that their minds can be set at rest and they can lift up their heads again."

"In 1957 I said: 'We must bring about a political climate which has both centralism and democracy, discipline and freedom, unity of purpose and ease of mind for the individual, and which is lively and vigorous.'

"Any mistake that the Center has made ought to be my direct responsibility. There are other comrades who also bear responsibility, but the person primarily responsible should be me . . . Those of you who shirk responsibility . . . who do not allow people to speak . . . ten out of ten of you will fail. You think no one will dare touch the arse of a tiger like you? They damn well will!"

Mao spoke again of class struggle. "In a socialist society, new bourgeois elements may still be produced." The old exploiting classes would still attempt to come back. That was why the mass line, democratic centralism, was so important. "If in our nation we do not fully extend . . . the people's democracy [proletarian democracy] then we cannot establish a socialist economy."

To acquire understanding of the objective world of China, of the real issues of Chinese society, had not been easy. Now faced with socialist construction, they were all still groping. It had taken three hundred years for capitalism to reach its present stage. It would take China a century — "if less . . . then that will be a splendid thing . . . The next fifty or one hundred years or so will be an earth-shaking period . . . such as history has never seen . . . Living in such a period, we must be prepared to carry out great struggles."

Mao then referred to Liu Shao-chi's draft report with gentle irony: "Sixty regulations on our work in the countryside, seventy regulations on industrial enterprise, sixty regulations on higher education, forty regulations on scientific research. . . . All have . . . already been implemented. . . . They will be revised in the future . . . some may have to be greatly revised."

At the close of this meeting Mao seems to have left for Shanghai. In the debate on economic matters which followed, Liu was not able to win a majority to dismantle the general line, the Great Leap Forward and the communes. It was Chou En-lai who at this juncture rose to defend Mao Tsetung's policies.

In 1967, in his self-criticism, Liu would say: "At a central work conference convened in January 1962 I delivered a written report. . . . A still greater event took place there . . . from February 21 to 26, 1962. When the financial policy was being discussed, *a deficit was found*. . . . I thought such a deficit normal. We let first-grade Party members discuss it and express dissenting opinions. . . . As Chairman Mao was not in Peking then I went to him and delivered a report . . . Chairman Mao was not at all in agreement with my appraisal."

Liu would also table for discussion the case of Peng Teh-huai, ex–Defense minister. Liu seems to have endorsed a proposal for a reversal of the 1959 verdicts upon Peng and others, saying that "much of what he wrote was in conformity with facts. . . . There should be a reconsideration." "Opposition to Chairman Mao is only opposition to an individual. . . . We should review the case . . . so long as there is no collusion with a foreign country." Peng Teh-huai was then still vice-premier of the State Council, vice-chairman of the National Defense Council, and a Politburo member.

To the disagreements over financial policies and over Peng Teh-huai's case was added discord over external policies. The right wing suggested at the time what is known in capsule form as "the three reconciliations and one reduction." The gist was: reconciliation or striving for better relations with the United States, with Soviet "revisionism," and with the western countries as a whole, and reduction of the aid program to the developing countries of the Third World. This was, in effect, a capitulation to the status quo.

"I committed myself to the right-inclined line in the summer of 1962," said Liu Shao-chi in his self-criticism of 1967. But as usual he blamed others for his having done so.

The meetings ended without any agreement having been reached. In March, after the Supreme State Conference, and with Chou En-lai voicing his strong opposition to Liu's practices, four vice-premiers, among them Finance Minister Li Hsien-nien, went to Shanghai to call upon Mao — an indication of the gravity of the dissension.

The National People's Congress, scheduled for March, was delayed by these prolonged discussions. It was finally held behind closed doors. Even Chou En-lai's usual report on the work of the government was not published in full but only summarized.

While the NPC sat in session, an editorial of March 29 in the *People's Daily* repeated the formula of the Liu economics: "Proceed slowly and steadfastly on a firm foundation." *Red Flag* also carried an editorial against "haste."

Mao openly stated his intention to continue the revolution (economic and political) along the lines of the previous Leap. There would be no pause, no stagnation. And Mao won, by a narrow majority.

In June, Foreign Minister Chen Yi said to the author: "There will be no change in our foreign policy towards imperialism or towards the Third World just because of temporary difficulties. Nor will we give up the 'Three Red Banners'" (the general line, the Leap, the communes).*

The foreign policy of "three reconciliations and one reduction" was denounced by Chou En-lai in his report on the work of the government, at the National People's Congress in March. Chou quoted Mao:

---

* Author's interview with Foreign Minister Chen Yi, June 1962.

"The east wind prevails over the west wind." The tide of history was irresistible; there would be no compromise with revisionism; none with imperialism and its peace tricks, intensified war preparations and arms expansion. Aid to the Third World would continue and expand.

In that summer, the two lines were demarcated even more sharply in preparation for the tenth plenum of the Eighth Central Committee.

In June, Peng Teh-huai wrote a long memorandum which contained a demand for reversal of the verdict against him of 1959. The standing committee of the Politburo, with Mao presiding, decided not to allow Peng to speak at the forthcoming tenth plenum; he was still "under investigation." An article entitled *Strengthen the System of Democratic Centralism* appeared, containing veiled references to the Peng case: "Some leadership persons at the higher level . . . when they take disciplinary action or pass sentence on a Party member . . . will not allow him to appear, to make representations in person."

Liu Shao-chi called for reinforcement of "Party spirit" and Party discipline when his book was reissued that June. Liu would now battle Mao for control of the Party apparatus, as Mao indicated that he would now look more closely into implementation. A decision on the planned interchange of important leading cadres of Party and government organizations would be issued in September, and this in effect somewhat curbed Liu's power, abolishing the two channels of action.

During that summer, what appeared to be a concerted move by the Kennedy administration and the Chiang regime on Taiwan to initiate invasion of the South China coast occurred. Washington on June 21 announced "concern" over troop movements in Fukien, opposite Quemoy Island. Broadcasts from Taiwan (heard in China) announced the reconquest of the mainland; and in the prevailing disarray in the countryside landlords and rich peasants rejoiced openly and threatened the poor peasants. Chiang urged "revolt" in China against Mao. But the U.S. made an ambiguous declaration that it would defend the offshore islands only if an attack on them was part of an attack on Taiwan. The British opined that the world would be a safer place if these islands were transferred to China. On September 10 the Chinese brought down a U-2 spy plane — from Taiwan. The meetings at ambassadorial level continued. The crisis petered out.

Yet another enlarged Politburo conference was held at Peitaiho in August. Mao repeated his objections to the economic policies promoted by Liu. He also brought up again the subject of class struggle. The tenth plenum was imminent, and support for Mao was growing.

At this point, early in September, Teng To suddenly stopped his anti-Mao publications with a final article on *Thirty-six Stratagems*. "Of all the stratagems, the best one is withdrawal [when in a weak position]," he wrote. For now Mao Tsetung was returning in strength, to dominate the tenth plenum.

And it was then that the cultural revolution was conceived.

II

THE CULTURAL REVOLUTION AND AFTER

1

Prelude, 1962–1965

We must be fired with great, lofty proletarian aspirations and dare
to break paths unexplored by people before and scale heights yet unclimbed.

— Mao Tsetung, 1962 (reported 1966)

Matter becomes spirit, spirit becomes matter.
— Mao Tsetung, 1963

At the tenth plenum of the Eighth Central Committee (September
23–27, 1962), Mao again grasped "the weapon of class struggle." "Before that plenum, we could no longer hear Chairman Mao's voice . . . it
was kept from us."*

There never has been, in the continuing Chinese revolution, a time
when one or the other line in the seesaw struggle has achieved total
victory, gathered all the winnings. Dialectically this would be unrealistic, since the "unity of contradictions" can only allow preponderance of
one over the other, not total effacement. Always hostages for the next
fray remain; circumstances and situations change, new contradictions
crop up. But in this zigzag course the great ship of China advances,
churning towards the goal with more or less momentum. And Mao, the
"helmsman," would utilize even "negative" features to advance the
revolution.

The existence of a right wing, an entrenched establishment, pre-
sumes a left-wing dissenting minority — radical groups which Mao
would now proceed to enlarge and to invigorate with "rebellion"
against the "bourgeois headquarters" within the Party.

The role of Premier Chou En-lai, of Finance Minister Li Hsien-nien,
of Foreign Minister Chen Yi and other able men in the government
around Chou En-lai would be, at this juncture, crucial. Though all

* Author's interviews in many communes and factories with workers and peasants during the cultural revolution.

were more or less savagely attacked during the cultural revolution, it is because Mao could count on this sizable portion of able administrators, who supported him with great loyalty even when reviled by the Red Guards, that the cultural revolution when it occurred did not produce a major dislocation in the work of the government.

Chou En-lai had not built up a following as Liu had. Through the years his untiring capacity for work and integrity had commanded respect and rallied to him a number of cadres, intellectuals, and also the masses. Workers and peasants really began to know him, to esteem this frail man who worked so unselfishly. Chou En-lai would own up that he had in the past committed mistakes. He had been one of the twenty-eight Bolsheviks sent by Stalin, under Wang Ming, to control the Chinese Party. "But I did my self-criticism and I stuck to it."[*] In 1961 he again confirmed Mao's trust by countering Khrushchev at the Twenty-second Congress of the CPSU in Moscow. In 1962 it was Chou who defended Mao against Liu Shao-chi at the Meeting of the Seven Thousand. It was the economists working in Chou's State Council who would uphold the Mao line for the third five-year plan, due to begin in 1966.

On a mellow September morning in Peking, at the tenth plenum, Mao gave his now celebrated, abundantly quoted, still unpublished speech which started the cultural revolution.

Mao began by recalling how often he had spoken of class struggle, contradiction between superstructure and base, contradictions among the people. Class struggle continued, contradictions were present in socialist society, relapse into capitalism was possible, and it began with revisionism. "It is incumbent upon our country to grasp, understand and study this problem carefully."

Revisionism was happening now in the Soviet Union, which was "changing color," a change insidious and peaceful. "If the generation of our sons should espouse revisionism . . . which although called social- ism would actually be capitalism . . . then our grandsons will definitely

---

[*] Author's interview. This fact, unknown in history, is reported with the assent of Premier Chou himself. Many of the twenty-eight Bolsheviks, it must be stressed, had rallied to Mao Tsetung and turned against Wang Ming, their leader, who persisted in a dogmatic, unrealistic "line" dictated by Moscow. It was against the Wang Ming line that Mao Tsetung had fought for a decade. The Long March, which under the orders transmitted by Wang Ming began as a rout, became a signal triumph when Mao took over its military conduct in January 1935 at Tsunyi. The Great Rectification of 1941–1944 was also designed to combat Wang Ming's ideas in the Party. See *The Morning Deluge*, Part I chapters 11 and 12, Part II chapter 4.

stage an uprising to overthrow their parents because of mass disaffection. . . . Class struggle must be talked about every year, every month, every day."

During the Leap there had been blunders, in agriculture, in industry; the main one was excessive procurement when there was not enough grain, "but we insisted that there was." Most errors had already been corrected by the end of 1960. Now it was necessary to pick up again where the Leap had stopped. If only pessimists were heeded, the Chinese Revolution would never have taken place.

Mao spoke of Khrushchev, narrating the various occasions on which Khrushchev had tried to impose his views, insulted the Chinese Party "on our own rostrum." This showed there were contradictions between socialist parties and countries, a class struggle on the international level. Khrushchev was now a representative of a new bourgeoisie emergent in the USSR.

Yet the situation was favorable, both internally and externally. Externally, peoples in the world were opposed to imperialism. But now there was revisionism, a very great danger, a great help to imperialism.

Mao then turned to right opportunism in China. Perhaps its name should now change to "Chinese revisionism," he said. The problem of revisionism was also one of methods of work; and at the 1962 January conference (of the Seven Thousand) he had pointed out that without a people's democracy the dictatorship of the proletariat could not be consolidated and political power would be unstable. The possibility of a capitalist restoration was always there; the exploiting classes would sooner or later attempt a comeback; if only professional methods of subduing counterrevolution (arrests, physical liquidations, etc.) were used, they would be unsuccessful. Only the mass line, mass participation, would cope with this problem, not suppression or repression.*

Revisionism, the "bourgeoisie" within the Party, could be handled at present as a problem of methodology, as had been done in the rectification movement of 1942–1944: criticism, self-criticism and then unity. "If such a [revisionist] comrade should change himself earnestly, we should welcome him. If the erring comrade recognizes his errors and returns to the Marxist stand, we will then align ourselves with you. *I welcome several of the comrades here.*"

Thus plainly, Mao indicated there were revisionists in the Chinese

---

* This is one of Mao's numerous criticisms of the public security services. Like Lenin, Mao wanted no terroristic apparatus, illegally arresting people under pretense of enforcing "security."

Communist Party. "I wish to advise comrades who have colluded with foreign countries or engaged in anti-Party cliques that if they would expose everything and speak out truthfully, they would be welcome . . . nor will we adopt the method of execution." Mao was obviously referring to Peng Teh-huai and several of those who had been demoted with him. "But we cannot rehabilitate someone who has not erred," he added, recalling Liu's plea that actually there was "reason" in what Peng had said. Nor could there be blanket rehabilitations. The Lushan plenum had spent three weeks on the Peng problem. "We cannot afford so much time now."

In a jolting aside Mao added: "Isn't the writing of novels very popular now? To utilize novels to engage in anti-Party activities is a great invention. In order to overthrow any political power, one must first create public opinion and engage in ideological and philosophical work. This applies to the revolutionary class as well as to the counter-revolutionary classes."

At the time, a novel had been published designed to rehabilitate Kao Kang. Perhaps Mao was alluding to it; he did not allude to the scarcely veiled attacks against him in the *Notes from a Three-Family Village* and *Evening Talks at Yenshan* series, nor to the play *The Dismissal of Hai Jui*.

"Taking agriculture as the foundation and industry as the leading factor" was the basic line launched at the tenth plenum, putting an end to the "consolidation and readjustment" motto of the ninth plenum of 1961. The priorities would now be: agriculture, light industry, and heavy industry in that order.

The resolutions and the communiqué issuing from the tenth plenum make the point that it will take a longer time for technical than for social reform in agriculture; that twenty to twenty-five years may elapse before agricultural mechanization is completed; "although we have been somewhat slow in assuming this mission," it must now be done "with flexibility rather than rigid uniformity, with dispatch rather than protraction." The resolutions repeat what Mao had been saying since 1956: that the rural areas are the greatest internal market for heavy industry; that light industry accumulates funds more quickly; that heavy industry must be oriented towards supplying rural areas with machinery; that the ratio of investment for each sector of the national economy must be redetermined in conformity with agriculture as the foundation, and a larger share put into the latter. In twelve clauses the resolutions substantially develop Mao's thinking expounded since 1956, and are therefore a return to the spirit and the methods which brought about the Great Leap Forward.

Oddly enough, at the same time this document was enacted, a policy directive was sent to the communes which turned out to be a revised draft of the Sixty Regulations on agriculture which Liu had been circulating since 1961. It still incorporated, despite revisions, the reward and punishment system and household quotas, and forbade any new small enterprises "for many years" and also any not directly related to agricultural pursuits. "Liu always sang a tune contrary to Mao," is the Chinese description of this deliberate countering.

The tenth plenum decided, in order to increase economic and political momentum, on a socialist education movement, regarded now as the prelude to the cultural revolution. In itself such a movement was not new, since we have already encountered it several times since 1949, when Mao had stated the need for socialist education of the peasantry.

It is not certain that in September 1962 Mao was planning the cultural revolution as it happened. As he would say himself, "straw sandals shape themselves as one weaves them." Mao was probably thinking of something like the Leap, but better organized. He was thinking in term of mass arousal, as had been tried before. After all, the Leap had been a cultural revolution as well as an industrial, agricultural and technological one. There is nothing to indicate that at the time Mao was discarding Liu. Until 1965 Liu would still be acting through the regular channels of Party organization and the Party executive. Mao still seemed to hope he could bring Liu around to his way of thinking. Although at the tenth plenum the "two channels" of executive and ideological authority were abolished, they continued to manifest themselves, for Mao was inhumanly busy, unable to attend to everything, and nothing is more difficult to budge than an entrenched bureaucracy with established lines of command.

Investigations throughout the winter revealed the state of flux in the countryside, with intense and bitter class struggle and ugly features of return to the past.* On May 20, 1963, Mao's first draft resolution on *Some Problems in Current Rural Work* was passed by the Central Committee. This document, known as the First Ten Points, is considered the first document of the cultural revolution.†

* Seen by author in 1961, 1962, 1963, 1964.
† Mentioned as such in *Liberation Daily* April 18, 1966. The document has not yet been officially published.

The First Ten Points exhibits the usual Mao way of *stating* ideological problems and guidelines, thus arousing initiative to deal with them. It points to responsibility for errors at the top level, insists that this is where the fault lies, not with the grass-roots cadres. It denounces the recrudescent activity of landlords and rich peasants *at this moment on the offensive* in the countryside. Leadership and power in some communes had fallen to them through corruption. Speculation and profiteering of serious proportions had occurred — buying and selling of land, usury and extortion. "Not all comrades see this . . . some . . . turn a blind eye to reality." The main thrust is a specific demand for the removal of "those in the Party in authority who are taking the capitalist road." "The socialist education movement is a great revolutionary movement . . . *This is a struggle that calls for the re-education of man . . . the new man.*"

Here, again, Mao goes further than before: to voluntary remolding. Man, facing himself, must change himself, must "fight self" in order to "repudiate revisionism." It is a problem of "world outlook," for each and every person. He entertained no illusion that all would change in one or even several such movements, but something could be done. Sixty to 70 percent of the poor and lower middle peasants, Mao firmly believed, wanted revolution and socialism. They were the mainstay of such a movement in rural areas. The peasant associations must hence be the prime movers in the change; all decisions on important problems must be made through full discussion with the masses, who must fully express their views "to expose bad people and evil deeds," the mass line in action.

When introducing the First Ten Points in May 1963, Mao Tsetung, in a vivid aside, took time off to reply to some of the attacks on the philosophical level which had been made against him by Yang Hsien-chen, the "Marxist" theoretician already mentioned.

Yang Hsien-chen in early 1962 had been calling the Leap "idealistic" and "due to one man's initiative only." It was necessary "to summarize historical experience and educate the cadres" in the errors of the Leap, he said. This attack on the theoretical plane, coming at such a time, coincident with the Seven Thousand conference, was far more deadly, in a system where ideological correctness is all, than any other form of attack. Yang denied the relation between matter and consciousness, between base and superstructure.

"Where do correct ideas come from?" said Mao. "Are they innate in the mind? No . . . they come from social practice and from it alone."

Thus from practice to knowledge and back to practice, in a continuing motion; this was the acquisition of understanding. Here also Mao went a step further in his enunciation of the relation between ideas, habits and customs which produce behavior, and the material and tangible ways in which they change the material environment.

"*Some comrades . . . do not comprehend that matter can be transformed into consciousness and consciousness into matter, although such leaps are phenomena of everyday life.*" "It is man's social being that determines his thinking. Once the correct ideas characteristic of the advanced class are grasped by the masses, these ideas turn into a material force which changes society and changes the world." Yang's philosophical precepts were actually, even though not worded that way, based upon the concept of an unchanging human nature, which is rejected by Marxism. For man does change, conditioned by the system he lives in; and though he has six thousand years of class society behind him, and it may take some centuries to eradicate certain of the traits which pull him back into a barbaric exploiting past, yet man can choose what he becomes, and this implies willful unremitting awareness of himself, perpetual self-remolding. Revolutions are conscious changes, and are becoming more and more conscious as the majority of the world's peoples heighten their awareness. This act of will by millions of people who want revolution is accompanied by an act of will towards the self, which also must change; and so man's future is to change himself, doing away consciously with the so-called "instincts" of greed, selfishness, and inhumanity towards others.

This moral dimension, generating a change consciously known and performed, accelerates the revolutionary process and is the key to the future. Hence all revolutions are not only acts of violence by which one class overthrows another, but also immense exercises in self-change. This inner revolution must accompany the societal one, and the eradication of old customs, attitudes, ideas, and prejudices is as essential as the breakdown of old societal structures. In fact, one cannot be performed without the other.

Thus Mao Tsetung was establishing the philosophical foundation of the *continuing revolution*, deepening the scope and giving the role of conscious man the forefront position in the great battle against injustice, exploitation, and barbarism.

But how could a party which, at the highest level, received its directives from a "bourgeois headquarters" ensconced within it, which issued regulations and directives subtly distorting Mao's ideas, and persistently refused the concept of mass supervision, criticism and participation, carry out Mao's program?

Would it not have been easier for Mao arbitrarily to replace the top level in the Central Committee and the Politburo who opposed him? This kind of "palace coup" had been performed by Khrushchev. But Mao Tsetung had deliberately limited his own power back in September 1948, trusting to consensus, to persuasion, to education, to his own power of debate and reasoning. It was their own distortion and sabotage which would reveal the "capitalist-roaders" in the Party.

Mao's main preoccupation is to *teach* the masses. "The people are our wall of bronze." But the people must understand all the issues. He wanted to provoke confrontation, to awaken, stir into defiance against these high leaders the middle and lower levels of Party cadres, who must get out of the habit of blind obedience, ponder and try to understand the essence of the thinking behind Mao's circulars, and discover the discrepancies between word and deed. Only thus would new contingents of true revolutionaries be built up. It was upon this arousal of awareness — among the masses, the cadres, the Party — that Mao placed high hope. Paradoxically, only those who would protest and rebel against the distortions, exercising the right of dissidence, could close the existing gap between Party and people.

The socialist education movement was involved from its inception with a campaign known as the "four cleanups," so called because of demands from counties and communes that cadres involved in corrupt practices be checked. Account books, stocks of grain in public granaries, work points, bribery and usury were mentioned among items of corrupt practices. This occasion was seized upon by the establishment, loath to really "stir the masses," and preferring a straightforward police job of cleaning up accounts, granaries, establishing rules, awarding punishment — not the ideological education process which Mao conceived. "The four cleanups campaign in the rural areas should be a socialist revolutionary class struggle . . . basic construction in politics, economics, ideology and organization."* The masses were to discuss, criticize, and judge whether the cadres, after self-criticism and repentance, would remain in their positions. The supervision of cadres by the masses was a right Mao spoke about constantly, but it was seldom exercised until the cultural revolution.

* Chou En-lai's report on the work of government, National People's Congress, December 1964.

Between May and September 1963 fourteen rural areas were exposed to the socialist education and four cleanups campaigns. In September 1963 another directive came out, called the Later Ten Points.* These Later Ten Points purported to clarify the First Ten Points, but stressed that the movement must be controlled *from above,* against Mao's express injunction that it must come "from below . . . because . . . the masses are the real heroes, while we ourselves are often childish and ignorant."

The key to the problem lies in the leadership, says the Later Ten Points. The basic Party organization and the existing cadres must do the work of cleaning up — a concept contrary to that of the masses doing the work through their own associations.

It is odd how much a person's style, in revolution as in everything else, reveals him. Liu Shao-chi had always favored work teams since that faraway job in land reform he had done in 1947 (and which had been ultra-left in performance).† Now again work teams were sent to carry out intensive socialist education for three months in selected communes. They were empowered to replace, condemn, punish, lead the masses against local cadres guilty of corruption. Work teams would listen to one or two reports, usually from a cadre at a higher level, himself perhaps guilty of embezzling, who would now happily find a poor peasant cadre as a scapegoat, and the peasant masses, frightened and confused, would echo docilely the accusations launched against the unfortunate man.

One interesting feature of the Later Ten Points is the way it spells out protection for the sons and daughters of landlords or rich peasants who have contracted marriage alliances with cadres or become cadres.

The Later Ten Points refers to Liu's Sixty Regulations for agriculture of 1961 as guidance for the socialist education movement. Under this guidance the four cleanups movement became a drive to "knock down the many to protect the few." The attitude was of punishment, not self-change. Cadres who had erred, Mao had said, should "come clean . . . then wash their faces and go straight back to work," accepting the criticism and supervision of the peasant organizations. But with the emphasis on punishment, the prime aim of the cadres would be subterfuge.

---

* *Some Concrete Policy Formulations of the Central Committee in the Rural Socialist Education Movement.* Not officially published.

† For Liu's "ultra-left" performance in 1947–1948, see *The Morning Deluge,* pages 481–482.

"How can peaceful coexistence in politics, muddle-mindedness in organization, and perfunctoriness in economy build socialism?" Mao asked in one of his famous offhand remarks, to awaken the conscience of "some comrades." The orientation, instead of "lifting the lid off the class struggle . . . by exposing all kinds of contradictions," was deviated to individual punishment. By proceeding as a police action, the socialist education movement as revised was not exposing class struggle or contradictions in the rural areas, only making individual errors the target of attack.

But not everything was distorted, for the creative fertilizing element in the drive was producing offshoots, some to become mighty trees. One of these was the writing of history from the proletarian point of view, a total change of evaluation of historical material which has transformed and revivified all critical studies of China's past as well as given a great impetus to archaeological research.

China's historians of the older type were able; but "orthodox" historical studies had started again in the early 1960's and produced a spate of resurrected corpses, many old-time "heroes" of imperial days now being propped up as models, including Confucius. Historical research was in the direction of "honoring the past and slighting the present." Mao Tsetung recommended that the socialist education movement also collect records of peasant struggles — not only the enormous peasant revolts which in the past had shaken the dynasties and toppled so many, but also the post-Liberation struggles for land reform and the establishment of the communes.

The "four histories" — personal and individual records of poor peasants and workers and what they endured, the story of their region or factory or village, the story of struggles for liberation, and the national history — must be assessed again, with priority given to the history of the downtrodden, the slaves, those who really made history. Thus the workers and lower technicians of the railway station at Tientsin gathered to write the history of the station; so did the mine workers of Anyuan, and workers in many other places. This new sifting of what history really is Mao Tsetung called "establishing the family tree of the proletariat." Accepted "heroes" were often tyrants who had suppressed revolts, while the "wicked people" were indeed revolutionaries.

History conditions and molds awareness. It was necessary to reorientate history away from emperors and Confucian "good" heroes, towards the real bone and blood of creation, the people.

This drive for historical reinterpretation was pointed up in Szechuan, in Kwangtung, with clay figures showing the exploitation of the past, unknown to the young born after 1949. Museums were opened in communes; a literature for young children, in a series entitled *Never Forget the Past*, appeared on book stands; stories of hitherto unknown peasants and their revolts jostled with books about prim Confucian magistrates and "heroes" of previous dynasties. Never was the two-line struggle more clear than in this literature for children.

The socialist education movement would produce the rivalry of two models in the countryside: the Mao model, the Tachai brigade in Shansi province; the Liu model, the Taoyuan brigade in Hopei province.

Located in the midst of the arid loess which covers a million square kilometers of North China, Tachai was a desolate huddle of seven gullies, eight hills and one slope; its fifty families lived in scooped earth caves, eking out of their waterless fifty-three hectares a mere 50 kilograms per mu (750 per hectare) of millet and sorghum. But the Tachai people had guts. Tachai became a higher cooperative in 1955, a brigade in the Leap, and under the leadership of the splendid poor peasant Chen Yung-kwei* and the woman cadre Sun Li-ying (who had been a slave child sold to a landlord) dug itself out of misery by its own efforts, rearranged its gullies and hills, terraced and planted and read philosophy, held nightly debates on Mao Tsetung's writings, grasped dialectics, organized an honors work point system, refused grants and loans from the state even when overwhelmed with natural calamities, refused the "new economic policy" of Liu and the "four freedoms," and sold to the state in 1960–1962 double its assigned quota of grain. Throughout, Tachai stuck to the socialist way, to self-reliance and frugality, the cadres laboring along with ordinary members and wanting no higher remuneration. The result was a leap in production, and also a change in people. To stay in Tachai a few days is a psychological experience — the impact of a new moral climate, an osmosis of goodness which has nothing spurious about it. The fact that everyone in Tachai can argue philosophy and politics far better than "educated" intellectuals is an unforgettable experience.

Liu Shao-chi set up his own model brigade at Taoyuan, with the help of no less a person than his own wife, Wang Kuang-mei. Taoyuan is a rich, well-watered brigade, with three times the land of Tachai, and good land. Wang Kuang-mei brought a work team, announced the

* Now vice-premier of the PRC.

"four cleanups." Thirty-four out of forty-five grass-roots cadres were interrogated, and according to some reports hung by the thumbs to confess misdeeds, or beaten. Allowing for some imagination on such an occasion, it still remains true that Wang Kuang-mei's "style of work," which relied on arbitrary methods and secret police information, was not socialist education. Wang Kuang-mei left a large sum of money and a monument to her visit. Her report on Taoyuan was circulated throughout the Party as a study document. Chou Yang ordered playwrights and film directors to make a film and write scripts based on this "rich experience." As late as January 1974, at a North China theater festival, a laudatory play based on the Taoyuan brigade would be shown and create some indignation.

Mao, though busily engaged with Sino-Soviet polemics in the summer of 1963, toured the countryside and came back dissatisfied. He summoned a work conference of the standing committee of the Politburo. Had the four uncleans been wiped out? The poor and lower peasants mobilized? Were the cadres doing manual labor? Had a good leadership nucleus been established in each commune? What had been done about the five bad elements (landlord, rich peasant, counter-revolutionary, capitalist and hooligan)? Was production increasing or decreasing?

Eighteen organizational rules to strengthen the peasant associations and a revision of the Later Ten Points would then be promulgated. The revision begins: "Only by freely mobilizing the masses can this movement achieve complete victory." The study of Mao Thought concerning class struggle was a prerequisite for the movement. But the revision bypassed the cardinal issue of class struggle; it talked of "intertwining contradictions" between "clean and unclean." In short, a document "left in form but right in essence," which would lead to dissension among the masses and between them and Party cadres.

"I did not learn to grasp Chairman Mao's Thought . . . nor did I make reports to Chairman Mao," Liu would say in 1967 of the socialist education movement.

In January 1965 Mao came to the conclusion that he could no longer go on working with Liu Shao-chi, although he would still give him some chances to rehabilitate himself. This facing up to a split is clearly foreshadowed in Chou En-lai's report on the work of government at the National People's Congress in December 1964. The way in which the socialist education movement was conducted, said Chou, was a question of world outlook, of basic class stand, and therefore of great ideological importance. "Serious and acute class struggles exist in our urban and rural areas . . . such are necessarily reflected inside the Party . . . the crux of the movement is to purge the capitalist-roaders within the Party. . . . These stay behind the scenes in some cases. . . . Some of their supporters come from below and some from above." In a socialist society, new bourgeois elements were ceaselessly being generated in the Party, government organs, economic organizations, cultural and educational departments — they linked with the older bourgeoisie in trying to restore capitalism.*

In January 1965 Mao would place before the Politburo a draft program for the cultural revolution to come and a draft program for China's economic advance.† Part of the first, concerning the socialist education movement in the rural areas, is known as the Twenty-three Articles. The economic program would only become known ten years later.

The Twenty-three Articles repeats all of Mao's theses. "Our Party will not betray the trust and the hopes of the people of the whole nation and of the peoples of the world." What was being done in China had an international significance; it was to keep China from changing color, to stop any chance of capitalist restoration in China, that these measures were necessary. The essence of the movement to come was the contradiction between socialism and capitalism. The key point was to rectify those people in authority within the Party who took the capitalist road; there were such people at every level, even in the Central Committee. Some harbored among their own friends and in their own families people who engaged in capitalist activities.‡

The Twenty-three Articles repeats the need for high-level personnel to labor, "squatting at points,"§ staying there to live, eat, work with the peasantry. It stresses that the majority of cadres (95 percent or more) are good or relatively good. It repeats the "save the man by curing the disease" methodology. But two new concepts are introduced.

First: where mistakes had been very serious, where leadership had been taken over by counterrevolutionaries or degenerate elements, there must be a seizure of power, to be achieved *with* the masses and

* The speech of Chou En-lai quotes Mao almost verbatim.
† Mentioned in Premier Chou En-lai's report to the Fourth National People's Congress in January 1975. See page 385.
‡ This was a clear hint about Liu Shao-chi, who was still writing to his land-lord family. See Liu Shao-chi *Collected Works* (Hong Kong 1968).
§ An expression meaning staying to live and labor there, in order to become thoroughly acquainted with all the issues and problems of the situation.

by arousing them. This new concept of "seizing authority" from a degenerate Party leadership is the crux of the cultural revolution and the rebellion it taught. Second: where Party organs had become degenerate, and before a new leadership nucleus could be formed, the right was given to the poor and lower middle peasant associations to seize power temporarily, not to replace the Party but to wield authority on an interim basis until the Party could be reformed locally. This also was startling and new.

Point 20 of the Twenty-three Articles says that all communes and brigades must learn from the People's Liberation Army, which carries out political democracy, democracy in production, in financial affairs, and military democracy. For it was now clear to Mao that he could no longer use the Party organization, because the Party was being used organizationally against him. The Party must be shaken; a great wind must blow, blow till the tree shook off its deadwood from the top; shaken until it would toss off all its withered leaves. . . . Meanwhile, there must be a stand-in. And that would be the PLA.

Besides confrontation from below, Mao would generate a surge from above, from within the superstructure itself. In every Party committee, at every level, and also among the non-Party intelligentsia, there must be awareness of revisionist tendencies and stimulus to revolt against the unnamed "capitalist-roaders" in authority in the Party. Again, it seems a very circumambulatory way of doing things; would it not have been simpler just to depose Liu Shao-chi?

But Mao's primary concern is to *teach* people, teach them political awareness, self-reliance, daring to speak, to act, to think on their own. This education against submission, docility, blindly obeying orders from a higher level, was perhaps particularly difficult in a China still imbued with Confucianism, in a Party which was reproducing so rapidly a Confucian mandarinate.

Mao's thoughts turned back to the beginnings of the revolution, and so to the army. It is not clear when Mao first thought of writing the PLA in the cultural revolution as an alternative organized body of men, as pace setter, and checkmate to a possible right-wing insurrection. Peng Teh-huai in 1959 had almost threatened Mao with a "Hungarian type" of counterrevolution. The cultural revolution would be a civil war, as Mao himself would aver in conversation with visitors. It was essential that the PLA not fall into the hands of "capitalist-roaders," to be utilized against socialism and the people.

Mao was founder of the PLA as well as of the Party; the Party had been reborn from within the small force he had led, after the holocaust of 1927, in the Autumn Harvest Uprising.* The armed struggle of the next twenty-two years had been accompanied by internecine struggles against the wrong tendencies both in the Party and in the army. Mao had forged the army as the instrument to achieve the Party's aims in the war against Japan and the War of Liberation against Chiang Kai-shek. At Liberation in 1949, it was the PLA who had supplied the necessary administrative cadres for liberated areas. Mao said then: "The army is a school for cadres. . . . Our field armies of 2,100,000 are equivalent to several thousand universities and secondary schools. We have to rely chiefly on the army to supply our cadres."

But time, age, the demobilization of veterans into other jobs (such as state farms in Sinkiang and in Manchuria) and the sovietization under Peng Teh-huai had modified the PLA. Like the Party, it now had a majority of unseasoned men. There were, in 1961, 17 million Party members, 70 percent of whom had been enrolled after 1953. In the army, one out of three of the rank and file were Party members, but the same proportion held. The difference was that the PLA rank and file was in majority composed of poor peasants' sons and workers' sons, with less admixture of intellectuals and petty bourgeois than in the urban Party branches. Veteran Long Marchers, although now in civilian posts, still had main links with the PLA (such as Chen Yi, Chou En-lai, Teng Hsiao-ping). And most of the commanders were tough erstwhile guerilla leaders of peasant origin.

The army's political role ("the Party commands the gun, and never the gun the Party") would mean a return to the spirit and the methods of the epic period 1935 to 1949. Both sides were now acutely aware that in case of a showdown the PLA's role would be a major factor in ultimate victory. Hence the obstinate demands for the reversal of the verdicts on Peng Teh-huai and his acolytes.

The locus of power in military affairs resides in the Military Affairs Committee, directly linked to the Politburo. The Party chairman (Mao Tsetung) is also chairman of the MAC. The entire spectrum of military affairs falls within his purview, and it is he who holds substantive power. Added to this was Mao's enormous prestige as military leader and strategist. Mao Tsetung had already begun to reshape the PLA before Lin Piao became minister of Defense to replace Peng Teh-huai, and the commanders gave allegiance to Mao, not to the minister of Defense.

* See *The Morning Deluge,* pages 173–180.

While the Party constitution of 1956 had written Mao Tsetung Thought out, the PLA from 1960 onward wrote Mao Tsetung Thought into its curricula as a compulsory course. After 1959 the dual command system, with a political commissar of equal rank at the side of every regional commander, was revived. In three strategic areas, Fukien, Inner Mongolia, and Sinkiang, both posts were combined in one individual.

Lin Piao's accession to Peng Teh-huai's post, often regarded as a sole move by Mao, was the result of a consensus, but with Mao's approval. Lin Piao had been moving upward since 1953, and he was the optimal choice. Until his fall in 1971, the belief that he was Mao's most devoted and faithful disciple held sway everywhere, both in China and outside. Much internecine conflict in the Party conclaves is *not* aired until many years later.

Lin Piao's biography and previous career are curiously dualistic. For instance, he is not mentioned at all in *History of the Modern Chinese Revolution* published in 1959* (the only one ever published, and afterward withdrawn). It is now denied that as a young schoolboy he was an activist, early joining an association affiliated to the pre-Communist nucleus set up by Tung Pi-wu in Hupeh province (Lin's birthplace). It is also averred that he came from a small landlord family with some landholdings. Episodes of conflict with Mao, buried in silence for decades, are now scrutinized.

After the famous conference at Kutien in the winter of 1929–1930, Lin did not uphold Mao's line, contrary to what was circulated after 1960. Quite the opposite, he proved a pessimist, saying: "How long can the Red flag be kept flying?" and advocating dispersal of the Red base Mao was building and a return to functioning as roving guerilla bands. This can be verified, for until 1948 Mao's critical epistle *A Single Spark Can Light a Prairie Fire* was a letter addressed openly: To Comrade Lin Piao. But in 1948 Lin Piao asked Mao that this document make no mention of him, and Mao agreed. From then onward the document was labeled "written . . . in criticism of certain pessimistic views then existing in the Party."†

Lin's fractiousness in Yenan, when he rushed off to carry on his own

---

* Ho Kan-chih *History of the Modern Chinese Revolution* (English edition Peking 1959).

† *A Single Spark Can Light a Prairie Fire*, January 5, 1930. *Selected Works of Mao Tsetung* (English edition Peking 1961–1965), vol. I, page 117. See also pages 105–114, *On Correcting Mistaken Ideas in the Party*, written after the Kutien conference, December 1929. This also refers to Mao's ideas on what the Party and Army should be.

guerilla war, is documented by secret Kuomintang papers. His refusal to obey Mao's directives during the Manchurian campaign, and particularly the taking of Peking and Tientsin, is today the subject of intense study. We now understand Mao's repeated references to "mountaintoppism"* and his stream of telegrams to army commanders, including Lin Piao, during the war against Chiang Kai-shek.

Lin's refusal to have anything to do with the Korean War and in 1960 his advocacy of "reunion" with the USSR are now exposed. But these exhumations of past conflicts are not sufficient to condemn Lin Piao out of hand. For as Chen Yi, the forthright, popular, and humorous general and foreign minister, was to say sarcastically: "Which of us has not at one time or other opposed Chairman Mao? Only comrade Lin Piao has not . . . he is truly a great man." This gibe (for it was one) nearly cost Chen Yi his life at the hands of a resentful Lin Piao.

Mao does not expect docility from his colleagues, nor has he ever resented reasoned contradiction, and that is his greatness. But Lin Piao's claim that he was the only one who never differed with Mao was to promote his own career and ambitions. His reproach was not that he differed with Mao, but that he never operated a self-change, harbored and nursed his power lust under a mask of loyalty. "Of them all [the major derelicts of the Party], he was the worst, because he was able to conceal his real motivations for so long."†

In today's catalogue of his crimes, we find little about Lin Piao between 1959, when he became minister of Defense, and 1966, for during these years his career was pinned on Mao's success.

The study of Mao's works in the PLA, and the "little red book" of Mao quotations,‡ often attributed to Lin Piao, is the work of the PLA General Political Department, under Hsiao Hua. The little red book of quotations was necessary in that transition time, when a whole new generation was beginning to read; it is no longer necessary when we find whole villages able to read. Lin Piao appended a preface to the second edition, after the book had already been in circulation for nearly eighteen months.

PLA reorganization in 1960 was impeded by the abrupt withdrawal of Soviet equipment, which posed a problem of weapons supply, solved to some extent by cannibalizing parts from airplanes or tanks or

---

* Mountain-toppism is acting like a warlord, inaccessible in his "mountain fortress" and wishing to grasp power by military means.

† Author's interviews with many ordinary people.

‡ *Quotations from Chairman Mao Tsetung* (in English; Peking 1966).

machinery. The supply problem was solved by the PLA's starting its own spare parts program. The formation of eight ministries of machine building in 1962–1963, five out of the eight said to be connected with design and production of military matériel, made the PLA independent of outside sources of equipment for ordinary weaponry, but below the level required by modern conventional forces. This facilitated in some respects the orientation away from highly technical professionalism, but also left unsatisfied demands from some army sectors for modern sophisticated equipment (such as electronic material, an important issue for military technology, which was to come up in 1969–1970). Strategic dispersal of arsenals and weapons manufacturing plants, parallel to industrial dissemination, was to make every region self-reliant in basic defense needs. The militia were to rely on local production of weaponry to relieve strain on major industrial plants. And the nuclear program absorbed a large part of the military investment, while conventional equipment came second.

From 1960 onward the PLA was deluged with political movements, on the principle that man, not weapons, is the decisive factor in war as in peaceful construction. All drives are meant to elevate morale and conduct. In October-November 1961 a military-political conference was held to strengthen political control. Indications are that Lin Piao was reprimanded for slackness in not dealing energetically enough with cases of corruption, arrogance, among army officers.

Lin Piao himself might be ambitious, self-serving, and degenerate into a traitor, but the PLA by 1964 had become a model of proletarian virtue.

A campaign to grasp "living thinking," in order to prepare the PLA for grappling with problems of propaganda and political education during the socialist education movement, was instituted in 1963. "Cherish the people" and "cherish the army" drives reinforced the links between people and army. Units were sent into each commune to train militia, disarm landlord-led bandit gangs, dig wells, level hills, build roads, organize afforestation.

In 1964 the PLA was ready for total participation in the socialist education movement, with Party branches at company level, cells in the majority of platoons, and 250,000 new Party members among soldier activists. The PLA organized cultural teams to propagandize the countryside, reverting to its educator role; PLA teams also led rural construction programs, which saw a great expansion in 1964–1965. One hundred million people were in the rural militia by 1965, ready to repulse any invader.* Despite all this, it is curious to note that not until May 1965 was all distinction of rank and uniform, established by Peng Teh-huai ten years previously, abolished by decision of the State Council. Surely, it seems, this could have been done before?

The slogan "Learn from the PLA" brought out emulation models, the outstanding one being Lei Feng, a young soldier who sacrificed his life to save others in a train accident. Undistinguished except for a remarkable zeal for doing everything ordinary with modest thoroughness and self-effacement, this non-hero was a people's hero because he was the typical "masses," a poor peasant's son, and all he wanted in life was to be "a stainless screw" performing service for the people with a perfect heart. However childish it may sound (he sewed buttons on comrades' clothes, swept floors left dirty by others, sent money anonymously to someone's father), he was outstandingly the stuff of saints, and great historical movements need such anonymous saints. He was always happy, never lethargic, nothing to him was humdrum, and his virtues, because they were so ordinary, made him lovable because he loved others more than himself. Among the urban educated youth, captives of cynicism and the pursuit of "high official jobs," Lei Feng stuck out. "I want my limited life to serve that limitless cause, the revolution," he wrote.

In 1964 demobilized officers and men were brought into administrative departments, meshed into the civilian superstructure, in a reinforcement of political education in the cities. A movement of exchange between civilian and military, to "learn from each other," took place. "Think sweet" was the motto of the candid PLA soldiers, and so they did, resistant to sarcasm, modest, humble and thorough. "Learn from the PLA in political education and ideological work" † accented the purpose of this infiltration. Every commercial unit, bank and ministry, even the Foreign Language Press, acquired its PLA contingent, come to help with the "four cleanups," to learn how to run things. Living Lei Fengs, they were as irresistible as water, unarmed, pleasant, unobtrusive, and they shamed some of the bureaucrats, for purity has a strong power.

Each school and university saw its small PLA contingent; the soldiers taught physical training (indistinguishable from military training). Six hundred thousand young students and staff employees from

---

* In 1965, with the war escalation in Vietnam, many believed that war between the U.S. and China was imminent.
† *People's Daily*, February 1964.

various institutions would go on a summer course of camping, swimming and practice shooting in that year. Physical fitness, moral goodness, application to study was the program; this sounds very boy scout, but revolutions were never made by sybarites.

Mao's poem was quoted:

> This land of bewitching beauty
> Has bred numberless heroes to do her obeisance,
> But to find those who truly serve her,
> Seek them today.

And today the common man, the Lei Fengs of China, millions of them, were coming into their own heritage. The future of the revolution was in their hands; the PLA was to be the pace setter to that future.

The socialist education movement in industry was far less active. It was buried under fulsome and bombastic reports of advance from its very beginning, being more under the control of the Liu "headquarters." The "four cleanups" in many administrative units were sheer formalism, not rousing the masses. The movement in the cities was first known as the five "antis": against cadres guilty of corruption, not speaking the truth, nepotism, bureaucratism, not cultivating relations with the masses. An exodus of surplus cadres from the cities to the rural areas took place, and by 1965 over a million had been sent to grass-roots organizations in the communes.

According to a *Red Flag* report,* members of the petty bourgeoisie among the workers had brought in nonproletarian ideas . . . There was slackening, shoddy work, lack of revolutionary fervor. Perhaps the divergent economic policies had to do with this decline. As late as February 26, 1965, *Peking Review* in an article, "Industrial Management in China," by Ma Wen-kuei, stated that there were still "many irrational rules and regulations" in industrial units.

A national conference in January 1964 was held to strengthen political and ideological work in the industrial sector. Socialist emulation campaigns to raise standards and improve management, to practice economy in raw materials were devised. The State Economic Planning Commission took a hand in this in February, convening political units

---

* Article by Ku To-chun in *Red Flag*, January 1964.

in each industry to get rid of "listless and procrastinating bureaucratism."

"We must emulate the Liberation Army, we must emulate Taching oilfield," said Mao. As Tachai was the agricultural model, so Taching oilfield became the industrial model proposed by Mao. The workers who in 1960 had gone there from the older oilfields of Karamai and Yumen were demobilized PLA veterans; they had achieved remarkable results, for by 1964 China was self-sufficient in oil because of Taching. The hardships they had endured, the pace at which they had worked, form an epic story of devotion and heroism by "ordinary men." In 1961 they had rejected Liu's orders to close down. In 1964 ten thousand educated young people from Shanghai's schools and universities were sent to Taching. The PLA's connection with Taching was, perforce, intimate, since the oilfield is in Heilungkiang province, neighboring the USSR.

From all reports, industry during this period did not do badly. There were certainly major advances, notably the tripling of chemical fertilizer plants, the establishment of new industries, the streamlining of others. Liu would subsequently be accused of having preferred to buy machinery from abroad rather than rely on native ingenuity, but a cooler assessment must do him the justice of seeing that there are certain things which no amount of native ingenuity can fabricate from scratch. An "all-around upsurge" in industry, proclaimed in early 1965, was real. If the small and medium industries were sacrificed, or limped along, at least the major and large complexes were run more or less efficiently (even if along capitalist lines, with problems in the future to come). And though the elitist system was maintained, it cannot be denied that there was also an effort at self-reliance. "We have progressed from copying to independent designing," said Po I-po.*

Some foreign observers in 1965 detected nervousness among industrial management teams that a reinforced political line, another "leap," would damage rather than strengthen industrial advance. But this point of view, which took into consideration only "production" in large complexes, was a "capitalist" point of view, not the thinking which would liberate the tremendous human potential of China into effective action.

"Training successors for the revolution is the Party's strategic task." In 1964 Mao posed the problem of successors as a vital issue, a "life and death" matter for the Party. The words "Red and expert" reap-

* *Far Eastern Economic Review*, October 1, 1964 (issue on China).

peared; Mao's strictures on education were again circulated. *Red Flag* No. 14, 1964, warned that U.S. imperialism pinned its hopes on a degeneration of the third and fourth generation. "Who can dismiss this view as entirely groundless?" Mao is quoted as saying.

The only way to avoid Khrushchevian revisionism, to ensure that China would not change color, was to train not a few, but "millions of successors." At the present time a very acute class struggle was going on in China, with frantic attacks by the exploiting classes, who had not given up.* Leadership in certain grass-roots organizations had been usurped. Old age was also upon the Party; "at present, the average leading cadre in the grass-roots organizations is more than forty years old, while the number of Party members over forty is very large . . . what will happen in ten or twenty years' time?"

Now there was, in Mao, a sense of urgency. Too swiftly had degeneration set in in the USSR. He remembered that cold snowy November 1957, when he had stood in Moscow, looking at the upturned eager faces of the thousands of Chinese students sent to study there in the "socialist motherland" . . . how many of them were revisionists now? And this invisible rotting at the heart must stop, though at the time he could not warn them, except to repeat that "the world is yours. . . . You young people full of vigor and vitality . . . our hope is placed on you . . . China's future belongs to you." But there had been too much belief in pap-feeding socialism. There must be the release of one previous quality, revolt, now smothered in a new orthodoxy. Revolution is dissent, its purpose to make the world young, to fashion new tomorrows. A new generation must come forward, fearing neither hardship nor death, to take up the burden when the old ones would depart.

Again, as at the Leap, the part study, part labor method of education was promoted. Since its inception in 1958, the Kiangsi province part study, part labor university had endured and expanded. While other academic institutions reverted to the old system, shutting the factories and workshops on the campuses, it had opened feeder schools "up the mountains and down the plains," recruiting peasant children. The students grew their food, built their dormitories. By 1970 they would have trained 140,000 agronomists, veterinarians, plant and soil technicians essential for China's intermediate technology in rural areas.

But elsewhere the practice of throwing out or humiliating workers' and peasants' children had not stopped. A certain middle school, admitting 2,181 such children in 1952, in 1956 took 173, and in 1961, 17.

* Various editorials and articles during 1964.

There was sound economics as well as sound politics behind the reform in education, for preventive health measures had brought down infant mortality and increased longevity; by 1964 probably half the population was less than twenty-one years old. Yet the courses were very long; it was only at twenty-five or twenty-six that a graduate engineer or doctor had finished studying; only one year of manual labor was required for him then, a year he was most disinclined to "lose." The cost of this kind of education to the state was large, and increasing, and this vast army of the educated all wanted to be white-collar workers.

In 1958, in Shanghai, a spare-time engineering college had been set up which took in 3,100 veteran workers, irrespective of age. Eight hundred graduates from 437 different factories came out in 1964 who had on the average worked fourteen years. No formal examination was given; the workers had been graduated by working on practical in-novations or designing new projects or machinery. By 1965 there were 1,051 part work, part study schools in Shanghai with 118,000 worker students, one-fifth of the total enrollment of full-time secondary schools in the city.

But obstruction and hostility to the part labor, part study system was strong. Amid the balderdash of enthusiastic articles recording as "al-ready basically achieved" what some of the men in charge of education had no intention of ever starting, one can discern the stubbornness of the conservative wing. Buttressed in their institutions, protected by the Ministry of Higher Education, eminent universities had restored longer years of study, classically orthodox degrees, prolonged postgraduate research . . . for the fortunate few. Very curiously, the children of workers and peasants found themselves shifted into the part work, part study system; the Ministry of Lower Education announced a vigorous all-around development of this lower system.

Again the fish was drowned in a flood of verbiage, but Mao's anger, and forcefulness, come through. "You have not been told the truth," he said bluntly in February 1964 to a Nepalese delegation on education who had been shown around. "Since ancient times, those who create new ideas, new ways of thought, have often been young people with-out much learning." The education system was killing imagination, initiative, vitality, and making a lot of young people shortsighted too. It alienated them and turned them into revisionists and dogmatists, with petrified minds.

Three hundred and twenty thousand young urban "knowledge bear-ers" (intellectuals) were to leave the cities to "go up the mountains and down to the plains" in 1964; in 1965 from Shanghai sixty thousand young went to Sinkiang, where Premier Chou and Foreign Minister Chen Yi visited them and encouraged them to settle down.

Like a tree in the wind, an establishment complies, stretches, then snaps back. So the Liu headquarters thought they would let the Mao storm pass and wear itself out. But "though the tree would like to be still the wind does not cease." Bureaucratic repose was no longer possible because Mao had started something which answered latent demands in the youth sector, raised the problem of the succession to his revolutionary generation. Among the students, lecturers, teachers in higher middle schools and colleges and universities, a good many debated the problems of education; others who had volunteered for labor during the Leap Forward were politicized by this contact with the realities of China. Dissent and criticism of the methods and the teaching in universities and colleges was suppressed, however; the education authorities confined debate within closed rooms and "regular channels." But small nuclei of incipient rebels sprang up and could not be stifled. In some universities these dissident groups were placed under surveillance or isolated for "study," their salaries docked, or they were sent off to the countryside in socialist education teams — from which they returned more radically ardent than ever.

The persecution of the "Maoist" element from 1964 to 1966 was insidious; it would become open ill-treatment only by 1966. To stifle real dissent by creating appearances of debate, the ministries of Education held conferences paying lip service to Mao's ideas but emphasizing "a well-thought-out and *long* process of educational reform . . . five years' experimentation, ten years' popularization," and prudence. All the formulae of inertia.

One case in point was the Communist Youth League, great reservoir for "successors" in the Party. Mao had listed in 1964 five main requirements for successors.* But the Youth League was described in 1964 as "dormant." Only 13 percent of 100 million eligible youths in rural areas had joined, only 10 percent of production teams in the whole country had Youth League members (one or two). Whether this was because recruiting of Party members in the countryside had been stopped (some poor peasant applications for Party membership waited fifteen years for a reply which never came) is not clear. And the leaders of the Youth League were often middle-aged men.

* *Training Successors for the Revolution Is the Party's Strategic Task* (English edition Peking 1965).

Suddenly in 1964 and 1965 the Youth League opened its doors wide and admitted in one swoop nearly eight and a half million new members, the greatest enrollment in its history, but without any investigation into class origin and with only formal requirements. Landlords' and rich peasants' sons, even the offspring of counterrevolutionaries, joined en masse. The admission of such a huge number, so suddenly, was certainly an attempt by the right wing to counter Mao and his youth policies. It would render the youth "problem" during the cultural revolution so much more complex. The Youth League was suspended in late 1966 and only revived in 1971.

"Tell the Ministry of Public Health that it works for only 50 percent of the people, and that of this 50 percent only the lords get real service. The broad masses of the peasants do not get medical treatment. The Ministry of Public Health is not that of the people; it is better to rename it the Ministry of Urban Health . . . or the Health Ministry of Urban Lords" (Mao, July 1964).

"Medical education must be reformed . . . The important thing (for medical students) is to improve themselves through study in practice . . . A vast amount of manpower and material has been diverted from mass work for carrying out research in rare diseases . . . no attention has been paid to the prevention and improved treatment of common diseases" (Mao, June 1965).

Oriented to the rural areas, with prevention as their axis of work, medical teams from the cities comprising eminent medical men and their students toured the countryside that year, some of them for the first time in sixteen years of revolution! The "barefoot doctors" system now came into being, as did clinics and hospitals at commune level, and family planning services; preventive measures (which between 1960 and 1964 had almost lapsed) were to lead to cooperative medical care, by which each commune member pays a small fee per year as medical insurance. By 1973 there would be over one million "barefoot doctors." They manned a web of public health services, medical care, access to hospitals for the sick, and education in hygiene and disease prevention. But it took Mao, and the cultural revolution, really to bring medical care to each village at last.

"The first problem is: Literature and Art for whom?" (Mao, 1942). Art and literature are the sensitive apex of the superstructure. This height would also be stormed, and from this storming emerged a radical group during the cultural revolution with a great impact upon its course. Among them, symbol of the revolution in art, would be Mao's wife, Chiang Ching.

Chiang Ching was busy from 1950 on investigating the scene of art and literature, although without a voice in any decision. Wu Han's play on the dismissal of Hai Jui (1960–1961) drew her attention. From 1962 onward she became very active, visiting artists and actors and musicians, expounding Mao's line in literature and art to them, and stirring them against the revisionist "headquarters" in the Party.

After 1960 the imitations or reproductions of Russian plays, operas and ballets which had previously been current tailed off, but nothing original or new replaced them; there was a return to the old plays; new plays on contemporary themes were few in number and often short-lived.

But the favorite all over China is opera in its various forms, its rich provincial varieties, and this enormous field had remained untouched. All that happened was that old scripts were resurrected; many operas propagated feudal themes like chastity of widows, filial duty, and such age-worn virtues of feudalism. Automatically the officials of Culture and Propaganda rejected, or sat upon as technically inferior, the work of young workers and peasants or "unknowns."

In 1963 Mao spoke forcefully on the Chinese opera, the vehicle capable of the deepest reach among the people. "Operas should develop what is new from what is old, rather than what is old from what is old. They must not sing only of emperors, kings, generals, and beauties."

Encouragement to write "prolifically on the last thirteen years" was voiced by the mayor of Shanghai, Ke Ching-shih, who produced an analysis of the reasons why new, revolutionary artistic expression was stiffed. "Problems abound in all forms of art," wrote Mao on December 12, 1963, "and the people involved [in maintaining these obstacles] are numerous; in many departments very little has been achieved so far in socialist transformation. The 'dead' still dominate . . . the social and economic base has changed but the arts as part of the superstructure which serve this base still remain a serious problem . . . Isn't it absurd that many Communists are enthusiastic about promoting feudal and capitalist art, but not socialist art?"

The revolution in opera, in the ballet and in music began in 1964, with Chiang Ching in a pioneer role. The new productions met with obstruction and harassment. No theaters vacant; no place to rehearse;

no publicity; no costumes; political criticism of the young breakaways.
. . . Finally an opera festival was held in the autumn of 1964; among
classical items, a modern opera and a modern ballet were shown. The
opera was to become the famous *Shachiapang*, at the time named *Fire
Among the Reeds*. The ballet was *Red Regiment of Women*. This was
the first time in history that the Chinese opera had taken a leap of
many centuries, and the innovation in the ballet, adapting western
choreography to a Chinese theme, was also a landmark.

At the festival Chiang Ching delivered a speech on the revolution of
the Peking Opera, which went unreported until 1967, three years later.
Opera "experts" criticized the new operas as "not genuine." Peng Chen,
the Peking mayor, tried to alter the title and the main character of *Fire
Among the Reeds*. In Kuangchow the new creations were obstructed.
A "struggle" to wrest the best singers and actors away from the revolutionary operas began. The ballet *Red Regiment of Women* put a stop
to the poor imitations of *Swan Lake, Giselle*, which no peasant or
worker ever saw or wanted to see. But it was a battle all the way.

"It is inconceivable that the dominating position on the stage
throughout our socialist country, which is led by the Communist Party,
should not be occupied by the workers, peasants and soldiers, the real
creators of our country," said Chiang Ching. There were three thousand theatrical companies in the country (not including amateurs),
and of these twenty-eight hundred were opera companies. There were
ninety drama companies. None of these staged anything but feudal
operas and plays or foreign plays. "What about the 600 million peasants, workers and soldiers, who are not portrayed? Where is the artistic
conscience you are always talking about?"

The intention was not to liquidate traditional operas, but to select
good ones. However, the accent must be on new creations. Chiang
Ching aptly remarked on the difficulty of creating positive characters,
for Chinese opera portrays its heroes larger than life. Yet this portrayal
must now be of the ordinary laboring people, the majority in the
world, the real heroes. It called in question the whole goal of artistic
creation, the glorifying of the common working man.

The new operas became immediately very popular. Articles then
suggested a coexistence of old and new in the name of "letting a
hundred flowers bloom"; new plays and contemporary Peking operas
were to be allotted one-third of the time, space and facilities given to
the old.

In ballet, the ballet officials insisted that choreography was a western art and could not be adapted; "the old must serve the new . . . things foreign should serve China," Mao retorted. The ballet could be Sinicized. The same for music. The new troupes started using western instruments on Chinese melodic themes.

The refusal to orient culture towards the masses also extended to the reform of the written language, a reform essential for mass literacy. "Over my dead body," shouted in the author's presence a vice-minister of the Ministry of Culture, pale with anger. Such was the reaction, almost psychopathic, to anything which might erode the class privileges of the new literocracy.

In literature, too, the trend towards stepping backward into the past was obvious. Poems culled from the Tang and Sung dynasties were translated by the Foreign Language Press.

After Mao's warning of December 1963 Chou Yang called impressively for "carrying high the red banner of Mao Tsetung Thought in literature and art." And did nothing. Six months later Mao came out with another serious warning directed against the Culture and Propaganda officials: "In the last fifteen years these associations . . . [the literature and art organizations such as the Federation of Writers], most of their publications (it is said that a few are good), and by and large the people in them (that is, not everybody) have *not* carried out the policies of the Party. They have acted as high and mighty bureaucrats, have not gone to the workers, peasants and soldiers, and have not reflected the socialist revolution and socialist construction. In recent years they have slid right down to the brink of revisionism. . . . Unless they remold themselves in real earnest . . . they are bound to become groups like the Hungarian Petofi Club."[*]

Chou Yang affected to see in these words an encouragement: "The situation in literature and art is good . . . apart from a few people." He omitted to remember how, in early 1962, he had gone about calling for a literature of the whole people, in imitation of Khrushchev's line at the Twenty-first Congress proclaiming "a state of the whole people" in the USSR. He also forbore to state how he had called the Leap "a tragedy," asked for "truthful depiction" in 1962.

When a bureaucrat is driven "up a cow's horn," he seeks a scapegoat among his subordinates. Writers Chou Yang had encouraged were now criticized. One of them, Shao Chuan-lin, had urged writing about mid-

[*] Instruction of June 27, 1964.

dle characters, not the forcefully "positive character" depiction of socialist art, and was encouraged by Chou Yang and "welcomed by a number of writers."* He was now criticized. Mao Tun, a distinguished non-Communist writer and minister of Culture, left his post and it was taken over by Lu Ting-yi.† "The methods some people use today are much more subtle. While they mouth high-sounding phrases about supporting the policy of the Party on literature and art, they are doing their level best to advertise nonrevolutionary things."‡

Mao was now forging ahead for another fourfold revolution, a cultural revolution as the motive power for accelerated advance. "Grasp revolution and promote production" was once again heard. Mao Tsetung Thought was lauded everywhere in a renewed bout of personality cult, similar to that in Yenan in 1944–1945.

In mid-1964 a committee in charge of the cultural revolution was formed. It was headed by Peng Chen, the mayor of Peking, than whom no more unlikely person could have been selected. Why did Mao not organize a committee of his own followers only, peremptorily refuse Peng Chen, who by now he must have known was an opponent of Chiang Ching's revolutionary innovations in art and in favor of control from above of any mass manifestation?

That is not Mao's way. His intention was to expose the revisionists by their own actions. He was also giving his opponents a last chance.

---

* *Peking Review*, December 25, 1964.

† It is stated that this retirement was due to ill-health. Mao Tun has been seen recently at official parties.

‡ *Peking Review*, December 25, 1964, probably quoting Mao.

2

Revisionism and Imperialism

The revolutionary peoples are more than nine-tenths of the population
of the world . . . victory will be theirs in the end.

— Mao Tsetung, June 1960

While launching this internal restructuring, Mao was at the same
time carrying on a campaign against Khrushchevian revisionism and
against American imperialism, both part of the same struggle, to keep
China unfaltering in her revolutionary duty towards the world. Revisionism in the USSR would give rise to what Lenin had called social-
imperialism, "even more perfidious" than the old type of imperialism,
for it would cloak itself in Marxist homilies.

After the Cuban missile crisis of October 1962, American involvement with the USSR was psychologically deeper than Kennedy's advisers ever noticed or analyzed. Khrushchev had succeeded in forcing
parity, a dialogue on equal terms, a tacit partnership of power, upon
the American administration. The bright brains around the American
President found themselves, without knowing it, dangerously inclined
to accept the Russian reports of China's irrationality and danger to the
rest of the world.* From that time on, the American administration
would look towards the USSR to help it in sticky situations, and this
priority given to the Russian connection would leave Khrushchev's
hands free for rearmament,† while the vision of a dangerous and bellicose China clouded the minds in Washington.

This fuzzy perception gave the Kennedy administration its rationale
for escalation in Vietnam. "The fundament of present Soviet-American
relations . . . is that they must be tacit . . . the two superpowers, both
eager to avoid a world war and worried about China, are simultane-

* David Halberstam *The Best and the Brightest* (New York 1972).
† James C. Thomson, Jr. "On the Making of U.S. China Policy, 1961–1969,"
China Quarterly no. 50 (1973), page 220.

ously both explicit enemies and implicit allies," wrote C. L. Sulzberger in a superb appreciation.* From the Washington window, the framework in which all foreign policy was conducted was the containment of China through military presence of the U.S. in Southeast Asia. And this obsession made a larger aperture for dialogue, despite the continuing ambassadorial talks now transferred to Warsaw, almost futile. The domino theory was sustained, an ingenious child's tale, visualizing the countries of Southeast Asia falling one by one to China. Any liberation movement could not but be instigated by the "Chincoms"; the desire of the local population for independence and social change was ignored. America was a prisoner of her own marvelously rhetorical dogmas of freedom, without an inquiry into the basis of freedom for others.

The almost indecent haste with which both superpowers signed the atomic test ban in July 1963 indicated this error of evaluation, well noted in the Kremlin. According to some European sources there were even talks between Kennedy and Khrushchev in which a joint preemptive operation upon China's nuclear plants was discussed.†

To oppose modern revisionism (that is, becoming like the USSR) was for Mao "our main task at present and for a long time to come."

China's aid program to the Third World increased. In the winter of 1963–1964 Premier Chou En-lai, with about sixty technicians and experts in various fields, made a ten-week tour of countries in Africa and Asia. The object of this voyage was to acquaint countries of the Third World with Chinese internal and foreign policy. The aid program figured prominently; Chou acquainted himself with the specific and real needs of each country, and money flowed out, in gifts, in loans with no interest or very low interest, and at very long term, for projects designed to aid the recipient country without dependence on China. Chou elaborated the "eight points of aid," proving that China was not supplying aid to benefit herself, but to help other nations to independence and self-reliance. Chinese experts and personnel would live at the standard of the country they were in, without extra amenities or privileges. China is today a big aid donor, in terms of benefits without indebtedness, beating the Soviet Union easily, and demanding no privileges or economic say in the recipient country.

"Things are different now, we don't need the Chinese any more." Khrushchev thus insulted the Chinese delegation to the Soviet Party

* *New York Times*, January 17, 1966.
† Joseph Alsop, "Go or No-Go," *New York Times Magazine*, March 11, 1973.

Congress in 1962. Mao Tsetung would notice that whenever Khrushchev needed support he would soften towards China, and harden again when this need vanished. In February 1963 Khrushchev called almost politely for a cessation of polemics, for he was at the time under pressure in the Kremlin, where his attitude towards the United States alarmed the diehards.

In December 1962 China appeared to consider favorably a request for another international consultation of Communist parties. Khrushchev, who had been against it, now urged it. For a while Mao Tsetung seemed to agree, but reserved the right of reply to all the attacks to which the CCP was subject in the press of the "socialist camp." It was agreed to have a preliminary meeting in July in Moscow. But by April 1963 Khrushchev was bouncing back and full of vituperation.

On June 14 Mao Tsetung would launch a most important document, which was in part a reply to a Khrushchev letter of March 30 which had condemned the "splitting activities of the Albanian dogmatists." It is a full statement of the Chinese case. It does not mention Khrushchev by name, is reasoned and mild in tone, but it contains a comprehensive indictment of the policies and theoretical statements of the Soviet premier since 1956.*

The gist of the June 14 document, described as "a frank presentation of our views . . . conducive to mutual understanding," is that the central issue of the differences is whether people still living under imperialism and capitalism need or do not need to make revolution; and whether those already on the socialist road need to carry their revolution forward "to the end." If the general line of the international Communist movement is "peaceful coexistence," "peaceful competition," and "peaceful transition," it violates the principles of the previous conferences (the 1957 declaration and 1960 statement).

Khrushchev's erroneous propositions are listed, among them that the contradictions between imperialist countries can be reconciled by international agreements among the big monopolies, and that through economic competition a world without wars and of all-around cooperation can be attained. The comment also implies that the USSR is making deals at the expense of other socialist countries, or even inciting

---

* *Proposals Concerning the General Line of the International Communist Movement* (also known as Letter in Twenty-five Points, and as First Reply), June 14, 1963; reply from the Central Committee of the CCP to the March 30, 1963, letter from the CPSU. The enormous number of letters, aricles, and comments through which Sino-Soviet debate has been carried on must now total more than two million words at least.

war against a socialist country by a capitalist country (this probably refers to India's attempt in 1962, openly aided by the USSR). A scornful attitude towards national liberation movements was a very serious offense. A broad united front against imperialism should be organized, relying on those who refused to be slaves of imperialism, including "kings, princes, and aristocrats." The Letter asserts that it is wrong to reject legal forms of struggle when they can and should be used, but one must not fall into "parliamentary cretinism" and advocate this as the only form of revolution. The peaceful development of revolution is "very seldom to be met with," Lenin had remarked. In fact there was no historical precedent for a peaceful transition from capitalism to socialism. "Some people" exaggerated the role of peaceful competition between socialist and imperialist countries, saying that imperialism would automatically collapse; all the oppressed peoples had to do was "to wait quietly for the advent of this day."

The Letter goes on to many other topics (altogether twenty-five): the principle of independence and equality among Communist parties; the complete banning and destruction of nuclear weaponry; peaceful coexistence between independent countries with different social systems but never between oppressed and oppressor nations or classes. A sixty-thousand-word document, it is the most comprehensive and well-reasoned exposé of Mao's thinking as yet penned, and a guide to all China's foreign diplomacy and policies as well as her relations with the Third World and with capitalist countries.

The Yugoslav writer Fetjo* has called the Letter in Twenty-five Points "a new Communist Manifesto," adapted to the present epoch. It spells out, above all, the role of liberation movements in the Third World and their importance. The possession or not of nuclear weapons will not alter the rise of nations wanting independence, liberation from exploitation. Seeing the state of the world today, we can only acknowledge that Mao saw correctly the direction of history.

In this document Mao warns that capitalist restoration in a socialist country is wholly possible, hints that this is already occurring in the USSR and is a warning to all socialist countries, "including China, and to all Communist and workers' parties, including the Chinese Communist Party."

The Letter lists four major contradictions in the world by order of importance, the first being the "contradiction between the socialist and the imperialist camps," as the formulations of the 1957 and 1960 meet-

---

* François Fetjo *Chine-URSS, de l'alliance au conflit* (Paris 1973).

ings in Moscow had it. But six years later, at the Ninth Congress of the CCP in April 1969, the main contradiction was listed as that "between oppressed nations on the one hand and imperialism and social-imperialism on the other." By then the Soviet Union, first socialist state in the world, had degenerated into becoming an imperialism "more ferocious" than any other. And in April 1974 at the United Nations the leader of the Chinese delegation, Teng Hsiao-ping, was to declare that the socialist camp had ceased to exist, and that the united front of the Third World, among which China counted herself, was based on the struggle against the dual hegemony of two imperialisms.

There are passages in this Letter in Twenty-five Points (as well as in the Nine Comments and numerous other replies, etc.) which bring us back to the young Mao of 1927. "The imperialists and colonialists tremble before the great revolutionary tempests . . . they say: 'It is terrible, terrible.' But the revolutionaries acclaim it and say: 'It is good, it is excellent.' " Mao has reproduced here exactly the style and almost the words of his first exposé, *Report on an Investigation of the Peasant Movement in Hunan,* when he revolted against the wrong line practiced then in the Chinese Party.

On June 18, 1963, the Central Committee of the CPSU in a plenary session announced the Chinese letter would not be published. It was "unwarranted . . . groundless and slanderous." Three Chinese embassy officials and some students were expelled for distributing copies of it. However, the Romanian Party printed the Chinese letter, and this placed Khrushchev in an impasse. The Soviet reply, dated July 14 (eighteen thousand words), in the form of an open letter, accused the Chinese leaders of being prepared to sacrifice hundreds of millions of lives, of belittling Soviet aid, wishing for world war, thinking that "wearing rope sandals and eating watery soup . . . is communism."

On July 19 a spokesman for the Chinese Central Committee ironically said that both the June 14 and the July 14 letters would be broadcast "in many languages." The Soviet letter was "a remarkable piece of work." To quote a Chinese poem:

> A remarkable work should be enjoyed together,
> And dubiety scrutinized in company.

It was "superlative material for learning by negative example."

Pravda in September denounced the "neo-Trotskyist" Chinese leadership and called for a conference to "rebuff the schismatics," saying that fifty-two parties, in great indignation at the Chinese attacks, had asked for this move.

Mao Tsetung kept up the great flood of comments, massive tonnage of words, effective bombardment of the ideological positions of Khrushchev. This cannonade had three purposes: one was the genuine one of "talking revisionism to death"; another was to force all Communists in the world to interrogate themselves and clarify their own minds; and the third was to teach the Chinese people and the "revisionists" at home. It also had the effect of preventing the latter from making any move for reconciliation or capitulation for two years.

In Comment No. 4, October 22, 1963, *Apologists of Neo-colonialism*, Mao denounced Khrushchev as a lackey of imperialism, wanting to share in a dual hegemony to enslave the world. Nuclear blackmail is denounced, and the tacit agreement between the two superpowers to settle "peacefully" all national and territorial conflicts, which would lead to wars by proxy and was an implicit consent to the American invasion of Vietnam.

Mao's great verbal war was to end with two comments directly condemning Khrushchev. The last comment was to be issued on July 14, 1964, the first anniversary of the CPSU reply to the June 14 document.

To someone who asked Mao, "When will these polemics cease?" he answered: "The sky won't fall, trees will grow, women will have children and fish will swim, even if we go on forever," and then added that it might take "a thousand years."* Lenin, in a minority, had battled the Second International when it went rotten with revisionism. Mao Tsetung in that winter of 1963–1964 was a young seventy, and growing younger with the vigor of a battle in a just cause.

The image of the CPSU as the center of proletarian internationalism was being chipped by the syllabled shrapnel. "Such a party . . . is incapable of accomplishing the great historical mission of the working class." No longer was Khrushchev a deluded abbot; he was the white-boned devil himself. Mao would call for the formation of "true Marxist-Leninist parties."

In October 1963 Khrushchev offered to deliver again industrial equipment and spare parts, and to return the technicians to China. He also offered to negotiate the brewing Sino-Soviet frontier dispute,

* Ten thousand years, according to other reports. In Chinese parlance, a thousand and ten thousand are not actual figures, but simply denote a very long time.

which had started with the clashes in 1959 and 1962 in Sinkiang. But he added the proviso that the frontiers had been "formed by history."

On March 8, 1963, the *People's Daily* had recalled nine unequal treaties which former Chinese governments had been forced to sign. The matter would not have been publicized had not Khrushchev in the previous December raised the question of Macao and Hong Kong, accusing the Chinese of making "concessions to British and Portuguese colonialists." The Russian position was that the "unequal treaties" *must* be accepted as binding and legal, for "no one makes history all over again." The Chinese standpoint was that China would never recognize the unequal treaties as equal, though she was ready to accept them as basis for an overall settlement of the frontier. Meanwhile the status quo should be preserved. "This is our stand for the last ten years."*

Mao's first talk with Khrushchev in 1954 must have raised the problems of the boundaries and the unequal treaties.

Boundary negotiations began in Peking in February 1964, but were suspended without results in May. And then on July 10, speaking to a group of Japanese from the Socialist Party of Japan, Mao said, "There are too many places occupied by the Soviet Union." The Japanese people were claiming the four Kurile Islands, occupied by the USSR since World War II.

Now each side accused the other of systematic border violations. Among China's neighbors only the USSR and India had deliberately created border disputes with China.† Chou En-lai had concluded boundary treaties with Korea, Afghanistan, Burma, and Outer Mongolia as well as Pakistan.

Russian aid was "neither a one-way affair nor gratis," said the Chinese. China had had to pay for everything, and had paid; the repayments of food products alone amounted to more than 2 billion rubles, and in minerals and rare metals essential for missile production 1 billion 400 million new rubles. Loans to China had been used for the purchase of war materials during the Korean War, when Korea "made the greatest sacrifices" and China had made sacrifices too, standing in the forefront so that the USSR was not involved. "For many years we have been paying the principal and interest on these Soviet loans." The letter reproaches the Russians with their extortion, the 1960 withdrawal of experts and scrapping of contracts, which had caused enormous

---

* The same policy applies to the frontier with India, which, historically, has never been demarcated.

† Letter of February 19, 1964, from the CCP to the CPSU.

damage to Chinese industrialization. "Now you have again suggested sending experts . . . to be frank, the Chinese people no longer trust you. . . . You have for years used trade for political pressure . . . you violate the independence and sovereignty of fraternal countries . . . oppose their efforts to develop their economy independently."

During the same period, a steady stream of articles and statements against imperialism issued from Mao, denouncing the escalation of war in Vietnam (August 29, 1963), calling for opposition to racial discrimination against American Negroes (August 8, 1963), upholding and supporting the struggle in Panama (January 12, 1964). Imperialism was the "most ferocious enemy of the peoples of the world." On every occasion Taiwan's occupation by U.S. troops was also mentioned. There must be a great united front of all peoples of the world against imperialism, including the American people themselves.

In November 1963 the assassination of the American-backed Ngo Dinh Diem in Saigon revealed the baffling morass into which the United States was sinking. The undeclared war was going badly; and though Kennedy was hopeful of a satisfactory settlement through the good offices of the USSR, there was a growing realization that it would take much more than military muscle to conclude the adventure.

A shift was perceptible in that autumn in America — a growing number of voices dissenting on the rigidity of U.S. policies towards China. Although Dean Rusk could not be moved in his hostility to "Red China," and the China Lobby* was still very powerful, not all his aides were of the same mind. Even Kennedy, on November 14, 1963, in his last press conference, would have to say that "we are not wedded to a policy of hostility to Red China." In December, two weeks after the assassination of Kennedy, it was left to Roger Hilsman of the State Department, a major critic of the Vietnam War, to make a speech which conveyed that "Red China is here to stay," the first time it was openly acknowledged that the policies of inflexibility might not be entirely correct.

The death of Kennedy did not change the foreign policy options for President Lyndon Johnson, a declared "hawk" on Vietnam. Seeking a solid foundation for his own presidency, he thought it best to continue as his undeservedly popular predecessor had done, and was thus compelled to "more of the same" in Vietnam. The division of opinion in the

---

* A lobby of American pro–Chiang Kai-shek personalities, which for years continued to sustain him.

United States concerning China policies was momentarily muted in the mounting thunder of the ever-growing Vietnam War, now represented as a great crusade to save the free world.

After the publication in China, on February 4, 1964, of the Seventh Comment, entitled *The Leaders of the CPSU Are the Greatest Splitters of Our Time,* the Soviet leadership decided on drastic action. Mikhail Suslov, who had had a long and bitter controversy with Teng Hsiao-ping in 1960, prepared an indictment, in the form of a letter sent to all Communist parties except the CCP, openly advocating the toppling of Mao at an international conference. "There must be . . . a struggle against the Trotskyite views and the sectarian and undermining activities of the Chinese leaders." Suslov's indictment was not published at the time, at the Romanian Party's request, and for some weeks the Romanians tried to mediate. Meanwhile, the Chinese reinforced all-out aid to Albania and to Vietnam.

On March 31, the Eighth Comment, *The Proletarian Revolution and Khrushchev's Revisionism,* called Khrushchev the greatest capitulation-ist in history and advised "leading comrades" of the Soviet Party to throw him "on the rubbish heap of history."

Khrushchev made his strongest attack yet on Mao in Budapest in April (altogether he made twelve speeches in under a fortnight in various countries), accusing the Chinese of "hegemony," irresponsible gambling, great China chauvinism, and so on.* The Chinese were behaving as political enemies; a conference must be called in which majority rule must prevail.

But now the size of the opposition to Khrushchev's scheme to ex-communicate China had grown. The Italian, Norwegian, Romanian, Indonesian and Cuban parties, Wladyslaw Gomulka of Poland and Janos Kadar of Hungary, all in various ways asked for delay; the Albanians (China's staunch supporters), the North Vietnamese, North Koreans, Japanese and Yugoslavs all dissented.

On July 28 the Chinese Party definitely rejected the calling of a world Party conference which Khrushchev was now pressing. The Chinese called it a "schismatic meeting" whose purpose was to split the international Communist movement. "Since you have made up your

---

* Great China chauvinism: an arrogant assumption of superiority over other races. This accusation is particularly inept, since Mao had battled against all chauvinism for many years. See the denunciation of chauvinism in *On the Historical Experience of the Dictatorship of the Proletariat,* 1956.

minds, you will probably call the meeting . . . or you will become a laughingstock. . . . If you do not call the meeting, people will say that you have followed the advice of the Chinese, and you will lose face. If you do, you will land yourselves in an impasse . . . dear comrades, we appeal to you not to attach too much importance to face. But if you . . . are determined to take the road to catastrophe, suit yourselves. We shall only be able to say: 'Flowers fall off, do what they may;/Swallows return, no strangers they.' "*

Two days later, on July 30, the CPSU invited twenty-five other Communist parties to send delegations to Moscow on December 15 to plan for a world conference to be held in 1965. However, the invitation specified that the meeting would "excommunicate" no one . . . because by that July, a host of parties no longer wanted to condemn China.

In August 1964 occurred the Tonkin Gulf incident and the first bombardments of North Vietnam. This purported attack upon U.S. vessels by the North Vietnamese has now been revealed as a fabrication† by Americans themselves.

The plot was for the purpose of justifying escalation; systematic bombing of North Vietnam would "bring them to their knees" and end the war in South Vietnam quickly. Underlying this assumption was the view that one could count on the USSR to be frightened and pressure the North Vietnam government to cut off equipment and supplies to the South Vietnam liberation forces.

When the bombardments took place, Hanoi protested and duly informed Moscow and Peking, asking for support; Khrushchev's reaction was irritation. He affected not to believe Hanoi, although Moscow was aware through its ordinary diplomatic services of an intended escalation, already discussed in the press and in Washington. Far from supporting socialist North Vietnam, a member of the socialist camp, Khrushchev advised Hanoi to bring the case to the Security Council of the United Nations!‡ This was a deliberate insult. In view of Peking's denunciations of the bombing, and promises of help and support ("the Vietnamese and the Chinese people are as brothers . . . as lips to teeth") and effective flow of aid and supplies, it was one of the incidents which led to the downfall of Khrushchev the next month.

---

* This quotation from a Tang dynasty poem is Mao's particular touch.
† See *The Pentagon Papers*, with commentary by Neil Sheehan and others (New York 1971), pages 258–270.
‡ The Democratic Republic of North Vietnam is not represented at the United Nations at the time of this writing.

But then, all that summer Khrushchev had been out of luck. Not only were most of the parties reluctant to be rushed into a conference (and the Vietnamese had protested in April against a "hasty conference without adequate preparation"), but he had other troubles as well. One of his best supporters, and the most hostile to China, Maurice Thorez of the French Communist Party, died on July 11 on his way to Moscow. Palmiro Togliatti of the Italian Party expired in August. Before his death Togliatti wrote a long document, called his testament, indicating his serious reservations on the strategy and tactics of the Soviet Party in the dispute. Rather, he wrote, do as the Chinese did: continue the polemics, but with reason and in an objective manner; "Let us fight the Chinese by facts and not by phrases." Although opposed to the Chinese ideological stand (Mao had written a hundred thousand words exposing Togliatti's erroneous thinking), he was unhappy about the way the USSR behaved, especially towards other Communist parties.

A wave of dismay swept the other parties. Why did the USSR allow the bombing of a fraternal socialist country, member of the socialist camp? Khrushchev had so often boasted that "any war" could be stopped by the might of the USSR.

And in China great banners, U.S. AGGRESSION AGAINST THE VIETNAM DEMOCRATIC REPUBLIC MEANS AGGRESSION AGAINST CHINA, warned the United States not to go too far. Fifty thousand PLA men were moved to the frontier; forty thousand workers would be in North Vietnam keeping the railway between the two countries in good condition through the next few years. A constant flow of weapons, ammunition, rice, cloth — all without charge — would flow to the North and to the South Vietnam liberation forces for the next ten years. In fact, China had already begun aid to Vietnam in 1960.

On August 30 Mao wrote scornfully to the Kremlin: "In your eyes, all fraternal parties are puppets . . . we shall never be taken in by your fair words, nor submit to your threats."

The Romanians issued a declaration that unless participation was unanimous, no conference should be held. As for Albania, who from the start had fought side by side with China, she was unquenchable, and some of the best documents produced in this great war of ideas are from the Albanian Party.

In September *Pravda* went off at a tangent, accusing China of claiming one and a half million square kilometers of Russian territory. This totally unfounded assertion was the start of a Yellow Peril campaign among the Russian peoples which continues to this day.

Khrushchev went to Sochi in the Caucasus for a rest at the end of September. During his absence a carefully prepared palace coup against him took place. On October 13 he received a phone call from Leonid Brezhnev asking him to return to Moscow for a meeting of the Presidium. Faced with a hostile Presidium, Khrushchev thought he would again do what he had done in 1957 — ask for a meeting of the Central Committee and win. But in 1957 the Central Committee had been stuffed with Khrushchev's men; this time it was not so, and the Red Army did not intervene in his favor. Suslov, faithful to Khrushchev for some years, now demanded his resignation. On October 14 Khrushchev was superseded.

On October 16 China exploded her first atom bomb. This was greeted with joy throughout the Third World; the Africans were jubilant; so were even such sworn enemies of communism as Tunku Abdul Rahman, prime minister of Malaysia, who expressed his "happiness" at the Chinese bomb.

Immediately the Chinese renewed their demand* for the total destruction and interdiction of manufacture of all atomic weapons. They insisted that they had given themselves nuclear weapons solely to break nuclear "monopoly and blackmail," solemnly promised never to be the first to use nuclear weapons whatever the provocation.

"From the very first day China developed her nuclear weapons, her aim has been to break the nuclear monopoly of big powers and realize equality among all countries, big or small, and eventually to eliminate nuclear weapons. We firmly stand for the complete prohibition and thorough destruction of nuclear weapons and have repeatedly declared that we will never be the first to use nuclear weapons. We believe that we will certainly attain our goal."

With this success, "due to self-reliance," China's position in the world had now changed, said Foreign Minister Chen Yi. And Washington remarked that "the way was open . . . for a dialogue on atomic disarmament." But "the decisive factor is man," reiterated the Chinese. And on October 22 the *People's Daily* declared that China had a weapon far more powerful than nuclear weapons: "the Thought of

* See letter from Premier Chou En-lai to all heads of state and government, demanding total destruction and interdiction of all nuclear weapons, August 2, 1963 (Peking 1963). See also the Chinese Government Statement of October 16, 1964, and Premier Chou's cable to government heads of the world on October 17, 1964. Also repeated at the United Nations by the Chinese delegation in 1972, 1973, 1974.

Mao Tsetung, the direction of the great, glorious and correct Chinese Communist Party, and the superiority of the socialist system."

What would Khrushchev's successors be like? No one in China expected radical improvement. Nevertheless, Mao Tsetung, Chou En-lai, Liu Shao-chi and Chu Teh sent warm congratulations on October 16 for the nomination of Brezhnev as Party first secretary and Alexei Kosygin as premier, hoping "the unbreakable friendship between the Chinese and Soviet people would continue to develop." Chou En-lai and six other leading personages visited Moscow in November for the fifty-seventh anniversary celebrations of the Russian Revolution.

At the Kremlin, Chou was given a standing ovation by the assembled delegates, spontaneous admiration of many, even if they did not agree with the Chinese theses, for China's courage and steadfastness, Mao's brilliant polemical campaign, and of course the fact that China was now a nuclear power. But in his public speech on November 6, and in "frank and comradely talks" with Chou En-lai, Brezhnev indicated clearly that the new leadership would continue Khrushchev's foreign policy. The plans for an international conference would go on, as there was an "urgent necessity" for unity.

On the 14th Chou En-lai went back to Peking, and again Mao was at the airport to welcome him. That very day the Russian press started polemics again. On November 20 *Red Flag* in Peking published an article entitled *Why Khrushchev Fell*. The Chinese brushed off suggestions of ill-health, methods of work, age; Khrushchev fell "because he vainly tried to obstruct the advance of history." Many charges were laid against him: that he had tried to write off the achievements of the Russian people, to defame the socialist system under pretense of exposing Stalin and the personality cult; sought entire cooperation with imperialism, maintaining that only the heads of the U.S. and the USSR could decide the fate of humanity; obstructed national liberation movements (such as the Algerian war of liberation, which he had described as an internal affair of France); made no protest on the bombing of North Vietnam in August 1964 and thus allowed escalation; sabotaged Chinese industry, encouraged India in armed provocations, encroached on the internal affairs of fraternal countries, led the USSR back to capitalism . . . and now, should there be Khrushchevism without Khrushchev, it would end up in a blind alley.

The war in Vietnam provided more occasion for invective and denunciation.

In December 1964 – January 1965 the White House probed the Kremlin, asking it to influence Hanoi to stop supporting the South Vietnamese National Liberation Front and to engage in "unconditional discussions." The war was going badly, and the Staley-Taylor plan was being put in effect.* The probe was accompanied by a threat of bombing escalation. Far from rejecting this approach, the Soviet government agreed to transmit these proposals to Hanoi, and Kosygin went in person to give the message to Ho Chi Minh (February 6–10, 1965).

But Ho Chi Minh was no compliant satellite. The Vietnamese are an intransigent, ardently nationalistic, stubborn people, and they proved unbendable. Ho Chi Minh signified his anger to Kosygin, and the latter could pacify him only by promising more help to Vietnam. Ho Chi Minh and the National Liberation Front now made their positions clear in official statements. In November 1964 a major conference was held in Hanoi.† The view that the war must be stopped "somehow" lest it become a world war was rejected. The North Vietnamese laid down their conditions. The 1954 Geneva conference had recognized Vietnam as an independent, sovereign, *unified* nation; the provisional military demarcation between North and South Vietnam was supposed to be effaced by elections held in both areas. But the Americans had not allowed these elections. (Eisenhower in his own book *Mandate for Change* wrote: "I have never talked or corresponded with a person knowledgeable in Indochinese affairs who did not agree that had elections been held . . . possibly 80 percent of the population would have voted for Ho Chi Minh.")

Now the U.S. must withdraw all its troops and weapons from South Vietnam and let the South Vietnamese settle their own affairs, stop its acts of provocation and bombing of North Vietnam, and respect the 1954 Geneva conference agreements.

The argument that the bombing of North Vietnam would stop the war in South Vietnam was illogical, but it was the main argument of the Johnson administration to justify its actions. Had the USSR vigorously protested, and indicated all-out help to Vietnam, both North and South, there would have been no American escalation. And such

* Copied on the model used in Malaya during the Emergency 1950–1959: barbed wire around every village, and the death penalty for giving any food and supplies to the guerillas.

† See Anna Louise Strong *Letters from China* (3 vols., Peking 1963–1965). Letter of January 8, 1965, on the Hanoi International Conference, November 25–29, 1964.

firm action would not have led to a global war. But this was not done.

On February 7, 1965, the day after Kosygin arrived in Hanoi, the U.S. started regular bombing raids on Vietnam, adding insult to provocation. Kosygin flew to Peking on February 10, held talks with Mao Tsetung, Chou En-lai and Chen Yi. Kosygin was fulfilling an awkwardly shameful mission. He developed three points: (1) The danger of escalation to "total war" unless the Americans were given an honorable way out of Vietnam ("peace with honor"). This was tantamount to asking Mao to help pressure the Vietnamese for liquidation of their national liberation struggle. What about Vietnamese honor? asked Mao. (2) That the international conference of all Communist parties to be held in March was only a consultative meeting. Kosygin tried to persuade China to come, as a mark of unity. (3) "Unity of action" to aid Vietnam. Kosygin suggested an aerial bridge for weapons conveyance through China. A dramatic stance, totally out of step with the kind of war going on in South Vietnam, a guerilla war with "the countryside surrounding the cities."

Mao replied that an international conference in the present circumstances would only confirm the divergence of views, it would not bring unity. As to the cessation of polemics, he thought polemics should go on as long as necessary. He was willing to make it nine hundred years instead of a thousand, from a spirit of conciliation. As for unity of action, what particular unity did the USSR have in mind? Unity in making a deal to pressure the Vietnamese to give up? Unity to bargain with the U.S., using the Vietnamese as a pawn in a dirty game? How could there be unity of action to betray the revolutionary cause? As to "global" war, Mao said he did not believe it would happen over Vietnam.

Mao's view on the third point had been made explicit earlier that year in an interview with Edgar Snow.* The war in South Vietnam was a people's guerilla war, and if Americans increased their troops and weaponry they would only speed up the arming of the people against them. He thought the South Vietnam forces could win by their own efforts. Only if the American forces escalated and attacked China would there be a larger war. Probably the American leaders knew it and consequently would not invade China.

About the invasion of North Vietnam, Mao seemed quite sure (quot-

* Edgar Snow "Interview with Mao Tsetung," *New Republic*, February 27, 1965.

ing Dean Rusk) that there would not be an invasion of North Vietnam, only bombing, under the argument that this would stop the war in South Vietnam. "China's armies would not go beyond her borders to fight. . . . The Vietnamese could cope with the situation."

To an Italian Communist* Teng Hsiao-ping explained that the bombings would not solve the Vietnam problem for the U.S. Nor would troop escalation. America was bound to fail. If the Americans invaded North Vietnam, China would be forced to intervene. This, however, would still be a local war, like the Korean War. If the Americans bombed China the war would be enlarged, but whether it would become a world war depended not on China but on the U.S. and the USSR. And he clearly stated that China would not call on the USSR for help, despite the treaty of alliance of 1950.

As to the third point, Mao refused point-blank to allow Russian garrisons and an aerial bridge or airlifts. The whole of China's rolling stock was at the disposal of the USSR for sending any weaponry they wanted. In fact, the Chinese kept empty rolling stock tied up, waiting for Russian supplies which did not arrive, for months.

"Comrade Kosygin expressed agreement with our views at the time and stated that they [the new Soviet leadership] would not bargain with others on this issue [Vietnam]."† But when he returned to Moscow, Kosygin changed his mind.

The day after his return, on February 16, a proposal for reconvening the Geneva conference of 1954 on Indochina was made by Moscow to China and to North Vietnam. Without waiting for a reply, the USSR as co-chairman informed France and Great Britain of the proposal. On February 25 the United States would turn it down, saying it was not contemplating any "negotiations," though the Kremlin had acquiesced to "unconditional negotiations." The Chinese pointed out that such a conference would have stopped the Vietnamese from fighting but left U.S. troops in situ in South Vietnam. It was a "shameful betrayal" again.

As for the international conference of Communist parties, seven parties refused to attend; others accepted with many reservations. The conference (March 1–5, 1955) was a gloomy affair, filled with the

* Aldo Natoli article in *Il Manifesto* (Rome), November 15, 1972, on relations between Vietnam, China and the USSR. Reprinted in French in *Le Monde*, November 30, 1972.

† *People's Daily* and *Red Flag* Editorial Departments *Refutation of the New Leaders of the CPSU on "United Action,"* November 11, 1965 (English edition Peking 1965).

sound of bombs over Vietnam. All it could do was recommend a preliminary consultative conference to discuss the question of a new international conference in the years to come. Time and again the Kremlin would hold "international" conferences; none of them would oust China, nor could they restore the ideological prestige of the Soviet Party.* The socialist camp had begun to fragment. In 1974 at the United Nations, Teng Hsiao-ping would announce that it had ceased to exist.

In late March 1965 the Chinese denounced the conference as "illegal" and "schismatic." "The new leaders in Moscow have merely changed the signboard and employed more subtle methods in order better to apply Khrushchevism." It was "sham revolution but real betrayal."

The Kremlin leaders did, for a short while, deploy to some effect their new catchword phrase "unity of action" in aid to Vietnam. They hoped by this to introduce differences between the Vietnamese and the Chinese, between the Chinese and other Communist parties, by denouncing "obstructiveness" on the part of China.† They also hoped to revive the revisionist opposition to Mao within the Chinese Party itself.

As in a chorus, with point and counterpoint, the American stance towards China hardened. In February and March newspaper articles openly discussed war with China. The policy of "containment" was revived; Johnson's speeches showed an escalation along with U.S. bombings in Vietnam and the spectacular rise in U.S. combat troops there.‡ "China, not the USSR, is the enemy," proclaimed Defense Secretary Robert McNamara (February 19, 1965).

But the Chinese were aware that Johnson had inherited a mess not of his making; that his advisers were in favor of an extension of the war on the grounds that victory could be secured by "punishing" Hanoi. Johnson himself, as Hans Morgenthau pointed out in a perceptive article,§ had a far subtler mind than he was given credit for. But he had to carry on, hoping the mess would clear with a little more punch to the military arm; his numerous speeches, television appearances, strenuously explaining his policies ("we seek no wider war") to the

---

* This is occurring again at the time of writing (December 1975), when Moscow is calling for a pan-European conference and even previously docile West European Communist parties (such as the French) express reservations.
† This was denied by the Vietnamese themselves.
‡ Fifty thousand GI's in May 1965; 530,000 in May 1968.
§ Hans Morgenthau "War with China?" New Republic, April 5, 1965.

American people, his energetic obsession with Vietnam, with the fact that America must win or lose face forever, were indications of his own unease.

Mao Tsetung emphasized again that it was entirely possible for Vietnam to win through "self-reliance" (which does not mean self-sufficiency, for China's help was continuous). "A small and weak country can certainly defeat a large one," provided the cause is just and the people mobilized. It is a fundamental tenet of Mao's concept of people's war. On February 15, 1966, an editorial in the *People's Daily* quoted Mao: "The South Vietnamese people are sure to win and the U.S. aggressor forces and their lackeys will certainly lose."

The Kremlin leaders had gauged right in thinking that the slogan "Unity of action" would foment trouble within the Chinese Party itself. Mao Tsetung himself had said to Kosygin that "some" of his colleagues did not agree with his views. "Sometimes I am the only one who agrees with myself," Mao would say with wry humor in 1966.

Since the escalation, discussions had taken place in China on the possibility of an extension of the war to North Vietnam, when China would certainly intervene. This would mean war with the United States; and some PLA personnel, including the chief of staff, Lo Jui-ching, appeared convinced that war would occur.

A distinction must be made between those who genuinely believed that war was inevitable and the revisionists in the Party, who saw the advantage they would derive from it. Was Lo Jui-ching really sincere in his conviction, or was he anxious, as was Liu Shao-chi, almost to provoke war, or at least a war psychosis, in order to stop the cultural revolution program which Mao had announced in January 1965 and which he was determined to carry through?

Lo Jui-ching personally had differences with Lin Piao. He was unhappy with the state of weaponry in the PLA; a professional man, he organized tournaments where skill and military excellence rather than political knowledge were awarded prizes; he did not believe in close combat, body to body combat, but in conventional warfare. He felt that faced with a war threat, all other problems were secondary. The army should be deployed on a war footing, and there must also be "unity" within the Party in China to cope with the external threat. Lo's ideas are expressed in a May 1965 article in *Red Flag* entitled: *Commemorate the Victory Over German Fascism. Carry the Struggle Against U.S. Imperialism Through to the End!* Not that Lo recommended unity of action with the USSR; he did not. But he argued that "all dying reactionary forces . . . put up final desperate struggles."*

In April the USSR made two specific proposals, one for a tripartite meeting of the Soviet Union, North Vietnam and China on the Vietnam War, and the second for sending through China some four thousand Soviet military men to be stationed in Vietnam; the use and occupation of airports in China, to be manned by five hundred or more Soviet experts; the opening of an air corridor and free traffic for Soviet planes in China's airspace. This was only a repetition of what Kosygin had suggested in February. It was again rejected, for at the same time the USSR was pressuring North Vietnam for "unconditional negotiations" and backing an Indian proposal for a cease-fire which would allow U.S. troops to remain indefinitely in South Vietnam.

Mao Tsetung was convinced there would not be an American attack on China, nor invasion of North Vietnam. The battle against "modern revisionism" was the top priority. He would "carry the struggle against Krushchev revisionism through to the end,"† and also carry the battle against the Party right-wing, "Chinese revisionism," through to the end. They were "two faces of the same struggle."

It is not surprising therefore if the right wing endorsed Lo's military views. Mao's streamlining of the PLA‡ showed that he was preparing for internal showdown, not external conflict. And with Mao there is absolutely no compromise on ideology. As he would say himself: "When it is a question of principle, I . . . never let go."

The slogan "Unity of action" could be used to deviate this "to the end" threat. Articles pleading for reinforcing Party unity appeared, as they always appear in times of acute intra-Party struggle. Liu's book *How to Be a Good Communist*, Mao's writings, and study of Marx and Lenin were all praised as equally valuable to resolve all problems. Many stories appeared in the newspapers in which "unity and friendship" resolve quarrels, and "intransigence" is deplored.

Because of hints in military circles that a limited accord with the USSR should be considered in case of war with the U.S., on May 14, 1965, China exploded a second atom bomb to show its independence in nuclear matters.

In August the reprint of Mao's *Problems of Strategy in the Guerilla*

* Lo Jui-ching has since been rehabilitated.
† *People's Daily* Editorial Department *Carry the Struggle Against Khrushchev Revisionism Through to the End*, June 14, 1965 (English edition Peking 1965).
‡ See pages 226–232.

*War Against Japan** was a response to divergent views in the PLA on the priority of dangers. On September 3 the two opposite views were expressed on the same day — one view by Lo Jui-ching in a speech at a mass rally celebrating the twentieth anniversary of the victory over Japan, and the other by Lin Piao in the *People's Daily*.

The People Defeated Japanese Fascism and They Can Certainly Defeat U.S. Imperialism Too is the title of Lo's speech. Lin Piao's *Long Live the Victory of People's War* is a condensation of all that Mao had said or written on war strategy and tactics. It carries, however, a Mao-inspired expansion; the grand strategy of a world united front against imperialism follows the principles of people's war.

Lin Piao's article was given great publicity, while Lo Jui-ching was now criticized. In another month the cultural revolution would begin. The Soviet "united action" play had brought to the surface yet another contradiction within the PLA itself, but it did not stop the cultural revolution.

* Written in 1938. See *Selected Works of Mao Tsetung* (English edition Peking 1961–1965), vol. II.

3

The Cultural Revolution
Swings into Action

It is I who started the fire.
— MAO TSETUNG
October 1966

Throughout 1965, the still skin of that ebullient entity called China deceived both experts abroad and visitors within. The colossal turmoil which would shake the country was not guessed, nor was there indication of the final, abrupt division in the Party. Economists picked up divergences on policies for the third five-year plan, but the usual bias, stemming from a division of economic and political aims, prevented most from realizing how crucial was the debate, and how politically full of warning was Chou En-lai's report in December 1964 on the work of government. It was a question of two destinies for China, of a life and death struggle. Very few realized that the words "revolution through to the end" carried so much impending upheaval.

Indications that the policies and methods of the Leap of 1958 would be the ones guiding the Third Plan were abundantly clear in the *People's Daily* editorial for the sixteenth anniversary, October 1, 1965. "Long live the general line of going all out, aiming high, and achieving greater, faster, better and more economical results in building socialism," it was headed. But resistance to this policy continued, pugnacious, subtle, outwardly compliant, captiously hindering.

To all appearances, the cultural revolution already announced in 1964 was proceeding satisfactorily, or so the press proclaimed. The socialist education movement had certainly strengthened peasants' associations, which were getting more vocal. Great campaigns to study Mao Tsetung Thought, to emulate the PLA, were dutifully reported.

China's financial and commercial system was endowed with "strengthening" political committees manned by PLA demobilized veterans; strategic industrial units had similarly been reinforced. The intensive study of Mao Thought, it was said, had already effected great changes in thinking and doing; all successes were ascribed to it; and a pervasive Mao cult (boring in its loquacity) prevented critical assessment of the resistance to Mao Thought. Dialectical, "one divides into two" scientific thinking had led to success in solving medical, botanical, engineering and other problems. Exaggeration depresses.

The refutation of Yang Hsien-chien's heretical "two combine into one" theory silenced the opposition on the philosophical level. The down-to-labor movement among Party cadres now extended to Party secretaries, who criticized their own "mandarin behavior." University professors and students went in teams to rural areas. Industry was now "truly serving" agriculture; the volume of water conservancy works in that year (with PLA participation) had been the greatest ever — 1.3 million hectares were opened to irrigation in 1965 alone, of which 99 percent was funded by the communes themselves. Chemical fertilizers, cheaper and more, were now available, and the harvests were good. Tractors of various kinds were turned out. The policy of lending only to selected areas was canceled. Small industrial plants, hydroelectric, cement, fertilizer, agricultural implements, and light industries of various kinds increased in rural areas. Publishing services supplied more science books to brigades and production teams. Actors, musicians, drama troupes toured the villages, bringing culture and leisure to the peasantry. A wired broadcasting network was erected to web China's countryside, with every team and sometimes every house equipped with its own loudspeaker, bringing news, exhortation, medical and agricultural advice, weather forecasts, scientific knowledge and political study. The picture was of health, modest prosperity and achievement.

On the mental level, an understanding of what Mao Tsetung wanted for his people appeared to percolate through the masses and the Party. On October 18, 1965, the *People's Daily* published a revealing statement by a Party secretary. "We always think that the source of opposition lies . . . with the basic level cadres and the masses . . . we do not seek the reason in the directives themselves, but criticize the lower cadres. . . . This is wrong. . . . We were greatly shocked when we read Chairman Mao's teaching that 'to carry out directives from *upper levels*

Page 264 — The Cultural Revolution and After

blindly and without reservation' is the most subtle way of opposing or sabotaging such directives."

If everything was proceeding so well, then why was the upheaval necessary? In 1972 and 1973 one still heard it said aloud in China: "Was it really necessary to do it this way?" For the cultural revolution had to pay its cost, in errors, in extremism, in destruction.

The answer is a question of class outlook, of ultimate goals. The choice was either an unexplained palace coup, removing Liu Shao-chi, imposing Mao's line from above, or the way which Mao chose, which was to "rouse" the totality of the people in order to let them, through revolutionary practice, grasp the great issues at stake. Had the problem of Chinese revisionism been settled by a diktat from Mao, the people, and especially the young generation, would never have realized the ups and downs, the torment and conflict, the tortuousness and complexity of revolution. It had to be a revolution within the Chinese revolution, and in fact it amounted to a civil war (as Mao himself would aver). Only this could shock the Party and the people into an understanding of the continuing revolution; of the danger of assuming that all problems would be solved once a Communist Party took power; of the danger of docility and submission to orders "from above" without using one's own head . . . of what it really means to be a revolutionary.

Notwithstanding the comforting lullabies of articles proclaiming success from every angle and every day, what was taking place was actually reformism "from above," by no means as thorough as the reports would have us believe, and without the real participation Mao wanted to create by and of *the people.* The outside perfection of an authoritarian order was not fooling Mao Tsetung. The hard core of conservative thinking remained intact, and it had its strongholds. Some of these strongholds of the "bourgeois headquarters within the Party" were in North China cities, Shenyang, Tientsin and Peking. The Peking Municipal Party Committee was solidly pro-Liu. To quote Mao, "No needle can penetrate it, no water percolate through it" — it was a closed, tight nucleus of high Party officials who controlled "the Center." It was against this high bureaucracy that Mao went to war.

At the December 1964 – January 1965 meetings of the Central Committee, Politburo, and the enlarged work conference, Mao Tsetung had raised once again, and even more succinctly, the challenge to Liu. Addressing the provincial representatives present, he said: "If revisionism appears at the Center, what will you do about it? There is the possibility, and it is a real danger."

On June 14, 1965, anniversary of the start of the Sino-Soviet polemics two years before, the editorial *Carry the Struggle Against Khrushchev Revisionism Through to the End,* which bore Mao's style and imprint, indicated that the battle against revisionism was on the same level of importance as the battle against imperialism. On November 11, 1965, *Refutation of the New Leaders of the CPSU on "United Action"* accused the USSR of collaborating with the United States on the question of Vietnam, and predicted a period of "great upheaval, great division, and great reorganization" in the world, for which China must prepare. "Comrade Mao Tsetung has often said . . . that if China's leadership is usurped by revisionists . . . the Marxist-Leninists of all countries should . . . expose and fight them." This invitation to criticize China should she ever become revisionist was to be repeated in April 1974 by Teng Hsiao-ping, leading the Chinese delegation at the United Nations. Mao's hand and heart are revealed in the poetic quotation at the end:

> *With power and to spare, we must not cease the pursuit*
> *Nor halt in mid-course for the sake of idle laurels.*

Antirevisionism was the heart, the very core of the cultural revolution, and Mao pressed on, undeterred, to make China safe from revisionism. His contempt for revisionists burst in a poem.

> *Ants on the locust tree wear a great nation swagger,*
> *And mayflies lightly plot to topple the giant tree.*

But as always he pinned his faith and trust on the masses, on humanity itself:

> *The four seas are rising,*
> *Clouds and water rage. . . .*
> *Away with all pests!*
> *Our strength is irresistible.*

He was now seventy-two years old, reported failing, a nurse at his elbow. This outward aspect of physical decrepitude may have been put on to lure his opponents still deeper in their plots to overturn him and his policies. The next year the nurse had disappeared, and a jaunty, vigorous Mao would be launching the most dangerous campaign of his lifetime, engaging in the most strenuous physical and mental activity. Until the roof fell upon his head, Liu Shao-chi would not believe that Samson-Mao would shake the pillars of the edifice and produce "great havoc under heaven" rather than forswear the principles and the goal of revolution, rather than see China slide, unconsciously, peacefully, into revisionism.

And therefore, in between soothing propaganda pieces recounting how well everything went ("lullabies to send people to sleep") the press was studded with articles setting out, step by step, the blueprint of the cultural revolution to come. On October 1, 1965, *Using the Proletarian World Outlook to Create Our New World*° said that a break must be made with the "four olds": obsolete ideas, notions, habits and conventions. Destruction of the four olds would be the launching pad for the youth movement the next year. "The problem today is . . . that old ideas do not reveal themselves nakedly but generally clothe themselves in socialist terminology and slogans in order to survive and to spread."

In September 1965 another stormy work conference of the Politburo was held. Mao Tsetung pressed for implementation of the Party policies of the tenth plenum (September 1962). And he brought up, at last, the case of Wu Han's writings and the play *The Dismissal of Hai Jui.* "The crux of the play is the question of dismissal from office. The Ming emperor . . . dismissed Hai Jui. In 1959 we dismissed Peng Teh-huai. Peng Teh-huai is Hai Jui too." This was a political matter, not merely the literary vagaries of a frustrated intellectual who also happened to be the capital's vice-mayor.

The Group of Five in charge of the cultural revolution, headed by Peking's mayor Peng Chen, was to investigate the case. This test of intention Peng Chen did not pass. Peng Chen was possibly not pro-Khrushchev — in 1945 he had complained of the high-handed methods of the Russians in Manchuria — but he was against the mass line, preferring the tutelage model.

After the meeting Mao left Peking, and went traveling in South and Middle China and to Shanghai, where he remained that winter. Through the winter his supporters (the "radical wing" which promoted the cultural revolution) were engaged in peripatetic moves to recruit support for Mao and the "proletarian left." For instance, Chen Po-ta, apparently staunchly pro-Mao, went traveling as far as Szechuan province. In December, Mao received the foreign experts employed in

° *People's Daily*, October 1, 1965.

China in Shanghai, contrary to his custom of seeing them in Peking. With them he was his affable, humorous self; not one guessed what was going to happen.*

And yet, that November, the first bullet of the cultural revolution had been fired. It was an incisive piece of writing by Yao Wen-yuan, a young polemicist from Shanghai, on Wu Han's play *The Dismissal of Hai Jui*. Yao Wen-yuan had caught Mao's attention in 1957 by a cogent article criticizing the Shanghai newspaper *Wen Hui Pao*.† Yao's slashing attack on Wu Han's play was published on November 10 in this same paper. For his article Yao obtained documentation and support from Chiang Ching and Chang Chun-chiao, the latter a Shanghai Party Committee official, and now one of China's vice-premiers. When the article appeared, a telephone call came from Peng Chen. "Where is your Party spirit? Why did you not announce that you were going to publish this text? This probably comes from the Boss [Chairman Mao]. . . . But all are equal before the truth."

It would be twenty days (November 30) before the *People's Daily* in Peking reproduced Yao's article. "Why was criticism of Wu Han started in Shanghai and not in Peking? In Peking there was no one who would take it up," Mao said later (October 1966).

The *People's Daily* appended an editorial note to Yao's article saying that the criticism of Wu Han's play was an academic matter of how to deal with historical characters, thus denying that it was a matter of ideology, and put the topic on the academic page, where it stayed for nearly five months. For some weeks no one realized how important this attack was; it seemed bafflingly off center, immediately smothered under academic discussions. Yet Wu Han's case was actually the weak spot of Peking's impenetrable Party Committee. He was the collaborator of Teng To, one author of the scurrilous articles of 1961–1962 and editor of *Frontline*.‡ An attack on Wu Han, and the whole edifice would start shaking.

This is Mao's typical campaign style; first a skirmish, a test, a light jab hither and there, then "concentrate superior force to destroy the enemy forces one by one, choosing the point where he is weak."

Articles for and against Wu Han now appeared; the "academic" ones saw print in Peking. On December 30 Wu Han made a devious self-

* Interview by author with two experts who attended.
† See *People's Daily*, June 14, 1957, an article signed by the editorial board but emanating from Mao, who often writes under a pseudonym or as "observer."
‡ See page 188.

criticism, confessing to being carried away by "bourgeois ideas." Meanwhile a movement for a revolution in historical studies had started; Mao's radical minority was coming up, getting more and more support among young critics and writers. Other historians were now being taken to task for their outlook and their articles. The Peking Municipal Party Committee, hoping to diminish the importance of Wu Han's case in this flux of criticism, printed criticisms of other personalities. In January 1966 Wu Han's case was slowly fading from the Peking area newspapers. But in April Chi Pen-yu, another radical critic and writer, to rise high in the cultural revolution and then to fall just as precipitately, wrote *The Truth About the Reactionary Nature of Hai Jui*, which was denied publication in Peking but was circulated in other cities, notably Shanghai.

"Freaks and monsters are bound to expose themselves in the course of a movement." This is a Mao statement; unswervingly he believes it, and it seems to happen. "By their deeds shall you know them" applies well in the Aeschylean drama of the cultural revolution.

Mao had allowed Peking's mayor, Peng Chen, to chair the Group of Five in Charge of the Cultural Revolution, and then to investigate the Wu Han case. This placed Peng Chen inside the proverbial "cow's horn." Either he would condemn his vice-mayor, Wu Han, and thus himself for allowing years to go by without reproof, or he would pretend that he did not understand what Mao was driving at and report that Wu Han's play was merely an error of bourgeois methodology. He chose the latter course, presenting in February 1966 an *Outline Report on the Cultural Revolution*, supposedly the opinion of his Group of Five in Charge of the Cultural Revolution. The report was circulated to Party officials of Culture and Propaganda without being first read by Mao or the Central Committee. It is said that Peng Chen got Liu's assent by going privately to Liu's house; this may or may not be true.

The Group of Five convened a meeting on February 3 attended by eleven comrades (it could co-opt, like a work conference, additional members). The situation and nature of the current academic criticism was said to have reaped "tremendous achievements . . . a rich harvest" in the realm of criticism of bourgeois ideas. It was necessary to carry this out "under leadership . . . seriously, prudently. . . . Problems of academic contention are rather complicated." The report professed to see no connection between the play by Wu Han and Peng Teh-huai's dismissal at the Lushan plenum.

Yet the Group of Five had split over the *Outline Report*, Kang Sheng and two other members protesting against it.

Mao Tsetung received the report towards the end of February. In that same month a forum on literature and art was held under the aegis of Lin Piao in the PLA, presided over by Chiang Ching. This gave the PLA Cultural Department the imprimatur of Mao, and hoisted it as arbiter in the literature and art sector. From then onward authoritative statements on literature and art emanated from the PLA cultural groups. The forum's importance was signaled by Mao's revising its summary report three times. The report asserted that Mao's line on art and literature "meets the needs of the proletariat adequately and for a long time to come," denied criticism that it was simplistic, designed only for the Yenan period, inapplicable in more complex times. "We have been under the dictatorship of a black anti-Party and antisocialist line," said the report. The new Peking opera on contemporary revolutionary themes had marked a breakthrough. The bourgeoisie had established its own monologue on creating the new; the proletariat must break it. The forum praised Lu Hsun and his work. The intention of this forum was that other strongholds of the bourgeoisie, the ministries of Culture and of Propaganda in Peking, were now to be assaulted.

Also in that month there was another altercation between Mao and Liu, on the subject of agricultural mechanization. Liu seems to have blocked a report study from Hupeh province on the possibility of agricultural mechanization entirely funded by the communes themselves. In March yet another skirmish occurred when a Japanese Communist Party delegation visited Peking with a self-appointed mission to push for "unity of action" over Vietnam. Peng Chen saw them, declared that "both revisionism and dogmatism must be fought," and a joint communiqué was worked out which received the assent of other members of the Politburo. But when the delegation went to call on Mao, then in Hangchow, Mao became angry, insisted that the communiqué should append the words "a united international front against American imperialism and Soviet revisionism." Both were just as counterrevolutionary, said Mao. The JCP's idea that the world was divided between warmongers and peace lovers was dismissed by Mao.

In April Mao launched anathema, his words like claps of thunder, "frightening demons and ghosts," against Chou Yang and Lu Ting-yi. "The Department of Propaganda [of the Party] is the palace of the King of Hell. Down with the King of Hell! Liberate the little ones! I shall call to rebellion in the provinces, I shall call for rebellion against the Center . . . everywhere there must be innumerable wise monkeys,* they will rise and tear down the palace of the King of Hell." And in a final warning to Party officials: "The tenth plenum decided on class struggle. Yet Wu Han writes counterrevolutionary anti-Party libelous stuff, and the Culture Ministry does not care; it ignores the decision of the Center." It was a "black gang," said Mao, which suppressed writings from the left and protected anti-Party intelligentsia.

Editorials against the "black, antisocialist anti-Party gang" appeared. On April 14, at a meeting of the secretariat of the Central Committee, Kang Sheng denounced Peng Chen's trickery on the *Outline Report.* On the 16th the standing committee of the National People's Congress met to deliberate on the problem of Peng Chen's anti-Party activities.

And also on April 16 the socialist cultural revolution (this was its first name; only in August would it be named the Great Proletarian Cultural Revolution) was officially launched.

Mao's attack was pressing home. *Frontline* and the *Peking Daily,* on that same April 16, published criticism of *Notes from a Three-Family Village* and *Evening Talks at Yenshan.* It was acknowledged that these articles had been published "without timely criticism." Once more Yao Wen-yuan, now chief editor of Shanghai's *Liberation Daily,* took up his pen, blasting the reactionary nature of *Evening Talks at Yenshan* and *Three-Family Village.*† Denunciations of freaks and monsters, of anti-Party elements, were hurled from Shanghai against the bourgeois bastion of Peking. The radicalism of Shanghai, the great city of the working class, was to continue throughout the cultural revolution, and has continued until today. People still refer elliptically to "the Shanghai group" to denote the radicals who have now, through the cultural revolution, reached important positions at the top of the Party.

In May, to show that Shanghai was by now the base of Mao's ideas, a music festival took place there attended by the Party, the army, and many officials then in Shanghai.

Teng To was now in dire straits; he had earlier published a fake criticism of his collaborator Wu Han. The editorial department of *Frontline* (Teng To was the editor) now criticized Teng To. But these curious contortions could not save him. Yao wrote that the two series were a deliberate conspiracy, preparing public opinion for a return to capitalism, and he named each one of those involved in their composition.

---

* Referring to the classic Monkey of *The Western Pilgrimage.*

† Article published on May 10, 1966, in Shanghai's *Liberation Daily* and *Wen Hui Pao.*

On April 18 the PLA laid claim to the guardianship of revolutionary purity in an article entitled *Hold Aloft the Great Red Banner of Mao Tsetung Thought*. "Our People's Liberation Army . . . created and led by the Chinese Communist Party and Chairman Mao, is *the most loyal tool* of the Party and of the people, the mainstay of the dictatorship of the proletariat."

People's Daily was now swamped with letters from workers, peasants, intellectuals, soldiers against the authors of the villainous series which had "spread poison" everywhere in China (their noxious appeal was acknowledged; they had corrupted the minds of many innocent people). On May 4[*] *Liberation Daily* came out with *Never Forget the Class Struggle*. At last the criticism of Wu Han was moved from the academic page of the Peking *People's Daily* to page two, while page one was filled with articles on the cultural revolution.

On May 8, the article *Open Fire on the Anti-Party Antisocialist Black Line* went a step further. The abyss had now opened, waiting for its condemned. Teng To was dismissed, and a few days later Peng Chen. The fortress of Peking was crumbling. In July Chou Yang vanished. Hsu Kuang-ping, Lu Hsun's wife, participated in the long debate which then took place in literary circles, denouncing Chou Yang, thus picking up where her husband had been interrupted by death twenty-nine years previously, in his "fight to the dying breath" against Chou Yang.[†]

The dismissals of Peng Chen, Teng To, Chou Yang were not accomplished "from above" alone; their own subordinates refused them entry in their offices. They went home, remaining "suspended" until the mass arousal in the cultural revolution would drag them for public "struggle" and criticism in front of thousands of Red Guards some months later.

The criticism of Wu Han had truly been the spark that now set China ablaze with comment, discussion, debate on every aspect of the administration, the Party, the government. For some two years China would have the most extensive democracy possible, all rules in abeyance. Already in May the factories were full of big-character posters (*tatzepao*) denouncing the "freaks and monsters" of "the black line." But who were the freaks and monsters in the factory? Few had any notion how high the rot went. The city of Peking was seething with

---

[*] May 4, 1966, was the forty-seventh anniversary of the first cultural revolution of May 1919 (see *The Morning Deluge*).

[†] The author was attending the Emergency Congress of Afro-Asian Writers in Peking (June-July 1966) as an observer, and had a private interview with Hsu Kuang-ping (July 1966), then involved in the denunciation of Chou Yang by the Chinese writers. He has since reappeared publicly on September 30, 1975.

rumors. The big-character posters had not yet erupted on the streets, but stayed within each unit. The mayor of Peking and the officials of the Culture and Propaganda ministries seemed the highest of all the monsters to knock down.

In late April, Mao Tsetung returned to Peking. Liu Shao-chi, absent since March, came back from a round of travels.abroad. On March 26, as Mao was blasting the ministries and Peng Chen, Liu had left for some three weeks on a tour of Pakistan, Afghanistan, Burma. In between he returned twice to China, stopping in Sinkiang province to get the news of what was going on. He was not present in April at a Politburo meeting in Hangchow when Peng Chen was exposed, but returned in late April to attend a Politburo meeting in Peking and a Central Committee meeting which followed (May 4–18) in Hangchow.

At this meeting of the Central Committee in May 1966, the left-wing supporters of Mao came into prominence. Chief among them were Lin Piao and Chen Po-ta, both to fall some years later as traitors. But there were also very good revolutionaries in Mao's group, and Party men of long standing, like Kang Sheng and Chou En-lai, who sided with Mao. At the meeting's close a circular, known as the May 16 circular of the Central Committee, was distributed within the Party. It was published and given wide publicity as a "historic, epoch-making document" — a year later, May 16, 1967.

The May 16 circular castigates Peng Chen's *Outline Report* for falsifying, blurring, distorting the goal of the cultural revolution; turning into academic, formal discussion the political problem of Wu Han's play and its relevance to "the right opportunists" of the Lushan meeting of 1959; using "freedom of speech" and "everyone is equal before the truth" as specious excuses to allow only the representatives of the bourgeoisie within the Party to speak. The circular also notes that in many places the vast majority of the Party committees have not grasped the real issues; Peng Chen's recommendation to conduct the struggle against bourgeois ideology "with prudence" and "under leadership" was clamping a lid on mass arousal; "restrictions on the proletarian left . . . imposing taboos . . . to tie its hands" were preventing the real cultural revolution from taking place. Cadres who wanted to follow Mao Thought were being systematically persecuted, while free rein was given to all the "ghosts and monsters who for many years have abounded in our press, radio, magazines, books, textbooks."

The circular ends in a forceful call to carry out the cultural revolution and to seize the leadership in cultural spheres; "above all we must not entrust these people [capitalist-roaders in the Party] with the work of leading the cultural revolution. In fact many of them have done and are still doing such work, and this is extremely dangerous . . . once conditions are ripe they will seize political power. Some of them we have already seen through, others we have not. Some are still trusted by us and are being trained as our successors, persons *like Khrushchev . . . still nestling beside us."*

It would be another six months before Liu Shao-chi would be named "China's Khrushchev."

Among those who supported (or appeared to support) Mao, two personages were to prove ambitious opportunists, Lin Piao and Chen Po-ta.

In the developing thrust for power of Lin Piao, Chen Po-ta's role as a gray eminence, manipulator behind Lin Piao's ambition, is interesting. As editor of *Red Flag* since 1958, Chen's value was in molding public opinion. With the downfall of Teng To, Chou Yang, and Lu Ting-yi, Chen Po-ta's importance as spokesman for the Mao line became outstanding.

Chen Po-ta was not an almost unknown; a shadowy figure who called himself "just a small commoner," he is invariably described as Mao's "secretary" in biographies, but this is incorrect. Chen was a teacher in a middle school in Peking who in 1937 went to Yenan, at the time when there was a great dearth of intellectual talent. He seems to have worked in the Party archives, producing studies in political science and economics which received Mao's approval. In 1949, when Mao went to see Stalin, Chen Po-ta accompanied the group and distinguished himself by haranguing the intellectuals on their defects. The far more modest (and far more eminent) Kuo Mo-jo tried to explain and to persuade the intelligentsia to read and to study Mao's works; Chen shouted at them and was cordially disliked.

Chen Po-ta was the teacher of Yeh Chun, second wife of Lin Piao (they were married in 1965). In 1945 he was elected to the Seventh Central Committee as a representative of "social science bodies." He defended Mao's thesis of agricultural collectivization in 1955 but then adopted Liu's thesis of productive forces in 1956, and in May 1958 became editor of *Red Flag*. He pushed strenuously for "early communism" in the communes, again with Liu Shao-chi. Throughout, Chen Po-ta appeared a vociferous radical, and now in 1966 he was again among "the proletarian left," supporting Mao.

Lin Piao's May 18, 1966, speech to the enlarged session of the Politburo, two days after the May 16 circular which disbanded Peng Chen's Group of Five, was the first exposure of his own opportunism.

Lin Piao addressed the meeting in his capacity as vice-chairman of the Party and member of the standing committee. But it is possible to trace a further rise of his prestige to Mao's May 7 letter, addressed to Lin Piao, concerning the function of the PLA as initiator of the youth "successors to the revolution." A series of directives had been issued by the Military Affairs Committee and the General Political Department of the PLA concerning the training of young revolutionaries, but this letter of May 7 gave the PLA the responsibility of fostering successors even more concretely. It was a follow-up of the line of thought already heralded in an article* on January 17, 1966: *Boldly to Nourish and Select Young Cadres Is the Glorious Tradition of the PLA.* Mao had suggested that to prevent "Khrushchev revisionism" PLA cadres should be sent as models for teachers and students in educational institutions.† The birth of the Red Guards in 1966 is traceable to this introduction of PLA models within the schools and universities.

"In the absence of a world war, our army should be a big school. Even under conditions of a third world war, it can still serve as a big school . . . the army should learn politics, military affairs, and culture, and engage in agricultural production. . . . It can take part in mass work, factory work, and rural socialist education . . . to unite the army and people as one. Likewise workers should . . . learn military affairs, politics and culture. . . . (All should also take part in criticizing the capitalist class during these activities.)

"The students are in a similar position. Their studies are their chief work; they must also learn . . . industrial, agricultural and military work. The school years should be shortened . . . What has been said above is neither new nor original. Many people have been doing this for some time, but it has not yet become widespread. . . . Our army has been working in this way for decades."‡

Mao failed to see that his casual "Well done" or "This is excellent" immediately elevated the recipient above ordinary men. Such is the penalty of greatness; it mantles others, even unworthy. Now Lin Piao spoke, and round him hung the aura of Mao's approval.

The burden of Lin Piao's speech of May 18 is that there was an incipient counterrevolutionary coup d'etat in the making. "The greatest

---

* *Liberation Army Daily.*
† Address by Mao to Communist Youth League, June 1964.
‡ Mao's letter of May 7, 1966, to Lin Piao.

problem was the prevention of such a coup," said Lin Piao. Many measures had been taken by Chairman Mao in the last few months to avert this seizure of political power by counterrevolutionaries; hence Mao had "summoned personnel" and stationed them in the public security systems, the radio broadcasting stations, and other strategic points in Peking, "to prevent occupation of our crucial points." This was to explain the replacement of the troops garrisoning Peking by Lin Piao's own troops, in April-May.

Lin Piao hinted that Lo Jui-ching (arrested in February) and "others" had conspired to garrison Peking with provincial troops under their influence, and to seize and "probably assassinate" Mao.

Lin Piao's speech created tension. He enumerated the number of military coups actually taking place in the world, the ease with which such coups succeed. "There is a likelihood of counterrevolutionary coup d'etat, killings, seizure of political power, capitalist restoration, and doing away with all those associated with socialism." He then named the men allegedly involved in this conspiracy: Peng Chen, Lo Jui-ching, and Yang Shang-kun (of the secret police).

Mao had not spoken of a plot or a coup, only of a *peaceful slide* into revisionism and then into capitalism, through the expert manipulation of art, literature and economics, the public opinion forming media, the alliance with "the bourgeois intellectuals" outside the Party, and the policies of "profit in command."

Lin Piao's speech praises Mao and extols his genius. Already on March 11, in a letter entitled *Politics in Command* addressed to the armed forces, Lin Piao had written that Mao had elevated Marxism-Leninism to a completely new stage with "genius"; that Mao Tsetung Thought "has not grown up spontaneously from among the working people" but is the sole result of "Chairman Mao inheriting and developing Marxism-Leninism . . . on the basis of [his] great revolutionary practice." This separated the "genius," Mao, from the masses, their wisdom and living practice of revolution, to which Mao constantly referred and deferred.

"Mao Tsetung Thought is an everlasting universal truth, an everlasting guideline for our actions," said Lin, whereas Mao claimed only to be "adequate for the present period." "Chairman Mao . . . has his ideas, many of which we do not understand. We must resolutely carry out Chairman Mao's instructions *whether we understand them or not*," writes Lin Piao. Mao was the greatest genius to emerge "in the last two thousand years or so" — greater than Lenin, Marx, Engels.

Listening to this praise, Mao was worried, for he had said that to carry out instructions blindly without understanding them was wrong. But at the time he was in a minority, and the first task was to get rid of the "capitalist-roaders in the Party."

After the circular of May 16, what had been a Party affair involved everyone in China. Everyone debated about the "proletarian left" and the "black gang." And now, who should be in charge of the cultural revolution in universities and colleges but . . . Liu Shao-chi himself!

"It was to give Liu Shao-chi a last chance" is perhaps the best way to summarize the long and painful process of the tearing apart of bonds fashioned during thirty years between Mao and Liu Shao-chi. Had it been possible to make Liu see his errors, Mao would have preferred to keep Liu in the Party. But Liu could no longer change.

Liu abandoned Peng Chen, appointed Li Hsueh-feng to be acting mayor in the reorganized Peking Municipal Committee. He summoned Tao Chu, first secretary of the Southern bureau, to take over the Propaganda Department in Peking.

The Group of Five in charge of the cultural revolution having been abolished, another group was in the making. It was semiofficialized when on July 10 Hsinhua News Agency, reporting a banquet at the end of the Emergency Congress of Afro-Asian Writers in Peking, referred to Chen Po-ta as the "leader of the Group in Charge of the Cultural Revolution [GCCR] under the Party's Central Committee."

Control of the mass media in Peking that June passed to the GCCR, described as an "organ of power of the cultural revolution." In August the group would take over the work of the ministries of Culture and Propaganda, and also function partly as a general secretariat of the Central Committee until 1969. The first list of its seventeen members appeared on November 22; Chen Po-ta would head it, Chiang Ching being first deputy head. The Shanghai activists Yao Wen-yuan and Chang Chun-chiao were also on the first list, and they with Chiang Ching would be the only ones to remain with it till the end.

After the May meetings in Peking, Mao Tsetung left again for Middle China. He was weighing the great decisions to take, watching the developments he had started. "It was I who started the fire. . . . As I see it, shocking people is good. For many years I thought about how to administer [to the revisionists in the Party] a shock . . . and finally I conceived this."* The young Mao, in the 1930's, had said that when a person is (politically) sick, yet unwilling to recognize his state, one must shock him, shouting loudly in his ear: "You are sick!"

The first onslaught had been successful. The Peking fortress had disintegrated. But this was a mere beginning.

Mao's thoughts of the time are conveyed in a letter he wrote to his wife Chiang Ching on July 6, 1966. This letter, photocopied and circulated throughout China, by now has also been translated and reproduced abroad.† It describes Mao's feelings, both towards his opponents and towards his supporters. It shows his misgivings towards the man who appeared his most devoted, loyal and impeccable disciple, Lin Piao.

"I have received your letter of June 29. It is good that you should . . . remain a little longer where you are" (it seems Chiang Ching was then in Shanghai).

"Since my arrival at Pai Yun Huang" — mountains in Hupeh province where Mao had withdrawn — "ten days have passed. I read documents every day; they are of great interest. Great disorder across the land leads to great order. And so once again, every seven or eight years monsters and demons will jump out themselves. Determined by their own class nature, they cannot act otherwise. . . .

"The Central Committee is in a hurry to publicize the speech of my friend.‡ I am ready to agree. In it he refers particularly to the problems of a coup d'etat. Never has such language been used before. . . .

"*Certain of his ideas greatly disturb me.* I could never have believed that my little books could have such magical powers. . . . But now that he extolled them, the whole country will follow his example. . . . It makes one think of the story of the woman who sells melons, and overpraises her merchandise. . . .

"My friend and his partisans have forced me to act . . . apparently I cannot do otherwise than to approve them."

In what way did they force Mao to act? In getting Lin Piao's speech approved and distributed throughout the Party (which was done on September 22) or, in general, forcing him to move more drastically than he would have wished? Certainly the problem of revisionism was there, incarnate in Liu Shao-chi, and Mao had to battle against it. "It is

---

* Attributed to Mao, October 1966.

† Author was given the Chinese version to read in China in June 1973, along with Project 571 (see pages 347–348), and Chairman Mao's *Some Opinions* (see page 344). The letter is quoted here in extracts, not in full.

‡ This refers to the May 18 speech by Lin Piao.

the first time in my life that I am in agreement with the others on the essence of a problem against my will. This is what is called changing one's orientation without willing to do so."

Mao then quotes from a Chinese classic writer, Yuan Chi, who, commenting on a battle won by Liu Pang, the founder of the Han dynasty, had remarked: "The world being in need of a hero, this enabled a fellow like Liu Pang to make a name." Thus Mao hints, I too am a hero by default. "Lu Hsun was always correcting his satirical writings. My soul is in communication with his. He said: 'I dissect myself far more harshly than I dissect others.' After having stumbled several times, I often do as he does. But the comrades do not always believe this. I have confidence in myself, but I also doubt myself a little. I always have the feeling that when there is no tiger in the mountain, the monkey becomes a King. I became that sort of a King. But this is not eclecticism. There is a little of the tiger in me; that's the main part, and also a little of the monkey, that's a secondary part. . . .

"The more difficult the song, the less people capable of singing it. When one enjoys great repute, it is difficult to be worthy of it. These last two sentences summarize my case. . . . I have recited these words to a session of the standing committee of the Politburo: *What is called nobility in man, is the wisdom to know himself.* . . .

"At the Hangchow meeting [a meeting of the Central Committee in Hangchow in April, preparatory to the enlarged meeting held in May] in April this year, I expressed ideas different from my friend. But what could be done? He repeated the same things [he had said in Hangchow] at the conference in Peking in May. . . .

"In the present conditions, I can do nothing else but to let myself be carried along. I suppose they (my friend and his partisans) intend to beat the evil spirits with the help of Chung Kuei.* Now in the sixties of the twentieth century, I have become the Chung Kuei of the Communist Party!"

And then Mao shows his fundamental worry, and the choice before him: "There are more than a hundred Communist parties in the world. The great majority no longer believe in Marxism-Leninism . . . they have even reduced to dust Marx and Lenin. If this happens to them, why not to us? . . ."

Mao then goes back to the Lin Piao topic. He recommends that

---

* Chung Kuei was a mythical personage who had the power to exorcise demons. His picture is stuck on doors and gates on New Year's Day to prevent the entry of malevolent demons.

Chiang Ching pay attention to "this problem," not to let triumph go to her head. One must always think of weak points, defects and errors. "I do not know how often I have spoken to you about this. I also spoke about it in April in Shanghai.

"What I have said here [about other Communist parties] is rather similar to 'black talk' [talk by counterrevolutionaries]. . . . Don't the anti-Party elements talk like this? But the difference is that I speak of my own reactions, whereas the black gang aims at overthrowing our Party and myself.

"At present what I have just said cannot be made public [because] at the moment all the left speaks the same language. If one divulged what I have just written, it is like pouring cold water on them, and thus helping the right wing. Our task at present is to overthrow partly the right (not totally, for this is impossible) in the Party and in the whole country. In seven or eight years one will have to launch another movement to clean up [other] demons. . . . And this will have to be repeated many times. . . .

"Perhaps, after my death, the right will divulge this [letter] when it comes to power. It is possible that the right wing will use it to lift high and forever the black flag. . . . But if it does so, it will be doomed. Since 1911 . . . reactionary power cannot last long in China. . . . If a coup d'etat by the anti-Communist right-wing elements happens in China, I am sure they will know no peace either and their regime will be of short duration, because it will not be tolerated by the revolutionaries, who represent the interests of the people . . . 90 percent of the population . . . The right in power could utilize my words to become mighty for a while. But then the left will be able to utilize others of my words and organize itself to overthrow the right."

This letter shows us Mao, knowing, at the very beginning of the upheaval he would lead, its limitations, the possibilities of its misuse, and the objects of the men who were helping him. He *had* to use them, not because they were all truly dedicated but because the main task, the great priority, was to overthrow revisionism in the Party, headed by Liu Shao-chi. Later he would clean up other "evil spirits."

Did Lin Piao realize what Mao Tsetung thought of him? Lin's speeches carry a forcible, hectic note: "We will strike down those in power who take the capitalist road, strike down the reactionary bourgeois authorities, strike down all bourgeois royalists . . . strike down all monsters and demons."*

* Speech by Lin Piao at a mass rally in Peking, August 18, 1966.

For the dialectician Mao, weak men, criminals, all have their role to play, long-term or transient, positive or negative, in the drama of revolution. The man who could shake hands and drink with Chiang Kaishek, form a united front with him to beat Japan's aggression in China, would certainly utilize Lin Piao to beat down China's Khrushchev and then denounce Lin Piao, should the latter prove unworthy.

Liu Shao-chi too proceeded according to his nature, or to his style, as unchangeable as one's signature. He had always sent work teams to cope with movements. Again he sent work teams to all universities and colleges, and also to industrial complexes and factories. On June 2 the first work teams entered the universities and middle schools in Peking.

Student effervescence was at a high. It had begun in 1964, and in 1965 there had been some minor explosions controlled by Party pressures. "The children are no longer obedient," one Party official sourly complained to the author. But it was the May 16 document which removed the lid. On May 25 a big-character poster was put up at Peking University by six young lecturers from the department of social sciences and philosophy, among them a woman lecturer, Nieh Yuan-tze, who became prominent during the cultural revolution but is now undergoing reform through manual labor in a commune, because she became corrupted by power.

This poster denounced Lu Ping, the university chancellor, and the orientation of education. Mao saw it on June 1, called it the "first Marxist-Leninist poster . . . a manifesto of the Chinese Paris Commune of the twentieth century," and ordered its diffusion. Had there not been the asseveration in the May 16 document that there were representatives of the bourgeoisie within the Party, the poster would have been suppressed as "anti-Party" and "counterrevolutionary," because it attacked the Party Committee of the university in the person of its head, Chancellor Lu Ping. On June 1 the *People's Daily* (with a revamped editorial board) came out with a thundering article: *Sweep Away All Monsters.* Clearly, the target was monsters *in the Party.* On June 2, another editorial, *A Great Revolution That Touches People to Their Very Souls,* went more fully into what the role of revolutionaries (and of the young) should be. *We Are Critics of the Old World* on June 4 would become the slogan of the youth. Once again we find reference to the Hungarian episode of 1956: "It was a number of revisionist literary men of the Petofi Club who acted as the shock brigade in the Hungarian events." "The turbulent wind precedes the mountain storm. . . . Public opinion forming is always necessary before preparing the public for certain events." The prelude to counterrevolutionary restoration was "the obstinacy with which emperors and kings, scholars and beauties, foreign idols and dead men" had dominated the stage, art and literature during the preceding seventeen years of China's revolution.

In universities the work teams were greeted with happiness and joy. "Chairman Mao has sent work teams to help us." In Peking University the work team suspended Lu Ping on June 3. Lu was thus withdrawn from public execration, protected from having to face student accusation meetings. For already the students had organized public meetings calling to account their professors and lecturers. The work teams now exercised control in place of the university Party Committee.

On June 6 the senior third grade at a Peking girls' middle school wrote to the Central Committee and to Mao proposing the abolition of college entrance examinations, which served only to control the young by "reactionary elements."* Middle school graduates should integrate with workers, peasants and soldiers by living and working with them, and get their "ideological diplomas" by mass approval. Admission to university should be on the recommendation of the masses where the young worked.†

In response the State Council and the Central Committee issued a joint notice on June 13 abolishing entrance examinations in the universities, postponing for six months any new enrollment of students in colleges and universities to ensure "the successful carrying out of the cultural revolution through to the end, and to effect a thorough reform of the educational system . . . where bourgeois domination is still deeply rooted." The students on the verge of graduation that year would be automatically graduated.

The six-month limit was optimistic. It would be four years before universities would begin functioning again.

"To rebel is justified," Mao had said. And groups of "rebel" students, reading Mao, had appeared in each university and middle school.

Undoubtedly, in their first "rebellion," some of them behaved badly towards their teachers. Under the pretext of returning to the correct road, the work teams started another tyranny. The students were now

---

* By setting questions and subjects and judging the student by their own "bourgeois" values.
† *Peking Review*, June 24, 1966.

turned against many hapless lecturers and minor professors. It was again the "knock down the many to protect the few" technique. The work teams protected the higher Party cadres; they organized student groups for "study," but only the lower cadre echelon was accessible to the students to shout at, criticize and ill-treat. The work teams incited evil treatment, digging into past histories, demanding the death penalty for "crimes" committed before Liberation such as having had a love affair. As to big-character posters, the work teams decreed that they should distinguish between inner Party matters and external matters. Mao Tsetung was to condemn this in July; "to use the pretense of distinguishing between inner Party matters and external non-Party matters is to be afraid of revolution."

The work teams incited the students one against the other. Students whose parents were Party cadres thought that "to protect the Party is to protect Chairman Mao." They naturally sided with the work teams, concentrating on non-Party bourgeois and on the students and lecturers who had "rebelled" against Party injunctions. The work teams also compiled files against the "rebel" students. This was done by secret investigations, a good deal through the suspended former Party Committee. The leaders of rebel groups were called antisocialist and anti-Party, and public meetings were called to "struggle" against them. Thus factional strife arose on every campus and in every school, which was to mark the youth movement for the next three years.

After two weeks of such "revolution" the students realized that something was wrong. The editorials proclaiming "Mobilize the masses freely" (June 16) and the behavior of the work teams were at variance. The target, the editorials said, was the "handful of people . . . in authority in the Party." Where was the criticism of this handful? Now the masses were fighting the masses, students struggling against students.

On June 18 an incident occurred at Peking University; the rebels fought bodily against the work team. At Tsinghua University on June 24 a student leader, Kuai Ta-fu, questioned the work team and was criticized at a packed public meeting. On June 26 the new acting mayor of Peking, Li Hsueh-feng, was to say that "to oppose the work team is to oppose the Party Center." But the rebel students persisted though the majority of students were led to "struggle" against them. The Communist youth had received directives to "protect the Party against counterrevolutionaries." Everywhere the "rebels" were being beaten, jailed, some had excreta thrown upon them.

Liu's wife, Wang Kuang-mei, was reported as going herself to Tsinghua University, where she advised the work team and called the June 18 incident "counterrevolutionary." The students banded to "protect the Party" were praised as "activists and student leaders." Daily now in the streets of Peking processions of university and middle school students were seen with red flags flying and holding large portraits of Mao, going to the tall white glazed Peking Municipality building to bring news of their successes in fighting the bourgeoisie, and to pledge their loyalty to the Party.

And this was a distortion of what the cultural revolution was meant to be.

On the hot and sunny morning of July 17, in Wuhan, the triple metropolis on the broad Yangtze, about two hundred thousand people gathered on the banks to watch the annual swim across the river performed since Mao had initiated it in 1956 (a swim he had since repeated several times). That day they saw Mao himself in a white toweling robe standing on the bank; then, discarding his robe, he plunged into the river, where he swam for about an hour. From the sailboats that held thousands of spectators shouts were raised as he was recognized. "Chairman Mao, Chairman Mao!" The heads of ten thousand swimmers bobbed in the mile-wide water, and the crowd went delirious with enthusiasm.

The significance was not obvious until three weeks later. Then all China understood that Mao's swim was a symbol and a warning. He was plunging personally into the great tide of the cultural revolution, leading personally the youth to battle in the great stream of history. On July 18 Mao flew back to Peking.

In Peking, Liu Shao-chi had reached the same impasse as Peng Chen had in February. Had he carried out the cultural revolution by "boldly arousing the masses to criticize and to repudiate," he would have had to submit to criticism himself, and all his directives, since 1961. If he persisted in pretending he had "not grasped the Chairman's thought" (and this would be his main excuse in the next two years), then he had lost out.

A meeting of the standing committee of the Politburo was held in Peking when Mao returned. Through the last ten days of July, preparatory meetings took place as members arrived in Peking by air and by train. The eleventh plenum of the Eighth Central Committee was to begin August 1.

Kang Sheng, Chiang Ching, and other Mao supporters in the GCCR proceeded to various universities and colleges in Peking to investigate the situation. On the 22nd Mao received their reports. Chiang Ching, at Peking University on July 19, told the students that Chairman Mao considered the June 18 incident revolutionary and not counterrevolutionary. On the very same day all the students incarcerated by the work teams were released. Unfortunately factionalism, which was to plague the youth movement during the cultural revolution, was evident. Many different groups had sprung into being. One of them based itself on the "five good origins" — admitting to its ranks only those "born revolutionary": sons and daughters of revolutionary cadres, revolutionary soldiers or martyrs, workers, and poor and lower middle peasants. "A dragon begets a dragon, but a mouse can only dig a hole in the ground," they said. Chiang Ching changed the ditty they sang, "A hero begets a hero, a reactionary's son is a rotten egg," into "Father reactionary, son turns the tables, father a hero, son carries on." Chou En-lai also spent four days at the universities with the students.

At the meetings of the Politburo, Mao spoke about the evil wrought by the work teams, who had suppressed the masses, shut the university and college gates, allowed no one in or out, not even allowed students to telephone their parents. "The present great cultural revolution is a heaven and earth shaking event . . . like crossing a pass into another realm, the realms of socialism . . . do we dare to cross?" He told his colleagues that they must be prepared to endure a great deal; there would be mass arousal and criticism, but they must submit humbly to criticism; learn to listen to the masses to know what they really thought and felt. "You must lead the fire of the great cultural revolution towards yourselves. . . . You yourselves must fan the flames to make them burn you. . . . Some comrades are good at struggling fiercely against others, but they cannot struggle against themselves." Now the time had come for this self-immolation. "It won't do just to sit in an office and listen to reports." He upbraided some on their pusillanimity, their fear. "You put fear above everything else . . . replace the word fear by the word dare. . . . Be prepared for the revolution to come down on your own heads. . . . Leaders must all be prepared."

On July 24 the work teams were withdrawn from all universities. Tao Chu, once secretary of the Southern bureau, called to Peking in June by Liu, was now co-opted into the GCCR and placed in charge of the education sector. He established "liaison agents" in each educational institution, in place of the work teams.

On July 20 one of the middle schools attached to Tsinghua University officially reported its first organized Red Guards. Within the next three weeks every university and college had its Red Guards. Hundreds of such groups would spring up, involving millions of young people from fifteen to thirty years old, in that first month.

Mao spent the days conferring with his colleagues, but always he would return to the necessity of arousing the masses "thoroughly" in order to expose the "dark side" of the Party and to carry out the destruction of bourgeois authoritarianism. "Without this destruction socialism cannot be established, and the three great differences" — between mental and manual labor, city and countryside, worker and peasant — "cannot be resolved." As Mao saw it, the revolution would be in stages, with youth in the vanguard. The Party must undergo first "struggle," then "criticism," and the third stage would be "transformation" so that it would regenerate itself through this ordeal.

"Struggle, criticism, transformation" was to be performed in each factory, school, institution, organization. Each one would carry on its own cultural revolution by its own internal forces, its own masses, cadres, workers, administration, all confronting each other and thrashing out the ideological problems, exposing their views and ideas, putting up posters and denouncing the revisionist and feudal trends. No outside unit or work team could do this; for this would again be "from above" and contrary to the main thrust of the movement — to let the masses express themselves.

Mao recommended that all officials read the *tatzepao* which plastered the walls. Very shortly the posters would proliferate and cover the streets, every wall plastered with thousands of messages as each person sought to pour out his heart. The most moving sight was to watch workers, a large white sheet in front of them, brush poised, begin to write their views and ideas, then solemnly place their composition on a wall. Only anti-Party elements were afraid of these posters, said Mao. Articles and circulars by the Central Committee were not half so effective as these products of the people's desire for expression.

The university gates were flung open and hundreds of thousands of people streamed in, stimulated, curious, eager to listen. It was fantastic . . . peasants came in their best clothes from the communes to see what was going on — they had never dreamed of crossing the threshold of a university. The students formed relays to explain to the crowds what the movement was all about, and also began traveling in groups to other provinces, beginning these immense travels by China's youth called "big linkups," in which they visited remote parts of their country and exchanged experience with other youths.

On August 1 Mao Tsetung wrote a personal letter to the young. He had seen their big-character posters reprinted in the press (June 24 – July 4). He praised their stand, saying they were justified in expressing their wrath, denouncing the landlords, the imperialists, the revisionists, the bourgeoisie and their lackeys. "It is justified to rebel against reactionaries. . . . I offer you my warm support. . . . While supporting you, at the same time, we ask you to pay attention to *uniting with all persons that can be united with*. . . . As for those who have made serious mistakes, after their mistakes have been pointed out, they too should be given work and a way out for correcting their mistakes and becoming new men. . . . Marx said: 'The proletariat must emancipate not only itself but all mankind.' Without emancipating mankind as a whole the proletariat cannot achieve its own final emancipation. *Comrades, please pay attention to this truth.*"

This was a warning against internecine strife, against ill-treating people merely because they were *older,* against petty bourgeois radicalism. Some young rebels become leaders of groups, such as Kuai Ta-fu, were already drunk with newfound power. Kuai had distinguished himself by going against the work teams and had been praised for it. Now he would become arrogant and swiftly corrupted. However, for some months he continued to be held up as a hero and became very popular.

On August 5, during the meeting of the eleventh plenum, Mao Tsetung threw his bombshell. He wrote his own *tatzepao,* called *Bombard the Headquarters.*

Mao's poster praised the May 25 *tatzepao* put up at Peking University. "Comrades, please read it again. . . . But in the last fifty days or so some leading comrades from the Center down to the local levels have acted in a diametrically opposite way. . . . They have enforced a bourgeois dictatorship and struck down the surging movement of the great cultural revolution of the proletariat. They have stood facts on their head . . . imposed a white terror, and felt very pleased with themselves. . . . They have puffed up the arrogance of the bourgeoisie and deflated the morale of the proletariat. How vicious they are!"

Mao's poster "blasted the lid off the struggle between the two lines and between the proletarian headquarters and the bourgeois headquarters [within the Party] which had existed in the Party over a long period."* It was the final challenge to Liu, and Liu knew it very well.

On August 8 the decision of the Central Committee concerning the great cultural revolution was issued. This document was to be known as the Sixteen Articles of the Cultural Revolution. The plenum was guarded by the troops of Lin Piao. It has been alleged that the PLA kept out of the plenum certain members of the Central Committee; otherwise the left would have been outvoted. What is known is that those in the "black gang," such as Peng Chen and Lu Ting-yi, attended but were not allowed to vote, since they were under investigation. The enlarged plenum was attended by revolutionaries from the newly created Red Guard organizations and the members of the GCCR. The communiqué avers that "representatives of revolutionary teachers and students in Peking were present." Liu Shao-chi was present and cast his vote. As for the secretary-general, Teng Hsiao-ping, who Mao had complained "always sits far from me," he appears to have come to Mao's side either at the plenum or shortly after. Teng Hsiao-ping had not been a Liu devotee, though he seems to have shared some (not all) of Liu's opinions. Teng would accomplish a satisfactory self-criticism, and Mao would personally ask for his return to a high position in the Party in 1973.

The Sixteen Articles repeat that the present revolution is to touch people's souls, to change man. It is a new, broader, deeper stage of the continuing revolution. Old ideas, culture, customs, habits of the exploiting classes still mold public opinion, offering fertile ground for restoration of the past. The mental outlook must be transformed and new values created. The object of the revolution is to overthrow "those persons in power taking the capitalist road; to repudiate and criticize bourgeois academic authorities; to transform education, literature and art and all parts of the superstructure which do not correspond to the socialist economic base."

The main forces of the revolution were the worker-peasant-soldier masses and the revolutionary intelligentsia; now young pioneers (the Red Guards) in the movement were springing up, whose general orientation was correct in spite of certain shortcomings. They were to be

---

* *Red Flag*, nos. 13 and 14, 1966. During 1967 *Red Flag* came out two or even three times a month, but the whole of *Red Flag* from January to September 1967 is now regarded as "unreliable" because it was then controlled by the ultra-left. As a result, *Red Flag* was suspended for some months.

encouraged. Because the resistance was "fairly strong" there would be reversals, a tortuous course for the movement. The outcome would depend on whether or not Party leadership would exercise itself to arouse the masses. In many places the cadres stuck to outmoded ways and rigid rules, not understanding what leadership meant. In others the control was in the hands of the capitalist-roaders, who intrigued, backstabbed, and spread rumors to deviate the movement.

The masses were to be aroused, but things must not be done for them; they must emancipate their own minds, find out themselves what is right and wrong. Full use of *tatzepao* and great debate to argue matters out must be made.

More than 95 percent of the cadres and more than 95 percent of the masses were good or relatively so and should be united; only the most reactionary rightists should be isolated. Distinction should be carefully made between anti-Party rightists with a definite policy against socialism, and the usual run of people who had erred but were not themselves plotting a restoration.

The method of the movement was debate, reasoning things out, persuasion through reasoning. Any method of forcing a minority with different views to submit was impermissible. "The minority should be protected, because sometimes the truth is with the minority. Even if the minority is wrong, they should still be allowed to argue their case and reserve their views."

"Where there is a debate it should be conducted by reasoning and not by force." This clause was added personally by Mao himself. Another clause insists that there should not be incitement for "the masses to struggle against each other or the students to do likewise." The two clauses were not respected in the next few years. There would be violence, and there would be a great deal of factionalism.

There must be no suppression of the new organizations created by the upsurge of the cultural revolution; these were excellent bridges to keep the Party in close contact with the masses. It was necessary to institute a system of general elections like that of the Paris Commune for electing members to such mass organizations. The right should be given to the masses at any time to criticize members of these new organs of power and demand their replacement or recall.

Clause 10 speaks in detail of the revolution in education, one of the main goals of the cultural revolution. Another clause gives protection for scientists, technicians, and ordinary staff workers in departments of the government or those who have made contributions to the country, so long as they have had no "illicit relations with foreign countries." This was to ensure that the strategic industries and the work in the important research departments should not be dislocated.

But the words "illicit relations with foreign countries" would provoke regrettable and stupid behavior towards anyone who had ever had foreign friends. One family who returned to China after living abroad were harassed for three months under pretext of having had "illicit relations." A good many patriotic overseas Chinese were to suffer in a similar way. Chou En-lai would do his best to stop these excesses, and to redeem injustices done.*

Yet another clause decided that for the time being there should not be any cultural revolution in the communes or in industrial enterprises. In September 1966 Chou En-lai was to tell the students not to spread revolution in factories or rural areas "at present." "Any idea of counter-posing the great cultural revolution to the development of production is incorrect." Workers and peasants were to "make revolution at their place of work," unlike the students, who began to travel all over China by the millions.

The armed forces were to carry out their own cultural revolution in accordance with instructions of the Military Affairs Committee and the General Political Department of the PLA. This separation ensured its objectivity in its function as guardian over the movement.

Mao had expected to limit the Party upheaval, the "fire" to burn the dross in their souls, at first to the upper and middle levels of Party administrators. The mass criticism of this higher echelon would come "from below." But things did not work out that way.

Did Liu Shao-chi oppose the sixteen-point decision? Edgar Snow asked Mao Tsetung.†

He was very ambiguous about it, Mao replied, and thrown into consternation by Mao's August 5 poster, *Bombard the Headquarters*. Liu knew that he was the headquarters to be now smashed. Mao was ready to smash the machinery of the Party which Liu had built, and this to Liu was unthinkable, because the Party machinery was the Party. "It is not justified to rebel against the Communist Party," said Liu. Throughout the years, until today, it has been repeated many

---

* Chou En-lai's speech of March 8, 1973 (unpublished), which gave to many hundreds of foreigners living in China an explanation of some of the events of the cultural revolution.
† Edgar Snow *The Long Revolution* (New York 1971), page 18.

times that the cultural revolution was "entirely appropriate and timely." This is in answer to a continuous reluctance by certain members of the Party to accept that the revolution must be made with the masses and for the masses; that a truly revolutionary leader must be ready to suffer humiliation, torment, injustice in his dedication to one aim: to serve the people.

On the 10th of August, Mao Tsetung joined a large number of youth leaders in the enclosure of Chung Nan Hai, the official residence of the Party leadership. He talked with them, telling them that all the people "should concern themselves with state affairs." He was televised sitting cross-legged on the ground, looking vigorous and bronzed.

On the 12th the communiqué which wound up the eleventh plenum was broadcast. Its main point was the revisionism, both in China and abroad, which China was combating. Revisionism was allied to imperialism; to fight one was to fight the other. The communiqué approved all of Mao's directives as well as those of the tenth plenum of 1962; the socialist education movement as well as the long polemical struggle against the Soviet Union. "It is impossible to have united action with them. . . . We are now in a new era of world revolution. All political forces are undergoing a process of great upheaval, great division, and great reorganization."

Liu Shao-chi was downgraded in the Party hierarchy, along with Teng Hsiao-ping,* and Lin Piao forced through a vote the downgrading of Chu Teh and Chou En-lai from vice-chairmanships in the Party, so that he remained the sole vice-chairman.

After the eleventh plenum the GCCR practically replaced the Party secretariat. With three other organs — the State Council, the Central Committee (represented by the standing committee of the Politburo), and the Military Affairs Committee — it would form the center of command for the cultural revolution for the next four years.

---

* At this crisis in the Party, between May and August 1966, Liu Shao-chi wanted to call a full Central Committee meeting to condemn Mao, but Teng Hsiao-ping, as Party secretary-general, did not comply. This might explain his subsequent reappearance, to be given — as is Mao's habit — another chance to prove himself worthy.

4

The Tortuous Zigzags
of the Cultural
Revolution, 1966–1967

A revolution is not a dinner party.
— MAO TSETUNG, 1927

On August 18 the Red Guards, existent since May, made their first public appearance at a million-strong rally held on Peking's Heavenly Peace Square.

Clad in khaki soldier's garb, Mao Tsetung stood on the terrace overlooking the square and reviewed the battalions of the new revolution marching past and singing: "Sailing the Seas Depends on the Helmsman." From dawn to sweltering noon Mao stood there, occasionally taking some minutes off to retire to the cooler interior hall, drink tea, and remove his vest to wipe, unselfconsciously, his chest and armpits. To a Belgian Communist surprised by this lack of protocol Mao explained candidly: "It's unhealthy to let sweat dry on your body."

Seven more times until late November, Mao would hold those enormous rallies. From all over China came Red Guards, proclaiming a new world in the making. Thirteen million of them. "Let the rest of the country come to Peking, or Peking go to the rest of the country. Train transport is free, isn't it?" Mao said on August 21. And the young overcrowded the trains and came. At any time two million of them would be in the capital. The PLA, in charge of arrangements for feeding and lodging them, with the help of the local population, surpassed itself, providing six thousand trucks, drilling the young in march-past, latrine discipline, erecting canteens and dormitories. Everyone praised the "little generals," whose conduct was excellent, who sang "The World Belongs to Us," and who were very clean, well-behaved and polite. As the cold set in, however, epidemics were feared, especially among the light-clad southerners. In October the Red Guards were enjoined to stop coming by train but to come on foot, as transport was being disrupted by their numbers. They began long marches, walking to places as far as Sinkiang, Manchuria, Tibet to organize great linkups and "exchange revolutionary experience" with other Red Guards. Millions of them saw their land, with its people of many ethnic origins, for the first time.* This enormous cavalcade through China was very well absorbed, and no Red Guard went hungry or without a bed. To pinpoint the few cases of bad conduct is to ignore the discipline and good example of the great majority of these youngsters. "They left no dirt behind them . . . they did not steal anything." Never had China been so exuberant, so alive, so full of the sound of drums and cymbals and so colorful with red flags everywhere.

The Red Guards were not allowed to carry weapons, nor to arrest or try anyone, nor to arbitrarily replace any administrative cadre. They were to "criticize and repudiate," combat the "four olds," proselytize the masses, arouse them into a climate of total involvement. And this they did, spreading into every corner of every city and town, taking down old street names, pointing out how much feudalism still existed. Some of their actions were naïve, and some were brutal, especially when they began to conduct house searches among former capitalists, landlords, and counterrevolutionaries refugeed in the cities. But out of thirty million young people it would be unbelievable not to have a percentage of delinquents. The Red Guards performed a task no one else could have; they literally spring-cleaned the cities, turning up caches of gold and firearms, ferreting out many a secret agent and spy. Their propaganda action, carried out in the streets every day, talking to the people everywhere, did involve the population and disseminate the idea of criticism and debate. This leavening action was very important, for the dough of an older generation could not have been made to ferment otherwise. And very early in September they were already being attacked, and sometimes killed, by groups of workers and peasants, mobilized by the Liu faction in the Party and told that these youngsters were "attacking the Party and Chairman Mao" and were counterrevolutionary. "Repression is not allowed," Mao said when he was told of such conflicts in three or four provinces. The Red Guards had their shortcomings, but they could discipline themselves. And so they did. In Peking, Shanghai, and Manchuria they established

* There are fifty-five ethnic groups or nationalities in China, including the Han majority (93 percent of the total population).

their own disciplinary committees, to deal with misdeeds in their own groups.

On September 15 Chou En-lai, who kept in constant touch with hundreds of youth groups, told the Red Guards that the workers and peasants were well able to make their own cultural revolution at their production posts, and should not leave the factories and the rural areas to follow the Red Guards in their peregrinations. By now the factories were forming groups similar to the Red Guards, based on rebel workers who had resisted the work teams of Liu Shao-chi.

In the streets there were millions of *tatzepao* and the population was excited as never before. Mass supervision of the Party seemed now a reality, with open criticism of so many Party members, and the masses were round-eyed with reading things (not always factual) they had never dreamed could be said or written. The posters caught on and everyone wrote posters. Never had there been so much self-expression, all horizons open.

But factionalism plagued the movement. The youth groups multiplied, split, quarreled; the right wing, organizing fake groups of Red Guards, used this weakness thoroughly. The result was escalation of conflicts and of brutality. Although articles stressed that coercion and force "can touch the skin and flesh but not the soul," and although Chou En-lai and Chiang Ching spent hours and days enjoining "reasoning and not force," force was being used, and on an increasing scale, in quarrels between groups, and also and chiefly on Party cadres, now denounced as "freaks and monsters." The bad tendency to "strike down the many to protect the few" would remain; the Red Guards were searching for people to accuse, to parade, and to dunce-cap as enemies of Mao.

An ultra-right, almost fascist group of young people called the Lientung (associated action group) emerged. It originated from the notion that only the "five good" classes could become Red Guards; its leaders were often the sons and daughters of high cadres, and out of this elitism the right wing began to organize Lientung. Its members had abundant funds, vehicles, and always went in groups, wearing large silk sleeves instead of the small cotton armband which the Red Guards wore. They began beating, kidnapping, and even killing, put up posters condemning the GCCR, Chiang Ching and Chou En-lai, and openly supported Liu Shao-chi. One hundred and thirty-nine of their number would be arrested in early 1967, and the Lientung declared a counterrevolutionary organization.

A Red workers' army, consisting of workers from large complexes, was also organized by the right wing to beat and kill the Red Guards. Other such "armies," made up of peasants from suburban communes, were drafted to "protect the Party" and degenerated into looting bands. This increased the confusion and the scale of violence and discredited genuine Red Guards. Thus a reservoir of available violence which could be utilized against Mao's aims, *but in Mao's name,* was built up. In the profusion of organizations and grouplets, it was very difficult to distinguish true left from false; "who waved the Red flag to bring down the Red flag." Not once did any group claim to be anti-Mao. Factions clustered, coalesced, split, varied almost from hour to hour. The Foreign Language School in Peking alone had around forty such organizations. "Truly a Hundred Flowers bloom," commented the jovial foreign minister, Chen Yi. A factory in Shanghai boasted eighty-five such groups, later to fight each other with fists and sticks, and still later to fight with more dangerous weapons.

But the mainstream of the revolution went on despite factions. The youth movement had to find its own feet. The masses, through their own mistakes and stumblings, must find out what was right and what was wrong. "In a big country like ours one should not be upset by the disturbances caused by a handful . . . it tempers the young . . . helps them to understand that the revolutionary road does not run smoothly," said Mao.

In Shanghai, the Party Municipal Committee, anxious to protect itself, would try to deflect the attacks of the Shanghai Red Guards toward ready-made targets, the bourgeoisie, who lived in large houses and drew interest on their money. Some secondary cadres were sacrificed, to be paraded in the streets with dunce caps on their heads. Meanwhile the municipality organized its own "Red defense corps" from among the workers, sworn "to protect Chairman Mao and the Party" against the rebel Red Guards and others, who were now called counterrevolutionaries. This also happened in other cities.

This complex stage of the cultural revolution was rendered even more confusing, it is alleged, by the actions of Tao Chu. Tao Chu had been placed in charge of liaison between the revolutionary committees organized by the groups of Red Guards and the GCCR, of which he was a member (one out of seventeen), and a very prominent one. His liaison agents, apparently, did exactly what the work teams had done; they sought to impose rules and regulations upon the Red Guard committees. But now that so many of the early members of the GCCR are known to have been partisans of Lin Piao, it is open to question whether Tao Chu was really as guilty as he was made out to be, or whether most of the violence was not due to the covert incitation of the Lin Piao clique. Certainly Tao Chu could be counted as a "right-winger." But just as certainly Lin Piao in his public speeches at Red Guard mass rallies was inciting to violence. The words "destroy . . . destroy . . . destroy . . . knock down . . . knock down" were constantly found in his speeches. Lin Piao had a habit of repeating everything three times, and there is abundant evidence that the admonitions against the use of force figured minimally compared to the calls for more or less violent action in his speeches. Tao Chu, however, does appear to have used the liaison agents to bog down the youth movement, confining it to a middle level in order to protect the upper Party levels, inciting therefore to indiscriminate attacks on all cadres. "Apart from Chairman Mao and Vice-Chairman Lin Piao, everyone can be attacked" was attributed to him.

The liaison agents refused to deliver to the Red Guards incriminating material which had been gathered by the work teams against their leaders. Thus the files on many thousands of young activists were incriminating and rehabilitation was not forthcoming. In factories the same thing had happened. The matter of the dossiers was to assume very large proportions and contribute to Tao Chu's downfall.

Mao Tsetung and Chou En-lai disapproved of the dunce-capping and parading. To point up his disapproval Mao would invite to stand with him on the rostrum, at the seventeenth anniversary celebration of the PRC on October 1, several of the people thus treated, one of them an eminent woman doctor who had shown great fortitude and went right back to work after being paraded. A great-grandmother, she is a well-known and respected figure of China's post-cultural revolution society. At an October meeting of the Politburo, Mao Tsetung said he was surprised by the havoc created — never had he expected that all China would be thrown into such turmoil. Since it was he who had caused this turmoil, it was understandable if some people felt bitter against him.

Perhaps Mao had not expected so much anarchism from the young, especially from the university-educated. But this only proved how deficient the previous education had been in instilling true proletarian values and conduct. The youth had been brought up in an elitist framework, and despite all the slogans, what had emerged was petty bourgeois radicalism, not the real proletarian spirit. For the latter does not use violence when not necessary; it protects collective property, is not self-seeking, is both disciplined and innovative. Pseudo-radicalism had deluded many, Mao would say.* It would slow down the pace of the cultural revolution. But the mainstream of the movement had done what no rectification movement, no socialist education movement, had been capable of doing: revealed the "dark side" of the Party "in an all-around way and from below," and that is what Mao wanted. Mao added that it would take years before anyone, including himself, would really understand the cultural revolution in its entirety.

In October, Liu Shao-chi was called upon to make his self-criticism. Mao Tsetung seemed anxious and preoccupied with the viciousness which Lin Piao exhibited towards Liu, Teng Hsiao-ping, and others.† He reminded the meeting that it was also his fault; he had been anxious to leave things in order after his death, and so had agreed to "two channels" of command. But then he had not been consulted or informed about many things; for instance, Liu's Tientsin speeches to capitalists in March 1949. In the past many leaders had acted on their own, some openly, some secretly. Liu Shao-chi and Teng Hsiao-ping had always been open about their views, whereas Kao Kang and Peng Teh-huai had been two-faced. "Those who are secretive will come to no good end." Did Lin Piao, hearing this, secretly wince?

Tao Chu then made a strange, revealing remark. "Supreme power had slipped from your hands," he said to Mao. "I deliberately relinquished it," Mao Tsetung reminded him.

Mao thought that Liu should be allowed to reform and participate in the cultural revolution. "If people make mistakes, they can change, can't they? . . . Then everything will be all right." But Lin Piao and Chen Po-ta were intractable and insisted that Liu and Teng both be eliminated.

Red Flag, in October, stressed that "the handful of people in the Party taking the capitalist road . . . men of the Khrushchev type . . . are our most dangerous and our main enemy."

Posters appeared, leaking part of Liu Shao-chi's self-criticism and describing it as unsatisfactory. Liu and his wife, Wang Kuang-mei, were being attacked through recognizable cartoons put up at Tsinghua University in Peking, though not named. The phrase of Lu Hsun, "beat the dog in the water," was used to stir up the youth movement against

---

* In July 1967. Exact date not known, but reported also by Jean Daubier in *A History of the Chinese Cultural Revolution* (New York 1974), pages 307–313.

† Such as Chu Teh, whom Lin Piao insulted as "incompetent," according to Red Guard reports. (These must, however, be treated with caution for the period January to October 1967.)

Liu. "Smash his dog's head." Lin Piao's speeches at Red Guard rallies stressed the example of the Paris Commune, the inauguration of "extensive democracy," the unleashing of "the broad masses . . . to criticize and supervise the Party and the government, leading institutions and leaders *at all levels*." This was calling for a wholesale attack on Party cadres, not just "the handful of capitalist-roaders" within the Party. It is therefore not accurate to hold Tao Chu responsible for all the violence that took place.

Only on one occasion, November 12, did Mao break his self-imposed silence, when he seized the microphone to tell the Red Guards: "You must let politics take command. Go to the masses and be with the masses. You must conduct the Great Proletarian Cultural Revolution even better." The Peking Municipal Party Committee issued warnings of dire punishment on November 18 against youths who beat up people and held kangaroo courts. What no one knew was that the chief inciter to violence was Lin Piao himself.

In November a rally of twenty thousand actors, musicians, and other workers from the arts saw the incorporation of Opera Troupe No. 1 of the Peking Opera, and the Peking Symphonic Orchestra, into the Cultural Department of the PLA. Chiang Ching became adviser to the PLA cultural group (as distinct from the GCCR, which depended directly from the Central Committee). This was a harbinger of the role the PLA would soon be called upon to play, to put an end to the infighting threatening to dislocate all essential services. For now Party committees even at grass-roots levels were being attacked — accountants in production teams, the heads of street committees, ordinary clerks in offices, and factory foremen.

This incorporation enhanced the power of Chen Po-ta as head of the GCCR. In December, Tao Chu was dismissed from his post. In the next year he would be denounced by Red Guard posters as a Liu follower, who had "waved the Red flag to bring down the Red flag."

Chen Po-ta did his utmost to utilize Chiang Ching's great personal prestige, as Lin Piao rode to power on Mao's charisma. Chen Po-ta now recommended Yeh Chun, Lin Piao's wife and Chen Po-ta's pupil, to Chiang Ching. Whenever Chiang Ching spoke at mass rallies, Yeh Chun would be there, leading the clapping and the shouting of slogans such as "Learn from Chiang Ching" and "Long live Chiang Ching." In brief, what Lin Piao was doing with Mao, creating Mao's personality cult as a "genius," Yeh Chun was trying on Mao's wife.

By January 1967 Yeh Chun, who worked as a public relations official in the PLA, was in the cultural group of the PLA, and by year's end she had moved in as chief of Lin Piao's bureau in the Military Affairs Committee. By 1969 she would become a member of the Politburo.

In December 1966, Mao Tsetung officially extended the cultural revolution to the agricultural and industrial sectors. Directives went out to ask them to "grasp revolution and promote production at their place of work," to resist attempts by landlords and counterrevolutionaries to deviate the current of the cultural revolution.

Now that the right wing was attacked everywhere, an insidious "ultra-left," which is actually a disguised right, was manifest. Mao had already remarked how, as in layers, one tendency covered another; peel one off and the other came up.

On January 4, 1967, the Red Guards held a public exhibition of Peng Chen, Lu Ting-yi, Lo Jui-ching, former chief of staff, and Yang Shang-kun, head of the secret police. Photographs of the men at this exposure circulated all over Peking and appear to have been smuggled abroad, where they appeared in many newspapers.

This "trial"* is attributed by some early writers on the cultural revolution (including some living in China then) to Tao Chu's influence — Tao Chu sought thus to fix resentment upon Peng Chen and the others, in order to stop action against Liu Shao-chi. But the development of the cultural revolution cannot allow us to consider this verdict as final. The ceremony may have been part of the deliberate and planned attempt by the Lin Piao group to take power, an attempt which developed from December 1966 until September 1967.

In January several things occurred which confirm this suspicion. First, there was a sudden clamor among the Red Guards to "drag out the capitalist-roaders in the army." Such a demand could not have been made spontaneously. Posters attacking Chu Teh, Mao's companion in arms since 1927, Marshal Ho Lung of the PLA, and Foreign Minister Chen Yi covered the walls of Peking. And in the midst of it all, on January 15, came a fifteen-foot *tatzepao* attacking Chou En-lai.

At the same time, *tatzepao* exhibited lurid accounts of an attempted coup organized by Liu Shao-chi, Peng Chen, Lo Jui-ching and others in February 1966. It was patently a reproduction of the idea of a "coup d'etat" which had been the burden of Lin Piao's speech of May 18, 1966, and to which Mao had taken exception. To bring back in January

---

* Although the Red Guards were not to hold "trials," they did so increasingly under the influence of the "ultra-left" trend of the supporters of Lin Piao.

1967 this story, to strive to implicate Chou En-lai in the coup, was certainly not the work of the imagination of the Red Guards alone. The slogan "Drag out the handful of capitalist-roaders in the army" was also not due to the young; it was a deliberate attempt by Lin Piao and Chen Po-ta to discredit all military commanders who might oppose Lin Piao's rise to absolute power.

The main target (approached indirectly) was of course the downfall of Chou En-lai. Chou En-lai supported Mao and the cultural revolution, and Mao Tsetung trusted him, calling him "the housekeeper" of China. In order to get at Chou, attacks had to be from many sides, the main one being against Chen Yi, the foreign minister.

One telephone call from the GCCR to the main headquarters of the Red Guard committees in Peking put an end to the "coup d'etat" story. The posters against Chou also disappeared. But the onslaught against Chen Yi continued. Chou En-lai came out in person to see that his foreign minister's choleric temper and habit of blurting truths would not bring him to harm. The attacks against Marshal Ho Lung, another veteran, could not be stemmed. Ho Lung had differed with Mao on the question of equipment for the PLA, contending that there was no contradiction between democracy in the PLA and sophisticated equipment.* He was now indicted by the army cultural group as a revisionist. The attacks against him were mounted by Lin Piao, to seize the influential posts which Ho Lung's followers in the First Field Army occupied in certain regions of China. He also wanted to bring down Ho Lung's brother-in-law, Li Ching-chuan, Party secretary for Szechuan province, the "granary" of West China. Chen Po-ta had already attacked Li Ching-chuan the previous year during his trip to Szechuan. Li Ching-chuan was a veteran Long Marcher, who had studied under Mao in 1926 at the Kuangchow Peasant Institute which Mao was running. As Ho Lung's brother-in-law, Li Ching-chuan was violently attacked, but is now back, rehabilitated, as are so many of Lin Piao's victims. Groups of Red Guards under Chen Po-ta's influence went to Szechuan to mount a "popular uprising" against Li Ching-chuan in the spring of 1967.

Thus the "ultra-left" promoted by Lin Piao and Chen Po-ta was objectively right-wing and counterrevolutionary, since it was sabotaging the cultural revolution to bring about the personal power of one

---

* Ho Lung On the Democratic Tradition in the PLA (English edition Peking 1965). This was regarded as contradicting Lin Piao's article Long Live the Victory of People's War.

man. Both it and the Liu right wing were keeping violence at a high level: organizing and arming landlords and rich peasants, inciting workers into rival factions, "deluding" the young into demolishing all Party committees and all Party members, destroying the Party itself. This anarchism was expressed by the student Kuai Ta-fu, now an "ultra-leftist": "All the Party is bad . . . all must be destroyed." There must be, Kuai said, general elections by the masses, to assure the real dictatorship of the proletariat.

An editorial in the *People's Daily* of January 22 added to the intoxication, calling on its readers to "seize power, seize power, seize power . . . establish a *new* proletarian order," without any reference to Party cadres or to Party leadership. Yet Mao had made it clear that without the participation and *leadership* of Party cadres, the cultural revolution could not succeed, and had also said that "95 percent of cadres . . . are good or relatively good."

In the next *Red Flag* a measured and sober article by "Commentator" (who is sometimes Mao himself) asserted the need for *unity*, for heightening vigilance against "cunning enemies." But the ultra-left wave was at its beginning and growing strong. And within the GCCR were at least four of Lin Piao's and Chen Po-ta's own partisans, who were listened to by the youth groups.

The Military Affairs Committee, the Central Committee, the State Council and the GCCR combined to initiate important directives. In January 1967 they authorized the PLA to come out of its neutrality and to subdue "counterrevolutionary groups." This was not only to curb the violence, but also to assure essential services, and because attacks on PLA garrisons to capture weapons had begun. The PLA had not taken action, having been forbidden to use any weapons against the people. This had caused the death of many a young peasant soldier — as Chou En-lai would tell Edgar Snow, "hundreds of thousands of casualties," then and through the next years in the PLA.

Mao Tsetung had foreseen the possibility of using the PLA, and now the widespread attacks against low-level cadres necessitated this move. The PLA was enjoined to "support the left." The slogan "Drag out the handful of capitalist-roaders in the army" was denounced as inappropriate and incorrect. The PLA was maintained as a separate organism, indispensable for the final assault upon the entrenched and still very strong right wing.

By January 19 the PLA had already taken over the guarding of depots and grain stores, jails and banks and broadcasting stations. In February it would guard all communications and airports. By April 1, four hundred thousand men of the PLA would be manning all essential services. Almost two million PLA activists would be employed during these years of the cultural revolution to keep things going.

In March, the first directive to the PLA was clarified, because "Support the left" was extremely difficult to carry out. What was the real, true left? From all over came clamors of "repression and suppression" of youth movements by the military, some true, some fictitious. The PLA was given fresh instructions to support the revolutionary left, industry and agriculture; it was to exercise military control to prevent violence, and to take in hand the military and political education of the young. (Elliptically, this is known as the three support, two military directive.)

The calling in of the PLA marked the end of the first phase of the cultural revolution: the role of the young as stimulator and vanguard was already ended in December, when the working class had begun its own cultural revolution. Now the problem would be to take youth in hand and "remold" it as true revolutionary successors.

Mao Tsetung would give a broad view of the cultural revolution to a visiting foreign delegation in 1967. The first year of the event was for mobilization, arrangements and planning, or "lighting the fire." The second would be establishing new power structures based on the innovative genius of the masses, and revolutionizing thinking and the minds of men through the process of "struggle, criticism, transformation." The third year would be for tidying up. There is a strong resemblance to a Chinese cooking recipe in Mao's formula. As the Chinese chef first chops up meat, vegetables, and then puts it all in the hot pan, stirring briskly, so Mao threw all of China's social sectors into a tumult. Never in history did any leader seem to fear disorder so little, or have such confidence in the people, that out of their involvement and disorder would come a new awareness and order.

Mao defined for the delegation the role of the young and its limits. After the eleventh plenum of August 1966, where he had won by a bare majority, the enthusiasm of youth had been aroused; and this was a law of revolutionary development — young students were always in the forefront of revolt. But by January 1967 the situation had changed. The workers in Shanghai had been aroused, and the workers and peasants throughout the land had followed suit. The workers-peasants-soldiers were the main force in any revolution (soldiers were workers and peasants in uniform). Intellectuals were quicker on the uptake, but they had a tendency to opportunism. The young students had received a bourgeois education and "bourgeois thinking has somewhat got into their bloodstream." The world outlook of many of the intelligentsia, in or out of the Party, remained uncompromisingly bourgeois, and would have to be reformed.

The "January storm" in Shanghai was the rise of the Chinese working class to its true role of leader in the state.

The Shanghai working class is the largest and most skilled in China, with educated young workers in considerable numbers by 1965. Contact between workers and the Red Guards was early; nuclei of "rebels" formed quickly in factories. But the work teams of Liu Shao-chi and also the trade union leadership persecuted them and turned the other workers against them, calling them "anti-Party," docking wages, expelling or even jailing them. Nevertheless, the cultural revolution was making inroads, and the Red Guards of Shanghai were particularly active among the factories after September 1966. Yao Wen-yuan, whose attack on Wu Han had started the cultural revolution, and Chang Chun-chiao, at the time secretary of the Propaganda Department in the Shanghai Municipal Party Committee, were both from Shanghai; co-opted into the GCCR in Peking, they traveled back and forth between the two cities.

Although the Shanghai Municipal Party Committee resisted the cultural revolution, it could not go against Mao's December directive extending the revolution to industry and agriculture. No leading Party member in industry or mining enterprises was allowed to retaliate against mass criticism, dock wages, fire workers, or revoke the contracts of temporary laborers. Tao Chu fell that month, and the "black material" collected against students and workers was now exhumed from the Party files and burned publicly. At the same time, the All-China Federation of Trade Unions was suspended as a "revisionist" organism.

The first revolutionary workers' committee was formed by Wang Hung-wen, the young worker (now vice-chairman of the Party) who on June 12 put up a poster in the Shanghai cotton mill where he worked, attacking the "capitalist-roaders" in his factory. Wang was ostracized, went to Peking in October, and was encouraged to continue. He recruited, organized, and set up a Rebel Revolution Headquarters, attempting a coalition among scattered worker groups.

Then arose a wave of "economism." To sabotage worker rebellion, the right wing incited strikes which paralyzed the docks and public services. This was against Mao's recommendation that the way to make revolution was by "grasping production"; that is, that in each factory the revisionist line and management should be criticized, but work should not stop.

Factory managers revised scales of pay upward, issuing back pay for ten years. Sums for winter clothes were paid out, and large amounts to foremen, who were now exhorted to travel with their staffs to "exchange revolutionary experience," abandoning production. Bank accountants were to honor any chit presented by a worker, and this caused a run on banks. A spending spree set in, with stores emptied of bicycles, radios, watches, food. "Economism" spread to rural areas; landlords and rich peasants led bands to rifle stores, to loot the banks and commune funds.

Wang Hung-wen distinguished himself in the battle against economism. With Chang Chun-chiao he succeeded in grouping eleven main organizations of workers, won the adherence of Shanghai University and middle school Red Guards. This was no mean feat, when one realizes how difficult it was to get two groups of Red Guards to merge in other cities. Wang and Chang would reach four hundred thousand workers, versus the eight hundred thousand the Municipality had fostered in its "Red defense detachments" to "protect the Party." The Rebel Revolutionary Headquarters then proceeded to "seize power" as Mao Tsetung had recommended, first at the newspaper *Wen Hui Pao* on January 4, and at *Liberation Daily* on January 6. With the press in their hands, the Headquarters issued messages and an open letter to the people of Shanghai, denouncing "economism," disruption and losses in the factories, calling on the workers to rally to Mao's line, to promote production while making revolution, to renounce material demands. A First Front Command for production was set up. Workers, students, and the PLA manned the docks and kept utilities going. Within a month the "deluded" workers returned, and newspapers published eulogies of those who voluntarily returned radios, bicycles, or the funds issued to them. "We understood then that it is not money but power which the working class must wield . . . we began to see how money was a way to corrupt us."

Shanghai's events were a breakthrough; for this was, within the Chinese revolution, a revolution from below, with the working class seizing power and creating new institutions. The Headquarters' success in organizing a grand alliance of workers, Red Guards and revolutionary cadres created the first functioning representative proletarian power.

This "model" power seizure, vindicating the cultural revolution as a consolidation of the dictatorship of the proletariat, would now establish new government machinery. The first intention was to create a Shanghai people's commune, on the model of the famous Paris Commune of 1871.

The Paris Commune, established when a whole city's laboring people seized control and began creating revolutionary committees and running a new social order, has had perennial fascination for Marxists, including Mao Tsetung, although it failed. Its essential lesson is that the working class come to power cannot employ the ready-made state structure. Mao used the Paris Commune example in his polemics with the USSR to contend that revolutionary seizures of power *must* smash the bureaucratic and military machine of the previous class. Therefore, a policy of "peaceful transition" or "the parliamentary road" was bound to fail, since it would be merely inheriting a structure and trying to make it work.*

In March 1966 *Red Flag* had mentioned the Paris Commune as a lesson in "power seizure." In the Sixteen Articles, a passage refers to it. "It is necessary to institute a system of general elections, like that of the Paris Commune, for electing members to the cultural revolutionary committees and groups and delegates to the cultural revoutionary congresses."

But now Mao had second thoughts. Although the Shanghai commune was inaugurated on February 14 at a million-strong rally of Red Guards, workers, and PLA representatives of land, naval and air forces, Mao Tsetung called Yao Wen-yuan and Chang Chun-chiao, then busy in Shanghai with the commune establishment, to discuss the matter in Peking.

Practice, for Mao, is the supreme test. The experiences in the past six months now made him hesitate. The unquenched strife, the anarchist tendencies among the young, the violence which denied all authority, meant that a loose-knit and extensively democratic scheme such as the Paris Commune could be manipulated, split into endless squabbling small groups. The "small group mentality" was particularly strong among the intelligentsia. Power could then fall into the hands of a few

---

* *On Khrushchev's Phony Communism and the Lessons It Teaches the World* (English edition Peking 1965).

determined and unscrupulous careerists. Mao had read history and knew how "ultra-democracy" can be the seedbed of Bonapartism. "There are people who wave the Red flag to bring down the Red flag," said Mao — people who accused others of being counterrevolutionary, and were believed by the naïve workers, but who were themselves counterrevolutionary. It had not escaped Mao that in this wave of "ultra-democracy" the young were being instigated to call for the abolition of the Party itself, "and that won't do." Yet Chen Po-ta was calling for communes of the Paris type to be established everywhere, and in Taiyuan, and Peking, posters and leaflets were proclaiming the imminent formation of communes with "all power to the proletariat."

Mao Tsetung told Chang and Yao that the Shanghai victory had been brilliant and decisive for the cultural revolution by bringing the working class to its proper role as the main force; but the working class was still being split and divided, it had to clarify its ideology and unite. There were still seven hundred or more organizations in Shanghai's factories. Students of Shanghai middle schools and universities were already denouncing Chang Chun-chiao; they resisted the PLA take-over of the airport. The next few months would be crucial, Mao thought. A major assault against the positions of the right was to begin. To demand, as the Shanghai People's Committee had done, that Premier Chou En-lai do away with all heads of departments in the government offices was "extreme anarchism . . . downright reactionary." So was the slogan "Doubt everyone and overthrow everything," which youth groups clamored. Shanghai ought to create a revolutionary committee based on the triple alliance of revolutionary cadres (from the 95 percent in the old Party committees after due scrutiny), the PLA, and the masses. "Communes of the Paris type are too weak when it comes to suppressing counterrevolution."

Chang Chun-chiao duly reported this to a rally in Shanghai, and after much discussion it was decided to change the name to Revolutionary Committee of the Municipality of Shanghai. Some of the features of the Paris Commune were to be institutionalized in the revolutionary committees, such as elections, the right of criticism, and the right to recall bad officials.

Though their role was now over, it was by no means certain that the young would give up the carouse of revolution. Some of them had tasted a kind of power: leading groups with flags flying and drums and cymbals; holding "trials" and criticizing and abusing older cadres.

Some had a heady feeling that they were just as clever as any minister.

On February 8 a GCCR directive ordered all primary schools and lower classes of middle schools to open again. The great linkups and travels of the young were to stop. College and university students who traveled must henceforth pay for their own food and lodging. Higher middle schools would reopen by March 1.

Now revolution was to be made in each school, each deposing its own revisionists, then organizing a triple alliance (students, cadres, and teachers), and carrying through "struggle, criticism, transformation" to reform education, rewrite the textbooks.

But despite these formal orders, it would be weeks, even months, before middle schools could really function. On the one hand, it was difficult to get the children back (save for the primary schools), so much was going on all the time — people to criticize and condemn, posters to put up, parades and rallies. On the other hand, the teaching staffs would not return to work. "It is dangerous to be a teacher," they said, recalling ill-treatment, and stayed at home (everyone received full salary throughout the cultural revolution, whether suspended or not working).

Another "power seizure" in January became a landmark. In Heilungkiang the Party secretary of the province, Pan Fu-sheng, after due self-criticism, joined the "rebels" and led them against right-wing tank battalions. (Here the PLA seems to have been divided between left and pseudo-left factions.) Pan Fu-sheng appeared to be the first high-level cadre to come over to Mao's side and to form a triple alliance. This was a link between revolution "from below" and "from above," highly important when youth leaders were calling for the overthrow of *all* Party members, and proof that not all high cadres were revisionists. The true diehards were only a handful, Mao repeated; he called for speedy rehabilitation of the majority of Party cadres, who must join the masses to make revolution together.*

The greatest difficulties would be encountered in carrying out this policy because the "ultra-left" would continue to treat cadres most evilly. Appeals to "treat cadres correctly"† would continue for the whole of 1967 and 1968. Violence was "helpful only to the class enemy." "The danger of ultra-democracy lies in the fact that it damages or even completely wrecks the Party organization and weakens or even

---

* But Pan Fu-sheng was later demoted as too arbitrary; he seems to have tried a military dictatorship along Lin Piao's methods.

† See *Cadres Must Be Treated Correctly, Red Flag,* no. 4, 1967.

completely undermines the Party's fighting capacity . . . thereby causing the defeat of the revolution."

Power seizures were not always stable and final. Some of the new
revolutionary committee members "chased after motorcycles, tele-
phones, and a high standard of living." Therefore there were repeated
power seizures; and among them, some were manufactured by fake left
groups.

Yet in all this medley, chaos, confusion, Mao preserved equanimity.
It was all very good, he said; it exposed all the contradictions present
in society; it taught the minds of millions the many quirks and pitfalls
on the way to genuine revolution; and this was being done through
practice more rapidly than any amount of teaching could have
achieved.

The untiring Chou En-lai, meanwhile, was striving to promote a
grand alliance and unity among all the Red Guards, as well as their
return to school to make revolution in educational establishments. In
both these goals he was hindered by the ultra-left. Chi Pen-yu, a journalist working with Chen Po-ta, a member of the GCCR, sneered: "Go
back to school? Then everything will be just like before." Nevertheless,
Chou En-lai succeeded in assembling a Congress of Red Guards on
February 22 in Peking, which proclaimed a grand alliance. But this
unity did not last. Although many of the young were getting tired of
violence, and many would be going back to school within the next few
months, a sizable minority would disobey the orders.

Chou En-lai, throughout, refused to follow the Lin Piao instigated
ultra-left tide. He expressed his indignation, a very courageous thing to
do in the circumstances, against the ill-treatment meted out to cadres,
including the way in which Liu Shao-chi's wife, Wang Kuang-mei, had
been treated. "I am very upset, very upset," he said, when his minister
of Coal died of a heart attack after a forty-hour continuous grilling.
But Chi Pen-yu and Wang Li, another of Lin Piao's confederates and
also a member of the GCCR, continued to prod the young. "The only
way is to seize power, all the Party power, political and financial."
Later it would be revealed that Lin Piao thus did seize control of
certain major industrial complexes, utilizing the slogan "All power to
the proletariat" to do so.

While this was going on, PLA activists were helping the peasants
with the spring sowing and planting, and with subduing re-emergent
landlords and rich peasants and their armed bands. Though accused in

some places of crushing "true left" rebels, in others they put down counterrevolutionary bands. They sent propaganda teams into every industry where sectarian conflicts raged, and gave political training to teachers and students in reopened middle schools.

But the tendency to use the mailed fist was also present. In April, shooting was forbidden when dealing with mass organizations, whatever the provocation. So were large-scale arrests. There was to be no revenge against masses who stormed military garrisons or assaulted PLA men (Order in Ten Points, April 6, 1967). This abstention from retaliation was hard. Some PLA commanders and men gave very creditable performances in persuasive nonviolence, and became very popular thereby.

A mysterious episode known as the February Adverse Current now took place. At the time it was represented in the press as a determined counterrevolutionary move to resist power seizures and overturn "verdicts" on the revisionists. But time, and especially the revelation of Lin Piao's treachery, has allowed a reappraisal.

It was, in fact, a reaction among some of the ministers of the State Council, backed by a number of cadres, both central and provincial, against the violence to which they were subject. Tan Chen-lin, minister of Agriculture, took it upon himself to rehabilitate useful and necessary cadres in his ministry, and he stood up at a meeting to shout: "Too many cadres have been struck down and persecuted." Tan Chen-lin was not alone in protesting. Both in Shanghai and in other areas, military and civilian officials were not happy at the way they were treated. In particular, it seems, Tan's objections coincided with the movement which was shaping against Ho Lung, and also against Hsiao Hua, the head of the PLA General Political Department. It is very difficult, even today, to extricate facts from the confusion and the insidious maneuvers of that time, because of course both the right wing and the Lin Piao clique were also engaged in covert action. Tan Chen-lin was violently criticized and suspended; his actions were denounced as trying to upset the verdicts against the right wing. He had indeed laid himself open to the accusation of putting a technocratic line above revolutionary ideology. But he was not a plotter, and is now rehabilitated and in high position. As for Ho Lung, who seems to have been the target of a great deal of attack, he died of old age, and it is said that in his last days Mao Tsetung sent him a comforting message. He has been completely rehabilitated posthumously.

A renewal of the campaign against Liu Shao-chi, which had become bogged down in January, now took place. It was marked by an article by Chi Pen-yu on April 1, entitled *Patriotism or National Betrayal?* This brought up again the story of the film *Inside Story of the Ching Court* of 1950, which Liu had praised and Mao condemned. Chi Pen-yu in his article asked Liu Shao-chi to answer eight questions on his past life. They concerned his having been a renegade, colluded with the Kuomintang several times, and incited, in 1937, several Communists in the jails of Chiang Kai-shek to abjure in order to save their own lives. Red Guard posters appeared asking that Liu Shao-chi be handed over "to the masses."

Mao Tsetung commented with acerbity on the crop of posters about Liu Shao-chi and on the level of criticism against him. It was personal, not ideological; it missed the point. "It isn't enough just to write: smash the dog's head . . . this is not criticism." It was not Liu personally, but his revisionism, which had to be criticized. On May 8 an article entitled *Betrayal of the Proletarian Dictatorship Is the Heart of the Book on "Self-Cultivation"** would raise the ideological level of criticism. Millions of articles from commune members, factory workers, intellectuals, would criticize one or another aspect of Liu's book until 1973.

But Liu Shao-chi was stubborn. "In the proletarian cultural revolution, as to why I have advocated and promoted the bourgeois reactionary line, I myself am also not clear. Nor have I read any essay which can fully explain why I have made errors of line. After the eleventh plenum criticized my errors . . . others committed errors of a similar nature, but they also do not know why."

And so Liu remained obdurate, refusing to submit. Perhaps that is why Edgar Snow felt compassion for him,† and wrote of Liu's "dignity." But the manner in which Liu placed responsibility for errors on others, including his wife, is not something one can really admire.

"Factionalism shields counterrevolutionaries and counterrevolutionaries make use of factionalism," said Mao Tsetung.

Another group, called the May 16, to become notorious throughout China, came up in April or May. It was so named because of Mao's May 16 document of 1966. Also to become known as the 516 — because May is the fifth month — it was a semisecret society, with passwords

---

* *Self-Cultivation* is another title for Liu's book *How to Be a Good Communist.* The original title dates back to 1939, but since Liu in the book talks of "self-cultivation," everyone knew which book was meant.

† Edgar Snow *The Long Revolution* (New York 1972), pages 93–94.

and admission rituals. And it became Lin Piao's tool for fomenting disorder, although no one would know this until 1971.

The 516 was a plague; it spread in the cities; though its numbers were comparatively small, it terrorized a good many through its vandalism and murders. The woman lecturer Nieh Yuan-tze, whose *tatzepao* of May 25, 1966, had been commended by Mao, became somehow affiliated with them through marrying a Lin Piao follower. (She had been elected vice-chairman of the Peking Municipality Revolutionary Committee in April 1967.) The 516 had eight regional "armies," and liaison centers in Peking, Shanghai, Kuangchow, and other cities. One center was operating from the No. 1 Middle School in Changsha; another was at Tsinghua University. Kuai Ta-fu, the student leader, became involved in the 516.

The most curious feature of this extremism is the acquisition by the 516 of the cooperation of a small group of foreigners living in China, chief among them an American, Sydney Rittenberg. Rittenberg, who for a while occupied a great deal of space in Hsinhua News Agency reports as a representative of "proletarian internationalism," ran the foreign language broadcasts on Peking Radio. The 516 promoted an idolatrous cult of Mao and attacked anyone who did not conform. The cult now took on semireligious aspects; "loyalty to Chairman Mao" became the touchstone. Lin Piao said that "it does not matter what one does, so long as one has the correct orientation," and this was enough to permit the 516 to do anything. People were made to bow to Mao's image everywhere. At Chingkangshan, at Tsunyi, at other shrines of the revolution, all pictures of Mao's colleagues were removed, leaving only Lin Piao with Mao, the single faithful comrade in arms "who has never made a mistake."

The atrocities committed by the 516 were many. Dr. Fu Lien-chang, the medical practitioner who followed Mao to Chingkangshan in 1928, was one of their numerous victims.

In April the 516 acquired a recruit in the person of Yao Teng-shan, erstwhile ambassador to Indonesia, back in Peking as a hero after having sustained some minor injuries during a mob assault upon the Chinese embassy in Djakarta. Yao Teng-shan was probably psychotic, certainly power-greedy. He denounced Chen Yi and China's foreign policy as "revisionist" — an attack also on Chou En-lai as premier. He was echoed by Sydney Rittenberg, who even denounced North Vietnam, at that time heavily bombed, as "revisionist."

A series of incidents occurred on the diplomatic level, to culminate in the burning of the British embassy in August. Incidents involving foreigners in China escalated, and a strong streak of xenophobia became evident. Meanwhile, the cult of Mao was being assiduously pushed; newspapers which had denounced the "docile tool theory" of Liu Shaochi now called for absolute obedience to Chairman Mao; "whether we understand his instructions or not . . . we must establish Chairman Mao's absolute authority."* This was a repetition of what Lin Piao had said the previous May and again in August, that he obeyed Mao, whether he understood what Mao was saying or not. And it was exactly the opposite of what Mao was teaching, that "a Communist must use his brains . . . must always know the why and wherefore of things."

Mao was watching. An editorial in *Red Flag* warned that it was harmful to try to renovate completely the dictatorship of the proletariat. People with "ulterior motives" were trying to "overthrow all." This meant overthrowing the proletarian order already functioning and instituting a dictatorship of the bourgeoisie.

But the havoc created, and the decimation of cadres at all levels, hindered the work of forming new revolutionary committees. Chou En-lai, one of whose tasks was to examine the alliances formed and to watch over the revolutionary committees, was again subject to attacks. On July 1, 1967, the *People's Daily* warned that "nonproletarian ideas" were found in revolutionary ranks.

On May 13, youths armed with knives broke into the Ministry of Foreign Affairs to steal documents. A few days later the headquarters of the 516 handed Chou En-lai an ultimatum demanding that Chen Yi, Chi Peng-fei, and Chiao Kuan-hua, all trusted colleagues of Chou, be arraigned before a tribunal. Later they kidnapped and beat up Chiao Kuan-hua and paraded him in the streets.

On July 22, at a Red Guard rally, Chiang Ching again told the Red Guards that they should attack only by words. But since Red Guards were being attacked, she conceded they could defend themselves. The slogan "Attack by reason, defend by force" would lead to the formation of vigilante groups and provosts among the workers, to enforce order and to protect state property against hooliganism by the 516.

By now a good many young people were getting frightened and tired of the terrorist 516. Some groups began to criticize Lin Piao for saying that Mao was "greater than Marx, Engels, Lenin or Stalin." The

* Article of June 19, 1967, in *People's Daily* by Lin Chie, follower of Lin Piao and also a member of the GCCR.

516 grew more secret, coming out mostly by night to put up posters and to kidnap and terrorize people.

These posters said the right wing had a "backstage patron" (meaning Chou En-lai). Chou had protested the ill-treatment of a good many people, saying that such actions were not revolutionary or proletarian. In fact, Mao had banned all torture or physical ill-treatment. But the 516 did not care. "It is necessary to drag out a person that is more important that Chen Yi, one who does not belong to the cultural revolution group . . . and has stood guarantee for the greatest number of people . . . that person's name will astound you," said the posters. That was Chou En-lai, not a member of the GCCR.

Had Chou En-lai been brought down, China would be a Lin Piao fascist dictatorship today. Of all those Lin Piao sought to destroy, the frail but formidable Chou was the single most unifying force, after Mao, in the Party, and also with influence among regional commanders. The GCCR in that summer was almost overwhelmed by the Lin Piao group within it. And in the Military Affairs Committee, Lin Piao was extending his influence. The Central Committee was seriously weakened by the suspension of so many leading cadres, who were not all Liu followers but were indiscriminately accused. If Lin Piao could get rid of Chou En-lai, seize control of the Ministry of Foreign Affairs, he would relegate Mao (so he thought) to the role of a helpless deity, a supreme authority to be quoted and interpreted by Lin Piao, to enforce what Lin Piao wanted.

In July occurred the Wuhan incident.

During June and July discussions on the increasing severity of factional strife in many provinces were held in Peking, and the result was a series of investigative tours shared out between the leaders, including Mao himself. Mao would be absent from Peking for part of July and August.

The city of Wuhan had endured severe factional strife. Chou En-lai visited it in early July and advised the military commander, Chen Tsai-tao, that he should not back an organization called the One Million Heroes, while repressing the students of Wuhan University who with the steelworkers of the Wuhan steel complex had organized a rebel headquarters. Chen Tsai-tao replied that the students were anarchists and interfered with production.

Chou En-lai left, and on July 18 Hsieh Fu-chih, chairman of the Peking Revolutionary Committee and a member of the GCCR, arrived together with Wang Li, member of the GCCR and editor of *Red Flag* (and a Lin Piao supporter). With them was also Yu Li-chin, political commissar of the air force.

Wang Li addressed the students and steelworkers at their headquarters (known as the Mao Tsetung Thought Fighting Headquarters), assuring them of the Center's support. Instead of conciliating, he inflamed; in the torrid heat of Wuhan, tempers were extremely short. Commander Chen Tsai-tao took it ill, questioned whether Hsieh and Wang really represented the Center. That night one of his officers staged a surprise attack on the residential hotel where the Peking envoys slept and took them in custody. Chen Tsai-tao anticipated retaliation and began to reinforce defenses, placing Wuhan under curfew, with street patrols, announcing that "Chairman Mao's counter-revolutionary enemies must be smashed." On July 20 an airborne division and naval units were ordered against Chen Tsai-tao by Lin Piao, but before military operations took place Chou En-lai flew again to Wuhan. Though he was warned about being kidnapped, he was successful in mediating, and on the 22nd of July, when all seemed poised for civil war, Wang Li and Hsieh Fu-chih returned to Peking.

The Party Center called on "those who have erred to mend their ways, reminding them that if they do so sincerely and honestly, they will not be held accountable for their deeds." Chen Tsai-tao voluntarily gave himself up and flew to Peking to make his self-criticism. This typically Chinese denouement also shows the strength of Party authority, and Chen Tsai-tao is forgiven and well. The One Million Heroes organization dispersed, and within a week all was calm again in Wuhan.

Chen Tsai-tao's dilemma was that of other regional commanders. He felt that he knew the local situation better than "troublesome people" from Peking. And he also asserted that he was not clear about the functions of the GCCR. He said he did not know it was *also* in charge of the PLA, and acting as the replacement for the suspended secretariat of the Central Committee. Therefore he had questioned the authority of Wang Li and Hsieh Fu-chih. This challenge to the authority of the GCCR was indicative of growing restlessness among the regional commanders, who felt the GCCR backed the "ultra-left."

Returning to Peking, Wang and Hsieh were welcomed as heroes. The Lin Piao group thought the time had come, and Wang Li revived the slogan "Drag out the handful in the army who are capitalist-roaders!" This slogan would launch the 516 into raids against the regional commanders. "The proletariat must have a rifle in hand," wrote *Red Flag*, and thereupon attacks upon garrisons were intensified, and PLA commanders were violently attacked, even by name.* Looting of trains with ammunition for Vietnam and of arsenals occurred. Lo Jui-ching was again denounced, and on August 15 details of the Lushan plenum of 1959, when Peng Teh-huai, then minister of Defense, was demoted, were published for the first time. All this was to prove that there had been, and still were, "capitalist-roaders" within the PLA.

Lin Piao backed the "Drag out the handful in the army" slogan. The Wuhan incident was not fortuitous, he said after the incident, in late July, again hinting at an organized right-wing coup. In Lin Piao's July talks Chou En-lai was again indirectly attacked, for Lin Piao referred to the GCCR as the *"sole trustworthy"* repository of Mao Tsetung Thought, pointedly ignoring the State Council and its premier. Posters with "Down with the government" and "Down with the State Council" now appeared.

On Army Day, August 1, Mao Tsetung was proclaimed the prime mover of the Nanchang uprising of 1927. This uprising had been led by Chou En-lai.† In it had taken part Peng Teh-huai and Chu Teh, while Lin Piao was still a minor commander in the army. But now Lin was glorified as the victor at Nanchang, having followed Mao's directives faithfully. The museum at Nanchang was "renovated"; Chou disappeared from it while only Lin Piao and Mao figured in it.

But the regional commanders were irked. Wang En-mao in Sinkiang, Chang Kuo-hua in Szechuan, others elsewhere, were growing suspicious of Lin Piao and Chen Po-ta. The regional commanders seem to have made their discontent known, and on August 5 Lin Piao called some of the key commanders to Peking and spoke to them in a conciliatory manner, urging them to get in touch with him by telegraph or telephone, or if they had any problems to report them to the Central Committee. "We don't want any more Chen Tsai-tao affairs."

An editorial on August 12 in *Liberation Army Daily* extolled Lin Piao and said that the eleventh plenum "confirmed Comrade Lin Piao

---

* "Naming" is very serious in China; the person being criticized is named only when things have reached a point of no return. The Chinese are very cautious about accusing incorrectly; also, withholding the name may give the person a chance to see (and reform) his own errors. This taboo on naming makes tracing who is being criticized very difficult at times. Thus Liu Shao-chi, although caricatured for two years (1967–1968) and called "China's Khrushchev," was not named until the twelfth plenum of October 1968. Lin Piao, whose ideas had been criticized since 1969, was not named until after his death in 1971.

† See *The Morning Deluge*, pages 164–167, 180–183.

as the closest comrade in arms, best pupil of Chairman Mao, and the deputy supreme commander of the party." *"It is the greatest happiness of the people, the Party and the nation that the meeting confirmed Vice-Chairman Lin Piao as Chairman Mao's successor."*

There is something that smacks of a thriller, and also of the hieratic gestures of Chinese opera, in this story of plot, counterplot and intrigue which Lin Piao wove during the cultural revolution. It takes one back to the devious machinations of the warlord period, before Liberation. "He had that kind of brain . . . like an old-time warlord."*

As in a shadow play, real, and yet unreal, the moves to "drag out Liu Shao-chi" continued. Seven hundred Red Guard organizations, together numbering half a million, were to take turns for three weeks at a sit-in in front of the residence of the Central Committee, chanting, blaring loudspeakers, beating drums, making it impossible for the Central Committee to sleep. This picketing to "drag out Liu Shao-chi" was contrived and maintained by the ultra-left. Chi Pen-yu and Wang Li went among the young telling them it was the "central task" of the time to drag out Liu Shao-chi. Chi also told them that they had the support of the Central Committee and the GCCR in this action.

Mao had no intention of turning Liu Shao-chi over to the Red Guards. On August 5, anniversary of Mao's famous poster *Bombard the Headquarters*, the young were convinced that Liu would be handed over to them that day, and a stampede began at the gate as all pressed forward to be the first to "drag him out." Dozens were hurt as the various factions fought each other to get nearest the gate. The gate opened and out came Hsieh Fu-chih, chairman of the Peking Municipality Revolutionary Committee, admonitory and calm. He urged everyone, in Chairman Mao's name, to go home. Liu would not be handed over. And so the thousands trailed away.

But what most of the youngsters there did not know was that a group of the 516 were mobilized nearest the gate ready to seize Chou En-lai, for they were sure that it would be Chou who would venture out — he had confronted the young so many times. With Chou kidnapped (and possibly murdered), in the ensuing confusion Lin Piao and Chen Po-ta would speak of a "coup," and take over.

And in that same mid-August bands of the 516 seized the Ministry of Foreign Affairs; Yao Teng-shan became virtually foreign minister for

* Author's interviews with many Chinese, officials and non-officials, after the cultural revolution.

about two weeks. Chou En-lai was incarcerated for forty-eight hours in his offices in the Great Hall of the People, surrounded by clamoring hordes of the young intent on seizing the Central Committee files. By dint of braving it out, and talking to them in small groups, he talked them out, saving both the files and himself. But he could not intervene in the Ministry of Foreign Affairs, where Yao now issued orders withdrawing ambassadors and sending insane directives which led to incidents doing great harm to China's prestige abroad. Yao Teng-shan spoke of "not abandoning the Chinese minorities" in Southeast Asia, ordered the friendship associations in Cambodia, Nepal, and Burma to pull down the portrait of the nation's king or president which, in honor of peaceful coexistence, coexisted on the wall with Chairman Mao's picture. The British embassy was then burned down by a mob of the 516, despite the efforts of the State Council and of some members of the GCCR, including Chiang Ching, to stop the frenzy.

Because Mao was not there, and Chou En-lai was under attack, it fell to Chiang Ching to denounce the ultra-left, and she was the first to do so on August 6. "The May 16 organization . . . will not be tolerated . . . You must not be fooled by it. There are some people fishing in troubled waters."

The moment of victory is when defeat begins. August slid into September, Mao Tsetung returned from his tour of Middle China. He had investigated and conferred with regional commanders, and had visited seven provinces.

"*The situation in the Great Proletarian Cultural Revolution is not just good, but excellent . . . better than at any time in the past . . . never before has a mass movement been aroused so extensively and penetratingly.*" Thus spoke Mao, full of confidence, and his words dispelled the miasma of terror and evil. "Wang Li has committed more errors in forty days than Chen Yi in forty years." Exit Wang Li from the GCCR. Briskly, Mao set to cleaning up. On September 1 the Central Committee held a full meeting. The 516 was condemned, and Chen Po-ta (still unmasked) joined Chiang Ching in condemning it. Wang Li and four others in the GCCR were arrested. So was Sydney Rittenberg, together with some naïve foreigners he had decoyed into his organization. All were released except Sydney Rittenberg.

Such is the confidence Mao exudes that now all seemed changed. Yet there were figures of ninety thousand casualties in Szechuan, and a good many too in Yunnan. Kuangchow was ugly with summary executions by rival factions. Huang Yung-sheng, the military commander there, harshly suppressed Red Guards, who called him "the butcher of Kuangchow."

"The main thing at present is organizing triple combinations and great alliances, digging out bad people, ghosts, and monsters, and the revival of Party organizations."

The art of governing is to grasp the situation in its essence. Mao, by declaring it excellent, was restoring a sense of proportion. For however sensational the events, and high the violence, they were still, for a large country like China, pretty sporadic and limited. Though the actual numbers appear large, and the conflicts widespread and serious, throughout only a minority was involved, and the mainstream of the cultural revolution went on.

And now Mao Tsetung, having allowed all that seethed underground to come forth, was ready to summarize experience, pick up the constructive ideas which had expressed themselves among the people, and provide dynamic and vigorous leadership.

On September 5 Chiang Ching made a most important speech, representing Mao's views to a large meeting. The ultra-left had been ensconced within the GCCR itself, and Chiang Ching was deputy head of the GCCR (in no sense responsible for their depredations, for she was the first to fight against them). The responsibility was hers to denounce the 516 and its leaders. "The real manipulators behind the scene are very bad people." The slogan "Drag out the handful in the army" was a bad slogan; it had led to attacks on regional commanders. Chiang Ching defended the regional commanders. Most of them came from peasant or working class background, and were veterans of the War of Liberation; they had not always seen the issues clearly, but mistakes were unavoidable. She announced that anyone stealing weapons or assaulting the PLA would now incur the death penalty, for PLA weaponry and personnel were not to be touched.

Chiang Ching now began to suspect both Lin Piao and Chen Po-ta. Observers abroad reported a "rift" between her and Lin Piao, as if it were a capricious, subjective matter. The GCCR found its authority curtailed. Its prominent role was no longer necessary, and by 1969 it would begin to fade away.

Great restraint was shown by Chou En-lai, who told the meeting that the 516 had tried to sow dissension, "turning the spearhead first against me . . . to estrange me from the GCCR." But he recommended that the problem not be enlarged. The "few wicked leaders" would be detained, the "eight regional armies" of the 516 would be re-educated. This was done swiftly. The roundup of extremists was eagerly helped by the population itself; in some cities it took only three days to "tidy up." The young were sent off to state farms and reformed through labor, but each case was dealt with meticulously and in detail, those who had not committed any crimes not being punished. The re-education process was to be done with thoroughness; but throughout, the young were not held responsible. They had been "led astray, deluded." The responsibility was upon those who corrupted them.

Chou En-lai's refusal to enlarge the problem was sound tactics. For any large-scale move against the 516 at the time would have led to a return of the obstinate right wing. Chou En-lai added to his speech the firm warning that exposing the ultra-left did not mean reversing the cultural revolution, nor that the verdicts which had been pronounced on "capitalist-roaders" in the Party were now to be considered as denied.

But after the Ninth Congress of the Party in April 1969, when Lin Piao was officially designated as Mao's successor and his succession was even written into the Party's statutes, Mao Tsetung would order a full investigation into the May 16 group and its backers.

At the apex of success, Lin Piao would know the unsparing finger of investigation beginning to point at him. And in the end, he would not escape.

5

Construction After Destruction, 1968–1971

We are taught by mistakes and setbacks.
— MAO TSETUNG, many times
through the last forty years

Mao's program for the "construction after destruction" phase of the cultural revolution was an end to internecine strife, alliance between factions, the creation of revolutionary committees at all levels, and the reconstruction of a purified, regenerated Party.

The revolutionary committee was to express democratic centralism, to give as much voice as possible to the *masses* in a combination of Party cadres, PLA representatives and the masses, renewing the tripod Party-army-masses basic to the success of the Chinese revolution before 1940.*

The revolutionary committee was to exercise *unified* leadership, do away with the duplication of administrative structures which had existed since 1950. Within each, the core would be the Party branch. This would eliminate the inflationary bureaucracy which Lenin had foreseen among Soviet government employees. This new form of power organ should give rise to a renovated Party, a true vanguard of the proletariat, constantly subject to mass supervision in a unified structure.

Splitting and sectarianism were declared "the evil fruits of the bourgeois reactionary line of China's Khrushchev," whether they were right or left in appearance. The campaign to denounce "China's Khrushchev" started briskly again. The cities cleaned themselves of hooligans and murderous 516ers. Mass organizations of workers rounded up "wicked

---

* See *The Morning Deluge*, page 199.

people," collected the weapons and returned them to the PLA. The PLA hunted down the gangs. This caused an exodus of 516 members from North to South China, and also to Szechuan.

The Congress of Red Guards was ordered to get all students back to their units or schools within one month; school registration for those not returned would be canceled, and no jobs would be arranged for them. Chou En-lai also warned against phone tapping, stealing documents, and operating "intelligence organizations." Wang Li had apparently got Kuai Ta-fu to help him collect information among regional military units.

One problem was the cadres and their treatment. A good many cadres now felt reluctant to administer or to lead, because of the criticism, the suspension — and occasionally the physical duress — they had endured. Yet revolutionary committees could not do without cadres. The value of older and experienced cadres was reiterated. All ill-treatment of cadres must stop and the rehabilitation of cadres must proceed swiftly. Mao thought that with Party rebuilding, the infusion of "fresh blood," and "getting rid of the waste," it would be possible to hold a Party Congress in 1968.

Another problem was the severe conflicts — often armed, often with participation of ultra-left students — among the workers themselves. "Within the working class there is no basic clash of interests. Under the proletarian dictatorship, the working class has absolutely no reason to split into two hostile factional organizations," Mao said on September 14, 1967. Once again the PLA was called upon to restore unity. After briefings by Mao personally to thirty thousand top activists, PLA personnel formed Mao Tsetung Thought propaganda teams and once again descended upon each factory, each commune, to stop the strife, to help form the alliances which in turn would give birth to the revolutionary committees.

The workers united swiftly, far more swiftly than the university students. They formed "grand alliances" (Canton celebrated its alliance by year's end) and industry picked up remarkably. Agricultural communes were also tidied up; high-grade military commanders, including generals, went down to labor in communes and to hold study sessions with the peasantry.

But while doing this major work (and doing it well by most accounts), the PLA, like the Red Guards before it, was already being relegated to a secondary role. It was to monitor the new constructs, but voluntarily to efface itself after these were in place. On this point Mao was adamant. Despite the militarization which took place and the overwhelming PLA presence from 1968 to 1971, by 1973 the army was brought back under Party control. Civilian order was re-established. This demilitarization vindicated ideological leadership. "The Party commands the gun and never the gun the Party."

Party rebuilding would necessitate the admission of many young activists who had proved worthy. The Party was getting *old*, not only the leadership, but at all levels. The cultural revolution had been an enormous test of character. Admission of at least twelve million young cadres must have occurred to bring the Party from seventeen million in 1962 to twenty-eight millon by 1973. Admission was now to be heavily weighted in favor of workers.

The tripartite formula for the revolutionary committees was also to ensure young, middle-aged, and old members in equal proportion, so that the young would have access to command posts early, not have to wait endlessly for their elders to die off. Also there was the injunction (1969) that at least 30 percent of cadres in every revolutionary committee must be women, a figure achieved now.

In the economy, the slogan "Revolution stimulates production" was reinforced. To oppose one to the other, to waste or destroy state property, was counterrevolutionary. Red worker provosts were elected in each workshop to stimulate production. It was forbidden to put up posters tending to split, factionalize, disrupt or hinder unification. "There should now be an upturn," Mao said optimistically. Production had suffered through the factional strife since December 1966. "Such a world-shaking revolutionary movement of course exacts a certain price . . . we took account of this in advance," said Chou En-lai.

Mao would launch in 1968 the slogan "Fight self, repudiate revisionism," equating selfishness with opportunism, anarchism, sectarianism, petty bourgeois radicalism — manifestations of bourgeois mentality which would help revisionism. The heart-searching ethic of unselfish service was the proletarian world outlook.

Attacks against Chou En-lai subsided as Mao, without ambiguity, gave him his full support. Chou En-lai cleared the Ministry of Foreign Affairs of Yao Teng-shan; the latter was to be tried and sentenced to a jail term three years later. Chen Yi, severely ill with cancer, would be rehabilitated; he died in 1973.

The "ultra-left" was now condemned for trying to "subvert the proletarian dictatorship and restore capitalism." Revolutionary mass organizations must correctly understand what extensive democracy means. A few judicious executions of counterrevolutionaries (only four in Peking) gave point to the warnings of the death penalty for stealing weapons. All middle schools reopened, and a common sight was long files of children, framed by PLA men, marching and singing to perform useful tasks, sweep streets, clean railway stations, attend political study classes, help the communes with harvests. For about two years a militarized framework prevailed in schools; instead of classes, the children were divided into teams, squads, battalions. A problem was to persuade teachers to teach. Many of them refused to have anything to do with teaching, saying, "It is dangerous to teach," and remembering how ill-treated they had been, notably in the schools in Kuangchow, where extremism continued till 1969.

In that autumn the first drafts of a new Party constitution to prepare for the Ninth Party Congress and the election of the Ninth Central Committee were circulated for study. This introduced a climate of constructive debate throughout the country.*

The universities remained battlegrounds of various anarchists. Some of the youth factions protested that the aims of the cultural revolution were betrayed, that all was as before, and that youth was being suppressed. The ultra-left remained active, demanding, in March 1968, a purge of *all* existing Party membership. This position was "left in form but right in essence," denying Party leadership and also Mao's pronouncement that "only a handful" of cadres were capitalist-roaders, 95 percent were good or relatively good.

The Ninth Party Congress could not be called in 1968, for two reasons. Before it could be called, the case of Liu Shao-chi must be wound up, and the Party rebuilt. But Party building was going on very slowly, the rehabilitation of cadres taking very much longer than expected. Revolutionary committees also proved unstable and had to be overhauled.

Mao Tsetung would redefine the cultural revolution as a "continua-

* Drafts of the Party constitution and national constitution are circulated to groups at all levels and discussed by them — the revolutionary committees representing the masses, cadres, the PLA. Only after this process, which requires months, is the constitution in final form for submission to Congress (Party Congress for the Party; National People's Congress for the national constitution). The Party Congress was to elect a Ninth Central Committee in April 1969.

tion of the prolonged struggle between the CCP and the masses of revolutionary people under its leadership on the one hand and the Kuomintang reactionaries on the other, a continuation of the class struggle between the proletariat and the bourgeoisie." The identification of opponents of the cultural revolution as objectively "Kuomintang" included the notion of the battle against Kuomintang-style tutelage and military authoritarianism. Mao had already told the military commanders he briefed that winter that "to protect the masses or to suppress them . . . that is the fundamental difference between the Communist Party and the Kuomintang." This shift of emphasis, warning against authoritarianism of a military kind, can be regarded as Mao's first warning to Lin Piao that the PLA must not surrogate for the Party, and that it was Lin Piao who was opposing reconstruction of the Party.

"The current Great Proletarian Cultural Revolution is absolutely necessary and most timely for consolidating the dictatorship of the proletariat, preventing capitalist restoration and building socialism."*

Why was this assertion repeated? The validity, the course, and the shape which the cultural revolution had taken were being questioned. Two sectors both voiced such reservations. One consisted of ill-treated cadres. (It was found in 1974 that many cadres reported as suicides had actually been murdered by the 516.) It takes some saintly virtue to "fight self" to the extent of accepting ill-treatment for a cause. Many did, and have come out ennobled and strengthened in their devotion. "We always thought the enemy was the other, or outside. Now we understood the enemy was not a stranger, an outsider, it was ourselves, our fellow comrades, our work colleagues, often people we had known for years, but above all ourselves." Many of the cadres so ill-treated are working side by side with those who ill-treated them, and have no resentment. "We know each other better now."

The other and larger sector was made up of supporters of Lin Piao. Lin Piao by then realized fully that Mao was going to restrict the army and reconstruct the Party. If the Party were rebuilt, with 90 to 95 percent of the cadres "washed clean," Lin's chances of actual power were weakened.†

---

* Communiqué of the twelfth plenum of the Eighth Central Committee, October 1968.

† Not more than 3 percent of Party cadres seem to have been expelled at higher levels, and fewer than 1 percent at factory or commune level.

It is very clear that Lin Piao and his clique would hinder Party rebuilding in all ways — not only by deliberately keeping a good many cadres suspended or "in cattle pens" (that is, in very poor physical conditions) and inciting continued attacks against them for another eighteen months, but also by prolonging under pretext of unsettled conditions what amounted to a military tutelage which was taking the same form as that practiced by the Kuomintang under Chiang Kai-shek. Hence Mao's warning was double-edged.

By September 1968, however, just before the twelfth plenum was due, revolutionary committees had been set up for the twenty-nine provinces, municipalities and autonomous regions throughout China, but this did not mean the Party branches were rebuilt. PLA dominance in these committees was very marked, and the "masses" represented, as Mao Tsetung himself warned, were often not given any right except to assent to what the military had decided. Chen Po-ta, however, would cover this up with a "left"-appearing slogan, trying to bring up at the twelfth plenum a resolution for "All power to the revolutionary committees." This in reality was trying to do away with the Party representation as leadership core and to maintain army rule.

It also became evident that some of the PLA units would not willingly step down from their principal role. In certain regions commanders rode roughshod over revolutionary committees. On Army Day (August 1) a joint editorial in *People's Daily* and other newspapers emphasized that the army must trust, respect, support, help and defend the revolutionary committees.

Indicative of this two-line struggle, from April to October 1968 articles condemning the theory of "more than one center" or "many centers" appeared. "Every group wants to become the nucleus power," said Mao. But the condemnation was aimed at Lin Piao, who in a speech said that "whether there will be a restoration or not of the bourgeois reactionary line in a restored Party structure depends on the army. . . . The army is the most important of all sectors, the center of centers and the key of keys. As long as the army does not change its color, there are ways to cope with the Party, the government and the people. Political power grows out of the barrel of a gun." But this heresy of Lin Piao's was not publicized at the time. Instead, obliquely, the "theory of many centers" (author unknown) was criticized.

In October 1968 the enlarged twelfth plenum of the Eighth Central

Committee was held in Peking. It wound up the case of Liu Shao-chi.

A report (October 18, 1968) by a special panel on "renegade, traitor and scab" Liu Shao-chi listed Liu's repeated surrenders to the Kuomintang, accused him of having betrayed his own Party organization in order to save himself, and expelled him "forever" from the Party. The list of these crimes stops, however, at 1929. This appears odd, since the mass criticism of Liu's policies deals with his "capitalist-roading" after 1949.

Leniency, reintegration for Party cadres who repented, confessed, and made their self-criticism was Mao's way. Wang Ming had committed glaring errors, yet Mao had insisted that Wang Ming remain a member of the Central Committee. In 1966 Mao was still insisting that Liu be allowed to participate in the cultural revolution.

But if Liu had been, as the report alleges, an agent of the Kuomintang masquerading as a Communist, had abjured and betrayed, then expulsion was compulsory. Mao had mentioned that there could not be renegades within the Party; purification of the Party ranks to get rid of renegades, enemy agents, was on the agenda for Party rebuilding.

"The Great Proletarian Cultural Revolution long ago swept China's Khrushchev . . . onto the garbage heap of history. He was long ago deprived by the revolution of all power and positions both within the Party and outside it," wrote *Peking Review*.* The twelfth plenum ratified the end of this long struggle.

Punctilious legalists point out that to deprive Liu of his posts was unconstitutional; the decision must be taken by the National Party Congress. However, the Party constitution also provides that a two-thirds vote of the standing committee of the Central Committee can perform such a function, provided it is later ratified by a National Party Congress.

After so much turmoil and passion, there could be no other conclusion. Liu Shao-chi lived, it is said, in a commune in Manchuria, and his wife is staying in a private house somewhere in Central China. He died of cancer in 1974.

The year 1967 had had its February Adverse Current episode. The year 1968 saw the Evil March Wind, another curious quirk of the cultural revolution.

At the time, the two events were linked, the second one being de-

* No. 43, 1968.

scribed as yet another attempt by the disguised right wing to reverse verdicts against the capitalist-roaders. But since Lin Piao's treachery and the exposure of his Machiavellian plans, and the return and rehabilitation of the cadres and military who were denounced and suspended during both these episodes, another assessment is necessary.

It was averred at the time that the downfall of the terrorist 516 in the autumn of 1967 had given rise to a renewed right-wing surge, on the principle that "one tendency covers and overlaps another." The *Anhwei Daily* of April 24, 1968, was to write that the episode had been "a vain attempt by the capitalist-roaders to recover their lost paradise."

A more cogent explanation is possibly the following. The dissatisfaction within Party and army ranks and the doubts about Lin Piao since the summer of 1967 (and also about Chen Po-ta), although unvoiced, were not appeased. There was certainly resentment on the part of other field army commanders at Lin Piao's rapid increase of power and the methods he used. There might possibly have been also some latent moves to try to rehabilitate some discredited military figures. Certainly there were protests on the part of Foreign Affairs officials. Lin Piao and Chen Po-ta seem to have taken preemptive action, which erupted in that March 1968, and whose victim was Yang Cheng-wu, the acting chief of staff who had replaced Lo Jui-ching.

Yang Cheng-wu was a Long Marcher, a good commander, popular, but had not served under Lin Piao. Suddenly on March 26 large demonstrations took place in Peking against Yang Cheng-wu, with posters and screaming youths accusing him of being a "splitter." There were also attacks against Fu Chung-pi, head of the Peking military garrison, and Yu Li-chin, political commissar of the air force. Other posters proclaimed that Huang Yung-sheng, the commander in charge of the southern region (and whom the southern Red Guards had nicknamed "the butcher of Kuangchow") had now replaced Yang Cheng-wu as acting chief of staff.

Today Yang Cheng-wu, Fu Chung-pi and Yu Li-chin are rehabilitated, whereas Huang Yung-sheng is either dead or in jail, for he was a co-plotter with "the worst renegade of all," Lin Piao.

Certain observers wrote at the time (and they got their information probably through Chen Po-ta, who controlled the press) that all three of the victims were associated with the 516; that Fu Chung-pi and Yang Cheng-wu had organized a coup to kidnap some members of the GCCR and sent a truckload of soldiers to do so; and that the whole plot was revealed by the woman lecturer Nieh Yuan-tze, whose prestige was still high in 1968, and who had been interviewed by Anna Louise Strong. Nieh Yuan-tze, whose famous poster was still quoted in 1969, had been vice-chairman of the Peking Municipality Revolutionary Committee since April 1967, and had married an officer close to Lin Piao. It appears that one night in March it was Nieh who came to reveal "the plot" to some members of the GCCR in Peking. But Nieh Yuan-tze herself, who does not appear to have been a conspirator but to have been made use of, was at the time deeply engaged in continued factionalism. She was agitating, together with the youths who considered her a great heroine, in order to bring down Hsieh Fu-chih, who was chairman of the Peking Revolutionary Committee, as a right-winger.

At the time, the remnant bands of students and erstwhile student leaders like Kuai Ta-fu had begun to degenerate into something approaching gangs, which they called "troops." They refused to return to school and kept on attacking this or that personality, and they were now joined by a lumpen proletariat of hooligans, gangsters and murderers who had escaped the cleanups by refugeeing themselves with university youths.* These campuses were now held by the student "troops" as fortified places, and from these the students issued to parade and to mount demonstrations.

It does seem that on March 8 some PLA soldiers in trucks did surround some of the buildings in which the GCCR was housed; but they seized no one, and Yang Cheng-wu and Fu Chung-pi denied having sent them.

Four secret high-level sessions were held to discuss the events. Yang Cheng-wu, Fu Chung-pi and Yu Li-chin were suspended and arrested. It was Lin Piao who came out to explain what had happened, and he accused Yang Cheng-wu. He said that Yang was conspiring with the others to overthrow Wu Fa-hsien, the air force commander (later to fall with Lin Piao as a co-plotter), in order to usurp the leadership of the air force; that Yang was trying to eliminate the regional commanders, notably Huang Yung-sheng (also to fall with Lin Piao) and to place his own friends in positions of power; that Yang, Yu and Fu were the people behind the 516 who had caused so much wreckage. He said that Yang had tried to tap Mao Tsetung's phone; that he pretended to be friendly with Chiang Ching but in reality plotted against her; and to cap it all also told a farcical story of Yang having sent a

---

* Some Red Guards had opened the jails and let out criminals and former Kuomintang secret agents, gangsters from the Chiang Kai-shek regime, etc.

woman relative to suborn an air force commander. He then added that Yang Cheng-wu had distorted Marxism-Leninism by his speech on Army Day in 1967, when he had said: "Thoroughly establish the absolute authority of Mao Tsetung Thought"; that Yang also wanted to establish "many centers" of power . . .

And yet it is clear today that everything that Lin Piao accused Yang of, he performed himself, and it was Lin Piao who spoke of the "absolute authority" of Mao Thought, who spoke of "smashing" anyone who did not recognize it. It was Lin Piao who was plotting in the GCCR, through Chen Po-ta and others, against Chiang Ching. In fact Chiang Ching showed her disbelief of Lin Piao at that session.

We shall probably never know the exact story. Because of this March squall there were shifts and removals of regional commanders and political commissars in nine out of thirteen military regions, which reinforced Lin Piao's power. Lin also brought Huang Yung-sheng from Kuangchow to the Center to strengthen his position, and brought more of his own supporters into the Military Affairs Committee, creating within it his own administrative unit. The chief liaison officer of the unit would be his own wife, Yeh Chun, called the "viscount" or the "chief of staff" by his appointees. The dispatch of "Center supports the left" liaison units by Lin Piao to all military regions and provincial military districts consolidated his own outposts in every province.

In revolutionary China there is no record of troops rising to defend a military commander, however devoted their officers may be to him, once he is denounced by the Party. The dismissals undertaken by Lin Piao of Ho Lung's erstwhile field armies' officers in 1967, and Yang Cheng-wu's in 1968, were extensive and enabled him to place many more of his own people in position. A Lin Piao cult developed in which an increasing spate of articles extolled him; they emanated from various sources, including the navy and air force. "Vice-chairman Lin Piao is the most outstanding, long-tested statesman, thinker, soldier and theoretician nurtured by Chairman Mao for our Party . . . his closest comrade in arms, best student, his most ideal successor." "He is the most brilliant model . . . in defending Mao Tsetung Thought . . . as the most supreme authority."[*]

Some of these litanies of praise ("he is the best, the best, the best . . . the highest, the highest, the highest") may have been penned by Lin Piao himself, for some were in his style of repeating an asseveration

[*] *Peking Review*, no. 10, 1968.

three times ("the losses in the cultural revolution are the smallest, the smallest, the smallest; the gains the largest, the largest, the largest").

All this points to Lin Piao's need to bolster himself. So does the renewed attack on Lo Jui-ching, who was "struggled against" by thousands of PLA activists. Perhaps Lo's denunciation of Lin Piao, when Lo was dragged by the Red Guards, with his leg in a plaster cast, to a public trial in January 1967, still rang in Lin Piao's ears: "Lin Piao is a traitor, a big traitor!"*

The most important event of 1968, the one which would mark the cultural revolution as a proletarian revolution, give it its vitality and originality and China its continuing strength, was the rise of the working class into power in the superstructure, and to begin with, in education.

"The working class must exercise leadership in everything," said Mao, "including all spheres of culture." "Power to the worker" began with the take-over of the universities by the factory workers in their hundreds of thousands in July and August 1968.

The various factions of embattled Red Guards in the two Peking universities† numbered only a few hundred now. They had among them gangsters and criminals escaped from jails. They fortified themselves with trenches and barbed wire, and raided other factions in other buildings.

On July 3 and again on July 24 orders were issued to cease all fighting in Kwangsi and in Shansi provinces; a clause specified that these orders were applicable *everywhere*.‡

On the morning of July 27, six thousand workers from the Hsinhua Printing Plant and five other plants in Peking, unarmed, and accompanied by a PLA propaganda team, appeared before the gates of Tsinghua University. In T-shirts, carrying posters declaiming STRUGGLE BY REASON, NOT FORCE; OBEY THE JULY 3 AND 24 DIRECTIVES OF THE CENTRAL COMMITTEE, they proceeded to cross the barbed wire and the

---

* Lo Jui-ching is said to have attempted suicide in 1966 but only broke a leg; hence the plaster cast. He has now been rehabilitated, and was last seen by the author on September 30, 1975, at the PRC twenty-sixth anniversary banquet, on the eve of October 1.

† Peking University and Tsinghua University.

‡ There was turmoil of the same kind in many cities among various youth factions. In Nanning (Kwangsi) factions of Red Guards organized into armies and machine-gunned each other. These sporadic little wars lasted until the end of 1968. See William Hinton *The Hundred-Day War* (New York 1973).

trenches. They began parleying with the students: "Lay down your weapons. Stop fighting."

Kuai Ta-fu ordered his faction to refuse. "Go back to your workshops. Grasp production and make revolution!" shouted the students to the workers. The workers surged forward, scaling the fortifications surrounding the buildings and singing: "Use reason, not force . . . turn in your weapons, form a big alliance."

The students and the hoodlums with them now attacked with hand grenades (homemade) and threw rocks with catapults. Detachments of spearmen charged the unarmed workers. Five of them died, and dozens, including women workers, were injured. Students assaulted and took workers prisoner and beat them up. One gangster tried to gouge out a worker's eyes, but was prevented by the students, while the worker went on saying: "Use reason, not violence." Another worker was badly beaten and later died of his injuries. Kuai Ta-fu issued a "message" that there was a "black hand" trying to oppress and put down the righteous uprisings of the masses (himself and his gang).

Through the day the battle raged; more and more workers from factories came to Tsinghua, until there were about thirty thousand of them, and they literally swamped the buildings. By midnight many youths had given up; some of them were horrified by the conduct of the gangsters among them. At no time did the workers use weapons or force on the students.

At about four in the morning on July 28, Mao Tsetung called some five of the student leaders, including Kuai Ta-fu and Nieh Yuan-tze, to come and see him. He received them; with him were Lin Piao, Chiang Ching, Chou En-lai, Kang Sheng, Yao Wen-yuan, and others. Mao Tsetung spoke with them earnestly for about two hours. He had warned them, he said, on previous occasions about anarchy and factionalism. But they had not heeded his words. The students must dissolve their fighting battalions, or there would be military occupation of the campuses. "I sent the workers' propaganda team," said Mao. "I am the Black Hand."

Although it seems that Kuai Ta-fu (who came late to the meeting) went back professing that Mao had "encouraged" him, workers' propaganda teams in their thousands now invested peacefully every campus and school in China and put a stop to the childish but dangerous madness.

The campuses (many gutted, ruined, some of them foul with unburied corpses) were tidied up. Workers interviewed have always been reticent about their wounded and their dead; they always repeat that "it was not the students' fault . . . they were misled by bad people."*

On August 15 *People's Daily* published Mao's latest directive: "Our nation has seven hundred million people, and the working class is its leading class. It is essential to bring into full play the leading role of the working class in the great cultural revolution *and in all fields of work.*" The working class was to educate itself, raising its own political consciousness, in the practice of power wielding and struggle for building New China, and lead in the reform of education.†

Factional battles had made "struggle, criticism, transformation" impossible; now the process was speeded under the supervision of workers' teams and their leadership. "The workers' propaganda teams should stay *permanently* in the schools and . . . they will always lead the schools. In the countryside the schools should be managed by the poor and lower middle peasants . . . the most reliable ally of the working class."

This is the single most significant achievement of the cultural revolution, the one with the greatest impact upon the future: education, tool of elitism, would be in the hands of the working class. To show his appreciation of the way the workers of the Hsinhua Printing Plant had handled Tsinghua University, Mao Tsetung sent them mangoes, as he did to other exemplary factories.

"It is still necessary to have universities; here I refer mainly to colleges of science and engineering," Mao asserted. But these should follow the example of the Shanghai Machine Tools Plant, which had established within the plant its own technical college, promoting and training technicians from its own workers. Students of universities must be selected from among workers and peasants with practical experience, who would later go back to production.

On August 18, anniversary of Mao's first attendance at a grand rally of Red Guards, the newspapers stated the line for revolutionary youth. Youth was the vanguard, but it was the workers and peasants who were the basic strength of the cultural revolution. There was only one criterion to judge whether a youth was revolutionary or not: whether or not he was willing to integrate, and did in practice integrate, with workers and peasants. "We would like to advise those college students

* Author's interviews with many workers who took part.
† Yao Wen-yuan *The Working Class Must Exercise Leadership in Everything* (English edition Peking 1968).

who look down upon the workers and peasants and think themselves great to throw off their affected airs."

Thus the revolution in education was accomplished. Mao had brought the proletariat into the university world. It would take another four years of constant discussion, experimentation, debate to make the new system work. Since 1968, almost every day throughout the land there have been debates and articles on education and how it should be run.

A new system which precludes elitism and alienation is being evolved. Debate starts at the very bottom, with workers and peasants themselves writing their ideas on education. Workers and peasants lecture college youths; the latter, by the million, would be sent "up hill and down dale" to be "re-educated" through manual labor. The "factionalists" were sent to army-run farms. Millions of good Red Guards from middle schools were also persuaded to volunteer for labor, and in that winter two million volunteered to be re-educated through manual labor. They went to state farms, production units opening new land, communes ready to receive them. The best after one to three years are admitted to technical colleges or universities or medical schools for further study; they are chosen by mass selection and sponsored by their production unit or commune.

Cadres were also to undergo re-education through manual labor. They went to "May 7 schools," the first one being set up in Liuho, Heilungkiang province, in 1968. Cadres built their houses, tilled the fields, and studied Marxist-Leninist works. All cadres except the old, the weak, the disabled must go. This schooling was not punishment, but integration with their own people, and had a profound psychological effect. It was, said Mao, something permanent, "an excellent opportunity to study again."

Through the new education system workers and peasants would develop their own intelligentsia, theoreticians, innovators, research scientists, technological experts, cadres, Party leaders. And these will remain integrated, as it is compulsory for all cadres to labor: two hundred days a year for low and mid-level cadres, one hundred days a year for the higher level. The first contingent of the "proletarian intellectuals" whom Mao, in 1956, had looked forward to were graduated in the spring of 1974. There were two hundred thousand of them for all China. The first teams of historians, Marxist theoreticians, artists, writers are coming up from the proletariat.

In the countryside, the poor and lower middle peasants would be in charge of the urban-educated sent down for manual labor. This would break the "three big differences," create a way to accelerate development, increase the intellectual capital of the country, emancipate thinking, and keep China revolutionary.

In the winter the drive to get roving students back to school intensified. "Isn't it time you went back to your post of duty?" the newspapers asked pointedly of some thousand Shanghai students who had been sent to Taching oilfield in 1965 and had returned to Shanghai to "make revolution." There was the problem of integrating overage youngsters into the education circuit; the universities would not really start functioning until 1970–1971, and by 1974 would still be taking only about half the number of students they could have taken. And every year jobs have to be found for a new crop of eight to ten million young.

"Workers should only run factories . . . what do they know of education? They don't know the situation in the schools . . . how can they tell us what to do?" Thus the older, hostile intelligentsia. But resistance broke down. Reluctant teachers and professors found the workers full of understanding, generosity and balance. Mao issued injunctions that even diehard bourgeois authorities in universities and schools "be given a way out . . . to do otherwise is not the policy of the proletariat." This prevented the development of yet another "struggle."

On September 7, 1968, at a rally celebrating the formation of provincial revolutionary committees all over China, Chou En-lai spoke of the role of the working class and of the necessity for the young to integrate with workers and peasants. Chiang Ching made an impromptu speech to say: "You young revolutionaries and Red Guards have done a very good job in the cultural revolution. . . . You have made mistakes but you can learn from them. . . . The working class . . . *must not be led to repress you. . . . It must protect the young Red Guard fighters, help them and educate them. I am saying this on Chairman Mao's authority.*"

"The overwhelming majority of the intellectuals both new and old could integrate, and when they do they *will be* welcomed by the workers, peasants, and soldiers," wrote Mao.

"Intellectuals make mountains out of molehills . . . it takes a lot of patience to solve their problems"; "You've got to handle each case individually," said the workers. It was in this general climate that the workers' teams took on the responsibility of solving "big and difficult problems" in the universities.

In that same year the cooperative medical system would come in force in the communes. Public health and medical care took root in the villages. The educated who went down became barefoot doctors or teachers in the new rural schools.

By 1974 there would be 170 million children from seven to fifteen in primary and lower middle schools, but no one could go to a university who had not "integrated" with labor in communes or factories. The majority in universities, 95 percent, were workers, peasants, soldiers, or the offspring of workers, peasants or soldiers. One hundred and sixty thousand of these were admitted in 1974.

If there was anything he wanted to be called, Mao said to Edgar Snow in 1970,* it was a "teacher." Endlessly he repeated exhortations, advice. Examples of people, places, which had put in practice the study of Mao and scored successes appeared in the press. Endlessly there were meetings, debates all over the land; people attended Mao Tsetung Thought study classes, wrote posters, criticized. "The proletariat cannot emancipate itself if it does not emancipate all mankind." As dissension faded, Mao called: "Help more people, narrow the target of attack." Cadre rehabilitation became the top priority. Preparations for the Party Congress became vigorous. There was to be a changed Party constitution; the 1956 Party constitution had admitted anyone without class distinction, had done away with the study of Mao Tsetung Thought. It was impossible to "purify Party ranks" under it.

On December 5, 1968, *People's Daily* carried an article describing Lin Piao's boundless loyalty to Mao. It particularly stressed his obedience to Mao in the conduct of the campaign in Manchuria (1946–1948), whereas Liu Shao-chi had tried to sabotage this campaign.

This propaganda for Lin Piao, intensive and designed in relation to the Party Congress to take place in early 1969, when Lin Piao's succession to Mao would be ratified, was later to be proved a lie. In 1974 Lin Piao's "bourgeois military line" during the Manchurian campaign, and particularly his disobedience to Mao's orders in the campaign for Peking and Tientsin (1949), when he is said to have deliberately allowed the Kuomintang to escape, were the subject of many denunciatory articles. The facts are that a close reading of Mao does show that he was not always obeyed in his suggestions to commanders, and that Lin Piao did not follow the Mao directives. So Mao Tsetung must have

* See Edgar Snow "A Conversation with Mao Tsetung," *Life* magazine, April 30, 1971, page 46.

known that all the propaganda for Lin Piao was a lie. Yet he kept silent, waiting for an opportunity. And the opportunity would come.

For about a year preceding the Ninth Party Congress of April 1969, the draft of the new Party constitution had been circulated and debated at all levels. But how much of this debate was not PLA-guided? The main weakness was residual ultra-leftism, persistent and insidious. For instance, the student leader Kuai Ta-fu, openly now an anarchist — and Mao had disowned anarchism — obtained a certain number of supporting votes to become a delegate at the Congress. This was not fortuitous. Lin Piao's tactics seem to have been to manipulate young people (who were heavily present in preparatory sessions to choose delegates to the Party Congress), in order to "wipe out" older Party cadres and obtain a vote in his favor.

Of the nine questions discussed in the draft, the question of Mao's successor was the main one. In overwhelming majority the delegates demanded that Lin Piao, who "has never made a mistake," Chairman Mao's "closest comrade in arms for forty years," who had "always upheld the great Red banner of Mao Tsetung Thought," should be his successor, as a guarantee that Mao's policies would always be followed.

The revolutionary committees were heavily PLA-dominated; the delegations were elected, but the final *selection* was still influenced by the PLA. Many delegates did not know Chinese history well, and many were convinced by the propaganda. And so the successor clause was voted through.

Why did Mao allow Lin Piao to be nominated his successor? To this question no straight answer is available. According to some, Mao was against it but could not do anything at the time. On the other hand, there was certainly a vocal opinion that "the masses feel . . . no one should have the same power as Chairman Mao."*

Mao saw the prevailing climate of exaltation and enthusiasm. The Ninth Congress coincided with Russian attacks on the border,† which heightened the psychological need for militant (and military) leaders. The nation felt on the point of war, and demonstrations against the "new czars" were taking place. The need for an assertion that there would not be a reversal seemed to hinge upon assurance of a worthy successor.

Mao also knew that for over two years people had held an image of

* Author's private contacts with ordinary people.
† See pages 354–356.

Lin Piao as a brilliant leader. To go against the public will at this moment would introduce confusion. Unity was the main platform. And though he had reservations about Lin Piao, he did not know the extent of Lin Piao's ambition — "It took some time for us to know him," Chou En-lai would say in 1971.

There were 1,512 delegates at the Ninth Congress. Its presidium had 176 members, among them a good many who had been reviled during the cultural revolution, such as Chu Teh and Chen Yi. It is said that Chen Yi said humorously to Mao: "How can I be at the Congress? I am supposed to be a 'rightist,'" and that Mao replied: "Well then, come and represent the right."

"I hope that this will be a good Congress, a Congress of unity, a Congress of victory," said Mao in his opening speech. He then recalled how, forty-eight years ago in 1921, when the CCP came into being, twelve delegates had been present, of whom only two remained, Tung Pi-wu* (now acting chairman of the People's Republic) and himself. He briefly recalled the Party's history through its many vicissitudes, and added that "we must unite . . . to win still greater victories."

Lin Piao as Party vice-chairman was to deliver the main speech. According to what is said now, his own first draft was not accepted. The ideas he developed were against Mao's policies, against the cultural revolution and its aims. He propounded erroneous economic theses on "productive forces" being the principal spur to progress — exactly the same that the much reviled Liu had proposed in 1956 at the Eighth Congress. In both cases the originator of the theses was the same man, Chen Po-ta!

Since the authentic draft is unavailable, it is not possible to know what Lin Piao did propose to say. The spate of articles which appeared right after the Ninth Congress was not fortuitous, however, and the articles were aimed at Lin Piao. The difficulty, even for experts, is to pick out the exact allusion ensconced in many thousands of words which gives a clue to what is really the target.

Lin Piao's speech was revised, redrafted, and rewritten for him, which is probably why the films of the Ninth Congress show him stumbling over some words. According to this speech, for which Lin Piao was the unwilling mouthpiece, Mao had sought a method to arouse the broad masses so that they might expose "our dark side," that is, the Party's errors, defective methods, bureaucracy, arbitrary autocratic conduct, and even an erroneous line, if such existed, "openly, in

* Tung Pi-wu died in 1975.

an all-around way, and from below." The answer had been the cultural revolution.

Party consolidation and Party building was now the outstanding task. The Party must be composed of the advanced elements of the proletariat, must be renewed, invigorated, ridding itself of the stale and taking in the fresh. The two-line struggle within the Party, reflecting contradictions and class struggle in the society at large, would continue.

In the new Party constitution Lin Piao was declared Mao Tsetung's "close comrade in arms *and successor.*" Priority admission went to workers, poor and lower middle peasants, revolutionary army men or "other revolutionary elements."

To ensure open expression of different views and dissent within the Party, a clause was inserted: If a Party member holds different views with regard to the decisions or directives of the Party organizations, he is allowed to reserve his views and has the right to bypass the immediate leadership and report directly to higher levels, up to and including the Central Committee and its chairman. *"It is essential to create a political situation in which there are both centralism and democracy, both discipline and freedom, both unity of will and personal ease of mind and liveliness. . . .* Without democratic centralism political power would be unstable" (Mao, 1957).

As for economic policies, the theme would be "politics in command," the strategy of development outlined by Mao in 1956, the methods of the Great Leap Forward.

"It is wrong to speak lightly of the final victory of the revolution in our country; it runs counter to Leninism and does not conform to facts." "We cannot speak of final victory, not even for decades. We must not lose our vigilance." The warning that an era of major upheavals and crises in the world is dawning is urgently repeated. "The next fifty to one hundred years, beginning from now, will be a great era of radical change in the social systems throughout the world, an earthshaking era without equal in any previous historical period. Living in such an era, we must be prepared to engage in great struggles which will have many features different in form from those of the past." The cultural revolution was made to prepare China for her role in this era to come.

Unity was again the burden of Mao's speech at the first plenum of the Ninth Central Committee on April 28. "The purpose of uniting is to win still greater victories." The Soviet revisionists were attacking China, and there should be preparedness against war. "Others may come and attack us but *we shall not* fight outside our borders . . . but if you should come and attack us we will deal with you."

There must be economic preparedness and also psychological preparedness for war. Every region must be self-sufficient, not only in grain but also in defense.

As to the Great Proletarian Cultural Revolution, it was not ended. "In a few years we shall have to carry out another one." One cultural revolution was not enough. Much more minute detailed work remained to be done in this one. There were committees in industrial complexes where the leadership was not in the hands of Marxists. There were places where too many cadres had been arrested or suspended. Mao inveighed heavily against arbitrary arrests. Only those who had committed proven crimes should be arrested. Some very good cadres had erroneously followed Liu's line. "Some have been shut up for two years, shut up in cattle pens. . . . They should not be held, they should be liberated." This reference is to the fact that in some of the PLA-run May 7 schools for cadres, the PLA treated the cadres more like prisoners than like people there to study and do their own soul-searching.* "I have faith in some of the old comrades who have made mistakes in the past," repeated Mao. In this speech, the clearest indictment against Lin Piao and his manner of dealing with cadres was already evident, but very few saw it at the time.

Lin Piao was now plainly substituting a praetorian army dictatorship for the mandarin type of authoritarianism which Liu Shao-chi had tried to impose through the Party. This militarist take-over became clearer when his first attempts of 1967 and 1968 had failed.

When it was evident that Mao had no intention of installing a military regime, Lin Piao saw his chances of being a "successor" receding. Even though he was designated as successor, a reinvigorated Party would be a perpetual challenge to his personal supremacy. And he knew that Mao would not hesitate to change the "successor" if necessary.

For decades Lin Piao had been praised as a genius (far more outside China than in China), a brilliant strategist, a military expert. "My head is first quality," he used to say, and remark on the mediocrity of other military commanders. "What do you think you are," he shouted at Chu

---

* As Mao himself hinted to Edgar Snow in the December 1970 interview (*Life* magazine, April 30, 1971, page 46).

Teh. "It was I, not you, who fought." His persecution of Chen Yi, Ho Lung, and others revealed his meanness.

In early 1969, at a work conference, Mao had remarked that in quite a few revolutionary committees the masses were not represented, had little to say. The primary role was that of the workers and peasants, who must exercise supervision and criticism towards the cadres. This must not be left to the army. Mao criticized the attempt by PLA Party committees to exercise veto control upon the civilian revolutionary committees. Even in August 1971 he stressed: "Now that the regional Party committees have been established, they should exercise unified leadership. It would be reversing matters if things already decided by local Party committees were turned over to army Party committees for further discussion."

This struggle by Mao to re-establish Party leadership and curb army power was all the more difficult since the notion that "the PLA man is always right" had been cultivated among the masses, and the PLA was on the whole popular for having restored "order." Authoritarianism still has a strong appeal because it represents security.

The rebuilding of Party committees was very slow throughout 1968 and early 1969. By the end of 1969 they existed at commune and factory level, but there were very few county Party committees.

How was Mao to dislodge the military and return to civilian order? It looked difficult, but Mao had one great weapon: ideological authority. Party loyalty in the PLA went to Mao as Party chairman. This cuts across every other tie, even if the military commanders are recalcitrant. When it was evident that there were differences in view between Mao and Lin Piao, Lin Piao could no longer command Party loyalty in the PLA; he was left with the gun, but without the ideology.

The first army attack on Lin Piao is an article by the personnel of the Military Academy on September 15, 1969, in *People's Daily*. The article is an attack on the "theory of productive forces" of Liu Shao-chi, but the persistence with which this point is driven home shows that it involves a new "Liu Shao-chi."

Now that we are told that Lin Piao's first draft for his speech at the Ninth Congress contained this economic heresy, "a refurbished version . . . of the same revisionist trash that Liu Shao-chi and Chen Po-ta had smuggled into the resolution of the Eighth Congress,"* we understand the target was Lin Piao.

---

* Some argue that Chen Po-ta excoriated Liu Shao-chi for producing this theory, and hence cannot have been its originator. This denotes an incomplete knowledge of how criticism and self-criticism work in the Party. The individual

Other articles stressed the Party as "the highest form of organization of the working class," the only *"center of leadership"* over *"all sectors and all other organs,"* including mass organizations (such as the revolutionary committees) and of course the PLA. The insistence on rehabilitation of 95 percent of cadres after due processing, to be done "with open doors" through the masses and not through PLA action, continued, and there was a growing campaign against "arrogance" and "conceit," repeated admonitions on the importance of studying modestly, "to be good at *learning* . . . is important." One of the main points brought out in private conversations about Lin Piao is that "he never studied . . . did not read anything. He thought he knew everything."

Mao and Lin Piao, though appearing together for another two years in what looked like perfect amity, were actually engaged in a growing conflict all the more serious for being impersonal and ideological.

This is what Lin Piao wrote about Mao: "Today he uses this force to attack that force; tomorrow he uses that force to attack this force . . . Those who are his greatest friends today will be his prisoners tomorrow."* And still he went on waving the little red book, calling out, "Long live Chairman Mao."

Lin Piao invented nicknames for Mao: B-52, Emperor Ch'in (the first emperor who had defied Confucianism and burned the Confucian books). Lin Piao would have to find a moral and political justification for going against Mao.

In 1970 Mao began to cut down on his own personality cult. A personality cult, Mao had remarked in 1965, is sometimes necessary. He had invoked his prestige and popularity among people and used it as a tool to recover his authority. Mao began making humorous remarks about those who wore Mao medals (some of them were growing to the dimensions of small plates). "Give me back my airplanes!" he said, meaning: All this metal gone to adorn the chests of eight hundred millions! "The little red book . . . is somewhat formalistic," the author was told in the summer of 1970.† The ritual appellations of Great Leader, Great Helmsman, Great Supreme Commander, Great Teacher which plastered Mao's portraits everywhere also disappeared. Statues were removed.

---

who has upheld a wrong theory is required, after due self-criticism, to be the very one to castigate it. Examples of this abound in Liu's speeches—so why not Chen Po-ta?

* May 1971, Lin Piao in Document 571, seen by author in the original Chinese in June 1973.

† Author's interviews with officials, June 1973.

Embedded in the mind of every Chinese, the Confucian classics with their venerable rolling phrases have an enormous emotional appeal. Lin Piao must have gone back to his house seething with frustration and anger, and calmed his spirits with Confucian classics and calligraphy.* The fallback into the past, in search of an older, venerable code which would prove him right, was inevitable. In 1969 he gave to his supporters four scrolls he had written: "In all times and in everything, what is important is to restrain oneself and return to the rites" (the old institutions). But what Confucius had meant by "the rites" was the slave system, with a "superior man" supreme and the "small people" absolutely obedient.

The pre-revolution Chinese compradore bourgeoisie had not been able to create its own system of ethics. Even some early revolutionaries, as they grew older, when defeated would fall back into veneration of Confucius. So did Chiang Kai-shek, whose New Life Movement of 1934 was unadulterated Confucianism. In China the choice lies between straight Marxism and Confucianism; there is no other ethical system between them. And under the skin of many a Party member the old sage still resides.

"Heaven never changes," wrote Lin Piao to his son Lin Li-kuo. "Neither does man. Impatience in small things destroys big plans." Lin Piao countered the ideological criticism by articles praising himself and his superior "genius." Until September 1971, when he died, such pieces were still appearing, and a book on his military prowess was circulated. As was a second little red book, *Quotations of Vice-Chairman Lin Piao*, which was distributed in Peking among the cadres. At every shrine of the revolution, carefully prepared propaganda showed visitors Lin Piao as the only man accompanying Mao Tsetung in decisive actions.

But the critical pieces castigating "arrogance and complacency" intensified. One could see in Peking and other main cities large cars in which fat military men and their wives and children rode to do their shopping. This bad work style, "bureaucratic, subjective, formalistic," was excoriated. It lasted, however, until 1971.

At least five out of the thirteen military regions were under Lin Piao's appointees (some abandoned him). Six of his followers and his wife, Yeh Chun, were ensconced in the Military Affairs Committee. He had a web of his own appointees in some important revolutionary committees. There was a dominance of military personnel in the Central Committee, 110 out of 279. In it the air force was represented, with

* A traditional mode of behavior among Confucianists.

eight of its top commanding staff, the navy with seven, instead of the single man in the previous Congress. In the Politburo sat Yeh Chun and the head of the GCCR, Chen Po-ta. Out of seventeen members of the Politburo, barring himself and Mao, Lin Piao would have six supporters. And in the standing committee of the Politburo (five members including Mao), Lin Piao and Chen Po-ta confronted Chou En-lai and Kang Sheng.

Attacks against Chou En-lai began again. Chou distinguished himself by a minimum of red book waving and adulation, a maximum of blunt truth, and an extraordinary amount of real work. He was also known to millions of young Red Guards. The renewed attempts against Chou En-lai took the form of references, over provincial broadcasts, to the "twenty-eight Bolsheviks" who had opposed Mao in the past and hints that there were not twenty-eight but twenty-nine. The broadcasts suggested that there were still "capitalist-roaders" in top positions in the Party, and that "the *most veteran leaders* must undergo thought reform."

No National People's Congress had been held since 1964, and the state constitution promulgated in 1954 was now out of date. Mao Tsetung was obviously anxious to call such an assembly, which would open the post-cultural revolution stage and ratify the changes brought about.

The draft of a new state constitution began to circulate among revolutionary committees in the winter of 1969–1970. The earliest copies contained a provision for electing another head of state in place of Liu Shao-chi, but this provision was deleted at a meeting of the Central Committee and the Politburo in March 1970. "We do not need a head of state," said Mao — no new whim, for he had already manifested his own reluctance at being a head of state in 1958 by resigning. But the implications went further. To Lin Piao, the deletion, and further rephrasing of clauses pertaining to the ministry of Defense and the increased power of the Party over the army, was evidence that Mao was thinking of a collective leadership both in the Party and in the state machinery. Even though Lin Piao had been consecrated as successor in the Party constitution, it was evident this post would be weakened in the state constitution. Mao was also insistent that the people's militia, placed under the PLA during the cultural revolution, now be led by the committees of the workers in factories and the communes in rural areas.

In the first quarter of 1970 county Party committees had become established; articles stressed "unified" leadership, emphasizing that this meant Party leadership over PLA units "and all sectors of the economy." In August, again at Lushan, the scene of the August 1959 struggle with Peng Teh-huai, the first overt clash in the major struggle against Lin Piao took place.

It was the second plenum of the Ninth Central Committee, and a heavy agenda had been drawn up: economic decisions of great importance, "clarification of ideology," formulation of concrete policies for the next period, formation of Party committees at provincial level. The last had to be carried out swiftly, for Mao did not want to let the PLA remain in charge of executing the directives to come.

Suddenly Chen Po-ta, backed by Lin Piao, Yeh Chun, and some top military leaders in the Politburo, tried to change the agenda. They suggested that instead of Party committees being in charge, a procedure should be followed such as that prior to the Ninth Congress: congresses of *activists* should be held, and from these a new People's Representatives Assembly (or National People's Congress) should be elected. This was to bypass the Party; activists could be manipulated by PLA Party committees. The whole plan purported to carry out "extensive democracy." But Mao knew it would work against the interests of the masses. The calling of a national assembly before the Party was totally rebuilt and unified was a way of introducing confusion, not unified leadership.

The revised draft constitution was submitted. A committee with Chou En-lai presiding had deleted a clause extolling the "genius" of Mao Tsetung as well as the head of state clause. Chen Po-ta now made a "surprise attack" against Chou En-lai, circulating a memorandum in which he proved that the word "genius" and calling Mao a "genius" was Marxist-Leninist, and quoting both Marx and Lenin on the subject.[*] Anyone who did not recognize Mao's genius was counterrevolutionary. Then there was the question of the head of state. "Without such a post," said Lin Piao, "orders will not have due weight and people will not know who is in authority or not." He suggested that Mao be head of state. A demand backed by four military commanders, among them Chief of Staff Huang Yung-sheng, for a change in the agenda was then placed before the presidium.

The whole point of this intricate move was to place Chou En-lai on the defensive and obtain a vote against him, and to get a head of state

[*] Document shown to the author in the original Chinese version in June 1973.

post reinstated in the constitution. If Mao refused the appointment, it was arranged to have another vote and that the chairmanship should go to Lin Piao. The unsophistication of some of the provincial members of the Central Committee, the weight of the military presence would, Lin Piao hoped, pull the vote in his favor.

Lin Piao was quite right in thinking that the designation of "successor" was rapidly hollowing. In the revised draft for the state constitution, Mao was named leader of all the nationalities of the country and commander-in-chief of the nation and its armed forces. A second paragraph described Lin Piao as Mao's "close comrade in arms and his successor," the vice-commander-in-chief of the nation and its armed forces. But as minister of Defense in a reconstituted government, Lin Piao ranked below Premier Chou En-lai and even below Marshal Nieh Jung-chen, head of the Scientific and Technological State Planning Commission in the State Council.

For two and a half days the conspirators kept up the attack. And then Mao acted. He wrote a short seven-hundred-word note called *Some Opinions*. "Like a drop of alcohol killing off a colony of bacteria," his curt words reversed the situation. He reminded Lin Piao and Chen Po-ta that he had already six times before refused to become the head of state. "We do not need or want a head of state."

Some Opinions says:° "Comrade Chen Po-ta and I have had many divergences for many years . . . Now certain comrades act as if 'the earth would stop turning and Lushan mountain be blown flat . . . But this will not happen. The earth will continue to turn . . . Lushan will not be blown flat. . . .' As for the question of genius, we both [Lin Piao and himself] have discussed this and must still study this question . . . *of standing on the side of idealism or materialism;*† of whether history is made by genius or by slaves."

By criticizing Chen Po-ta but not Lin Piao, Mao divided his enemies; he would in September call for criticism of Chen Po-ta's ideas, and the self-criticism of those who had sided with him. To those who can read Mao between the lines, it was quite clear that he was accusing Lin Piao of "idealism," and when he now called for "study" and self-criticism by *all* Central Committee members, hoped Lin Piao would comply. Lin was being given a last chance.

Now the plotters were in disarray; all support melted away and the

---

° Document seen by author in Peking in June 1973.

† This is the key sentence, raising the debate on the ideological plane, but not attacking Lin Piao directly.

motion was hastily withdrawn. Yeh Chun, Lin Piao's wife, is said to have wailed: "Then what will happen to the succession?" — giving away the whole design.

Within the next few weeks the detailed scrutiny, review of Chen Po-ta's life, deeds and words, would begin. All those who had shared in the maneuver would also have to make their self-criticisms.

On September 15 Mao wrote a directive, as Party chairman, demanding a "rectification movement" against "apriorism, arrogance, and metaphysical ideas" in the Party. This meant Lin Piao's ideas and behavior. From then on Lin Piao could no longer count on anyone in the PLA except some top men who felt too deeply involved to withdraw.

The communiqué of the plenum called for a struggle against idealism and metaphysical ideas and "to smash the handful of counterrevolutionaries who undermine the revolution and socialist construction."

By April 1971 Chen Po-ta was denounced — not yet by name — as a "big careerist, who called himself a little commoner." In the summer his connections with the 516 became current knowledge.

After the plenum, provincial Party committees were established swiftly; it was no longer possible for Lin Piao to hinder their formation. The ideological struggle was demolishing Lin Piao's prestige, although his name was never mentioned and he still appeared to be Mao's devoted successor. Mao tried to "recuperate" him in the interests of unity; this, among Marxists, means a continuous ideological discussion.

Mao now began to "give medicine" to Lin Piao, again by way of the press. Everyone was exhorted to study Marxism-Leninism. An army rectification campaign was started, based on this study and the study of Party history. The lessons of history were valuable, said Mao; the Kutien conference (1930)* was brought up as a reminder. "The important thing is to be good at learning . . . from past mistakes." "Always bear in mind the historical experience of inner-Party struggle between two lines," wrote *Red Flag*.† Choice extracts from Mao's previous works were reprinted. Criticisms of apriorism then began, emanating from cadre schools, Marxist-Leninist institutes. Thinking that one can know and understand instinctively and without practice was "metaphysics." Thousands of articles from workers and peasants against "genius" and "heroes" clamored: "It is the slaves who make history."

---

* See *The Morning Deluge*, pages 222–225. Lin Piao had disagreed with Mao at that conference, but this was not known to many Party members.

† Nos. 7 and 8, 1971.

There were constant reminders that the PLA should be a great school . . . and learn from the masses (reversing the "Learn from the PLA" slogan).

In the torrent of exhortation, admonition, criticism, instruction coming from below, from people who had discussed the philosophical issues and the "world outlook" involved, Lin Piao was drowning. Many who wrote had no notion that they were writing against Lin. They knew "a wrong tendency is . . . to be repudiated."*

Yang Hsien-chen's "two merge into one" thesis was resurrected for criticism on February 1, 1971. This was to remind Lin Piao that in 1960 he also had recommended an accord with Khrushchev.

There was also (again) a dispute on external policies. In December 1970 the change in American policy towards the People's Republic of China was clear, and Mao in his interview with Edgar Snow had invited President Nixon to Peking. But at the conference held by the Politburo to discuss the matter, Lin Piao objected, contending that "imperialism will never lay down the butcher's knife." On August 1, 1971, Chief of Staff Huang Yung-sheng in his Army Day speech made a virulent attack on U.S. imperialism, which must "get out of all Asia," but failed to say one word against Soviet "social-imperialism" despite the Russian attacks on the Chinese borders in 1969.

Besides the dispute on foreign policy, there seems to have been another dispute on the question of weaponry and supply to the PLA. Lin Piao contended that the PLA needed highly sophisticated equipment and the electronic industry should have priority. Mao contended that steel must be used in priority for rural mechanization. "The sinister aim of sham Marxist political swindlers who preach that the electronic industry should be made the center . . . is the vain attempt to undermine . . . socialist construction."†

Lin Piao, his wife Yeh Chun and son Lin Li-kuo‡ were in Soochow in the spring of 1971, ostensibly on a vacation tour. It was there that the plot to launch a military coup d'etat and perhaps to assassinate Mao began. One of the first schemes discussed was to attempt to seize Peking and other cities by paratroopers, who would hold key points and broadcast the story that a counterrevolutionary seizure was being

* See Hsinhua releases July 12 and September 6, 1971, for philosophical essays against apriorism.
† *People's Daily*, August 12, 1971.
‡ Lin Li-kuo, despite his youth, had been promoted to vice-commander of the air force, which Lin Piao thus controlled.

averted and that Lin Piao had taken action to save Chairman Mao. The arrest and elimination of Chou En-lai, Kang Sheng and others of the Central Committee would then take place. Another scheme was to organize "dare to die" teams from discontented factions such as the 516, who felt that the cultural revolution had betrayed them, and had hidden in cities. Lin Piao thought he could rely on some of the cadres who had been demoted, and in the countryside on the landlords and rich peasants, who would happily rally to him. He counted on winning their allegiance by restoring them to authority in return for support. Lin Li-kuo went to see some air force leaders in Shanghai and in Hangchow to plan for air force support. The navy as well had a Lin Piao faction.

The conspirators drew up their manifesto, called Project 571 (the Chinese sound for 571 is the same as for "armed uprising").

Project 571* begins with a moral justification for the intended coup. The peasant masses are persecuted, the economy is stagnant, the people dare not speak up any longer. The "clique in power" is corrupt and alienated from the masses, there will be power struggles between its various factions, and therefore instability.

"B-52 [Mao] constantly resorts to the techniques of coup d'etat, favoring those who struggle with the pen rather than those who struggle with the gun . . . we must put a stop to this by a violent and radical revolution . . . otherwise no one knows how many heads will roll or how the Chinese revolution will be delayed."

"A new confrontation is inevitable. Unless we seize the leadership . . . we shall fail. *After several years of preparation,* our forces have already obtained remarkable results on the military and ideological plane . . . we have a material and an ideological base . . . throughout the land, our forces are progressing."

Lin compares his "flotilla" (the forces at his disposal) to those of the forces which made the October Revolution of Russia in 1917 and finds them "by no means inferior."

The support of the air force is assured. Regional commanders who are not won over can be dealt with in local operations. He lists the various forces and army corps at his disposal (some of them under pseudonyms) and notes that Huang Yung-sheng, the acting chief of staff, would put the "administrative sector" under control.

"Secret negotiations have already taken place with the USSR." Lin

---

* Seen by author in June 1973.

Piao mentions that Soviet troops would "make pressures and neutralize other military forces."

"But our strength is still not at a maximum of preparation and the cult of B-52 is deep among the masses." "The contradictions within the armed forces are particularly strong, which makes the constitution of a united front [of all the PLA] under our control difficult." "B-52 rarely comes out in public . . . security measures round his person are strict."

But an unstable equilibrium exists between "B-52 and us." A crisis impends. "It is a life and death struggle. Either they win or we do."

B-52 is "getting ready to devour us . . . and we are in great danger." Mao must be seized, as well as the Central Committee. An important Party meeting would assemble "all elements to eliminate. . . . We must first eliminate his unconditional supporters, then force B-52 to accept this palace revolution." "We must utilize all methods, poison gas, bacteriological weapons, kidnappings, urban guerillas, motorcar accidents." "*When B-52 has decided to make someone lose face, he never stops halfway.*"* The document then promises protection and political amnesty to all those who "suffered persecutions from B-52."

The conspirators were sworn to secrecy according to the oath of Bushido, the Japanese samurai oath.

Meanwhile, Mao was preparing to counter Lin Piao, adopting three tactics. He would define them as "throwing stones, mixing sand and soil, and undermining the wall."

Throwing stones: Calling for the self-criticism of Chen Po-ta and other top military leaders, and thus disrupting enemies at the second plenum, and distributing these self-criticisms at a work conference in April 1971 for perusal by all the Central Committee.

Mixing sand and soil, a gardening technique: "When soil is too tight, one puts sand in it to let it breathe," said Mao. It meant approving and publicizing the reports of regional commanders who took energetic measures in rectification of work style, arrogance and complacency, thus raising their importance — and diminishing Lin Piao's prestige as always ideologically correct. And adding new personnel to the MAC to counter Lin's appointees.

Undermining the wall: Reorganizing the Peking military region. This was carried out in December 1970. A corps command from Nanking and one from Fukien were also moved to Peking in June 1971. Thus a coup at the Center became impossible.

When the author was in China in the summer of 1971, some places

* Author's italics.

were strangely reticent about Lin Piao. For instance, in Sian in August, a month before Lin Piao's plane crash, all portraits of him had disappeared, and the political commissar of Sian would not discuss Lin Piao's role at the Anti-Japanese University in Yenan, where Lin Piao was director for eighteen months in 1936–1937.* "Nobody is sure a revolutionary is a real revolutionary . . . until he is dead."

In Szechuan† a great hunt for "ultra-leftists" was proceeding and each shop, each house had the slogan, "Drag out the ultra-left."

In Tsunyi, in Kweichow province, at the historical museum, on the contrary, the cult of Lin Piao was still profound, though it was September 14. The museum had not yet been informed of Lin Piao's death, which had occurred the previous day.‡

In August 1971 Mao had made a tour of Middle China and conferred with the regional commanders of the Nanking and Central and South China regions about "the Lin Piao problem."

"Practice Marxism and not revisionism; unite and don't split, be open and aboveboard, and don't intrigue and conspire," said Mao. He reviewed briefly the fifty years of the Party's history, during which there had been "ten big struggles" on the question of line. *"The correctness or incorrectness of the ideological and political line is the key; it decides everything."* Every attempt to split the Party on this matter of line had failed.

The tenth struggle had been in September 1970 at the Lushan conference, against Lin Piao and Chen Po-ta. It had lasted two and a half days and the opponents had been underhanded and mean. "They were not as open as Peng Teh-huai," said Mao. But Mao had shielded Lin Piao then and "no conclusions had been drawn about Lin Piao." "After I return to Peking I must seek them [the plotters] out again to have a talk. If they do not come to see me I will go to see them. Some of them may be saved, others it may not be possible to save . . . It is difficult for someone committing major errors of principle to reform." There must have been sadness in Mao's tone as he said this. But he reasserted that "we should still operate the policy of curing the disease to save the patient.

"When it comes to questions of line, questions of principle, I take a

---

* See *The Morning Deluge*, page 386 (Lin Piao in Yenan as head of the university).
† Visited by the author in September 1971.
‡ See *The Morning Deluge*, pages 278–282, for the Tsunyi conference, January 6–8, 1935.

*firm hold and do not relax my grip. On major questions of principle I
do not make concessions.*

"There has never been any supreme savior, nor can we rely on gods
and emperors, we rely entirely on ourselves for our salvation," said
Mao, talking of the fallacy of expecting "genius" or "superman" to save
mankind. "The International" must be sung, and studied, as well as
Lenin's article on its composer Eugène Pottier. Here "we have been
singing 'The International' for fifty years but people have tried to split
our Party ten times."*

He warned again of struggles to come. Even when communism was
reached, there would still be struggles, between new and old, correct
and incorrect, good and evil.

Mao returned from Shanghai by train, and on September 11 there
appears to have been an attempt by Lin Piao to assassinate him on the
way. Because there are not one but several versions of the same story,
it is not possible to be sure of details. Chou En-lai spoke of a "wild
attempt to assassinate Chairman Mao."

The attempt failed. Lin Piao and his wife Yeh Chun, six of his fellow
conspirators and his son Lin Li-kuo then decided to flee to the Soviet
Union. They commandeered a Trident and flew off, but the plane
crashed at Undur Khan in Inner Mongolia. The grounding of all planes
in China for three days from the night of September 12 was the first
indication that something unusual had taken place.

A meeting of the enlarged Central Committee was held in the western hills near Peking following Lin Piao's death. The October 1 march-
past at Tien An Men was canceled and replaced by a far more agreeable
program of opera, plays, open-air dances in parks — enjoyment for
the population. But the wildest rumors circulated, and it was only
on October 7, with a sigh of relief, that the people of China knew that
Chairman Mao was safe, for he was seen on television with Emperor
Haile Selassie of Ethiopia.

From October 20, documentation on Lin Piao began to be dissemi-
nated at all Party levels. Lin Piao's writings on Confucius, his Project
571, and other documents were read, debated, studied. In May 1972
the first semiofficial revelations came out, but it was not until the
summer of 1972 that the matter became openly commented on. By

---

* "The International" has the words: "There is no supreme savior."

then a major purge of all Lin Piao's followers and a shake-up in the PLA had been almost completed.

What were Mao's feelings? They are epitomized in a line quoted on October 20 by Peking Radio: "The enemy is nothing to fear. . . . What hurt and disappointed me most was the sinister arrow fired at my back by my ally, and his smiling face after I was wounded."*

* Words taken from the journal of the famous writer Lu Hsun.

6

China and the World

Wind in the tower, / Herald of the approaching storm . . .
— Poem quoted by PREMIER CHOU EN-LAI at
the Tenth Party Congress, August 1973[*]

There is today . . . great turmoil under heaven. . . . The situation is
excellent. . . . When the tree falls the monkeys scatter.
— Quotations attributed to MAO TSETUNG and repeated
in numerous articles and in editorials and speeches over
the last three years

At a rally held in June 1971 to greet the general secretary of Romania's Party, Nicolae Ceausescu, Premier Chou En-lai said: "China will not be a superpower, neither now nor ever in the future. We will always stand together with the oppressed countries and people in firmly opposing the power politics of superpowers."

The assertion shows the leap into world importance which China achieved between 1949 and today, and her leaders' consciousness of her potential.

China does enjoy an unprecedentedly favorable position. She is the only country in the world with total independence, both economic and diplomatic: initiative in her own hands, freedom from internal or external debt, and the ability to plan her own future on her own principles. Neither of the two superpowers, despite their gigantic accumulation of lethal weaponry, is as independent as China; their collusion and contention for world hegemony has manacled them to each other; neither can make a move without taking the other into account at all times. "Autarky is well and thriving in China," one American observer has remarked. No other country has more zealously pursued the goal of economic self-sufficiency and self-reliance without self-seclusion, but with selective trading guided by political goals. Nei-

[*] Author's translation.

ther has any country undertaken with such daring the upheaval of its society, the destruction of its misery and backwardness. The cultural revolution was a creative historical undertaking: the launching of China into a new era.

In China's relations with the world, it is some years since the myths of China's self-imposed isolation, of Mao's ignorance of world affairs, have been routed by the wisdom displayed in the conduct of China's foreign relations, the skill, adroitness, and brilliance of her diplomats and negotiators. Mao Tsetung was predicting the world of 1975 when, in Moscow in November 1957, he spoke of the swift rise of the Third World, of an era of disorders and splits, "great turmoil under heaven," of "earthquakes" in the affluent minority of industrial nations.

The cultural revolution was a voluntary, hardheaded, long-term calculation for political and strategic preparation of China for its future role in the world. "China . . . ought to have made a greater contribution to humanity. Her contribution over a long period has been far too small. For this we are regretful," Mao had said in 1956. In July 1967, speaking to a foreign delegation in Peking, he visualized China as "making her contribution" and becoming "the technological and industrial arsenal" upon which the liberation movements, the revolutions for independence in the future, could count for support. "But we must remain modest and prudent . . . not only now, but in the decades to come."

In January 1967 Leonid Brezhnev openly deplored the cultural revolution as a "great tragedy for all real Communists in China." Thirteen Russian divisions were moved to China's frontiers. The cultural revolution infuriated the Kremlin, which condemned "Mao and his group" by name, and called for another international conference to condemn it. The CCP, describing the Kremlin leaders as "renegades," did not send a delegation to the fiftieth anniversary of the Bolshevik revolution in Moscow in November 1967.

By 1968 the energetic handling of the excesses of the summer of 1967 had won back China's international prestige, imperiled by the aberrations of those weeks. Despite adverse propaganda, the fire and fervor, the germination of new ideas which the cultural revolution was causing throughout the Communist parties of the world were having effect in Eastern Europe. China's defiance of the Soviet "conductor's baton" was admired by many. As a result, signs of a turning away from Moscow's emprise appeared. In Czechoslovakia the tendency was towards a liberalization which China did not approve; disgust with socialism was due to the evil effects of revisionism and the high-handedness of the Kremlin, said the Chinese, who denounced exploitation by the Comecon of other Eastern European economies, and asked: "Would any other Party dare to make a cultural revolution in their own country?"*

In August 1968 the Soviet Union occupied Czechoslovakia with six hundred thousand troops and put an end to the Alexander Dubcek regime, a move which "unmasked the hideous features of the Soviet revisionism" in Chinese parlance. It shocked the world, but it also showed that the division of Europe was a fait accompli, and the new powerlessness of the United States, bogged down in the war in Vietnam.

Within the western world the looming economic crisis, President Johnson's withdrawal in April 1968 from seeking re-election, the unending Vietnam conflict, and the new and disturbing aggressiveness of the Soviet Union in the Mediterranean and in other parts of the world were forcing the American government to reconsider its policy towards China. The invasion of Czechoslovakia ruptured the socialist camp, for both Romania and Yugoslavia (and of course Albania) protested. To quell the incipient rebellion Brezhnev in December 1968 was to expound, with scarcely veiled threat, the doctrine of "limited sovereignty," justifying Soviet intervention "when socialism . . . is threatened . . . by actions threatening the common interests of the socialist camp." This was the preliminary stance to "detente," and would justify the Soviets in ignoring subsequent detente agreements.

In January 1969 small-scale attacks by Soviet troops began again on the Chinese frontiers at various points. On March 2 a fairly large-scale attack was made on Chen Pao Island on the Chinese side of the Ussuri River, a branch of the Amur. The USSR claimed the island as part of its territory, which contradicted both international law and its own "unequal" treaty of 1860 with China. The treaty of 1860 named the Ussuri River as the border between the two states, and according to regulations for safeguarding the state frontiers of the USSR, the stipulation was that the state boundary of the USSR on navigable boundary rivers runs along the center of the main channel or the thalweg of the river,† according to international usage.

* Chen Yi, in his speech at the conclusion of the Emergency Congress of Afro-Asian Writers, June-July 1966 at Peking.

† See Neville Maxwell "From the 'Unequal Treaties' to the Sino-Soviet Border Clash," *Monde Diplomatique*, March 1974. The principle of "'thalweg" is accepted by the USSR for its boundaries with all countries except China.

Chen Pao Island hugs the Chinese bank of the river, separated by a rivulet dry part of the year. The Kremlin now insisted the frontier was on the Chinese bank of the river, which would deny free use of the inside of the river to the Chinese. Moscow claimed right of possession and sovereign jurisdiction over the Amur and Ussuri rivers in their totality.

In the attacks of March 1969 the Russians employed tanks and flamethrowers, killing around eight hundred Chinese fishermen and militia who had resisted. The USSR lost thirty-one dead and fourteen wounded. Clashes continued until August.

Huge demonstrations took place in China, involving three hundred million people waving banners and posters, DOWN WITH THE NEW CZARS. Moscow then started an astonishing diplomatic offensive. Ambassadors and ministers of the USSR approached their counterparts in Washington, Paris, Bonn and London to discuss the enormous danger to the world of China's "chaotic internal situation," and suggested concerted measures against China. The Yellow Peril myth was once again resurrected throughout the USSR, and the poet Yevgeny Yevtushenko, seized with a fit of racist inaccuracy, wrote about defending the "Holy Sacred Soil of Russia" from the Huns, forgetting that the Huns were not Chinese, and had invaded China from the western steppes of Siberia.

In the middle of this clamor, on March 21, Soviet Premier Alexei Kosygin telephoned Peking, urgently demanding to speak to Premier Chou En-lai. He was told that there were normal diplomatic channels through which he could communicate. This strange telephone call the Chinese regarded as part of the usual ploy to create panic. But there was no panic in China. Cool-headed and prudent, Chou En-lai and his Ministry of Foreign Affairs staff had already come to the conclusion that this military provocation had a purpose, but not the purpose of a war on China. "They want to negotiate something, somewhere," their long experience with Khrushchev told them. Mao viewed it as a feint, with multiple intentions. And indeed on March 29 the Kremlin suggested that negotiations on the frontier, interrupted since 1964, be resumed, meanwhile continuing border attacks and deploying its immense propaganda apparatus everywhere to denounce China's aggressive intentions and territorial ambitions.

It seemed to the Chinese that the border attacks, occurring at the same time as preparations for a new international conference of all Communist parties, were meant to cover up a disadvantageous situation in the wake of the Czech invasion. The manifest defeat of the United States in the Vietnam War heralded a difficult but obvious necessity for a rapprochement between the U.S. and China. The shift of policy in Washington was already beginning; it had been noted with anxiety in Moscow in that very January. The Soviet diplomatic approach to Washington (and to other countries) was a failure, as sympathy in the world went to China.

It is also suggested that the Soviet leaders sought to disrupt the Ninth Congress and strengthen the position of Lin Piao as designated successor. There was also a note of smug relief in some western countries. If China and the USSR went to war, the western world might save itself from the impending financial crisis, already looming in 1969.

Mao Tsetung gauged that the Soviet aim was more subtle. The USSR leaders were trying to divert attention from their real target, Europe, and to push forward the European security conference, Moscow's primary aim since 1954. And there were the hard-liners in the Red Army who looked with suspicion at disarmament, even in words, and felt Brezhnev's policies of detente were a danger to the Soviet Union. By this action against China Brezhnev could smother the dissidence and proceed with "detente" with America. The next move would be revelatory, for it would indeed be a steady buildup of Soviet forces on the European front, until today there are three to four times as many units and far more nuclear and sophisticated weaponry on the western front than on the Chinese frontier. "They shout towards the East but their target is the West," said Mao. "The Soviet Union and the United States are rivaling each other for hegemony all over the world, with Europe as the focus of their contention." The Mediterranean, the southern countries of Europe,* the Middle East, and the Persian Gulf would now become the stage for their conflicts by proxy.

But pretense still overlay reality. A nonproliferation treaty achieved in 1968 between the two superpowers continued the hoax of the test ban of 1963. It was denounced by the Chinese Ministry of Foreign Affairs as a "dirty deal, collusion on a global scale for the monopoly of nuclear weaponry by nuclear overlords." Today the nonproliferation treaty is denounced by many other countries of the Third World; some are acquiring nuclear weapons, and both the U.S. and the USSR, as well as European countries, are vying with each other to sell weapons to all Third World countries.

---

* Portugal, Spain, Italy, Yugoslavia, Greece.

In October 1968 the Kremlin also began to make approaches to Chiang Kai-shek's regime in Taiwan, through the person of a mysteri-our Soviet journalist named Victor Louis and some trade representatives. Mao Tsetung concluded that the USSR was now baring its paper tiger teeth and demonstrating itself a young imperialism on the offensive. The United States would find it difficult in the future to defend what it had; for everywhere the USSR would now compete, including in the Atlantic and Pacific oceans. The USSR, in his eyes, was now the chief enemy of the peoples of the world, even more cunning than the U.S., "cheating many people who have not seen through it." The anti-Chinese propaganda from Moscow drew from Mao an ironical remark: "The ghost of John Foster Dulles has now taken residence in the Kremlin."

Would the United States choose to join with the USSR against China? In any case the latter must be ready to repel any attempted invasion. Whether or not both superpowers would drag in a few "lackeys" — in this case meaning India and Japan — was also envisaged, and "we have made full preparations to be attacked by all four at once," said Chou En-lai.*

But India had her own contradictions with the USSR, though more and more subject to economic spoliation and pressures.† As for Japan, although the Chinese made for a while a great show of denouncing Japanese militarism, the fact remained that they did not believe Japan was ready for any war with China; the Japanese people would be hostile to it.

China's policy was a combination of prudence and boldness, subtlety and daring. "Prepare for war, prepare for natural calamities, and do everything for the people." "Dig tunnels deep, store grain everywhere, and never seek hegemony." China's preparation for the defense of all her people, by building well-stocked underground cities and storing grain, began.

Mao Tsetung would take particular care to distinguish between the Kremlin leaders and the Soviet people, who, he asserted, were friends, and who would one day overthrow revisionism. There would be no racist crusade in China.‡

---

* Author's interview with Chou En-lai in 1971.

† The recent abrogation of "democracy" in India, applauded by the Kremlin, may have reinforced the Soviet hold. It will solve none of the country's economic difficulties, but sharpen class struggles and hasten revolutionary change.

‡ But Mao would make the point that the American people, should the USSR become imperialist, would be the people on whom his hopes were pinned. See

In 1970, Mao Tsetung looked at the state of the world. "Countries want independence, nations want liberation, and the people want revolution." This had now become the "irresistible tide of history." As a result of the monopolistic concentration of nuclear and other power in the hands of a dual hegemony, the erstwhile major capitalist countries of Western Europe were now themselves victims of "control, interference and bullying by the two overlords." The Third World of Asia, Africa, and Latin America, and the Second World of Europe, Oceania, Canada, were both the scenes of their competition, which would necessarily lead to arms escalation everywhere. Europe was the focus of this hegemonic rivalry.

"Since the two superpowers are contending for world hegemony, the contradiction between them is irreconcilable; one either overpowers the other, or is overpowered. Their compromise and collusion can only be partial, temporary and relative, while their contention is all-embracing, permanent and absolute."

From then on, China was unperturbed by all the talks of detente, rashes of summits, and other attempts not to face the reality of hegemonic rivalry. All this was "a façade and a deception."

There were two main possibilities. Either a world war would eventually occur, and in its wake it would bring revolution in many countries, or the rising tide of world revolution would stop world war. "The danger of a new world war still exists, and the people of all countries must get prepared. But revolution is the main trend of the world today."*

In January 1975 the consensus of Mao and the collective leadership created to succeed him was that both the possibilities of war and the possibilities of revolution had increased; it was a race between the two.

Hegemonism would create its own antithesis, revolt against it. Of course there would be reverses, tortuous and difficult passages, but the end of imperialism, in all its manifestations, would come. "This new period of history has already begun," said Mao Tsetung.

In June 1969 an international conference of Communist parties was assembled in Moscow. There were gaps — the Vietnamese were strikingly absent, as were other Asian parties. Brezhnev had been foiled in

Edgar Snow "Conversation with Mao Tsetung," *Life* magazine, April 30, 1971, page 46.
  * Mao Tsetung, May 20, 1970.

his attempt to condemn the cultural revolution and Mao, and the conference was uneasily haunted by the ghost of Czechoslovakia. Mao's remark on this search for respectability on the part of the Kremlin was: "The Soviet revisionist clique is like a notorious prostitute who insists on having a monument erected to her chastity."

Brezhnev utilized the conference to suggest an Asian collective security pact. Its meaning was plain. The USSR intended to step into Southeast Asia, into every place, territory, or base which the United States would vacate in its withdrawal — and American withdrawal was already in the air by 1971.

But improved Sino-U.S. relations might lead to a different balance, with China acquiring more influence in Asia and in Southeast Asia in the wake of American departure. Mao Tsetung had already warned that "the affairs of Asia must be run by the Asians themselves." And in the new diplomatic relations China would establish with Asian countries of the Pacific, a very forceful clause opposing "any hegemony" in the region would be introduced.

Hence the USSR since 1970 has redoubled its efforts to obtain influence and to pressure Japan; to establish control in the Indian Ocean; and to obtain a footing in the Philippines, Hong Kong, Singapore, in an attempt to encircle China. In 1971 the treaty of friendship and alliance with India permitted the latter to realize its ambition of smashing Pakistan by leading a military expedition under the pretext of liberating East Pakistan (Bangladesh). Actually the move was to prevent a genuine revolution in Bangladesh, which would have threatened India's Bengal (the other half of Bangladesh, with the same Bengali people, separated by the British at their withdrawal from India in 1947). This treaty with its military (secret) clauses would consolidate the Russian position in South Asia, although the Asian collective security pact itself met with little success among Asian countries desirous of good relations with China. "This so-called collective security is only an anti-China military alliance, but it will not disturb a hair on our heads," said Mao. Since then both Chou En-lai and Teng Hsiao-ping, in talks with Asian heads of state from Thailand and the Philippines, have warned them to be careful, "when they repel the wolf from the front gate, not to let the tiger in the back door." Yet another attempt which failed was an approach made in Washington by the enterprising Victor Louis to test State Department officials regarding joint action against China's nuclear installations. This elicited a cold negative.

Negotiations regarding the contested USSR-China border are still frozen. The Chinese replied affirmatively in June 1969 to the March-April letters from the Kremlin suggesting negotiations. The situation was further clarified in September with a meeting between Kosygin and Chou En-lai which took place at Peking airport.

North Vietnamese leader Ho Chi Minh died in September, leaving in a testament the hope of a reconciliation between China and the USSR. Chou En-lai and Kosygin, as representatives of their respective countries, both flew to Hanoi. On his return trip from Hanoi, Kosygin stopped in Peking, on September 11, for a two-hour meeting with Chou which was described as "frank."

Chou En-lai made three proposals to Kosygin as the basis for negotiations. There was to be an agreement on maintenance of the status quo on the border and the prevention of conflicts; this could be achieved by withdrawing the forces on both sides to an agreed distance from the boundary in the disputed area. The agreement would include a provision for non-use of force and for mutual nonaggression, with no radio and press attacks while negotiations proceeded. A Chinese statement reiterated the Chinese stand for an overall settlement which would not imply acceptance of the "unequal treaties" of the past. The recognition in principle that they were unequal is basic to the Chinese stand, yet the Chinese make no claim to the territories wrested from them — although Lenin had in 1919 condemned all unequal treaties, and in 1920 explicitly declared that the USSR would annul "all the treaties concluded with China by the former governments of Russia, and renounce all seizures of Chinese territory." The Chinese asserted their willingness to take the unequal treaties as the basis for settling the boundary question. In effect, the Chinese want a new, equal treaty, made without military pressure or interference, to replace the old treaties, and a new overall delineation of the frontier, but they do not lay claim to the territory previously wrested from them.*

Despite the understanding Kosygin evinced and verbally reached with Chou at Peking airport, attacks against China were renewed as soon as Kosygin went back to Moscow. The USSR still refuses to agree on maintenance of the status quo on the border, the prevention of armed conflicts, or troop disengagement. "What can their real intention be if not to deceive the Soviet people and world public opinion?"†

---

* Exactly the same procedure was laid down for settlement of the Sino-Indian frontier problem — but this has been, so far, refused by the Indian government.

† Speech by Premier Chou En-lai at the Fourth National People's Congress, January 1975.

In June 1971 Moscow suggested to a convocation of the five nuclear powers (U.S., USSR, PRC, France and Great Britain) that they "examine the problems of nuclear disarmament." The Chinese rejected this offer, which they considered an attempted bribe to establish a "nuclear club." "All the countries of the world, great or small, are equal." "There cannot be a monopoly of decision by a few powers; the question of nuclear disarmament is one which all nations must debate, and not only the few possessors of nuclear weapons." China's nuclear weapons were defensive, she stood for the total elimination, interdiction, destruction of all nuclear weapons, and would never be the first to use one. Would then the U.S. and USSR engage themselves solemnly before the world, as China had done, jointly or separately, never to be the first to use nuclear weapons? And to dismantle nuclear bases outside their territory?

This offer was repeated in 1972 at the United Nations by the Chinese chief delegate, and again in 1973 and 1974. But there has never been a word in reply, either from the U.S. or the USSR.

In October 1971, after the death of Lin Piao, a sudden escalation of virulence against "the Mao faction" occurred in Moscow's propaganda media. It called for the overthrow of Mao, accused of "sowing tension in the Balkans, trying to provoke a military conflict between the U.S. and the USSR, expansionism and great-power chauvinism."

This new verbal assault was related to the visit of Henry Kissinger to Peking in that summer and again later in the year, which provoked accusations of "collusion with the United States," and also to the role of Romania in acting as go-between for America and China.

Romania, Canada and Pakistan all took part in the China-U.S. rapprochement. China gave help to Romania in the calamitous earthquake and floods of 1970, with supplies and an interest-free loan of 250 million dollars. Yugoslavia was also improving her relations with China, and Poland and Hungary showed interest in good relations.

Fury at the Lin Piao failure may also have been a reason. Unofficial views in Peking state that Moscow's rage was as much due to this as to other causes. Another reason was probably that in October 1971, after twenty-two years, the People's Republic of China was admitted to her lawful seat in the United Nations — the greatest diplomatic victory in the history of the U.N.

The rising demand within the United States for a change in policies toward China could not be stemmed forever. Already in 1966 Secretary of State Dean Rusk had had to reply to seven hours of fairly sharp questioning on his foreign policies.[*] Rusk, whose great gifts were marred by a passionate, unreasoning hostility to "Red" China, conjured up visions of "a billion Chinese armed with nuclear weapons over-running Asia." Far from making Americans hysterical, Rusk's anti-China outburst was denounced by James Reston of the *New York Times* for its "yellow peril" flavor. Rusk was accused by Alexander Eckstein — no friend of China's, but in the best American tradition of objective appraisal — of "doing the nation a disservice by picturing a China which is militarily expansionist and aggressive . . . whom have the Chinese overrun? They fought in Korea but that can be clearly documented as a defensive war."

Denunciations by courageous Americans and by a sizable American West Coast business community increased. The embargo on China of 1951 was depriving the U.S. of a market but not depriving the Chinese of required goods, save for some strategic items still today under review.[†]

In January and June 1967 there had been the usual meetings between the U.S. and PRC at ambassadorial level (more than one hundred and thirty by then). The meeting in January 1968 was the only one for that year. In November 1968 the American elections were watched with great care, and the Chinese Ministry of Foreign Affairs then repeated, for clarity, China's stand: withdrawal of U.S. military forces from Taiwan and Taiwan Strait, and conclusion of an agreement on the five principles of peaceful coexistence, would begin the improvement necessary for normalization of relations. Chou En-lai had already told Edgar Snow in 1960 that "the specific steps on when and how" the United States should "withdraw . . . are matters for subsequent discussion."[‡] The Chinese were ready for a period of patient and flexible dialogue and a piecemeal approach, though as a matter of sovereignty always refusing the Dullesian proposal to eschew force in the liberation of Taiwan.

As long as American involvement in the Vietman War continued, and China was committed to total support of the Vietnamese liberation forces "through to the end," Mao and Chou felt that the Taiwan question must not appear to be used as a bribe to influence China's con-

---

[*] Before the Senate Foreign Relations Committee, February 18, 1966.
[†] Nor did it hinder European countries from trading with China.
[‡] Edgar Snow *Red China Today* (New York 1971; revision of *The Other Side of the River*).

duct; the priority was for aid and support to the Vietnamese. China was therefore prepared to wait for normalization of relations with the U.S. until the whole of Indochina was liberated, rather than give up support of Vietnam and Cambodia. In the latter country, a coup instigated and supported by the United States installed the military dictator Lon Nol in March 1970, ousting the chief of state, Prince Norodom Sihanouk. This gave rise to a five-year war of liberation, conducted entirely by the Cambodians themselves, which ended in total military victory, confirming Mao's dictum: "A small and weak nation can certainly defeat a large one . . . Man, not weapons, is the decisive factor."

In August 1969 President Nixon paid a visit, together with Secretary of State Henry Kissinger, to Romania. The central problem of foreign policy discussed with Romanian leaders was relations between the U.S., the USSR and China. Nixon emphasized that the flow of American blood must stop; the Vietnam War must be "Vietnamized." He also regarded communism as no longer a monolithic bloc directed from Moscow. He used the signal phrase "The People's Republic of China" in a toast proposed to Romania's President Nicolae Ceausescu.

In the next few months some small tokens of relaxation occurred. American tourists to Hong Kong were authorized to purchase up to one hundred dollars' worth of Chinese goods (none were permitted before) and American subsidiaries abroad to trade with China. By year's end the Seventh Fleet, patrolling Taiwan Strait, was taken off alert status. American newsmen tried to approach pro-Peking Chinese in Hong Kong and elsewhere. But in 1967–1968 an interdiction had been clamped on Chinese personnel abroad; no talking to Americans. Mao Tsetung would also mention to Edgar Snow that an ultra-left group had opposed Snow's visit to China in those years. The interdiction was lifted in 1970; it is now traced to Lin Piao.

On December 4 an "accidental" encounter at a cocktail party between Chinese and American diplomats led to another ambassadorial level talk (they had been suspended in 1968). But the scale of bombing in Vietnam intensified; and in March-April 1970 the disastrous American invasion of Cambodia and the Lon Nol coup d'etat froze the situation again. Mao gave support to the government of Prince Norodom Sihanouk, the legitimate chief of state, because the coup was patently from outside, not internal. A summit conference of all the Indochinese people attended by Prince Norodom Sihanouk saw Chou

En-lai pledge China's support. All this slowed down the small steps taken by the U.S. and China towards each other.

Lin Piao opposed any rapprochement throughout the year, or any kind of talk with the United States, contending that "imperialism will not lay down the butcher's knife." Quite true, Mao replied, but one must make use of all the contradictions in the enemy camp. There were vast contradictions in America's position; vis-à-vis the USSR, the Third World, Vietnam, and within America itself. Nixon was trying to extricate America from Vietnam. Inflexibility as to principles, but suppleness as to the means of achieving the principles, is Marxist dialectics. "Different forms of flexible tactics in struggle are required . . . in the fight against the enemy."

It was now the Americans who had to wait, and by autumn of 1970 the patience of State Department officials was being sorely tried. Then, on October 1, Mao asked Edgar Snow and his wife to stand next to him on the Tien An Men rostrum. That was a return "signal." In December 1970 Mao finally gave a response in a long interview with Snow. He would be happy to talk with Nixon, since he was the American people's choice, either as a tourist or as President. Nixon was welcome to visit China.

Edgar Snow's report of his interview with Mao Tsetung was published in *Life* magazine, April 30, 1971. And in April, young American ping-pong players had come to Peking — the first break in the wall of containment erected around China. Then, with the arrival of Henry Kissinger in July 1971 to see Premier Chou En-lai and to prepare for Nixon's visit in February 1972, the preliminaries were concluded. The relief and excitement with which Americans greeted the news showed how much it corresponded to what the public wanted.

The spectacular entry of China into the United Nations made it all the more imperative for the United States to mend relations with Mao. The "two-China" and "one China, one Taiwan" policies suddenly crumbled.

The Chinese people, meanwhile, were being educated about the diplomatic change which would occur. Mao's 1940 *On Policy* and 1945 *On the Chungking Negotiations** were reprinted. They contained the essence of Mao Thought on how to deal with various enemy contradictions. Mao asked the Party to be good at grasping the opportunities offered by any struggle, loopholes, or contradictions in the enemy

* See *Selected Works of Mao Tsetung* (English edition Peking 1961–1965), vol. III.

camp, and at waging all kinds of struggles in a flexible manner. Mao had not balked either at negotiating with Chiang Kai-shek; "negotiating is also a form of struggle."

Meanwhile a tidal bore of countries established diplomatic relations with Peking, and the tree-lined highway from airport to city saw a steady stream of heads of state, bunting, flags, dancing, beribboned girls chanting, "Welcome, welcome."

In March 1971 Chou En-lai went to Hanoi, to inform the Vietnamese of the new situation. Korean President Kim Il Sung was also informed, and the Cambodian head of state, Prince Norodom Sihanouk. Chou pledged China's continued and undeviating support to the Indochinese struggle; "not flinching from the greatest national sacrifices." For a while it did look as if the war in Vietnam would be escalated, despite the Paris negotiations between the U.S. and North and South Vietnam.

"Line determines policy, and policy embodies line. Chairman Mao formulates not only the general line and policy but also tactical principles and specific policies for each historical stage."[*] Most of the Chinese people seemed to respond favorably to the idea of normalizing relations with the U.S., though there were reservations. Chou told visiting delegations that if all went well, that would be good, but if nothing came out of Nixon's visit there would be no disappointment either. The fact that the president of the most powerful nation on earth was coming to visit Mao Tsetung, and was excited as a schoolboy, "caught by the magic of China," as *Life* reported, was mentioned without derogatory remarks. With equanimity came hints delineating what China was prepared to talk about and where she was not prepared to compromise.

"Affairs in the world require consultation. The internal affairs of a country must be settled by the peoples of that country, and international affairs must be settled by all concerned through consultation. They must not be decided by two big powers."[†]

Serenely, Mao saw many visitors from the Third World and thanked them. "It is through you that we have regained our seat at the United Nations." He appreciated Nixon's courage in breaking through twenty-two years of determined hostility. When Watergate befell, Mao did not forget that whatever Nixon had done wrong, he had also rendered his country and his people a service in regard to China.

Nixon's arrival in Peking on February 21, 1972, was the most fully

[*] *Red Flag*, no. 9 (September), 1971.
[†] Editorial, *People's Daily*, January 1, 1972, quoting Mao.

televised, commented on, and watched event in the world (bar the American moon landing in July 1969). On the very afternoon of his arrival he met Mao Tsetung. Some hint of what they might talk about had been given to Edgar Snow the previous December, when Snow had an interview with Mao. Mao, in his usual bland, unemphatic way, but full of hints to ponder, had said that there might be self-criticism on both sides; each side finding fault, not with the other but with himself. Since the notion of self-criticism is strange to an American, Mao meant that in order to establish a climate of mutual trust and frankness, there would be no discourteous recriminations. Mao Tsetung kept his word. He was frank about the backwardness of China and about what had been the difficulties in the cultural revolution. This was not a suppliant stance, but fearlessness. He showed that he knew the Americans were no fools; they were fully aware of China's weaknesses but also in need of China. There would be no time for devious quibbling. This establishment of a climate of mutual frankness was important, for it brought out in the subsequent, clear-eyed conversations both the areas of thorough disagreement and those in which improvement in relations could be augured.

In his two previous visits of 1971, Kissinger had developed for Chou En-lai what almost amounted to a personality cult. "Kissinger just fell in love with Chou En-lai," said an American.* Chou's dedication, his self-forgetfulness, appealed to the brilliant but certainly not so modest Kissinger. Kissinger and his aides had prepared the President for his interview with Mao, but Mao created his own all-prevailing weather of humor and good sense, and lucidly went to the heart of the problem. Nixon, never at ease with anyone, hiding his insecurity under a ploy of aggressive phraseology, understood the earthiness, candor, and ease of Mao Tsetung.

"Mao had the quality of being at the center wherever he stood; it moved with him wherever he moved," Kissinger is reported to have said.

"The week that changed the world" was a week of very hard negotiations. From the long hours spent at the negotiating tables issued the document known as the Shanghai joint communiqué. It confirmed the irreversible change that had taken place. There would not be a war between America and China now. Mao's faith that the two peoples, the Americans and the Chinese, would inevitably become friends again

* To the author.

one day, expressed so often through the years, had now seen fruition. And although the important event was not played up by the Chinese — who refused the strident propaganda of a "summit" characteristic of the Nixon-Brezhnev and Ford-Brezhnev encounters — their very caution, denoting a step-by-step approach, showed how seriously they were taking the whole event. There was also perhaps a lingering suspicion that the U.S. might turn back on this policy (although this disappeared after the Nixon-Brezhnev summit and its palpable hollowness).

In the course of the week's negotiations Chou En-lai brought down to hard realities the phraseology of Washington. He told Nixon that the U.S. should first solve the problem of Indochina. "If you remain there, tensions will continue and perhaps escalate . . . How can you then say you will withdraw your bases from Taiwan?" Chou En-lai also told Prince Norodom Sihanouk and the Vietnamese that only U.S. withdrawal would ensure normal relations and the solution of the Taiwan problem. In his banquet speech to Nixon, Chou recalled that in 1955, at Bandung, he had publicly stated that China did not want war with America and was willing to sit down and negotiate. "This is a policy we have pursued consistently."

And so to the joint Sino-U.S. communiqué (the Shanghai joint communiqué) after "extensive, earnest and frank" sessions. The Chinese part of the communiqué stated what Mao in substance had said many times. "Whenever there is oppression, there is resistance. Countries want independence, nations want liberation, and the peoples want revolution . . . this has become the irresistible trend of history. . . . China will never be a superpower and it opposes hegemony and power politics of any kind . . . it firmly supports the struggles of all the oppressed peoples and nations for freedom and liberation." The communiqué restated China's attitude on the main problems in Asia, including Korea, India and Pakistan.

To sabotage Nixon's visit to Peking, the Soviet Union had, since the previous December, launched rumors of an imminent invasion of North Vietnam by the United States, and supplied a great deal of new weaponry to Hanoi. Bombing of North Vietnam had escalated from the American side. This fresh deployment, which bore no relation to the Sino-American situation, nor altered fundamentally the situation in Vietnam, was meant to introduce into the negotiations in Paris elements of disarray which would sabotage the Peking talks. Before Nixon's visit to the USSR in May 1972, Brezhnev would be so anxious to make the meeting a success that he would ask the North Vietnamese in Paris to become more amenable, so as not to "jeopardize . . . delicate negotiations . . . for detente." But it was during a hail of bombs upon North Vietnam, including Hanoi, that Nixon, to bolster the prestige of America, went to Moscow. To show that they did not compromise on principles, the Chinese shipped more weapons and signed a new accord for help to both North Vietnam and the South Vietnam liberation forces a month before the arrival of Nixon in Peking.

The American side of the Shanghai joint communiqué was remarkable for one sentence: "No country should claim infallibility and each country should be prepared to re-examine its own attitudes for the common good." This sentence the Chinese regarded favorably, almost as genuine self-criticism, and worthy of respect. The second paragraph of the U.S. communiqué accepted the principle of peaceful coexistence between states with different social systems, and agreed that international disputes should not be settled by "threats of force." It accepted the right of the peoples of Southeast Asia to shape their future free of military threats. The phrase removed any logical basis for continuing the war in Vietnam on any ideological grounds.

On the question of Taiwan, the joint communiqué states: "The United States acknowledges that all Chinese on either side of the Taiwan Strait maintain there is but one China and that Taiwan is part of China. The United States government does not challenge that position. It reaffirms its interest in a peaceful settlement of the Taiwan question by the Chinese themselves . . . with this prospect in mind, it affirms the ultimate objective of the withdrawal of all the forces and military installations from Taiwan." In the meantime, there would be progressive reduction "as the tension in the area diminishes."

In December 1975 President Ford also visited Peking. His visit was publicized beforehand in America as not directed toward any substantial change in relations with China. "This is not the time for any change on Taiwan," a shrewd American diplomat told the author in 1975, six months before Ford's arrival. Facing the 1976 election, the President could ill afford any major policy moves, and this the Chinese understood well. Vice-Premier Teng Hsiao-ping and other officials had repeatedly stated before the visit that "we are not in a hurry" over the question of Taiwan, which was an internal affair of China's. Although it was well known that if the Chinese should attempt a military takeover of their own territory of Taiwan, the security pact between the

U.S. and Chiang Kai-shek (who died in 1975) would remain a dead letter, they were too statesmanlike for such a show of force. They knew the American people, disgusted and tired with the Vietnam War and defeat, were not going to engage in any military ventures, not even certainly committing themselves (as the Gallup polls showed) to the defense of Western Europe in case of Russian invasion. As Teng Hsiao-ping stated at the banquet in honor of President Ford on December 1, "a problem of greater magnitude confronts us . . . the international situation." Precisely the country talking most noisily about peace and detente constituted "the most dangerous threat of war."

The Chinese made no bones about their view of the phraseology of detente as immoral and dangerous; it lulled the American people into a false sense of security. The Soviet Union was aggressive imperialism, fully deployed. There was implicit blame for Kissinger's hyperintellectual policies. Kissinger seemed to the Chinese to think that by compromise he could "soften" the Kremlin leaders; that because the USSR had great shortages in agriculture (a 60 million ton deficit in grain, with production down to the 1917 level) and consumer goods it would not jeopardize, by aggressive conduct, the supplies, loans, and scientific techniques sorely needed for development. But, the Chinese argue, it is precisely this lack which spurs the "hawks" in the Russian military to further bellicosity; for the whole of the Soviet economy today is lopsided, entirely devoted to yet further aggrandizement of its weaponry, to which other sectors are sacrificed. "Detente" has worn thin as the world's statesmen realize that the Soviet interpretation of the Helsinki agreement* is widely different from that which European and American statesmen hoped it would be. The hardening stand of Soviet doctrinaires, who now urge other Communist parties in Europe to give up "the parliamentary road" and to engage in armed struggle in order to topple "the capitalist system," also shows how little Moscow will abide by any agreement it signs. The Chinese feel that the views of the erstwhile U.S. Defense secretary, James R. Schlesinger, correspond to reality. "Hegemonism . . . despises the soft and fears the tough."

" 'Wind in the tower,/Herald of the approaching storm . . .' and the wind is blowing ever stronger." The Chinese speak of a "new Munich agreement," and recall the deceptive period of 1938, when Chamberlain and Daladier announced "peace in our time" after their visit to

---

* Statement (August 1, 1975) of the summit Conference on Security and Cooperation in Europe, held at Helsinki.

Hitler. "We rely on ourselves, our independence . . . millet and rifles," said Teng Hsiao-ping, recalling Mao's answer to the Americans in 1945, when they tried to persuade him that he could not win because Chiang Kai-shek was so formidably armed (by the United States). "Time and history are on the side of the revolutionary peoples of the world," said Mao Tsetung.

China is part of the Third World, not its leader, but an equal among others. The idea of a new Chinese comintern is far from China's plans. Although the prestige and influence of China in the Third World is great, and many Third World leaders look to Peking as a moral and economic model, Mao enjoins the Chinese leadership to remain "modest and prudent." The speeches of China's delegations at the United Nations, clarifying principles, policy, and issues, have a great effect upon Third World nations. The consistent Chinese support of Third World demands for more equality, for an end to the exploitation to which these nations are subject, introduces a new element of "revolt" on the international scale. But the Chinese do not expect miracles. They well realize the Third World is weak, divided, and will be the battlefields of many more wars by proxy.

Chinese aid to Third World countries is impressive. Between 1955 and 1965, 1.2 billion dollars were given by poor and backward China to Third World countries, and double this (not including the contributions to the wars of liberation in Vietnam and Cambodia) from 1965 to 1974. There are never any conditions or privileges attached to the interest-free (or very low interest) loans, whose repayment time limit is extended whenever necessary. The aim of Chinese aid is not to elicit dependence upon China but to make the recipient country independent and self-reliant, thus denying another base to imperialism. Low-cost projects yielding quicker results, chiefly in light industry, are designed to increase the income of the recipient country and to satisfy its peoples, diminishing economic dependence on cost imports. The training of local technicians cuts out most of the need for continued Chinese presence.

In Western Europe, the place of China is growing steadily; for some years encouragement to a European Common Market strong enough to withstand pressures from the USSR and the U.S., and capable of creating a third independent focus of power, has been Chinese policy. It is consistent with China's main priority, which is a "world united front against dual hegemony." The European nations of the Common Market, on the other hand, are eager to establish good relations, both in trade and in diplomacy, with the People's Republic.

"If one day China should change her color and turn into a super-power; if she too should play the tyrant in the world, and subject others to her bullying, aggression and exploitation, the people of the world should identify her as social-imperialism, expose and oppose it, and work together with the Chinese people to overthrow it."

These words by Teng Hsiao-ping in April 1974 at the United Nations General Assembly were a quotation from Mao, who had already said the same in 1962. For Mao does not believe that any country, even China with her prestigious revolution still with her, can be regarded as faultless, or forever the fount of truth. And it places a responsibility for a critical attitude towards China upon all the peoples of the world.

In his book-lined study, so familiar to the world today, Mao Tsetung has seen history vindicate his fifty years of battles. "Wind in the tower,/Herald of the approaching storm." Today a great wind was sweeping through the world of men, and for Mao it was the wind of dawn, of a new day to begin.

7

Mao Tsetung, Confucius and the Future

Revolution can change everything.
— MAO TSETUNG

Poet and peasant, classicist and Marxist theoretician, master of the strategy of modern war, and liberator of the creative energy of his people, Mao in his thinking and his vision of the world transcends national boundaries. The most important thing he has taught all men is that there is no end, only perpetual beginnings, in a revolution. At eighty-two Mao is as ready as at twenty-two to launch into the future; as determined to press on as when he wrote the poem "Seize the day, seize the hour!" For he knows time unforgiving to the laggard. The acceleration of history, with which this book began, is still the spur for those who make history. "What we have done so far . . . is but a step in a Long March." There remains a great deal to be done.

To change the world and to change man has been man's age-old dream; Mao has shown that man's self-willed transformation is a determining factor in societal change. All moral and ethical values of the past are challenged in this self-remolding; so often they are but props of ancient tyrannies. "History has set us a great task, not only to know the world, but to transform it," said Mao, quoting Marx and speaking as a Communist, in the vanguard of a proletariat whose historical destiny it is to change the world. But for this the proletariat must remold itself as well; the vanguard must constantly overhaul its own assumptions; all too easily can it be perverted and become the very exploiter it sought to lay low. "Socialist society, born out of the old exploiting societies, is . . . still stamped with the birthmarks of the old society from whose womb it emerges," Marx had said. And Mao repeats it.

Another lesson which Mao has taught the world is that in socialism there must be revolution within the revolution; that the people must have the right to revolt against the leadership when it errs. The legitimation of dissent, revolt, is the guarantee for preserving revolutionary purity; as recently as July 1975 Mao stated it was "healthy for our state and our Party" to put up big-character posters, accusing high-ranking officials in the streets of Peking and other cities.*

This perpetual "blooming and contending" is seized upon by those who have not understood Mao's thinking as evidence that China's revolution will fail. There is talk of power struggles and of tensions, instability and internecine conflict at Mao's death; withering corruption and warlordism. How can China achieve the drive, popular mobilization and technological competence for the gigantic task still before her without using material incentives? Zeal and abnegation sooner or later will yield to "revolutionary fatigue." The rising tide of consumer expectations will inevitably catch hold of the Chinese people. Complacency and inertia will slow down, not accelerate, China's progress. So runs the argument against Mao's line today. Mao Tsetung would be the last man to gainsay such dire predictions. "Who can say . . . these are without foundation?" he asked when discussing these expectations of internal degeneration voiced by John Foster Dulles in 1956. "We should maintain the same vigor, the same revolutionary enthusiasm and the same daring, death-defying spirit we displayed in the years of revolutionary war." Every day, for the last five years, the Chinese press has warned against the dangers of revisionism, of capitalist restoration in China. Every day there are exposures of errors and misdeeds; frank and revealing articles debate the two-line struggle and the class struggle which goes on among the eight hundred millions and in the Party.

"Enemies at home and abroad all understand that the easiest way to capture a fortress is from within," said Chou En-lai at the Tenth Party Congress (August 1973). The unconscious slide into revisionism, most dangerous of all enemies, begins in the Party itself, in the superstructure. "It is much more convenient to have the capitalist-roaders in power who have sneaked into the Party do the job of subverting it . . . than for the landlords and capitalists to come to the fore themselves."

Because this danger is ever present, Mao Tsetung and his fast-disappearing generation are striving to accelerate both political and

---

* At the moment another *tatzepao* movement is going on in many educational institutions. Foreign journalists and visitors have been invited to see them and to mingle freely with the students and teachers (December 1975).

economic advance, since one propels the other, and since Communism cannot really be practiced until there is an abundance of material goods to fulfill all needs. Already the next generation (between thirty-five and sixty) are taking over the implementation of major policies. They are the ones who remember the bad old days before 1949; contrast and experience has matured and strengthened them. But what of the next generation? — those born after 1949, or too young to remember what the past was like? It is difficult — unless one has a contrast — to seize the essence of a problem, said Mao. In today's security and modest prosperity, in a society where candor and honesty prevail, how will the young be vigilant enough not only against outside dangers, but above all against the enemy within their own selves? "We must learn to arm ourselves against ourselves," said Madame Soong Ching-ling.* This is even more true of the third generation, those under thirty-five now rapidly filling sectors of activity in China.

Since 1971, and Lin Piao's death, the consciousness of this danger — revisionism, capitalist restoration — has haunted Mao more than ever. In 1966 already he had written to his wife Chiang Ching: "If the right stages an anti-Communist coup d'etat in China, I am sure they will know no peace either and their rule will most probably be short-lived . . . because it will not be tolerated by the revolutionaries who are 90 percent of the people."† But because the system was not yet consolidated enough, "if people like Lin Piao come to power, it will be quite easy for them to rig up a capitalist system."‡

It is in the full knowledge of this danger that consolidation and political education movements have been undertaken since 1971. The Tenth Party Congress of August 1973 and the new Party constitution; the National People's Congress of January 1975 and the new state constitution which replaces the 1954 constitution; the movements against Confucius and for the establishment of the dictatorship of the proletariat — all are geared towards the ultimate goal: speeding up the continuing revolution of China to attain communism as swiftly as possible.

The stimulus which made this acceleration possible is undoubtedly the Lin Piao affair, since criticism of Lin Piao, linked to the anti-Confucius drive, is still going on years after his death.

---

* Author's private interview with Madame Soong, who is vice-chairwoman of the National People's Congress.
† Letter to Chiang Ching (see pages 277–279).
‡ Said by Mao in 1972 or 1973.

"A bad thing . . . can turn into a good one." The negative lesson of Lin Piao brought about a profound psychological change among the Chinese millions. One instance is the succession issue.

As we have seen, Mao, after his visit to Moscow in 1957, was perturbed by the changes in the USSR and the crisis of succession after Stalin. He then tried to establish a succession, for he was aware of the deep-rooted tradition of the Chinese people that demands incarnation of supreme authority in one individual. Even up to the early 1960's peasants would come to kneel before the portrait of Mao in Heavenly Peace Square in Peking and say: "We have a new emperor." This, and the manifestations of the personality cult, were difficult to eradicate, both in the people and in the Party. In fact Mao himself was to use the personality cult deliberately (as he told Edgar Snow in 1965*) to rally adherents when preparing for the cultural revolution and to redress the "ultra-left" situation of 1967. He was also the first to cut it down in 1970.

By 1964 Mao's views on succession had changed; no single person could be really entrusted with an authority compared to his own. He was beginning to doubt Liu Shao-chi, and he realized that a collective leadership could not stand up against a single unscrupulous figure, who would not exhibit the integrity, forbearance and compunction Mao had shown in using power, because the masses were still not aware of the danger. Mao's most fetching quality is perhaps his candid and prolonged faith in his colleagues and comrades. "People can change, can't they?" he said in October 1966, when he was still trying to save Liu Shao-chi. But in 1971, after Lin Piao's treachery, it was a sad Mao who observed: "It seems very difficult for those who have committed gross errors of line to change." Undeniably, Lin Piao's betrayal caused Mao great personal grief.

In order to assure his heritage, Lin Piao had utilized a tradition far older than Marxism: that of the Confucian ruler, superman, genius, representing heaven's will, adhering to "the rites" and tradition. "Collective leadership weakens personal responsibility," said Lin Piao. "On his part there was a process of development and self-exposure, and on our part there was also a process of getting to know him," said Chou En-lai later (August 1973).

In 1964 Mao began his great campaign for training a generation of "successors," not one but "millions of them." This is to be the Party's central task; it enforces a handing over of power, not to a small clique

* See Edgar Snow *The Long Revolution* (New York 1972), pages 19 and 71.

but to the masses in general. And it makes collective leadership essential. The new constitution of January 1975 repeats: "All power in the People's Republic of China belongs to the people," who are to exercise this power through elected people's congresses at all levels, and have the power to supervise the deputies elected and to replace them at any time according to provisions of law.

The shock of Lin Piao's treachery and death (and it was a shock; in Peking itself posters representing Lin Piao were still up until about three weeks after his death) was salutary; it wrenched millions away from their traditional demand for a father-image incarnation of power; suddenly the two-line struggle made sense for many who had been puzzled by it.*

Lin Piao's short dominance represented a tendency ingrained in the minds of the Chinese people: the acceptance of authoritarianism. "There's something wrong in our minds and we've got to eradicate it." That something wrong was grounded in Confucianism. Hence the denunciation of Lin Piao and Confucius together, representing everything retrograde, evil, counterrevolutionary, and revisionist.

The discovery of betrayal "among the highest" made the idea of a collective leadership acceptable and popular. It was now imperative that there be more and better understanding of political theory, so that it would be more difficult for another Lin Piao to rise. "We should study more, read more Marxist-Leninist works," said Mao. Lenin had said that "On the ground cleared of one bourgeois generation, new ones continually appear as long as the ground gives rise to them."

Besides the positive features arising from the Lin Piao affair, there is an obverse, a mood of disenchantment and cynicism among some of the young educated people and the young workers. Lin Piao had utilized the appeal of fascism (the 516), promising power and prestige to some of these youths. And now the hard facts were anonymity, abnegation, and manual labor for the young to prove worthy successors. The affair also helped to revive some of the right-wing arguments. "So Liu Shao-chi was not so bad after all" was a comment heard in Peking when Lin Piao was condemned as a "superspy . . . who wanted to capitulate to Soviet . . . social-imperialism."†

However, these reactions do not represent the mainstream, which is the vigorous prosecution of revolutionary advance, based on educating

---

* This puzzlement was expressed by a good many in private interviews with the author. "Like peas in a frying pan, we couldn't see what was outside the pan."

† Chou En-lai at the Tenth Party Congress, August 1973.

and bringing up "contingents of Marxist-Leninist theoreticians" from among the workers and peasants. This means a very prolonged grounding and practice in the Marxist classics.

The Lin Piao affair pinpointed the danger of recrudescent warlordism. This too was tackled with success. Nowhere is the Party's ideological strength more evident than in the restoration of civilian authority (with Teng Hsiao-ping, vice-premier, as chief of staff and Chang Chunchiao, another vice-premier, as political commissar of the PLA). By 1972 temporary military organs of management had vanished from schools, factories, and communes. The purges of Lin Piao's adherents in the PLA cut a wide swath in the central military units, but there was little change in provincial and regional units. Forty-one military and four "masses" members of the Ninth Central Committee were dropped (this includes ten* who died); seven members and one alternate member of the Politburo were purged; 75 percent of the leaders removed or shifted belonged to Lin Piao's former Fourth Field Army. The militia (twelve million compared to less than three million in the PLA) were placed under revolutionary committee control in factories and in communes; the militia are being increasingly armed, thus making a military coup exceedingly difficult. The reinstatement of twenty-six former Party secretaries, of military leaders whom Lin Piao had purged or humiliated, the placing of the Ministry of Defense under Party aegis, with the chairman of the Central Committee as commander-in-chief in supreme control of all the armed forces, are all measures destined to curb military power, retain the PLA as essentially a work and production force serving the people and obeying Party policies. "Without a people's army the people have nothing."†

Another substantial gain was the marked rise of mass membership at the Tenth Party Congress, 75 percent of the Central Committee now being of worker, peasant or soldier origin (soldiers are the "masses" inside the PLA). This significant broadening of the political base, a promotion of younger successors, the reinstatement of 90 percent of Party units at basic level all indicate the "overall leadership of the Party over all sectors . . . including the army."

Despite rectifications and purges, the cultural revolution seems to have hit no more than 1 percent of pre–cultural revolution Party personnel; possibly 2 to 3 percent among the higher ranks in central

---

* With Lin Piao in the Trident crash: six. Of old age: four.

† On *Coalition Government*, April 24, 1945. *Selected Works of Mao Tsetung* (English edition Peking 1961–1965), vol. III, pages 296–297. See also *The Morning Deluge*, page 437.

administrative units. The increase of provincial representation in the Tenth Central Committee, with only 37 percent of the members coming from central organs (77 percent in the Eighth, elected by the Liu-dominated 1956 Party Congress), also has made one-man rule difficult.

The active promotion of the continued revolution now hinges on the vital relationship between Party and masses, without the pressure of a military apparatus. There remains one puzzle; and that is whether or not Mao, who also sought to abolish in China the Soviet type of secret police methods (he is on record as having criticized methods which do not adhere to the mass line) has been successful in that sector too. Mao has always strenuously fought against a KGB type of apparatus, which could be used by some clique within the Party towards right-wing restoration.*

"For a long time to come there will still be two-line struggles within the Party . . . ten, twenty, thirty times . . . Lin Piaos will appear again, and so will persons like Wang Ming, Liu Shao-chi, Peng Teh-huai." Thus Chou En-lai, quoting Mao, who had said that even when communism was reached, there would still be contradictions and struggles, albeit in a different form. Even then "some people like Chiang Kai-shek" might still emerge.

The difference is that now people expect such confrontations. The secrecy which surrounded intra-Party struggle and caused a shock every time a crisis occurred is being openly criticized by some of the younger "masses." There is at present possibly too much gossip about the continuing struggle, surmise about who is at loggerheads with whom, which caused Red Flag in October 1974 to admonish people "not to listen to alleyway rumor-mongering."

Because the masses now feel they have a right to know, and read the press with so much greater political acumen and critical sense than before the cultural revolution, the two-line struggle may somewhat change in aspect. Explosive situations peter out under the weight of public opinion (inevitable as the arguments develop), and new and as yet unpredictable forms of "struggle" may now occur.

"Chairman Mao has laid down for our party the basic line and policies for the entire historical period of socialism and also specific

---

* And which Liu Shao-chi seems to have used, as witness Mao's previous remarks on "secret" methods of public security. Any police investigation, Mao said in 1962, must also follow the "mass line."

lines and policies for specific work."* In the new Party statutes, and also in the new state constitution of January 1975, Marxism–Leninism–Mao Tsetung Thought is held as guide to thought and action. Thus Mao is consecrated as Lenin's true continuator (as is indeed obvious to anyone reading Mao). Abundant new quotations and publications of the works of Marx and Lenin, together with Mao's, are circulated for study throughout all China. Quotations from Stalin's writings, though mentioned in publications for external consumption, are very scarce in China itself.

The Tenth Party Congress sought to consolidate the new acquisitions of the cultural revolution by creating methods and channels whereby revolt against an erroneous leadership and dissent were legitimized. This meant a total break with traditional Soviet methods, and also with previous authoritarianism in the Chinese Party. The new Party constitution emphasizes the right of the masses to exercise supervision over cadres both in the Party and in state organizations, and the duty of cadres to "arouse" the masses in great movements. The right of dissent of the individual Party member himself is also established once again.† "If a Party member holds different views with regard to the decisions or directives of Party organizations he is allowed to reserve his views and has the right to bypass the immediate leadership and report directly to higher levels up to and including the Central Committee and the chairman of the Central Committee . . . it is absolutely impermissible to suppress criticism and to retaliate." Nevertheless, as both Chou En-lai and Wang Hung-wen (the young Shanghai worker now vice-chairman of the Party) made clear, there are still Party cadres who do suppress and retaliate. A recent example (July 1975) occurred with the setting up of big-character posters by some workers who complained they had been prevented from airing their views, despite this right guaranteed in the new constitution. These posters appear to have been torn down by the security police.‡ The new state constitution does indeed guarantee the rights of citizens to express opinions, freely air views, put up big-character posters; it guarantees freedom of speech,

---

* Chou En-lai, report at the Tenth Party Congress, August 1973.

† Already mentioned in the Party constitution of April 1969. This clause was added, it is reported, by Mao Tsetung.

‡ The author was told by some cadres in 1974 that posters put up were counter-revolutionary "nonsense" and removed to avoid "misleading the masses." But unless the mass line is applied and people trusted to judge for themselves and to debate, arbitrary removal may diminish trust in the leadership; in some cities posters were freely displayed to the author, even when they were utter nonsense.

inviolability of correspondence, freedom of religion, association, demonstration, and freedom to strike — the latter expressly inserted into the constitution by Mao Tsetung himself. But even with all these, the "two-line struggle" against authoritarianism will certainly continue; criticism of cadres who still "cannot bear to hear a different opinion" appears frequently in the Chinese press. It is important for China's future development that a new permeability and communication between the Party and the masses be achieved, "a political situation in which there are both centralism and democracy, both discipline and freedom, both unity of will and personal ease of mind and liveliness" (Mao, 1957).

A reinforcement of Mao's democratic centralism was the promotion of the slogan "Going against the tide," launched at the Tenth Party Congress. It had begun as a series of discussions, one of them concerning production teams who resisted the abolition of private plots in the "ultra-left" wave. This abolition was coupled with a distribution of all accumulation funds; both actions were harmful to the collective spirit and thus to socialism. Long debates ensued on what were "material incentives . . . capitalist tendencies," and what was "rational recompense for work done." In some factories the leadership of Party cadres returned to offering bonuses and material incentives to stimulate production from workers; workers denounced this as a reversion to "bourgeois thinking" and refused.

The principle of "going against the tide" was now affirmed as "a Marxist-Leninist principle." Both Lenin and Mao had gone against the tide in their day. "When like a surging tide the wrong tendency came up in the Party most people followed it, only a few withstood it," said Chou En-lai. "When confronted with issues that concern the line and the overall situation, a true Communist must act without any selfish considerations and dare to go against the tide, fearing neither removal from his post, expulsion from the Party, imprisonment, divorce, nor guillotine," said Wang Hung-wen, quoting Mao. Of course, it remains to discern what is truly "going against the tide" in order to promote socialism, and what are attempts against it.

Already in December 1973, shortly after the Tenth Congress, the *Kuangming Daily** was evoking a recrudescence of Party struggle, appealing to Party activists to prepare for the appearance of "an erroneous tendency" and calling for "going against the tide." Mao

* A Peking daily discussing mainly intellectual topics — literature, philosophy, etc.

Tsetung was said to have appealed once again to the Party to submit to mass criticism. A saying of his circulated, "Water too pure breeds no fish, too harsh a teacher has no pupils," as a warning to extreme purists and a hint that Party members must accept criticism. On June 30, 1974, an editorial for the Party's fifty-third anniversary called for all cadres to listen to the masses. Throughout that year there were sporadic rashes of posters denouncing the misdeeds of Party members in all of China's cities. There was also some turbulence, both in the factories and in universities. At the time the anti-Lin Piao, anti-Confucius movement was fanning out across the land, and "monsters and freaks" would come up. In this case it was groups active during the cultural revolution and later dissolved; they considered they had been unjustly treated. In Wuhan, the students of Wuhan University and the steelworkers once again united, as in 1967, and battled a local military commander of the garrison and another group of students from Hupeh University. In other cities there was hooliganism, and worker provosts and their militia patrolled the streets and the factories to prevent arson or other violence. It is certain that the new freedoms can also be used by counterrevolutionary factions. In the summer of 1974 there were rumors of a "wind of communization," with ultra-left manifestations, and the reaction from a majority of the people was hostile and fearful, in expectation of another 516 wave. It led to thousands of demands from overseas Chinese to leave the country to escape harassment (45,000 being granted exit permits that year). This explains why, in his major article *On Exercising All-Round Dictatorship Over the Bourgeoisie* (*Red Flag*, April 1975), Vice-Premier Chang Chun-chiao was to refer to the fears aroused by a "wind of communization." Such winds had been previously stirred by Liu Shao-chi (in 1958 during the Great Leap) and Chen Po-ta (in 1958 and during the cultural revolution in 1967). Some people who feared real communism deliberately provoked extremism, said Chang; they confused "contradictions among the people" with "enemy contradictions." On the contrary, the problem now was a "bourgeois wind" blowing about, which the present political drives must expose and eradicate.

All this illustrates the complexity of the continued revolution; its very advance and achievements give birth to new contradictions all the time. By October 1974 all the members of the Central Committee and the alternates, all provincial secretaries and secretaries of municipalities, trade union leaders, Communist Youth League leaders, and in some cases the entire leadership of a region had "gone down" to do manual labor, to live, eat and work with peasants and workers, in order to gain firsthand knowledge of the real problems among the masses. This is the recommended Mao procedure of personal investigation: "Do not rely on the reports of secretaries only."

The results were to shape the National People's Congress and the current political movements; to make possible renewed Party unity after what seems to have been eighteen months of seesaw debate. For the NPC was certainly much delayed, and the author was frankly told why. "We want to have even better unity before opening it."*

"Unite for one purpose, that is the consolidation of the dictatorship of the proletariat," Mao had said at the Ninth Party Congress (April 1969). The Tenth Party Congress, and the National People's Congress which followed, were decisively oriented towards the next step in political advance. For every Marxist must recognize and accept — otherwise he is not a Marxist — that in the transition from socialism to communism there is the dictatorship of the proletariat, which means that the bourgeoisie must not be allowed to subvert the state in any form whatsoever. To this end the constitution, the anti-Lin Piao and anti-Confucius drive, and the present movement against "bourgeois right"† and for the dictatorship of the proletariat have been personally launched by Mao Tsetung himself.

The anti-Lin Piao anti-Confucius movement started at the end of 1973. It is said to be "crucial," is a continuation of the cultural revolution, and strives to eradicate the "four old" tyrannies — ideas, tradition, behavior and customs — which still fetter and inhibit the minds of so many. In this movement the participation of women is of first importance. It is by far the most articulate drive yet undertaken, requiring a high level of reasoning, self-expression, and study and historical research from participants. It has seen erudite scholars and erstwhile Confucians engaged in new reappraisals of historical events; and the new contingents of Marxist theoreticians arising from the proletariat — "the main force of the movement" — are educating themselves in history, research, politics by continuous study and discussion, examining their own actions, thought and speech. The movement has witnessed an inspiring rise in woman consciousness and prowess. Already the cultural revolution was something of a watershed for woman's libera-

---

* Said to the author in Peking, September 1974.
† The legal justification for profit, private accumulation of wealth through exploitation, and other "rights" of the bourgeoisie.

tion, with women workers and women peasants of all ages participating massively in political activities. This campaign has mobilized them further by focusing upon the cultural and psychological pressures, the accepted tyranny to which women have submitted in the past. Every village, factory or urban street has seen women champion this drive, examine their own condition, debate all issues, great and small. Schoolchildren have questioned their teachers' dogmatism, and university students have voluntarily confessed that they reached the university "through the back door" — through the influence of a father who was a prominent Party cadre or PLA man — and have voluntarily given up their studies to return to labor, thus rejecting the Confucian ideal "Become an official and do honor to your family." Marriages between university students and peasants and workers are publicized; admission of women to the Party is now rising significantly. According to the figures, around 22 percent of the 28 million Party members in 1973 were women, but in 1959 it was averred that there were 18 percent. The percentage has not risen considerably, but now it must, and 35 to 40 percent of new Party recruits will probably be women. Revolutionary committees at all levels must be 30 percent women; many now exceed this figure, with up to 60 or 80 percent of the leadership (in textile factories) women cadres in top positions.

The drive furthermore stimulates the family planning movement, begun again in 1971 after a lapse during the cultural revolution.* Contraception and the liberation of woman go together; but the movement also is to achieve the necessary ratio between population planning and economic planning. The two-child family is now the ideal; girl children are to be considered "as good as boys," and to limit the family is a progressive "anti-Confucian" act. "Woman shoulders half of heaven," said Mao poetically. "Without the emancipation of women, there can be no fully consolidated socialism." In this Mao follows Lenin and Marx: "Great social changes are impossible without feminine ferment," said Marx; and Lenin: "The proletariat cannot achieve its own complete emancipation until it has won complete emancipation for women."

Many studies now shed light on the prolonged struggled between legalist and Confucianist schools in China's past. The legalists promoted scientific development and investigation and held a materialist

---

* Han Suyin "Population Growth and Birth Control in China," *The Conference Board Record* (New York), October 1973, and *Eastern Horizon* (Hong Kong), vol. XII, no. 5, 1973.

view of nature. Confucianism was responsible for China's scientific stagnation and lack of curiosity; it held that "nothing must disturb the harmony of heaven." "We should sum up our history from Confucius to Sun Yat-sen. This is important for guiding the movement today," Mao said. This self-analysis of a whole people, studying out of their souls their own prejudices, is indeed a feat of social engineering with no parallel in history. Rehabilitation of past "rebels," shunned by Confucianist China, includes that of the first emperor, Ch'in Shih-huang (220 to 209 B.C.), who unified China, promoted medicine and agriculture, completed many irrigation works, and burned Confucian books and killed Confucian scholars who sought to bring back the slave system of the past. Lin Piao had compared Mao to Ch'in Shih-huang. Confucianism is being "reasoned to death" to clear the foundations of the Chinese mind, and the movement may last "throughout the whole historic period of socialism." It will certainly take some decades to eradicate a mental tyranny of two and a half thousand years.

The Fourth National People's Congress (January 1975) was a milestone in this vast program for the consolidation of the political system and accelerated development of the economy. Communism cannot be practiced unless there is an abundance of material goods, and China is hastening towards both these goals, which are irrevocably linked.

There were 2,864 delegates, 74 percent of them workers and peasants who had won recognition in the great struggles of the past two decades. The range was very large, from erstwhile and remolded "bourgeois" academicians through nuclear physicists to poor peasants. There were representatives of all the national minorities and of the religions (one for the Christian religion). The oldest delegate was over one hundred years old, and the youngest barely nineteen.

Mao Tsetung was not present, deliberately so. The time to hand over power and responsibility had come, and this emphasis was obvious throughout the Congress; delegates revealed a solemn emotion and a sense of the new responsibilities, for they had to prepare themselves to carry out Mao's policies without Mao. It was evident that Chou En-lai, whose health was frail, was also handing over; Teng Hsiao-ping and Chang Chun-chiao were the new team to take his place.

But if China had already entered the after-Mao period, the policies and program for it had been drawn up by Mao. For by 1975, just as in 1955, Mao Tsetung had put the finishing touches to yet another accelerated strategy for development for China.

This was clear from Chou En-lai's speech, which was a summary of both past success and future goals. Thirteen years of good harvests; 190 percent industrial increase from 1964 to 1974, 330 percent in industrial chemical fertilizers and 650 percent in petroleum (100 million tons by 1976). And so on for many other items.* China's situation was excellent, her international prestige had never been so high. Quoting Mao repeatedly, Chou told how Mao in 1964–1965 had elaborated a two-stage program for development; the first stage, to begin in 1966, to build a self-reliant and relatively complete industrial and economic system by 1980; the second stage to achieve by the year 2000 the modernization of agriculture, industry, national defense, science and technology to reach "the first ranks of the world."† This splendid goal would now be carried out. To do so would mean hard and strenuous effort, dedication, unity, and of course politics in command. The superstructure must be constantly propelled forward to new and appropriate structures, not to lag behind the economic base. Revisionism, capitalist tendencies, servility, "snailism," waste and squandering must be criticized and curbed at all times. The slogans of the Great Leap Forward, self-reliance, doing away with old myths, burying servility and dogmatism and studying all experiences of other nations, good and bad, must continue to guide the accelerated strategy of development.

The new constitution, replacing the 1954 constitution, proclaimed that the PRC "is a socialist state of the dictatorship of the proletariat led by the working class and based on the alliance of workers and peasants," whereas the former had used the words "a democratic dictatorship of the people based on the alliance of workers and peasants." This meant that the main struggle now was the eradication of the bourgeoisie; again, not physically, but of its influence in all forms. For it was "bourgeois recurrence" which was the main threat, and "subversion by imperialism and social-imperialism" would be much easier with nests of bourgeois within China. These threats could be countered only by the dictatorship of the proletariat over the bourgeoisie to curb all manifestations of capitalist recurrence, large or small.

Immediately after the NPC sessions the new drive began, heralded by two major articles, one by Yao Wen-yuan, the polemicist and writer whose 1965 and 1966 attacks on Wu Han and others had started the

---

* Chou En-lai, speech on the work of government at the Fourth National People's Congress, January 13, 1975.

† This was the program on which Mao could not obtain consensus because of Lin's obstruction in December 1964 – January 1965.

cultural revolution in earnest, and the other by Chang Chun-chiao.*

There is no obvious bourgeois class in China; but the example of Lin Piao and his supporters showed how easily it could resurrect. Where, how, in what manner was a new bourgeoisie engendered in a socialist state? How could it be curbed and prevented from usurping power? This is the meaning of the "dictatorship of the proletariat" over the tenacious bourgeoisie.

In 1969 Mao Tsetung remarked that there were still a fairly large number of factories "whose leadership is not in the hands of genuine Marxists." And this is repeated in 1975 by Chang Chun-chiao. The latter — who since 1958 has been writing on socialist forms of owner-ship — warned at the NPC in January 1975 that in some enterprises "the form is that of socialist ownership but the reality is that their leadership is not in the hands of Marxists and the masses of workers." Apparently some are still in the hands of private individuals even today!

So after all these years the problem of industrial management still remains, even if on a minor scale. Despite propaganda, the Anshan Constitution promulgated by Mao is still not applied everywhere. And part of the turbulence in some factories† in 1974 was due to this state of affairs.

"There is no ten-thousand-li Great Wall between the working class and the bourgeoisie in the old society . . . in the transition period, *all* need to transform themselves" (Mao, 1974). The proletariat is not born with *a priori* Marxist correctness; it also has to remold itself; and only when it achieves the emancipation of all mankind will it also be eman-cipated. The lesson of the USSR was that a neo-bourgeoisie, a new exploiting class, could crop up as a "state capitalist monopolist bour-geoisie of bureaucrats and state functionaries" which would have even more power than ordinary capitalists, with no competition to curb it. The crux of the matter was in the problem of ownership. Who *really* owns the industries, agriculture, the various sectors of the economy? Who really is the decision maker?

Lenin had already analyzed the problem. "Small production engen-ders capitalism and the bourgeoisie continuously, daily, hourly, spon-taneously, and on a mass scale." "This also occurs among a section of

---

* Yao Wen-yuan *On the Social Basis of the Lin Piao Anti-Party Clique*, *Red Flag*, no. 3 (March), 1975. Chang Chun-chiao *On Exercising All-Around Dicta-torship Over the Bourgeoisie*, *Red Flag*, no. 4 (April), 1975.

† As reported in *Le Monde* and the *New York Times* in April-May 1975, a strike occurred in a factory in Hangchow. It was settled within a month.

the workers and a section of the Party members," added Mao Tsetung. "*Both within the ranks of the proletariat* and among the personnel of state organs there are people who follow the bourgeois style of life."

Already the various contradictions arising from the spurt of advance could be seen in China. To summarize them:

(*a*) *Recrudescent elitism in education.* The demand for accelerated technical progress, with the ensuing and very rapid rise in living standard in certain sectors, has led to another surge of elitism among highly trained students. In big-character posters, their views are exposed.* The need for accelerated technological progress requires an enormous upsurge in technical staff, yet the system is dead set against the emergence of a technocracy. In some universities a bitter wrangle has been going on, with students highly trained in automation saying: "We shall never be just ordinary workers." A poster war has been going on in Shenyang (Manchuria) for some weeks over this and other aspects of technical education.

The link uniting universities and factories is being reinforced; and as for the youths sent to the countryside (ten million of them in the last five years), correspondence courses are now available to them. In a number of cases rural areas found difficulty in integrating them. In some, the relations became very bad indeed, with ill-treatment and even rape of some girl students, but this is only a very small minority of cases. Now the educated youth "go down" with their teachers, and continue to study while doing manual labor. Cases of corruption, of the sons and daughters of high-ranking Party members getting into universities without going through mass selection, also figure in the "bourgeois thinking" which is assailed.

(*b*) *Malpractice among cadres.* This is now denounced very swiftly. Big-character posters are put up. There are occasional cases of retaliation.

(*c*) *Capitalism.* Capitalism in the countryside, the rise of "economism," and spontaneous capitalism have been noted recently.

(*d*) *Material incentives.* Bonuses, technocratism in industry, persistence of Soviet-type management.

Again Lenin is quoted by Mao: "In the first phase of Communist society (usually called socialism), bourgeois right is not abolished in its entirety but only in part . . . it continues to exist in the capacity of regulator (determining factor) in the distribution of products and the

---

* See Leo Goodstadt "Assessing a Worker's Worth," *Far Eastern Economic Review,* June 20, 1975.

allotment of labor . . . the socialist principle 'He who does not work, neither shall he eat'* is already realized . . . but this is not yet communism, and it does not yet abolish 'bourgeois right,' which gives to unequal individuals, in return for unequal (really unequal) amounts of labor, equal amounts of products."

Here then is the problem. It is "bourgeois right," and it prevails still in socialist society. "China is a socialist country. Before Liberation, she was more or less like capitalism [a capitalist country]," states Mao. "Even now she practices an eight-grade wages system, distribution to each according to his work and exchange by means of money, which are scarcely different from those in the old society. What is different is that the system of ownership has changed."

It is on this system of ownership that Chang Chun-chiao writes with clarity. A large part of the assets and resources is not yet the common property of the whole society but belongs to autonomous groups, such as communes. Although the new constitution recognizes only two kinds of ownership (by the whole people, and socialist collective ownership as in communes and a good many factories), who is really "in ownership" in decision-making power, and earning higher emoluments through it, is what matters. In the communes, the basic accounting is at production team level, which maintains inequality between production teams in the same commune. The communes are collectively owned, not state-owned. They comprise 90 percent of the land (state farms account for only 10 percent). The production teams still control over half the fixed assets in agriculture, and may refuse to "graduate" to the brigade or commune for accounting because it would mean the more prosperous ones would have to share with poorer ones. And in all these gaps lies the danger; it is also a hindrance to more speedy mechanization in the countryside. This breeding ground for inequality produces "bourgeois right." To maintain this inequality is to help capitalism recur.†

Another area lies in the differences in salaries, privileges, etc., which still exist between management, technicians and workers; mental and physical labor; town and country. It is to this situation that Chang Chun-chiao draws attention. Yet another is the method of distribution

* Quoted in the new state constitution of January 1975.
† In September 1974 the author attempted to discuss this question and to suggest that basic accounting should be at brigade level to mitigate inequalities and to help further mechanization. But the cadres in this particular commune reminded her sharply that "basic accounting at production team level is guaranteed for thirty years." This was certainly conservative on the part of the cadres!

of wages according to work points in the communes, which confirms existing and inevitable individual inequality.* Then there are the eight grades of wages in administration and in industrial units; actually they work out to thirty-odd gradations if length of tenure and marginal benefits are taken into account.

There is the "bourgeois style" of living — what Chang calls the "bourgeois wind," which is stirred up by those people "who have turned into bourgeois elements. Some are leading cadres . . . They scramble for position and gain and feel proud instead of ashamed of this. Some have reached the point of looking at everything as a commodity, including themselves. They join the Communist Party and do some work for the proletariat merely for the sake of upgrading themselves as commodities, and asking the proletariat for higher prices."

This wholesale denunciation of the "bourgeois wind" emphasizes the constant vigilance which must be exercised. This can only be done with the most open debate and permeability to criticism from the lower levels upward.

Only a proletariat imbued with scientific Marxist ideas, with a commitment to them, and occupying positions in all sectors, including the universities, the news media, and the administration, can curb and control this perennial rise of "bourgeois" ideas. Once the proletariat allow the newly engendered bourgeoisie — who resent participation in physical labor, who resist having their children work in the countryside and use influence, corruption, and pressure to get them into universities, who will spout but not perform; and who still put family ties, clan ties, above the public good — into positions where they can manipulate government machinery, then China will surely slide into the same state as the USSR, a "state capitalist monopoly bourgeoisie" of bureaucrats and state functionaries. For bourgeois right, finally, is propped up by those within socialist society who are stronger and more resourceful, the elite within the superstructure, who turn even collective ownership, even the new relations of production, to their own personal advantage because of the inequalities which still persist. And this is done by *legal* means, by the concurrence of habit and custom. Therefore, the mere conversion of the means of production to common property without removing the inequalities in status and in purchasing power or access to goods, without removing the inequality between

---

* Lenin has also written of the "inevitable inequality" between men, which the more resourceful will use to their own personal advantage rather than for the good of all.

town and countryside, mental and manual labor, elite and other personnel, engenders this neo-bourgeoisie all the time. The inevitable inequality of all men will continue to prevail as long as products are divided according to the amount of labor performed; and that is a standard kept in socialist society.

What, then, is to be done?

Just as in 1949, there are in China today a right tendency which wants no change, or change so slow that political advance is endangered, and a left wing which wants immediate and drastic change. Both will damage the goal of accelerated political and economic advance. It is necessary once again to read Mao Tsetung, to see how he functioned in leading the tremendous advance of the Chinese people, step by step, never faltering but flexibly, from medieval to modern times in less than three decades.

The meaning of "all-round dictatorship over the bourgeoisie" in all spheres and at all stages of development is precisely this awareness and curbing in the ideological sphere, in order to abolish all classes and all class distinctions, all the relations of production and the social relations corresponding to them which give rise to classes. This really means a wholesale revolution of *all the ideas* that result from past social relations. "It's dangerous to stop halfway," warns Chang; yet "within a short period no basic change" can be brought into the situation; no converting of all collective ownership (the three-tier level of ownership in communes) to ownership by the whole people, although this is the weak point of the structure. Only careful, vigilant restriction to prevent capitalism in the countryside from re-emergence can do it, and over a certain period of years.

Will this political leap forward jeopardize economic advance? Will there be resistance to it on such a scale that China will become "revisionist"?

The experience of the last twenty-five years disproves this contention. Despite all dire predictions, China has been advancing so swiftly in the building of her own prosperity because of, not in spite of, the swift ideological prosecution of the revolution. But it will mean that turbulent two-line struggling will continue. From now on it will consciously involve — for it must — the majority, the masses.

In September 1975 vigorous action was launched to implement this twenty-five-year Great Leap Forward to come. It started with agriculture. A month-long conference took place, attended by most of the top leaders and headed by Vice-Premier Hua Kuo-feng. It was designed to accelerate agricultural development by expanding still more the example of Tachai brigade. Mechanization of agriculture, said Hua Kuo-feng, must be basically completed within the next five years (by 1980).*

Restructuring of all the arable fields in China, to prepare for mechanization, was already visible in October, even in Szechuan and Tibet (visited by the author in October and November 1975). Nor did this effort at the agricultural base take place apart from the rest of the economy or the superstructure. At the same time, major conferences were held on the coal industry, on the steel industry; a Party rectification, again to shake the ever-recurrent evil of bureaucracy, began in November 1975, and a movement in education, with *tatzepao* and an "open door," in December.†

Meanwhile, the twelve million or more educated youths sent down to the countryside were also being taken in hand for more efficient service to the program. In Chengtu, in late October 1975, a major conference took place;‡ thousands of delegates flocked there, elected by the educated youth now in the countryside. This innovation will create for the youth their own representation, and voice, in the councils of leaders for future development — a wise and imaginative move, giving youth a greater stake in their own country's future than ever before.

In his speech at the agricultural conference, Hua Kuo-feng made it very explicit that the basic accounting system of the communes must change, with accounting taking place at brigade and commune level; otherwise mechanization would be impeded. This puts an end to the resistance to change of the wealthier production teams, which fell back on the 1962 directive (a Liu-inspired one) that there would be no change for thirty years.§

The New Year editorial of the *People's Daily* also stated clearly that although the two-line struggle would continue, no organization of "combat forces" or violence would be allowed — hence no repetition of the excesses of the cultural revolution.

All this would not be feasible had not China one great asset: oil. The

---

* See *Build Tachai-type Counties Throughout the Country*, excerpts from a report entitled *Mobilize the Whole Party, Make Greater Efforts to Develop Agriculture and Strive to Build Tachai-type Counties Throughout the Country*. National Conference on Learning from Tachai in Agriculture, October 15, 1975, reported in *Peking Review*, no. 44, October 31, 1975.

† See note, page 373.

‡ The author was present in Chengtu.

§ And it vindicated the author's remark made the previous year; see second note, page 388.

fact that she is not only self-sufficient but will become an oil exporter of magnitude, paying her way as she has done so far, without running into debt, is also part of the strategy of plenty which is now being put into action.

Nothing on this scale, or of this importance, has been attempted by any "socialist country," least of all by the USSR, where on the contrary political revolution was halted in favor of "economic advance" and there was a retrogression: inequalities are worse than ever; agriculture is at almost the same production level as before 1917;* and the USSR has changed into a predatory imperialist power, with vaulting ambitions of world domination, an economy totally militarized, but backward in consumer goods and amenities for the people.

By pushing her revolution forward China has turned her back on hegemonic ambition, and trusted not only her own people but all the peoples of the world to do the same one day, including the Russian and American peoples.

And who can say that, in the long term, Mao Tsetung's vision of the future will be wrong?

* See page 369.

Index

Copy 1   B
                                Mao

Han, Suyin
     Wind in the tower.
                                $12.95

We would appreciate your returning this
Library item by the due date so that others
in the community may have use of this material.

NATIONAL CITY PUBLIC LIBRARY
200 E. 12th Street
National City, CA 92050
477-5131

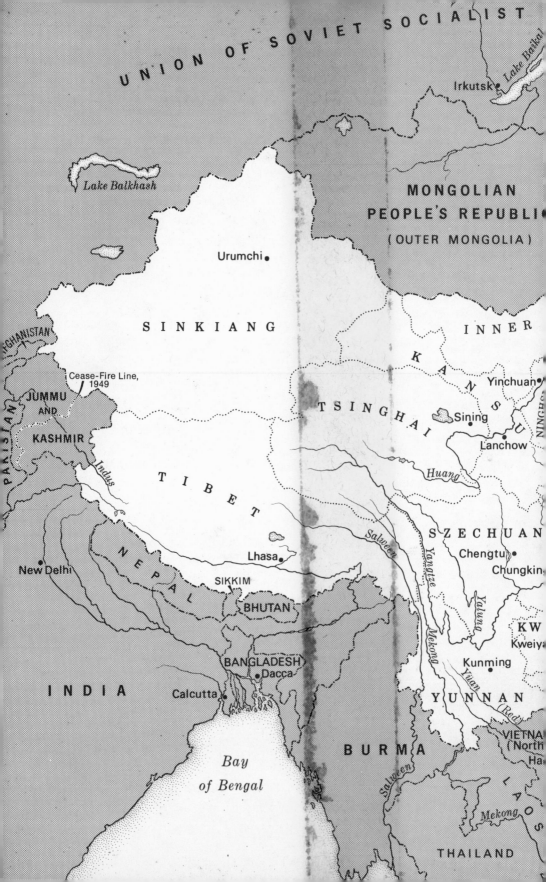